The Dilemma of Modernity

SUNY Series in Philosophy
Robert Cummings Neville, Editor

The
DILEMMA
of
MODERNITY

Philosophy, Culture, and Anti-Culture

Lawrence E. Cahoone

STATE UNIVERSITY OF NEW YORK PRESS

Published by
State University of New York Press, Albany

© 1988 State University of New York

All rights reserved

Printed in the United States of America

For information, address State University of New York Press, State
University Plaza, Albany, N.Y., 12246

Library of Congress Cataloging-in-Publication Data

Cahoone, Lawrence E., 1954–
   The dilemma of modernity.

   (SUNY series in philosophy)
   Bibliography: p.
   Includes index.
   1. Philosophy, Modern. 2. Culture—Philosophy.
3. Humanism. 4. Subjectivity. I. Title. II. Series.
B791.C18   1987   190   86–30195
ISBN 0-88706-549-X
ISBN 0-88706-550-3 (pbk.)

10 9 8 7 6 5 4 3

For my mother,
Mary Elizabeth Candelet
and the memory of my father,
Gerald Francis Cahoone

I had a dream of return. Multicolored.
Joyous. I was able to fly.

And the trees were even higher than in
childhood, because they had been
growing during all the years since
they had been cut down.

Czeslaw Milosz, "The Separate Notebooks"

Contents

Contents   ix

Preface: The Dilemma

We live in the later stages of a revolution. The on-going intellectual and social revolution of the Western world since the Renaissance has created a new culture, distinct from the medieval West and unique in human history, a culture that has never stopped evolving and following out the implications of its fundamental perspective. All of us who live in western and central Europe, Canada, and the United States are the direct heirs of that culture, and move within it as do fish in water. But the non-Western world has been powerfully influenced and shaped by this culture as well. Through colonialism, trade, and the export of ideology, the modern West has injected components of its own civilization into the indigenous cultures of non-Western societies. Most of the world's nations now resemble a kind of historical layer cake, in which social groups living side by side embody the lifestyles of different centuries, and this layering is largely determined by the extent to which a people has been influenced by Western modernity, either directly or indirectly. Most of the people of this earth are born into the world as children or step-children of modernity, whether they like it or not.

Just as undeniable as the phenomenon of modernity, however, is its contemporary debilitation in the West. The nineteenth century's anticipation of unimpeded progress and the nearly universal confidence of modernity are long gone. The unquestioning belief in the certainty and the eventual completion of the quest for knowledge in science and philosophy, like our previous faith in religious and political authority, now seems hopelessly naive. Philosophy and other forms of inquiry since the turn of the century exhibit a new tenor and impulse than that of inquiry before 1850, as if each author's sense of what could go without saying, what could be assumed without need of proof, has changed entirely. Decades of revolution in art, music, and literature have promulgated widely divergent notions of what art is, have denied the validity of representation, and have left the uncritical public entirely at sea. The religious sense and significance of human life and of morality is no longer a sufficient source of legitimation, strength, and purpose for the majority. Jefferson's belief in the agrarian basis of democracy, and most of the economic and social presuppositions of the founders of American democracy, have been stood on their heads in the last century. Technological innovation continues periodically to shatter whatever visions and expectations we may form about our collective future. And in two world wars the cradle of modernity, western and central Europe, has literally blasted itself to bits and now subsists in a state of seemingly permanent division and dependence upon its own cultural offspring, the Soviet Union and the United States.

Modernity, the amalgam of cultural principles on which post-Renaissance Western society has based itself, has certainly changed since the days of its sixteenth- and seventeenth-century infancy. And yet, in another sense, it has not changed. The words on all of our public monuments are the same, American political movements of every conceivable type drape themselves in the flag and quote our eighteenth-century constitution, the scientific and rationalist ideals of the seventeenth and eighteenth centuries are written into the introduction of every high school science textbook, and no one advocates a return to the Middle Ages. The question as to what has changed and what has remained the same, whether modernity is dead or merely asleep, whether its ideals can any longer serve as our guide, is the dominant question of our time. Should modernity be revivified, or should it be buried, perhaps with full honors at Arlington, or maybe in a vacant lot in the South Bronx? Or is the reversal apparent today the fulfillment of a modernity whose implications we never fully understood?

Consider the recent fate of modern humanism, the conviction that the human individual is the ultimate seat of value and the ultimate judge of truth in this world. The tremendous advances in the scientific understanding of the chemical, neural, and behavioral determinants of human experience and conduct, despite their benefits, make belief in the freedom, responsibility, and rationality of the human individual, and even the individual's qualitative difference from non-human species, harder and harder to maintain. Mass communication and the development of the political, legal, and commercial bureaucracies needed to manage the ever-increasing complexity of society continue to enwrap the individual in more and more complicated webs of social organization. The complexity of the contemporary economic system makes every man and woman more dependent on others than ever before; dependent not merely on family and local community, but on far-flung networks of national and international producers and consumers. It is now virtually impossible for an individual in the modernized portions of the globe *even to understand,* not to mention control, the manifold socio-economic influences on the concrete conditions of his or her life. These developments make human individuals seem ever less capable of understanding and determining the course of their own lives, less authoritative, less reliable as a repository for ultimate political and epistemic authority. They make the individual, untutored and unadorned by institutional and collective connections, seem ever less worthy of respect and trust.

Today, the West is plagued by seemingly incorrigible social problems (for example, crime, drug abuse, alcoholism, teenage pregnancy, pornography) that repeatedly raise in the public mind the question of how free the individual should be. The seeming breakdown of community traditions and public morality makes many worry that individuals cannot be trusted, that there is too much freedom in the contemporary West. These social problems, along with that on-going revolution we call the modern economic system, and its attendant social dislocations, add a constant supply of fuel to the fire of domestic anti-humanists who would abrogate democratic institutions and rights in order to institute their own programs of radical change. Despite the great power and seeming stability of some of the Western democracies, anti-humanist solutions are always tempting, and increasingly so. This is not to mention the fact that, globally, humanism is the exception and not the rule, and that forms of tyranny and collectivism constantly vie with humanism for the assent of suffering peoples, both in the developing and the developed world.

Lastly, the sheer power and violence of contemporary institutions as displayed in twentieth-century conflicts makes humanism seem naive and unrealistic. If millions can be killed in hours, millions who would presumably cast a strong vote against their slaughter, then how can a human being be considered free and self-determining? If human beings can be herded into pens, made to grovel and beg for food, programmed and de-programmed, gassed and burned, their very bodies mined for gold and hair, then what is the sense of claiming that such creatures contain some invisible, immaterial value, some sacred soul? If massive organizations and institutions alone can affect the course of life and history, if only groups count, then what nonsense is talk about the innate authority and rights of the individual who stands alone!

The modern world is caught in a dilemma. It has set into motion explosive waves of technological, social and intellectual change, waves that, for better or worse, pound against the very principles on which modernity based itself. Modernity is eroding its own cultural and intellectual bedrock. A combination of social change and intellectual attack is undermining the patterns of interpreting the world which have made those social changes and intellectual movements possible. Modernity hurtles forward, but we have less and less understanding of, and belief in, its nature and direction. The dilemma of modernity, and the question of how to deal with this dilemma, has been the greatest issue of the second half of the twentieth century, and will only become deeper and more wrenching in the decades to come.

It is noteworthy that, in this century of Western culture's growing self-doubt and humanism's insecurity, philosophy, which had played so prominent a role in the creation of the modern world, has been declared dead, most noticeably by the philosophers themselves. Philosophers of every stripe located along the long ideological arc stretching from Wittgenstein to Heidegger (or is it a circle?) have counted out their own discipline, numbering it among the many casualities in the heavy march of twentieth-century culture. People outside of philosophy find it increasingly empty of significance for their own social and intellectual problems. Those within philosophy flounder in a Babel of philosophic tongues seeking new ways to close out the philosophic epoch, to reduce philosophy to literary criticism or conceptual therapy, to deconstruct, analyze, and generally define their own discipline out of existence.

This spectacle might be amusing if philosophy were as isolated and lofty a phenomenon as many, both within and without it, believe. Fortunately or unfortunately, it is not isolated and what is at stake is more than the fate of philosophy and philosophers. Philosophy is a part of culture. It is one tradition within the on-going interpretation and reinterpretation of the world that is humanity's birthright. What afflicts philosophy today is indicative of global changes that are surging through the cultural life of the modern world. Contemporary philosophy's sense that it is cut off from its past, that pre–twentieth-century philosophy is out of date, naive, and irrelevant to present concerns mirrors the indifference to history that is increasingly characteristic of our culture in general. And the self-flagellation, the attempted intellectual suicide of contemporary philosophy, is part of a more pervasive strain of twentieth-century culture which cannot accept the eternal human project of integratively interpreting the totality of life and the world as a valid, possible project. This lack of acceptance does not mean that we are more skeptical, more fully critical, better at thinking than were earlier generations. It means that our imagination has shrunk, that we have little confidence in our ability to propose answers to questions, to take up a perspective, to create an interpretation and measure its value against its inevitable limitations. Philosophy today is no more or less fragmented, isolated, and self-absorbed than many other areas of our cultural life. Its alleged death is just one phase of the general self-decapitation of culture.

But aren't philosophy's insistent eulogists right, after all? Is it intellectually defensible to continue to engage in the kind of projects represented by Plato's *Republic,* Aristotle's *On the Soul,* Hobbes' *Leviathan,* Hegel's *Philosophy of Right,* Whitehead's *Process and Reality,* or Dewey's *Philosophy of Education?* It seems to many that this entire literary genre has been shown to be unsupportable. Or rather, is it only a tradition or series of traditions within philosophy that have run themselves onto the rocks, and not the whole unnumbered fleet of all past and possible philosophic projects? Are philosophy's critics confusing the demise of a kind of philosophy with the death of philosophy as a whole, thereby revealing the narrowness of their own conceptions of the aims of past thinkers and of philosophy's function within the orbit of human existence? Might philosophy someday rise to remind philosophers, like Mark Twain, that "Reports of my death have been greatly exaggerated!"?

This book is one philosopher's attempt to answer three related questions: What is happening, or has already happened, to the cultural principles that constituted the intellectual scaffolding of the modern Western world? Can we continue to believe in the humanism that has been an integral part of modernity, or have critical attacks and the heavy march of history rendered it indefensible and obsolete? Is philosophy, a chief architect of both modernity and humanism, dead, as some claim it to be?

I will suggest that one of the determining factors of the contemporary dilemma of modernity has been the progressive *self-undermining* of a problematic but important strain of modern culture. This process has led to the development of an anti-culture, to a de-legitimation or undermining of the value of culture, communication, and the sense of the significance of human acts and artifacts. Humanism and philosophy are neither dead nor illegitimate; it is only those interpretations of humanism and philosophy that were caught up in the self-undermining strain of modern culture that have revealed their untenability.

The interpretive categories that have shepherded modernity's achievements have succeeded so well that they have shattered the interpretive context that was essential to early modernity. The result is that in the twentieth century modernity has suffered a *de-contextualization* of its basic interpretive categories. The beliefs and modes of interpretation that once provided a context and a source of mediation for modernity's fundamental conceptions of subjectivity and objectivity have been delegitimated. This loss of context and mediation has affected the conceptions of subjectivity and objectivity themselves. Without a medium of relation their nature is drastically changed.

Many critics of late modernity fail to notice this dynamic. They tend to see in late modernity either a disintegration of public, community structures or a volatilization of the individual self. They fail to see that late modernity involves simultaneous changes in the interpretation of both public and private life, *and* that these changes are determined by a loss of context or mediation. The self-undermining of important parts of the modern tradition occurs through the progressive application and radicalization of certain elements of modernity which eventually burst the context in which they originally functioned. The result is that, while these elements retain their original meaning in one sense, they are fundamentally altered in another.

This dilemma is not insuperable. Modernity's technical, intellectual, and political achievements are not the cause of this problem; it is modernity's characteristic interpretation of those achievements, the prevalent way of understanding these successes, that leads to modernity's debilitation. Impaled on the horns of its dilemma, modernity is drying up, losing its confidence, its sense of a future, its sense of its own legitimacy. Modernity ought not to be allowed to die quietly, for with it would go its achievements, among which are humanism and democracy. Modernity needs to be reinvigorated. This does not mean a return to the beliefs of early modernity, of the seventeenth and eighteenth centuries. It means finding a new synthesis, a new set of ideas that can preserve the achievements of modernity without cutting off its future possibilities, that can provide a new context for modernity.

This book has both a historical and a constructive task. Historically, I will examine some of the problems of modern philosophy and culture and offer a theory of the development of modernity as a whole. My constructive aim is to go beyond some of the most problematic dichotomies of modern thought, to show that they are unnecessary, that it is possible to do theoretical work outside of these dichotomies and that, at the present time, the tradition of Western intellectual culture *needs* to re-examine and reinvigorate ideas that have been obscured by those unnecessary dichotomies. I will suggest that one of the pre-eminent tasks for intellectual work in our time (what Heidegger would call a task for thinking and Dewey would see as a call for "reconstruction") is the reinvigoration of the meaning and value of culture *per se,* the intellectual appreciation of the cultural dimension of human existence and a recognition of how essential such an appreciation is to the living future of human communities and the individuals in them.

A word of caution must be given to the reader. There is in this book a disparity of style. It is the result of relating what are usually considered two very different subject matters: philosophic texts and historical, general cultural life. Any writer convinced that technical and seemingly esoteric philosophy is in fact related to general cultural and historical matters, and that a full appreciation of either requires that both be discussed, must face the problem of alternating between the technical analyses of philosophy and the rich generalities and vagaries of cultural criticism within a single text. This almost inevitably means a disparity of writing style. Even more problematic from the standpoint of the critical reader, it entails a disparity of style of argumentation, for the criteria used to adjudge the adequacy of an argument about a philosophic doctrine are quite different from those appropriate to historical and cultural criticism. The reader has a right to expect a sound discussion in either case, but, as Aristotle reminds us, the nature of the particular subject matter rightly determines the investigative criteria and degree of precision that is required. Unless philosophers accept this kind of initial disparity and seek ways to overcome its strangeness rather than rejecting it out of hand, philosophy will deny itself relevance to some of the most important questions that human beings are asking themselves today.

In this regard, the reader is forewarned that Chapters 2, 3, 5, and 6, which constitute most of Part One of this study, are detailed discussions of the philosophic positions and arguments of René Descartes, Immanuel Kant, Edmund Husserl, and Martin Heidegger. Chapters 5 and 6 are particularly technical and textually detailed. These chapters are attempts to reveal macroscopic themes in microscopic artifacts, to show the development of a grand philosophic-cultural scheme as it is worked out in the nuts and bolts of particular philosophical texts. The less technically or historically inclined reader may want to skim these chapters on a first reading, especially those on Husserl and Heidegger.

The introduction and Chapter 1 set the stage for all that follows. The former defines the concept of modernity and discusses the relationship of philosophy and culture. The latter defines the crucial notion of 'subjectivism', the interpretive scheme which I will show to be one of the dominant traits of modern thought. My use of the term subjectivism is novel; it is *not* equivalent to frequently encountered philosophical talk about subjectivist ethics, subject-centered epistemology, subject as metaphysical substance, idealism, egology, or voluntarism. Part One demonstrates how subjectivism, since its classical formulation in the seventeenth century, has developed in such a way as to transform itself into a seemingly antithetical doctrine which nevertheless maintains the basic subjectivist categories. Chapter 4 is pivotal for this historical account. It introduces a new concept to describe the historical transformation of subjectivism, the concept of philosophical narcissism. Philosophical narcissism has nothing to do with egocentricity on the part of philosophers; it refers to the depiction of subject and object characteristic of philosophies whose subjectivism has been radicalized and, to an extent, broken down. It describes the late nineteenth and twentieth-century radicalization or purification of the subjectivist categories beyond the mediated, limited subjectivism characteristic of subjectivism's seventeenth and eighteenth-century founders and adherents.

Part Two concerns the theoretical understanding of modernity in general. It presents an original view of modernity, a 'cultural' theory, by way of a critical reformulation of the views of two of the most powerful writers on the subject, Theodor Adorno and Max Horkheimer. Through proposing this theory, Chapter 8 introduces a new concern into this study, the question of our concept of culture itself, of its meaning and value, and how this concept changes in the course of cultural history.

In Part Three, the theory of modernity and the question of the concept and valuation of culture from Part Two are brought together with the critique of philosophical subjectivism and narcissism from Part One. By using the changing conception of culture as a key, Chapter 9 shows how the development of philosophical subjectivism fits together with the theory of modernity as a whole, and how the alleged end of philosophy reflects broader themes in twentieth-century Western culture. Then, in Chapter 10 I suggest a philosophical alternative to subjectivism founded in a pluralistic theory of culture. The epilogue attempts to apply what has been learned about culture and its centrality in human affairs to the problematic position of humanism in contemporary American life.

It is my aim in this book to provide a better way of understanding the complex developments of modernity, and to show that it is possible to envision philosophy's future, its relation to culture, and the phenomenon of culture itself in a new way, through showing that certain generally accepted conceptual barriers to these new possibilities are unnecessary and illegitimate. The goal of this work is less to cajole others down the same intellectual road as myself than to convince the reader that there are alternative philosophical paths; paths leading beyond the roadblocks in front of which much contemporary intellectual traffic is now piled up. This study will be successful if it helps to loosen up this traffic jam and enable travellers to get on with their journeys, whatever their various destinations may be. For it is such journeys, in their very diversity and indeterminacy, that will constitute the on-going adventure of modernity. Modernity's reinvigoration depends on the recognition that the intellectual future is not foreclosed, but open, and is as rich as life itself in this strange and fascinating late-modern world.

Acknowledgments

This book is the product of years of interest in the problem of understanding the contemporary world, and of the conviction that philosophy can enrich our experience of that world, rather than distancing us from it. Many people have shared in my conviction, and my life, during these years, and have supported me in my work. They are all part of this book.

First and foremost, the book could never have been written without the unwavering help and loving support of my mother, Mary Candelet, to whom it belongs more than anyone. I dedicate it to her. My step-father Raymond Candelet contributed to my work posthumously, through the sweat of his brow. In their concern and support for my mother and myself, the rest of my family has helped make this book possible.

The manuscript has benefited from careful readings at various stages by Clyde Lee Miller, Sidney Gelber, Gerald Galgan, Patricia Athay, Patrick Heelan, Susan Bordo, Joseph Grange, David Hall, Elizabeth Baeten, and especially Edward Casey and Robert Neville, who worked with me from the beginning of the project. Jan Kott and David Allison encouraged me to write in this area long ago. I am grateful to William Eastman and the staff of the State University of New York Press for bringing my manuscript to the light of day, and Robert Neville for his help in this regard.

The Philosophy Department of the State University of New York at Stony Brook is a strange place, full of conflict and creativity, the kind of place where talented graduate students flounder and explore and, complaining to the end, produce original and important work. I am proud to have been a member of that community.

Two unique personalities have left their imprint on this book. Through his intellectual originality and integrity, Justus Buchler has made it possible for a generation of Stony Brook students to say that, thusfar in our lives, we have known at least one Philosopher. George

Breitbart, a man who treats conceptual schemes the way a wrecking ball treats a condemned building, has taught me more than I will ever be able to say.

Many people, some fellow students of philosophy, some fellow students of life, all friends, have shared in making this book what it is by sharing in making its author who he is. Too numerous to mention, but too important not to, some of them are Bette Snitzer, Ken Itzkowitz, Thomas Thorp, Susan Bordo, Todor Mijanovich, Tara Losquadro, Davin Wolok, Janice McLane, John Ryder, Kieran Donahue, Barbara Boutsikaris, Kevin MacDonald, Niall Caldwell, Ronald Scapp, Suhl Chin, Murray Gordon, Fred Evans, Mark Roberts, Edward Lee, Mario Moussa, Gary Aylesworth, Lou Levy, Pam Moskow, Tony Smith, Gerry Beaulieu, Margaret Ruggiero, Paul Colin, Dale Snow, Scott Brewer, Tony Mattera, David Sklar, Steve Beall, Arman Marsoobian, Kathleen Wallace, Laura Waddey, Amit Sen, Ed Marcotte, Brian Seitz, Jim Carmine, Peter Spurzem, P. J. Dwyer, Steven Odin, Laurie Miller, Dirk Leach, J. Barry, Larry Kupers, Phil Weiss, Charles Munitz, Theresa Rafferty, Robert Trudell, and the gentlemen at the Third Avenue YWCA in Brooklyn.

Thanks are due architect Paul Bennett for all diagrams, and my friends of the legal arts for smuggling me into the Brooklyn Law School, where the entire manuscript was written: Lew Lear, Ian Zimmerman, Fred Harrison, and Majer Gold. I am also grateful to my students who have enabled me to learn by teaching them, at the State University of New York at Stony Brook and at Old Westbury, at Nassau, Queensborough and Kingsborough Community Colleges, at C. W. Post College, Queens College and New York City Technical College, and at the Webb Institute of Naval Architecture.

Last but most, I want to thank my colleague, part-time editor, full-time best friend, and loving wife, Elizabeth Baeten, who has listened to all my ravings, who unaccountably believes in me, and whose presence makes me look forward to each new day.

Introduction: Modernity, Philosophy, and Culture

Modernity can be provisionally defined as the ideas, principles and patterns of interpretation, of diverse kinds ranging from the philosophic to the economic, on which western and central European and American society and culture, from the sixteen through the twentieth centuries, increasingly found itself to be based.

The historical starting point is impossible to fix; any century from the sixteenth through the nineteenth could be, and has been, named as the first "modern" century. The Copernican system, for example, arguably a cornerstone of modernity, dates from the fifteenth century, while democratic government, which can claim to be the essence of modern politics, did not become the dominant Western political form until very recently.

But the problem of defining the starting point is not as daunting as it may seem. In the ongoing debate over the nature of modernity the choice of starting point tends to depend on which principles are taken to be constitutive of *recent* modernity, that is, of late nineteenth-century culture. This is because the fundamental aim of the debate over the nature of modernity is to discern where modernity is going now through understanding its past and, furthermore, because the concept of modernity is founded on the conviction that we are heirs to a relatively *coherent* modern Western heritage of ideas. The concept of modernity makes sense only if we accept the notion that diverse sectors of modern culture and social life exhibit or have exhibited a common pattern or tendency; that, for example, the technological mastery of nature, democracy, the supremacy of the nation-state, modern science, secularism, and humanism all cohere in some way to form a spiritual-cultural amalgam, despite their differences and alleged contradictions.

There is, then, so single starting point of modernity, but rather there are many starting points, each marking the appearance of a piece of what would, by the mid-nineteenth century, become a dominant cultural force. The debate over modernity is primarily concerned with the

critical analysis of contrary tendencies in the present and with the proph-
ecy of the future, not with the past for its own sake; the past is examined
to find the roots of the various pieces of the present. Thus the choice of
starting point, within this context, is legitimately determined by present
concerns.

For a philosopher, the seventeenth century is a natural place to
begin, being generally accepted as the birth of modern philosophy. Given
this, the debate over modernity is the critical evaluation of the principles
upon which the post–seventeenth-century Western world increasingly
came to define itself. Of particular concern is the apparent change in
these principles since the late nineteenth century. What artistic and aesthetic commentators have called "modernism," and the more recent
movements which they, along with some philosophers, refer to as "post-
modernism" are all part of *late* modernity. The new artistic, literary, and
philosophic movements of the late nineteenth and twentieth centuries are
still within the orbit of modernity, but they represent the critical response of late against early modernity. The developments of late modernity do not imply that the principles and projects of early modernity
have disappeared, but that a variant branch of modernity has now developed to overlay the earlier tradition, in some ways supplanting it, in
other ways extending and fulfilling it.

The Modernity Debate

Three thinkers provided the background for the debate over modernity: Karl Marx, Max Weber, and Sigmund Freud. Marx could be said
to be the first critic of modernity. He developed a critique of the political, social, and cultural principles of modern Europe, claiming them to
be derived from the nature of the modern economy, capitalism. Marx
was the first to understand—and in a way that many contemporary
Marxists fail to understand—the deeply ambivalent nature of capitalism
as always both an oppressive and a liberating force. This point later
became a central tenet of the dialectical theory of modernity. For Marx,
capitalism oppressed the proletariat, but it also demystified oppression;
it tore the congenial illusion of paternalism from power relations and the
"sentimental veil" from the family and other social relations and institutions. Furthermore, by its very nature capitalism meant a "constant
revolutionizing of production . . . ." Capitalism is intrinsically revolutionary.[1] It is for this reason that Marshall Berman has called *The Communist Manifesto* "the first great modernist work of art."[2]

Max Weber, father of twentieth-century sociology, made a unique
contribution to the study of modernity. The key to the development of

the modern West, Weber argued, is "rationalization." Modernity exhibits a progressive rationalization of social life and bureaucratization of administration that gradually overcomes the mythical and irrational modes of organization characteristic of past ages. Anticipating the work of more recent cultural critics, Weber wondered if this process would eventually lead to a culture of, "Specialists without spirit, sensualists without heart; this nullity imagines that it has attained a level of civilization never before achieved."[3]

Freud's writings dealt a heavy blow to the psychological and anthropological notions characteristic of earlier modernity. Psychoanalytic theory undermines, for example, the notion of the determinative power of rational self-consciousness, a notion that had become a central tenet of influential modern economic and political viewpoints, such as classical liberalism. Freud's late work, as seen in *Civilization and Its Discontents,* presented a serious attack on the optimistic notions of social progress characteristic of much of nineteenth-century thought.[4]

The question of modernity was raised from various quarters with renewed intensity immediately before and after the First World War, especially in Germany. The unique historical experience of Germany within western Europe, its minimal development of a secular culture, lack of a democratic tradition, late emergence as a unified nation-state and subsequent rapid industrial modernization, its historical nationalistic antipathy toward more "enlightened" European nations, all seemed to make the conflicts attendant upon the rise of modernity especially intense in that country. Nietzsche was the first to foresee the coming elimination of Christianity as a ruling public force in the West.[5] Spengler's very influential *Decline of the West* prophesied the moral and spiritual death of Western culture.[6] The 1914–18 war, previously unthinkable in the scope of its destruction, permanently changed the climate of optimism and progress that had still been pervasive among intellectuals and in popular culture.

The sense of decline expressed by many theorists, fueled by both social progress and social trauma, gained impetus from artistic modernism and the avant-garde. The world economic crisis of the 1930s intensified the discussion, giving support to the Marxist critique of economic modernity and bourgeois, liberal society by seemingly confirming Marx's prediction of capitalist collapse. This crisis set the stage for the development that has given the debate over modernity its greatest and most frightening impetus: the rise of fascism.

It was in response to fascism that the "critical theorists" of the Frankfurt Institute incorporated psychological and psychoanalytic concepts into their Marxist social theory in order to address the most burning theoretical question of the war years: how could Europeans have willingly given up their hard-won freedom? How could fascism have arisen in the most enlightened, democratic, economically and scientifically advanced of civilizations? While the immediate product of the critical theorists was an account of the "authoritarian personality," the more general philosophical task was seen as the investigation of whether liberal, enlightened, modern society contained in *principle* the seeds of fascism. The result was a philosophical-sociological-depth-psychological analysis of modernity and of the fascism that had erupted within it, an analysis embodied most comprehensively and suggestively in Adorno and Horkheimer's *Dialectic of Enlightenment.*[7]

Adorno and Horkheimer defined the Enlightenment, the basic impulse of modern thought and culture, as the project of distinguishing and freeing the individual consciousness from the embeddedness in and determination by natural forces that was characteristic of the mythological phases of human history and culture. Their bold and radical contention was that this project is self-contradictory, that this contradiction has been historically realized in the development of Western society, that the vaunted modern freedom from natural determination and from the mythological identification with nature ends in a paradoxical reenthrallment with nature and a new mythology. This dialectical theory of modernity as negating its own fundamental principles is a powerful tool for understanding the complexities and seeming paradoxes of the late-modern world in which we live.

The dialectical theory is but one of the many answers our century's thinkers have tried to give to the question: what is happening to the modern West? The great events and the sweeping changes in the fabric of everyday life since 1914 force us to question the structure and direction of this accelerating revolution we call modernity. Are we more free, or less free than our great-grandparents? Have we fought off the rule of masculine paternalism, only to be smothered by the neutered mush of bureaucracy? Is our society ever more civilized or ever more barbaric? In overturning cultural rigidity and parochialism, have our arts become more creative and profound, or simply more meaningless? Are the democratic nations more, or less capable of conducting their affairs? Are we as a nation better educated than ever before or simply better *certified?* Has technological and military might made the West more secure, or are we less secure than ever? In our secular sophistication, are we more realistic and pragmatic, or are we, as Lippmann lamented, "sick with some kind of incapacity to cope with reality?"[8] And, depending on our answers to these questions, do we still believe in all those fine eighteenth century words: "due process," "equal protection," and especially, that all people "are endowed by their Creator with certain inalienable rights . . ."

The problems and paradoxes inherent in modernity have generated a broad and diverse literature, too large to be summarized here.[9] But the debate over modernity is not the exclusive property of our intellectual mandarins, either. It is an everyday topic for thinking people in the street and the lunchroom as well as the seminar room, and it pervades popular discussion in the media. Indeed, the major battles of contemporary American politics are centered on the problem of interpreting modernity.

For American conservatives, the earlier or classical phase of modernity culminating in nineteenth-century culture is the sole foundation for democracy, science, the rule of law, individual freedom, and personal and social morality. They see the cultural and social developments of late, or twentieth-century, modernity—the welfare state, the erosion of the patriarchal family, the assault on Western world leadership, the blurring of the distinction between the public and the private, non-representational and avant-garde movements in art, the rejection of communal moral absolutes, changes in sexual mores and the popular adoption of an ethic of individual desire and pleasure—as a tragic turning away from the foundation of the modern.

Liberals, on the other hand, view the recent movements toward greater individual choice and freedom of lifestyle, public control of private property and public assistance for private poverty, the liberation of racial minorities from the white majority, women from men and third-world nations from Western influence, the philosophic and artistic rejection of traditional concepts of truth and beauty, the loss of religious authority, and increasing hesitance about the use of American military force, all as the fulfillment of the project of early modernity. Liberals tend to see late modernity as continuous with early modernity, as, for example, a fulfillment of the democratic project embodied in the Bill of Rights and the Constitution, and this allows them to claim allegiance to both the early and late phases of the modern.

Contemporary American opinion oscillates between the liberal and conservative viewpoints; just when it seems that a general consensus has formed on one side, elements of the other seep through to muddy the waters. The cause of this oscillation is not indecisiveness; it is that both the liberal and conservative interpretations of the state of the union find ample evidence to confirm them in the contemporary world. Neither is obviously false; on the contrary, each has much to support it. But it is also true that each has obvious shortcomings and leads to absurdities when applied universally.

How is it that the liberal and conservative positions can each seem both true and false? The answer is that reality, which is to say, modernity, has become too complex for either view. While this has been more obvious in the case of liberalism, which has been an ideological shambles in America since 1980, it is no less true of the conservative and neo-conservative positions. The dialectical theory of modernity would contribute this important point: the economic-cultural amalgam which constitutes early modernity contains self-contradicting tendencies, tendencies which lead to modernity's negation. So, while late modernity is a product of early modernity, it is at the same time its contrary.

This view gives us new insight into the complexities of contemporary politics. In its light, contemporary American neo-conservatives are in error when they fail to see that the late modernity of the welfare state and the cultural avant-garde, which they attack, are products of the earlier "classical" modernity of entrepreneurial capitalism and the Protestant ethic, or rather, the product of the way these were interpreted. The ideologies of the late modernity they attack are a product of the early modernity they wish to embrace. In the same way, contemporary American liberals have failed to come to terms with the fact that early and late modernity, which liberals wish to see as continuous, are, in part, contradictory. When, for example, liberals approve of the avant-garde culture of late modernity as a culture of free expression, they fail to see that much of this culture ideologically undermines the positive conceptions of human nature and political society which alone provide a possible intellectual basis for such freedom. Many liberals reject religious values and the belief in a universal morality but fail to recognize that the commitment to individual freedom, which is one of the cornerstones of early modernity, itself implies something like a faith in a universal morality. Dewey is entirely correct when he tells us that democracy is essentially a moral faith.[10] In this regard, the alliance of the New Left with the civil rights movement hid a fundamental ideological chasm: the latter reflected the beliefs, characteristic of early modernity, that political reform must be intellectually grounded in metaphysical, ethical, and religious convictions, whereas the former's program was devoid of and even opposed to such justification for political action.

The complexities of the dialectic of modernity bear directly on that central problematic feature of both humanism and democracy, the attempt to organize society on the basis of individual freedom. The commitment to individual freedom is essential to *all* modernity, both early and late. But from early to late modernity, as we will see, the concept of the human individual changes in such a way that in late modernity the notion of individual freedom becomes extremely problematic. In particular, it becomes difficult to conceive of a *community* of free individuals.

This is part of the tragic narrowing of vision that has afflicted the liberal position in America in the last two decades. The liberal commitment to freedom seemed to require that members of society have no say in what occurs outside of their sphere of privacy; which in effect means that freedom exists only in privacy. Conservatives, repelled by this prospect, and wishing to maintain some notion of community, have often tended to reject the essence of modernity in reaction—to reject belief in the rule of universal or national law and individual freedom, and to turn instead to the wishes of the local community of like-thinking individuals or *Gemeinschaft*, to a religiously or racially organized community as an alternative basis for a less anarchic society.

The question of modernity has dominated political debates and crises on both sides of the Atlantic. It can be seen in the literature of those central Europeans who lived through the crucible of the years 1933–53. In Poland, as elsewhere in central Europe both before and after the war, the advocates of classical, democratic-individualist modernity were generally discredited and de-legitimated by both events and political rhetoric. They appeared to be the advocates of a hopelessly unrealistic and fragile democratic synthesis, an idealistic voice which could not conceivably withstand the coming onslaught of History.[11] Between 1930 and 1939 history appeared to demonstrate the weakness of democracy, and in the next six years seemed to reveal the pathetic vulnerability of human being itself, as well as the emptiness of its past ideals and the meaninglessness of the human individual *as* an individual. More and more, the only rational choice seemed to lie between two apparently antithetical political ideologies, both of which rejected the norms and ideals of classical, earlier modernity: namely, fascism and communism. If the dignity and inherent rights of the individual proved to be a sham, baseless in historical reality, then it seemed that some form of collectivism, either the racial-national *Gemeinschaft* or the international economic class, must constitute the only alternative repository of intellectual and political belief.

The tragic problem of the modern Western world in the twentieth century is that while modernity develops in such a way as to negate its foundations, those foundations are the basis for ideals which we cannot dispense with, for example, democracy, the rule of law, a culture which places an intrinsic value on the human individual. Two of the authors of the dialectical theory, Theodor Adorno and Max Horkheimer, wrote that despite their critique of early modernity, that is, of the Enlightenment, they could not escape the conviction that "social freedom is inseparable from enlightened thought."[12] The democratic, individualist, and rationalist convictions of classical or early modernity form the basis for a free society. But if we are to avoid being caught in the circle of recognizing early modernity as the sole basis for a free society, and yet seeing our modern impulses leading to a negation of that freedom, then we must look within the complex of principles and phenomena that constitute early modernity and distinguish within it the core of non-dialectical humanism, of the individualism which does not negate itself. We must dissect classical modernity and distinguish what can be left behind from what must be preserved.

Philosophy as a Cultural Process

The method and approach of this study treat philosophy as a part of culture and not as a super-cultural meta-activity devoid of practical aims and goals, uninfluenced by the events and tendencies of historical social and cultural life.

The belief that philosophy has little or nothing to do with the general cultural life of society is nonsensical, unless one believes that philosophy, unlike all other human activities, springs full-formed from the ahistorical head of Zeus. Philosophy is, after all, something some people *do* at various times and places, under the manifold conditions that affect all human doings, and for the multifarious reasons that lie behind any human actions. It would be exceedingly strange if we could forge an adequate understanding of philosophies without an appreciation of the social and historical context in which they are born and have their life.

The American philosopher John Herman Randall writes:

> The history of human thought, and the history of philosophical ideas in particular, exhibits with unusual clarity the general structure of social and cultural change . . . it is impossible to gain any real insight into the history of philosophical ideas without being led to formulate a philosophy of cultural and social change.[13]

The work of an individual philosopher is always the creative intellectual response of an individual to a double heritage, the tradition of specifically philosophical literature and the state and issues of contemporary culture. Each of these factors is, in varying degree, a product of the history of the other.

Randall remarks that the history of ideas:

> . . . is both cumulative and original. Ideas seized upon because they meet the needs generated by one type of experience, have a structure and implications of their own. That structure can be followed out by men who have the interest or motive. But men are always far more concerned to use ideas than to understand them; and when other elements of their culture, only remotely related to those ideas, have developed so far as to generate another type of experience, men feel the need of new ideas. So out of the ruins of previous structures they set out to build a new one . . . . No great philosophy has ever been refuted—it has been discarded as irrelevant to another type of experience.[14]

The question that is always most fundamental in determining the nature of a particular philosophic theory is "What needs to be understood? What requires, calls for, inquiry?" Individual philosophies, like all theories, are aimed at interpreting or illuminating certain questions, factors, or phenomena. Even if a philosophy is ultimately intended to apply to or interpret all of reality or all of Being, it must begin with certain questions rather than others, and with respect to those questions its author has in mind both a specific tradition of philosophical answers to which he or she must respond, and a hypothesis as to the location and nature of the real or key problems concerning these questions and answers. Philosophies, like all theories, have targets and are aimed at these targets with certain theoretical intentions and purposes already in mind.

For some time now, most philosophers have rejected the possibility of a presuppositionless philosophy, admitting that while certainty may obtain within the logical coherence of an argument, the conclusions of a philosophy or an argument can never be certain because they are based on fundamental premises which can never be proven, which are always in part the result of will, bias, perspective, and individual choice. Beyond this, the choice of topic, of subject matter, of the issue to be addressed is at least as important as the choice of basic premises, and makes any philosophy even more fully a product of individual decision and personal insight. The answer to the question "What calls for my inquiry?" is not imposed on a thinker, it is not determined by the obvious, impersonal state of a discipline; it is grasped in a combination of choice and intellectual vision. The philosopher must simply feel, or be convinced, that *this* question is vital, or that *this* belief must be legitimated or undermined, or that *these* phenomena more urgently require study than *those others*. The personal and even visceral nature of this does not in any way detract from a philosophy's logical coherence or its susceptibility to public debate, confirmation or refutation. Nor does it mean that the decision is arbitrary; on the contrary, if the results are to be fruitful, then the object of inquiry must be intelligently chosen, which precludes arbitrariness. Nevertheless, no algorithm, no logic can determine the starting point. It is incorrigibly the product of human intuition, desire, and decision, operating within a historical-cultural context. To paraphrase John Dewey, philosophies are choices.[15]

Philosophies are accepted or rejected on the basis of whether they address and offer fruitful or valuable interpretation of what the community of relevant listeners or readers feels most needs to be addressed. New types of experience put new demands for valuable, needed, or desired interpretation on all antecedently held philosophies. Philosophies compete for assent and acceptance not only according to their inner consistency and their conclusions *per se,* but also according to the relative importance of what-they-interpret-adequately versus what-they-interpret-inadequately, as felt by the relevant community.

Here we see the two points where philosophy's involvement with social and cultural conditions is most apparent, namely, in the selection of the problem to which the individual philosopher turns his or her attention before putting pen to paper, and subsequently, in the concerns and standards held by the community that reads or listens to the philosopher's finished product. The structure and dynamics of contemporary social life help to constitute *what is a problem* which can then be expressed intellectually, and further, makes some such problems more socially significant or more intellectually pressing than others.

The growth of a new and powerful science (for example, in the seventeenth century), radical changes in social organization (the rise of the middle-classes), legitimation and de-legitimation of kinds of authority (the decline of the religious and temporal power of the church), technological alterations of the general conditions of life, all of these and other changes in society have undeniable effects on what features of reality and segments of existing literature are felt by any particular philosopher to call for inquiry and interpretation. But this is only the beginning of the feedback loop through which philosophy and the general natural and social conditions of life influence each other. Not only does culture affect what is to become a philosophical problem, but the relevant community's evaluation of any philosophy will depend in part on the philosophy's aptness for the fruitful interpretation of current and, in the longer-run, future events. A philosophy, as a purposive human construction, must meet the test of new experience just as its creators must; it will become either more or less valuable with respect to various human purposes as these purposes confront new experience.

Can anyone doubt that Plato's *Republic,* Augustine's *City of God,* or Descartes' *Meditations* reflect the intellectual problems and basic interpretive patterns characteristic of their respective cultures? The fact of reflection does not mean that these works merely repeat cultural biases and presumptions common to their age, but rather that, in each text one can see a single great mind grasping what it conceived as the most important issues facing thought at the time and reinterpreting the conceptual tools at hand to deal with those issues. This embeddedness of a philosophic work in culture exhibits varying degrees of involvement. Clearly, the political philosophy of a Locke has a more obvious and direct connection to culture in general than do most theories of logic. But this only means that in some fields the relation is less direct, not absent, for the dominant theory of logic at a particular time affects other fields of inquiry both in and outside of philosophy, thereby influencing culture through a series of intermediary thinkers.

A philosophy's reflection of the problems and ideas of a historical community is not simple. Each philosopher's work is one piece of a constantly shifting mosaic that is the culture of a period and a place. A philosophy reflects and characterizes its culture not as a photograph characterizes its subject, or electoral results the will of a community, but as a part characterizes a whole. This is a complex relation, for different parts reflect or bear within themselves the marks of the whole and their relations to other parts in very different ways and in different degrees. One must be very careful always to recognize the manifoldness of these relationships. But they do exist, and a philosophy's participation in various cultural strains can be ascertained.

Further, a philosophy which is found to be valuable by a community provides ideas that guide action, thereby shaping the development of community life. Human social and cultural life are not, to be sure, ruled by conceptual categories or the logic of ideas. Societies do not think out all the logical implications of their ideas. But human beings do think, do use logic, and do apply and imaginatively explore lines of thought in their social life. When these lines of thought reach a dead end, when the limits of their logical implications are followed out in action, their implicit inadequacy for dealing with current problems is *felt* by various groups within society. Gradually, many people come to sense that the ongoing process of cultural interpretation has stalled in regard to the relevant problems. At first, people continue to act in accord with the older pattern of interpretation; then they begin to act differently, to cope with novel problems in a way that is not consistent with the old ideas, while still proclaiming the received interpretation. In other words, their actions adapt more quickly than their ideas. But this disparity makes people feel unsettled, less enthusiastic, and more confused as they become less and less able to match their inherited pattern of interpretation with the newly pressing social problems they face.

In a pluralistic society, people then begin to split into groups adhering to the inherited pattern and groups beginning to doubt and to endorse another way of thinking about the issues in question. Eventually, if the weight of reality and the narrowing of imaginable courses of action press heavily enough against the older pattern of thought, or if a new model emerges which has particular strength in meeting the test of the new while simultaneously maintaining sufficient continuity with those functions of the old way that are most dear, the interpretive center of gravity of the community will shift a few degrees, and a new cultural tradition becomes dominant.

Philosophies can enter into this process of cultural change and affect it. Philosophical literature and discussion are part of culture, like all forms of art and literature. As such, a philosophy provides views and interpretations that affect the thinking of the community encountering it precisely to the degree and in the respects that it is found to be valuable in interpreting felt problems.[16] The result is that certain lines of a community's thought and activity are reinforced and others are experienced as less legitimate than they previously were felt to be. The philosophical interpretation of the world, either directly or through layers of cultural intermediaries,[17] enters into the various determinants of a pluralistic community's activities in the form of general concepts and images that function to reinforce, de-legitimate, or skew relevant activities. These activities in turn contribute to the continual reconstruction of the conditions of community life, conditions that result in certain felt lines of stress, which then call for reinterpretation. Thus the loop comes back on itself.[18]

The existence of this cycle does not make philosophers mere reflecting prisms for deterministic super-personal cultural trends. Social and cultural reality is incorrigibly pluralistic and indefinitely complex. Its nature is fluid, its dynamics tidal. At any moment there are an indefinite number of variant unique expressions of creative intellect, collections and communities of which make up waves of influence that can alter the shape and direction of the culture as a whole, the current of the times. Moreover, this current is never monolithic; all sorts of materials are dragged along with the dominant stream, and may themselves become dominant at a later time. Even the degree of dominance is relative, so that a particular cultural shoreline may not readily exhibit a dominant character, or its dominance may be so hidden or tolerant that pluralism is maximized.

The individual thinker's products are almost never determined by culture because all but totalitarian cultures are too pluralistic to determine. Individual creativity does not mean a break with all of cultural tradition; rather, it is a selection of one cultural tradition over another, a reinterpretation and extension of one strain of culture and a turning away from other strains. The creativity and freedom of the individual thinker is a grasping of the novel relationships and significances of elements of given cultural traditions.

If proclaiming philosophy's involvement in culture seems today naive and forced, if it sounds anachronistic and foreign to the quasi-scientific sophistication of contemporary philosophy, if it rings untrue of the present day in which philosophy appears to be completely isolated from the rest of culture then *this too* tells us something about the state of the relationship of philosophy and culture. That two family members are estranged does not mean they are no longer related; it means that their relationship has changed, and this tells us something about the current mood of each of them. Contemporary philosophy's seeming isolation from culture is significant for both philosophy and culture; it reveals philosophy's idea of itself, and of its role and function in society, as well as the attitude of non-philosophers toward philosophy. Ultimately, however, the isolation of philosophy is a clue to a broader phenomenon, the fragmentation of culture in general. The processes and workings of science and art are as fully withdrawn from contact with non-practitioners as is philosophy; the difference is that the concrete effects of science and art are more visible than those of philosophy, but the greater visibility of the former implies no greater communion with or understanding by the public.

The days when a William James, a John Dewey or a Bertrand Russell could speak to an intelligent non-professional public seem long gone. Even more distant are the days of philosophers' active involvement in political governance and the growth of the sciences. In this light, it is interesting to note that the 'death' of philosophy proclaimed by many professional philosophers reflects the general public's view of philosophy. But appearances, as philosophers used to say, can be deceiving. It might be a good idea to postpone philosophy's burial a bit longer, lest we later find that we have confused the demise of a particular tradition within philosophy with the death of the patient as a whole.

PART ONE

The Dynamics of Subject and Object

Introduction to Part One

Recent decades have witnessed the publication of a number of attempts at interpreting and criticizing post-Renaissance Western philosophy in broad terms, attempts which see the traditionally opposed schools of modern philosophy—rationalism and empiricism—as sharing common assumptions and intentions. Richard Rorty's *Philosophy and the Mirror of Nature* is one of the most insightful and successful of these critical projects. Rorty views the 'rationalist' Descartes, the 'empiricist' Locke, and the 'transcendentalist' Kant as the dominant figures in a common modern philosophical tradition, a tradition characterized by the mind-body dualism, the primacy of epistemology and the 'problem' of knowledge over other philosophical interests, and the belief that philosophy is responsible for providing the epistemic scaffolding for all other cultural activities. In this, Rorty and other philosophers pursuing this global approach, by producing theories of philosophical modernity, have made modernity a more familiar philosophical topic.

The dialectical theory of modernity, proposed by Theodor Adorno and Max Horkheimer in the 1940s, is primarily concerned with modern social and cultural development as a whole, but an important and guiding part of this whole is a conception of philosophical modernity in particular. The dialectical theory suggests that the basic tendencies of early modern philosophy are, first, self-negating, and second, part of a general socio-cultural process, namely the self-negation of the spirit of the Enlightenment. The present study will try to determine to what degree and in what ways this theory is valid.

In Part One, I will show that the dialectical theory's first claim regarding philosophy is true, that there is a self negating strain or tradition of ideas in modern philosophy. However, whereas the dialectical theory implicates a wide range of ideas and 'isms' in this self-negation— including rationalism, humanism, scientism, etc.—I will argue that the self-negating strain of modern philosophy is a specific set of categories called subjectivism. Other ideas and doctrines may participate in this self-negation, but only if they are interpreted through subjectivism,

17

which alone is properly dialectical. Thus, for example, humanism *per se* is not implicated in this self-negation while *subjectivist* humanism is. This distinction is important for, as will be seen later, it holds out the possibility of answering the central, wrenching dilemma of the dialectical theory.

Adorno and Horkheimer straightforwardly admitted that they were "wholly convinced—and therein lies our *petitio principii*—that social freedom is inseparable from enlightened thought." Modernity, or in their terms, Enlightenment, is inherently flawed and these flaws have helped to create some of the worst historical crises and social problems of the twentieth-century West. And yet the Enlightenment has also been the irreplaceable basis for the highest achievements of the West, for example, social freedom. We cannot discard modernity, for modernity is the basis for freedom—both the ideal of freedom written into the constitutions and consciences of Western peoples and the reality of the very significant degree of liberty experienced in the Western democracies, whatever set-backs are periodically suffered. In their classic *Dialectic of Enlightenment,* Adorno and Horkheimer do not try to obscure the fact that they found no way out of this dilemma.

The only way out of this dilemma is to distinguish and isolate the self-negating strain of modernity from other aspects of the modern tradition which are not necessarily self-negating. Part One will focus attention on subjectivism as the self-negating strain in philosophical modernity, thereby paving the way for other modern ideas and traditions to be freed from the sweep of the dialectical theory's critique.

It is in Part Two that the second claim of the dialectical theory will be shown to be true, although again, with modification. The self-negation of philosophical subjectivism will be shown to be a part of the self-negation of subjectivism in modern culture in general. The concepts gleaned from Part One's analysis of philosophy will have an application to modern culture because the former is an aspect of the latter. But this participation of philosophy in cultural history cannot be understood through a neo-Hegelian dialectical scheme *à la* Adorno, Horkheimer, and others. Rather, philosophy participates in culture because of its nature as a human cultural product, and both develop as they do because of the contingent history of social events and the competition among manifold philosophical and cultural meanings to express and shape the on-going process of pluralistic humanity's interpretation of those events.

1

Subjectivism and the Transcendental Synthesis

Subjectivism is one of the most dominant and powerful viewpoints or categorical schemes in modern philosophy and culture. Subjectivist categories can be seen in early-modern thinkers as diverse as Descartes, Leibniz, Locke, Hume, and Kant, and in twentieth-century philosophers as different as A. J. Ayer and Martin Heidegger. Most of the contemporary attacks on what is commonly called 'subjectivism' are in fact critiques of egoism, egology, voluntarism, and the concept of the subject, and therefore fail to grasp the essence and scope of true subjectivism. Subjectivism is like an old and deep-rooted oak penetrating deep into the soil of modern thought, an oak whose branches many critics correctly attack while failing to grasp the trunk and the roots.[1]

Subjectivism is the conviction that the *distinction between subjectivity and non-subjectivity is the most fundamental distinction in an inquiry*. Although subjectivism can take on metaphysical, ethical, or other meanings, it is this methodological or systematic dualism which is most basic to it. Subjectivism is the view that the distinction between the subject and what is disclosed in or apparent to or internally related to the subject, on the one hand, and what is not the subject and/or is not internally related to it—in other words, what exists and is to be understood *independently* of any disclosure in or relation to subjectivity—on

19

the other hand, is the most fundamental distinction for inquiry. Every attempt at understanding the world systematically, methodically, must start somewhere, must use some concepts and distinctions as its basic tools to understand everything else. For subjectivism, the distinction between subjectivity and objectivity is the most fundamental tool for dividing up what is.

Now, it may appear misleading to term this perspective 'subjectivism', when what defines it is a dualism of subject *and* object or non-subject. Philosophies which are firmly realistic, objectivist, and anti-egological in their orientation, even those which deny metaphysical status to the subject, can be just as subjectivist as any absolute idealism or metaphysics of the subject, if they accept the dichotomy as fundamental for inquiry. Why, then, name this perspective 'subjectivist' rather than 'objectivist', 'dualist', etc.? The reason is that the making of this distinction is actually a selection of one particular type of thing—namely, subjectivity or what belongs to subjectivity—*from which* all other facets of reality are distinguished. In other words, out of the totality of discriminable factors or features of what is, subjectivism takes one particular feature of one particular type of being as fundamentally distinct from all other features of reality—which is to say, it takes the distinction between this feature and all else to be the most fundamental distinction for inquiry. The type of being is human being, and distinctive feature is individual consciousness or subjectivity, along with whatever 'belongs' to, whatever exhibits an internal relation to, or subsists 'within' subjectivity.[2]

Subjectivity is consciousness. That is to say, subjectivity is that feature or activity of human individuals by which humans have awareness of appearances or phenomena, by which things show themselves or are manifest or present to us; it is the awareness of anything whatsoever, the field or totality of appearances. Subjectivity is conceived in various and sometimes ambiguous ways: as an activity, as a metaphysical substance, as the things which appear, and that which allows them to appear.

The words 'object' and 'objectivity' carry multiple meanings. This is because 'subjectivity' or 'consciousness' has multiple meanings, and 'object' and 'objectivity' are generally the coordinated antitheses of the former terms. In the discussion of subjectivism, objectivity will variously mean: 1) reality, or the nature of existences independent of their appearance to individual subjects; 2) appearances or phenomena, which is to say, what appears to an individual subjectivity only insofar as and in the way that it appears; and, 3) the objective or apparent world, which is to say, that which, on the basis of what appears *as* it appears, is taken to exist independently of subjectivity, despite the fact that its entire existence, or existence *in-itself,* is not apparent. (Kant called these things-in-themselves, representations and appearances, respectively.)

The Pervasiveness of Subjectivism

The tremendous intellectual power and pervasiveness of the subjectivist dichotomy, its massive influence on the thinking of theoreticians and the public alike often goes unnoticed. Its obscurity is a measure of its power, of the degree to which we tend to view it as natural and inevitable. What could be more natural than dividing up all of existence into my own mental experience and thoughts, the inside of me, on the one hand, and the rest of the world, the outside in which I act and which I perceive, on the other? Even materialistic philosophers, who deny the mind's metaphysical difference from matter, generally hold that the *content* of subjective experience subsists in a fundamentally distinct order from that of material reality, although the latter determines the former. Obviously, thoughts and perceptions are not part of the being of things outside the mind; they subsist in subjectivity. Their *esse* is not their *percipi*. Idealists, on the other hand, despite their metaphysical grounding of matter in mind, make the same fundamental distinction between the content of the subject's experience and the objective reality of things outside of the subject, whether the latter are caused by a Berkeleyan God or bracketed by a Husserlian *epochē*.

What would it mean to deny subjectivism, to refuse to respect the subjectivist dichotomy? It would mean regarding the subject-object dichotomy as no more fundamental than other distinctions that might be made, for example, between appearance and reality, the finite and the infinite, matter and form, or trees and non-trees. It would mean regarding a subjective entity—for example, a thought—as no less relatable to, no more disparate from an objective entity—for example, a physical, public object—than two thoughts in the mind of one person, or two physical objects. This implies that a person's thoughts, ideas about, or perceptions of a natural entity which exists independently of the person may be internally related to the entity, may be actually a part of what the entity is as a natural, physical thing (not as a merely ideal entity or 'intentional' object). For most modern philosophers of any stripe—realists, idealists, analysts, and phenomenologists, and most non-philosophers as well—such a claim would be absurd and fanciful because it violates the almost universally accepted dichotomy between the order of things and the order of experiences, or objectivity and subjectivity. (I will argue in a later chapter, "The Metaphysics of Culture," that this claim is not absurd; rather, it is the subjectivism which rejects it in principle that leads to absurdity.)

There are, as we will see, a wide variety of terminologies and distinctions which are possible within a general subjectivist orientation. Some philosophers who appear to reject the concept of the subject altogether, such as Heidegger, are nevertheless subjectivist. What determines subjectivism is the acceptance of a fundamental distinction, not the explicit assertion of the primacy of subjectivity in inquiry. Even where the concept of subjectivity as such seems to have been rejected, if the *function* of subjectivity—to disclose, to make apparent—and the distinction between what is related to or taken up by this function and what is *not* taken up by it remains fundamental, then the viewpoint is subjectivist. For subjectivism, what appears (the totality of evidence available for inquiry) appears by virtue of some internal relation to subjectivity, to the disclosive function of human being. What does not have such a relation to subjectivity cannot appear, and thus cannot be considered evidence in the most primary sense. This position has certain immediate consequences.

First, all percepts, feelings, beliefs, and intentions of which I am conscious fall under the same category: they are all internally related to my consciousness. To adopt a subjectivist position automatically implies that ideas, intentions, and sensations, can be treated as members of a single class, at least initially. They can subsequently, of course, be analyzed into different sub-classes.

Second, the subjectivist position necessarily treats the world into which we can inquire as presentations or appearances. Subjectivism takes the world *as-it-is-for* an individual subject. Subjectivism puts out of bounds the possibility of any internal relation of subjectivity and subjective appearances on the one hand, with beings existing independently of any internal relation to subjectivity, on the other. Subjectivist philosophers do often speak of the latter, and often wish to establish an intrinsic relation between the two, but the fundamental distinction constituting subjectivism makes any such relation problematic. To talk of things existing independently of disclosure or subjectivity as constituting, producing, or being intrinsically related to what appears is *prima facie* to step outside of the subjectivist position and into some form of naturalism. Subjectivism and naturalism are antithetical viewpoints. This does not mean that they have not been historically conjoined; indeed, they usually are, resulting in a dualistic metaphysics.

When subjectivism is in force as a *metaphysical* doctrine it is generally characterized by two claims. First, subjectivist metaphysics identifies mind with individual consciousness. Mental events or qualities are events or qualities belonging to subjectivity. Second, nature or world or objectivity, insofar as they are not considered to belong to subjectivity, are defined as material and metaphysically antithetical to mind.

These two claims are simply the result of the translation of subjectivism as a fundamental claim about evidence into the domain of claims about the ultimate nature of things. That is, they are a result of applying to metaphysical inquiry the notion that the most fundamental philosophical distinction is that between what-is-subjective and what-is-not, thereby affecting the interpretation of various inherited concepts—mind, matter, mental substance, physical substance. Subjectivism in metaphysics is the view that mind and what-is-not-mind are metaphysical opposites.

This notion finds expression in monistic as well as dualistic metaphysical systems. The eighteenth-century idealist Berkeley accepts this principle no less than Descartes: matter and mind cannot be conceived as having anything in common, metaphysically speaking. Though both accept this principle, they derive antithetical conclusions, to be sure. Berkeley claims that consequently there can be no matter, whereas Descartes asserts that matter and mind each represent a different metaphysical substance.

This conception of mind and matter as metaphysically antithetical is, of course, not peculiarly modern, but the identification of mind, *nous* or *psychē* with subjectivity or personal consciousness is characteristically modern (post-Cartesian). It is in the context of this identification that the dualism of mind and matter becomes subjectivist. This identification makes the interaction of mind and the non-mental virtually inconceivable. For, in this context, the non-mental includes not just matter, but anything that is not or does not belong to an individual consciousness, for example, all of nature, social reality, and cultural artifacts. Furthermore, in this context, to be 'mental' a quality or event must be or belong to both consciousness and to an individual, since consciousness is individual. This view severely restricts the kinds of interrelation or the modes of interaction that can be asserted to exist between the mental-subjective and anything else we wish to talk about.

In metaphysics, ethics, epistemology or any field of inquiry, subjectivism invokes the relative distinction 'subjective–objective' and a whole set of roughly equivalent derivatives. In general these distinctions divide whatever phenomena are under investigation into two categories according to their degree of relatedness to the thinking subject as opposed to the non-subjective world. Now, distinctions between the subjective and objective are not inherently subjectivist: they are made subjectivist by their use, by their centrality in a particular inquiry. If they are made central, then, in effect, without necessarily asserting a metaphysical dualism of subject-substance and physical-substance, the inquiry in question has adopted the opposition 'thinking subject vs. world' as the basis for its orientation toward features of reality, and will inevitably divide those features along subjectivist lines. For example, in his inquiry into human knowledge, Hume divides all knowledge into two categories: that which is based on "relations of ideas" and that based on "matters of fact." Such a doctrine is subjectivist wherever it suggests, is based on, or coheres with—as it usually does—the division of human thought and knowledge into an order of necessary thought and an order of objective experience. Paraphrasing Quine, the former is usually taken as a purely internal order, under-determined by contact with the external world, and is therefore non-empirical, while the latter is treated as the order of the periphery where mind contacts and is determined by the external world, and therefore has empirical content.[3] This model and this manner of description, often characteristic of allegedly scientifically-oriented philosophies, is as rife with subjectivist implications as is any subjectivist metaphysical doctrine.

Subjectivism can serve as the partial basis for valuative and ethical inquiry. For example, within a subjectivist framework it is more or less inevitable that nature and physical reality have no *inherent* value, and that subjectivity be taken as possessing greater inherent or moral value than nature. Insofar as nature is material and devoid of spiritual, mental, or subjective properties, very hypothetical conditions or *ad hoc* doctrines would have to be invoked in order to grant a natural object inherent value. In general, subjectivism implies that the individual thinking subject is the only intrinsically valuable worldly entity, and consequently the center of all value within the bounds of the finite world.

Furthermore, in a subjectivist framework moral and psychological integrity requires the differentiation and consolidation of subjectivity over against the non-subjective. Human integrity is meant as both a moral and a psychological concept, which generally refers to the cognitive-practical-moral wholeness and directedness of the human person, a dimension of moral being that is coincident with the psychic-personal qualities of coherence of personality and strength of character. Subjectivist morality and psychology tend to find nature and the non-subjective world corrosive to personal integrity. Psychic and moral wholeness must be established and maintained by an active process of differentiating the truly subjective from the influences and incursions of the non-subject. For subjectivism, integrity tends to mean independence, non-affectedness, being in control in a variety of senses, not being subject to nature.

The moral-psychological value placed on integrity is not a defining character of subjectivism. The value placed on being "true to oneself," "*Eigentlichkeit*," becoming "what you are" has roots in Stoicism and in the Christian emphasis on the independent value of the individual soul. What is of concern here is the subjectivist interpretation of this integrity, and hence the definition of part of the subjectivist moral project. If the self is identified with the thinking subject, with personal consciousness, then the problem of the relation of the subject and the external world characteristic of subjectivist epistemology tends to reappear in subjectivist ethics, with, of course, specifically ethical connotations.

Subjectivism notwithstanding, consciousness or subjectivity must be conceived as a feature or characteristic of human being or human activity; it may or may not be a feature of other kinds of being or activity. The choice of making this particular feature the basis or primary region of evidence for philosophic inquiry has specific philosophic consequences due to the nature of this particular characteristic of human being. Subjectivism focuses philosophic inquiry on a specific kind of order, the order of what appears to or belongs to an individual consciousness.[4] Consequently, the special characteristics of this kind of order have determinative consequences for subjectivism.

Consciousness is in fact a property of individuals; it is purely personal or individual. The objects or contents of consciousness, naturalistically conceived, are not personal; they are common to an indefinite number of subjects. The consciousnesses of diverse human individuals are similar. But each consciousness uniquely belongs to a particular individual, just as does the individual's body. The 'having' of presentations or experience is purely personal.

If consciousness or subjectivity is made the basis for philosophic inquiry into the nature of things, then the things under consideration can only be understood or investigated in their being-for an individual consciousness, that is, in their status, configuration, or position within a personal, individual order of consciousness. Any other sense, meaning, or status of the things in question is excluded from consideration, as long as the subjectivist viewpoint is unambiguously in force.

Now, consciousness taken in this way as the primary realm of evidence is fundamentally *private*. Individual consciousness *in vivo* is not private; it is, as a property of a living human beings, in continual interaction with the natural and social world. But the theoretical consideration of the field of consciousness as an entity or realm of evidence, considered independently from worldly things as they exist in their own independence makes individual consciousness, thus construed, private. The exclusion of any other senses or meanings of, for example, perceived objects from the being of those objects *for* an individual consciousness is the very definition of privacy.

To say that the subjectivist notion of consciousness is privatistic does not mean that the field of consciousness is unchanging or empty. It remains the case that everything knowingly perceived or thought or felt is internally related to an individual consciousness in some way. But the assertion that the primordial evidences for philosophic inquiry are the totality of what appears to and belongs to an individual subjectivity, that the being-for-subjectivity of worldly things is the only or most basic feature of such things available for philosophic inquiry into their existence and nature, obscures the status of consciousness as a part of the natural and social world, as a feature of certain beings within that world, vulnerable to, affected by, and interacting with that world. The notion of a private consciousness does not necessarily signify a consciousness which has no content or which creates its own content; it signifies rather a subjectivity that cannot be conceived as interacting with an independently existing world. The status of subjectivity as an interactive member of an independent world which affects it is thereby relegated to a derivative, secondary position within philosophies constructed on a subjectivist basis.

Subjectivism is pervasive in modern and contemporary philosophy. From Descartes to Ayer, modern rationalism and empiricism, however much they are opposed, agree that the analysis of human knowledge of the world, and therefore the general characteristics of the known or knowable world, must begin with an analysis of the contents of the individual human mind or consciousness; or, differently put, an analysis of evidence *which is evidence at all* only because it has an internal relation to subjectivity. This priority of the subjective is not merely a matter of a rhetorical order of presentation. It reflects the beliefs that the contents or structure of mind are known most immediately, directly or certainly—in the order of knowledge they are logically, and perhaps temporally, prior to the world that is known through them—and, that the features of the world *that we can know* are all represented in mental contents, they are 'written' into consciousness, by whatever means.

Seventeenth- and eighteenth-century empiricists and rationalists differ over how this writing is accomplished, over the nature of mental contents, over the epistemic value of different categories of mental contents and the manner in which or means by which these differing types represent or reveal realities that exist independently of individual minds. They nevertheless agree that philosophic inquiry into human being and the knowable world is rooted in the totality of what is present to an individual human consciousness, in what the individual mind thinks, feels, and experiences, as the primary sphere of philosophic evidence, regardless of whether their particular philosophic system gives privilege to "sense impressions," "intuitions," or the "transcendental unity" of consciousness. Descartes' *Meditations,* Locke's *Essay Concerning Human Understanding,* Hume's *Inquiry Concerning Human Understanding,* Berkeley's *Dialogue Between Hylas and Philonous,* Kant's *Critique of Pure Reason,* Hegel's *Phenomenology of Spirit,* and Husserl's *Ideas* all share this conviction, that individual mind is the foundation-stone of philosophic inquiry, however much they wish then to go beyond that beginning point.

Beyond this initial identification of mind with subjectivity, a modern philosopher may, like Hegel, wish to demonstrate ultimately that individual consciousness is, upon philosophic analysis, identified with an absolute or universal mind; nevertheless, the first realm of evidence is what appears to an individual consciousness (for example, in Hegel's phase of "sense certainty"). Moreover, the individuality of the subjectivity that is this first realm of evidence does not mean that this subjectivity is presumed by those who adopt it to be unique or solipsistic. Quite the contrary, the philosophers in question usually presume and undertake to prove just the opposite. That is, they presume that their own analysis and description of the contents of consciousness can be repeated and confirmed by any other thinker or reader who engages in the same project, and they undertake to prove that the thought or experience of the individual subject reveals the traits of a common and objective world.

The Subjectivist—Transcendental Synthesis

The great philosophers of the seventeenth century, Galileo, Locke, Leibniz, Spinoza, and most of all, Descartes, made subjectivism a dominant force in early modern philosophy. They did so, however, in a way characteristic of their time, by *combining* the subjectivist perspective with ideas and doctrines that both served the philosophical aims of their age and mitigated the inherent limitations and difficulties of subjectivism. There are a variety of such difficulties, which will be explored in the course of the following chapters; but a particularly pernicious one, for which Descartes, to take one example, has been repeatedly criticized, is the problem of the relation between subject and non-subject. It is this problem in particular, to which subjectivism *per se* can *in principle* have no answer, that was mitigated by combining subjectivism with other doctrines or ideas. In the seventeenth and eighteenth centuries these ideas were characteristically 'transcendental' ones.

By transcendental I mean neither transcendental metaphysical notions nor Kantian conditions of possible experience, but simply the elements of otherwise subjectivist philosophical systems that transcend the subject-object dichotomy of those systems, and which serve as the conditions for the possibility of the interrelation of subjective and objective factors. Transcendental refers to a *function* that ideas may serve within subjectivist philosophy. In the seventeenth century, as we will see, the concept of God filled this function; in the eighteenth century the concept of reason, transcendentally construed, frequently served the same purpose.

Now, the transcendental elements incorporated into the basically subjectivist philosophies of early modernity were inherently incompatible with the underlying subjectivist categories. By definition, if the subjectivist categories are strictly and universally applied, there can be no sense in asserting the existence of factors which transcend the dichotomy. Indeed, twentieth-century criticism of the early-modern philosophers tends to focus on just this incompatibility. Nevertheless, despite this inconsistency, the transcendental elements were indispensable for making subjectivism work, and the systems formed by the synthesis of the basic subjectivist categories and transcendental factors were powerful, original, and world-shaping intellectual creations. Like most important philosophical systems throughout history, they were not *absolutely* consistent, but only *relatively* consistent. Like all philosophies, they were aimed at accomplishing certain intellectual purposes, aimed at understanding certain problematic areas of human thought about the world, and their adherents found their difficulties and inconsistencies less worrisome and significant than what they seemed to adequately interpret. The synthesis of the subjectivist perspective with non- and even antisubjectivist transcendental elements, elements whose assertion implicitly denies the universal applicability of subjectivism, became the most powerful interpretive weapon in the intellectual arsenal of early modernity and permanently altered the intellectual *Weltanschauung* of the Western world.

The subjectivist-transcendental synthesis is basic to many of the great philosophical systems of the seventeenth and eighteenth centuries. In Descartes' system, as will be seen in the following chapter, God and the light of reason make the subject's cognitive relation to material reality or *res extensa* possible. For Leibniz, the perceptions and ideas of individual subjective monads, which cannot influence or be influenced by any outside substance directly, are able to correspond to each other only because God provides their correspondence and relation. Likewise for Spinoza, God is the cause of all ideas and only through God can the human mind know the existence of any external body. In the philosophy of the empiricist Berkeley, perceptions, unlike mere ideas, are directly caused by God, thus assuring a common reality in a world without matter. And, as will be seen in Chapter 3, the synthetic, imaginative power of reason provides the glue to hold subjective experience and objective reality together in Kant's critical philosophy.

Nevertheless, despite the tremendous success of the subjectivist synthesis, the subjectivist philosophical systems could only be relatively coherent; there remained a tension between subjectivist and transcendental elements. The synthesis was tenuous and, generally, the persisting philosophic problems of these systems were centered on the fault line of this tenuous synthesis. The tension had to persist because the two factors in tension were ultimately, inherently incompatible.

The dynamics of subjectivist systems in modern philosophy involve the interrelation of three different factors or viewpoints: subjectivist, transcendental, and naturalist. The three stand in a definite relation.

Naturalism asserts that whatever is, exists within the order of nature. Thus, for naturalism, subjectivity exists within the natural order. Subjectivism, by adopting consciousness as the primary realm of evidence, is *prima facie* antithetical to naturalism, since subjectivism requires that the primary order for inquiry be the order of consciousness, within which nature must be located.

A consistent subjectivist philosophy, or, more accurately, an inquiry remaining completely faithful to its foundations in subjectivist categories, cannot make any positive claims about what exists independently of, what does not belong to, an individual subjectivity; such as nature, other subjects, and culture. If it speculates on their existence, and gives them a name—for example, things-in-themselves—it still cannot make positive claims about their nature or character. This is because there can be no relations between subjectivity and non-subjectivity in a consistent subjectivist system, and any claims about the non-subjective would in practice involve or imply some relationship between what belongs to a subject and what exists independently of any particular subject.

A consistent subjectivism would certainly be an impoverished philosophy. In fact, modern subjectivist philosophies were never and could not have been content with such a restriction. Modern philosophers like Descartes turned to subjectivist categories in order to forge what they considered to be a more adequate approach to crucial philosophical problems concerning the relation of mind to world, God, and society. They had no intention of cutting off the possibility of addressing such questions by giving up claims about what exists independently of individual minds.

In order to make claims about the nature of things independent of the subject, in order to establish the possibility of a relation or relations between subject and non-subject, a philosophy adopting a subjectivist foundation has two options, transcendentalist and naturalist. The transcendentalist option is to affirm the existence of characteristics, faculties or activities of or belonging to the subject which transcend the subject-object dichotomy, thereby establishing a relation between what-belongs-to-subjectivity and the nature of things that exist independently of any particular subjectivity. An example is Descartes' 'natural light'. The naturalist option is to introduce, however inconsistently, naturalist claims; for example, to claim that certain contents of subjectivity are caused by non-subjective existences. This involves a shift from the language of the order of consciousness to the language of the order of nature. Kant's use of the concept of sensation (sensations being, says Kant, the effect of the object on the mind) is an example of this.

The subjectivist philosophical systems of the seventeenth and eighteenth centuries are in fact syntheses of subjectivist, transcendental, and naturalist elements. It was only through combining transcendental and naturalist claims with the subjectivist viewpoint that the latter was made workable; without them, it is pure solipsism. While the naturalist claims are indeed important in the history of modern subjectivism, it is the transcendental notions that will be the concern of the present study, for it is the relation of the subjectivist categories with their accompanying transcendental ideas that is determinative for the historical dynamic of subjectivism.

It should be emphasized that the transcendental notions evident in the work of early modern philosophers did not serve as a mere *deus ex machina,* a device brought in to bandage up otherwise faultily constructed subjectivist systems. Historically, the relationship was more organic. Descartes, for example, clearly saw his transcendentalism and his subjectivism as part of one harmonious philosophical conception. Nevertheless, we can logically distinguish the two elements, just as Descartes implicitly distinguished them in his order of presentation in the *Meditations.* The history of modern philosophy has come rigorously to distinguish what Descartes saw as intrinsically connected, an historical process of distinction which correctly recognized the incompatibility at the heart of Descartes' position. This is not to say that the systems based on that recognition are superior to that of Descartes; it is only to say that they are more consistent in their subjectivism.

In the course of the development of modern philosophy, as we will see, the integral and synthetic relationship between subjectivist and transcendental ideas characteristic of early modern philosophy inevitably crumbled, and this crumbling is one of the factors that differentiates philosophy since the mid-nineteenth century from philosophy before that time and since Descartes. The cause of this crumbling is that, in the general competition between ideas that constitutes the philosophical tradition, at a certain time in history the historico-philosophical motivations and reasons for maintaining the transcendental doctrines became less important than the motivations and reasons that supported subjectivism. That is, because of their ultimate incompatibility, and because the two sets of ideas were in competition for the assent of philosophers, the synthesis could be maintained only as long as both sets of ideas were roughly equivalent in importance to philosophers. At a certain point, subjectivism's hold on the philosophical imagination significantly superceded that of the non-subjectivist elements of earlier philosophies. At that point, their incompatibility dictated that the latter be jettisoned.

The result of this process was a general breakdown of the subjectivist-transcendental synthesis, which become apparent beginning with the last decades of the nineteenth century. What had appeared in the centuries of Descartes and Kant as a plausible synthesis increasingly came to be seen as implausible. There ensued a general *delegitimation of the transcendental* as incompatible with the still-in-force subjectivist categories that continued to provide the underlying basis for much of philosophy. Subjectivism thus became radicalized, purified, and more universally applied.

But the most momentous fact about this process of radicalization remained generally unnoticed, even in the work of most of its twentieth-century proponents: the rejection of the transcendental radically *changed the subjectivist categories themselves*. These categories had been adopted by Descartes and others within a transcendental context and the loss of this context drastically altered the relations that could be conceived to hold between subject and non-subject, and this alteration of relations implicitly changed the conceivable nature of the subject and non-subject as well. Radicalized, non-transcendental subjectivism transformed the nature and relations of subjectivity and objectivity, turning them into something quite foreign to the work of their early modern proponents.

Before we can examine this transformation, however, we must explore the early phase of the historical dynamic of subject and object in the work of two of its classical authors, Descartes and Kant.

2

Forging the New
Standpoint: Descartes

Descartes is the founder of modern subjectivism. While his metaphysical dualism of thinking and extended substances is both well
known and almost universally criticized, few contemporary philosophers
notice that Descartes' underlying subjectivist interpretive categories remain powerfully in control of our thinking to this day. Most of us are
still closet neo-Cartesians.

In a letter to the Paris faculty of theology that accompanied the
second edition of his *Meditations On First Philosophy,* Descartes announced that the two chief questions addressed in his book would be
those of God and the soul; more specifically, of the former's existence
and of the latter's independence from and survival of the body.[1] He proposed to treat these questions philosophically rather than theologically.
The complete title of the second edition is in fact *Meditations on the
First Philosophy in Which the Existence of God and the Distinction
Between Mind and Body are Demonstrated.*

At the same time, the basis for Descartes' philosophy of nature can
also be found in the *Meditations.* He wrote in a letter to Mersenne:

> I will tell you, between ourselves, that these six meditations contain
> all the foundations of my physics. But please don't say so; because

32

those who favor Aristotle would perhaps make more difficulty about approving them; and I hope those who read them will accustom themselves insensibly to my principles, and recognize their truth, before noticing that they destroy those of Aristotle.[2]

Descartes is famous for his methodical doubt, his skeptical method, but religious and scientific ideas are just as central to his thought. Like most of his seventeenth-century colleagues, Descartes saw science, religion, and critical skepticism as quite compatible. For his age, science and religion were, after all, simply different aspects of the truth. And the aim of skepticism was not to debunk religion, but to debunk common sense, the manifold conflicting opinions of mankind which are born from the cloudy half-truths of the senses and their misinterpretations by the many. Interpretations of Descartes that devalue some aspects of his work, especially his theology, that cannot understand his abandonment of doubt and his embrace of religion, are guilty of importing today's modes of thought into Descartes' work. Such interpretations betray our contemporary difficulties over reconciling the claims of religion, the claims of science, and the claims of the critical spirit. On the contrary, the skeptical, scientific, and religious doctrines of the *Meditations* work together to form the uniqueness of the Cartesian system, as some commentators have seen.[3] Indeed, the attempt to find a common basis for religion, philosophy, and science, and therefore to harmonize the three, is precisely Descartes' aim and achievement. We may find the different aspects of the Cartesian philosophy incompatible on a *deeper* level, and so reject Descartes' attempted synthesis as ultimately inadequate, but this is not equivalent to claiming that such a synthesis is patently inconceivable.

Descartes forged a plausable synthesis of an anti-scholastic, materialistic physics and a spiritual, religious conception of human being. He did so by establishing a novel standpoint which, along with an associated method and set of concepts, makes his synthesis possible. Within the limits established by this standpoint the system works; that is, it gives relatively coherent answers to the problems Descartes was most concerned to address. But, as commentators noted even in Descartes' time, there are serious difficulties with the system. Some of these difficulties are the result of the very standpoint that makes the system possible. It is precisely the ground of Descartes' greatest achievement that at the same time determines what is most problematic in his philosophy. The fact of the widespread influence and enduring persuasiveness of Cartesian notions, despite their obvious difficulties, is due at least in part to the fact that the problems it caused were generally felt to be less significant than the questions it seemed to answer. This can be said as well of subjectiv-

ism in general, the prototype of which was formulated by Descartes in
his *Meditations*.

The Dichotomy

In Meditation One Descartes introduces the method of doubt
which he hopes will bring him a new and certain foundation for knowledge. In Meditation Two this doubting comes to a provisional end with
Descartes' assertion of the certainty of his own existence, based on his
awareness of his own thinking, and the further definition of his nature as
a "thing which thinks" (*res cogitans*). In Meditations Three through Six,
Descartes goes on to prove the existence of God, the existence of material substance—thus establishing the 'Cartesian dualism'—and to discuss
the nature of error and other topics.

Contrary to what is usually thought, the crucial step that defines
the Cartesian position occurs before the famous third paragraph of Meditation Two where Descartes presents the "I am deceived, therefore I
exist" argument. Indeed the certainty of Descartes' existence as a thinking thing is given from the start.

A clue to this pre-givenness can be seen in the second paragraph of
Meditation Two. Descartes writes that, "I imagine that body, figure,
extension, movement and place are but fictions of my mind."[4] A few
sentences later, but still antecedent to the argument that allegedly proves
his existence, he wonders, "Is there not some God, or some other being
by whatever name we call it, who puts these reflections into my mind?"[5]
In these passages Descartes makes reference to something, the existence
of which has evidently not been doubted: his mind or mental functioning. Descartes is writing as if there were a mind or some agency or locus
of thinking, which is subject to or entertains "fictions" and "reflections."
He certainly writes *as if* this agency or locus exists.

There is another term which Descartes associates with this existing
"mind," namely, Descartes' "I," which appears dozens of times before the
argument in paragraph three, Meditation Two. Whatever the referent of
the term "I" is, the existence of that referent is never doubted during the
so-called systematic doubt, although its existence has not been explicitly
affirmed. Briefly put, Descartes never doubts the existence of himself as
a mind or thinking thing, if we understand 'thing' in a broad sense, given
that Descartes has not yet defined the term. So, while in the pages preceding the middle of paragraph three, Meditation Two, Descartes does
not explicitly assert the existence of his mind, neither does he doubt it,
and indeed, he seems to presume it.

If one responds that this fact does not limit the range or validity of
Descartes' methodical doubt because to doubt the existence of one's own

mind would—as the whole doubt itself proves in the end—be impossible, then this assertion merely serves to call into question the meaning of the methodical doubt as a whole. It would seem that Descartes' doubt presumes what it seeks to prove, namely, the indubitability of the existence of Descartes' mind, of himself as a locus of coherent thinking activity.

If doubt proves that there must be a doubter, as Descartes subsequently argues, then by Descartes' own reasoning the existence of a doubter was already demonstrated at the *beginning* of the methodical doubt, not merely at the end, in a pragmatic rather than a discursive way. Descartes' method of doubt is not a method of argumentation and eventual proof, but is rather the methodical unfolding of a viewpoint. Even before the "I am deceived, therefore I exist" argument of Meditation Two Descartes has already established the primordiality and privileged status of an individual consciousness over all other realities as the starting point for inquiry by virtue of its indubitability.[6] He has begun with the position that, if we wish to know, to know anything at all, we must turn to the contents of an individual consciousness. The mind-body dualism and related Cartesian doctrines which Descartes unfolds later are already present here in implicit form. For what has been doubted?—only the existence of nature, the body, the world 'outside' of consciousness. The assertion of the I which thinks, of *res cogitans* or thinking substance, and of its antithesis in *res extensa* or extended substance, is the metaphysical justification for what has already been presumed as the standpoint from which the methodical doubt is enacted.

The Cartesian doubt cannot be fruitfully conceived as a simply negative process of subtraction, of removing beliefs in order to arrive at an indubitable, irreducible foundation. If Descartes' project of doubt is conceived in this way then it must be said that his doubt fails miserably: Descartes fails to question the integrity and existence of his own self or mind. He questions only his mind's opinions, sensations, and their sources or referents, external existences. If we adopt his own subsequent metaphysics as a measure, Descartes has put into question only one of the two kinds of finite substances in his methodical doubt. To conceive of his doubt according to the subtraction hypothesis, and to find it more or less adequate to this task, is to presume what the doubt ends by 'proving' (and, as I have argued, begins by presuming), namely, the primacy of mental existence.

Descartes' doubt is not a primarily negative, subtractive process. It is the tacit affirmation of a standpoint. The doubt enacts an affirmation of the methodological primacy of individual mental existence, of consciousness, as the standpoint from which philosophic and scientific thought should proceed. By presenting proofs of God's existence, and by legitimating the mathematico-scientific knowledge of *res extensa,* Descartes demonstrates that the chief questions he seeks to address can be fruitfully answered from the subjectivist standpoint he presumed in Meditation One and validated from within in Meditation Two.

The tacitly affirmed primacy of mental existence is one side of a dichotomy which is also being implicitly imposed by Descartes, and it is this dichotomy which is most essential. The failure to doubt mental existence and the fully enacted doubt of all independently existing things tacitly establishes the categorial distinction that Descartes believes to be the most fruitful, the distinction between what is or belongs to a subjectivity and all those things which do not belong to, which are not included in, a subjectivity.

This kind of dualism, subsequently given metaphysical justification in the doctrine of *res cogitans* and *res extensa,* but implicit in the methodical doubt, is given systematic expression throughout the *Meditations* and Descartes' other works. With this dualism, argues John Herman Randall, "Descartes effected a revolution in psychological theory and classification of the first importance . . . ."[7] Although this "revolution" is often glossed over by commentators, this dualism and the revolution it effected rest on Descartes' identification of mind with personal consciousness.

In Meditation Two Descartes asks himself, "What is a thing which thinks?" He answers that, "It is a thing which doubts, understands, affirms, denies, wills, refuses, which also imagines and feels."[8] Later, in asserting the indubitability of the contents of thinking *as thought,* he writes that:

> it is at least quite certain that it seems to me that I see light, that I hear noise and that I feel heat. That cannot be false; properly speaking it is what is in me called feeling; and used in this precise sense that is no other thing than thinking.[9]

And finally, in his *Principles of Philosophy,* he simply defines thought as "all that of which we are conscious as operating in us."[10] For Descartes, the contents of a thinking thing are the contents of its consciousness, the totality of what appears, the objects of awareness. This totality is the bedrock of indubitability for Descartes, as can be seen in the previous passages, and in the following: "If I mean only to talk of my sensation, or my consciously seeming to see or to walk, it [my assertion] becomes quite true because my assertion refers only to my mind . . . ."[11]

Descartes' equation of mind and thought with all of consciousness is a linguistic and a philosophical innovation. Anthony Kenny writes that:

French and Latin usage [of the words '*cogitare*' and '*penser*'] was never as wide as that found in Descartes; at no time was it natural to call a headache or a pang of hunger a *cogitatio* or *pensee*. In fact, Descartes was consciously extending the use of the words "*cogitare*" and "*penser.*"[12]

Philosophically, the Aristotelian-Scholastic tradition, which distinguished functional levels of soul, reserved the appellation 'mental' for acts of understanding and judgment, acts involving the grasping of universals. For the Scholastics sensation, feeling, and imagining are not mental events. Descartes' ascription of sensation to mind and thought

would have shocked the Aristotelian tradition, for which there is nothing whatever "mental" about pains: they are for it particular and individual bodily and material disturbances.[13]

Descartes initiated a concomitant change in the philosophical use of the word 'idea'. While there is some ambiguity over the word's meaning for Descartes, it certainly at times has a meaning as broad as "any content of mind." Kenny traces the modern use of the word through Locke back to Descartes who

was consciously giving it a new sense. Before him, philosophers used it to refer to archetypes in the divine intellect; it was a new departure to use it systematically for the contents of a human mind.[14]

The net effect of Descartes' identification of mind with thinking and his expansion of the meanings of "thinking" and "idea" is twofold. First, it pictures the human soul or mind as a uniform, homogeneous field of awareness. Descartes writes in *The Passions of the Soul* that, "there is within us but one soul, and this soul has not in itself any diversity of parts; the same part that is subject to sense impressions is rational . . . ."[15] Descartes' soul is not functionally differentiated according to Aristotelian-Scholastic levels; sensations, fantasies, and judgments are equally mental and therefore equally private, at least initially. That is, all functions of soul are equally related or unrelated to the external world. Second, the absolute distinction between consciousness and the non-conscious absorbs the distinction between the mental and the non-mental and rigidly enforces the privacy of the individual mind. The problematic external relation of mental to extended substance is visited indiscriminately on all mental activities.

What makes this Cartesian scheme subjectivist and radically distinct from earlier philosophical traditions is Descartes' determination of sensation (*aisthēsis*) and intellection (*nous*) as activities or characteristics of *individual consciousness*. In contrast to the Platonic and Aristotelian-Scholastic traditions, Descartes asserts that both mentation and sensation are first, essentially individual, and second, equivalent to or properties of consciousness or subjectivity. The effect of the Cartesian viewpoint is to move one particular aspect of human being—consciousness or subjectivity—to center-stage, thereby displacing other notions which had previously held the philosophic spotlight as the center of anthropology and epistemology. Mind, sensation, and other terms remain important, but they are now defined by Descartes in terms of the fundamental distinction between subjectivity and the non-subjective.

This Cartesian innovation has crucial epistemological implications. For Aristotle and for the Scholastics who translated his work into medieval Christian form, the knower and the known exhibit an internal or intrinsic relation. In both sensation and intellectual knowing the yet unperceived or unknown object, on the one hand, and the soul, on the other, embody different and complimentary powers. The mind and sense organs have the power to receive the intelligible and sensible forms of the object, while the object has the power to act on the sense organ and the mind. The "form" of a thing, its *to ti en einai* in Aristotle's Greek, is best translated as the "what it is to be" or "what it means to be" the thing.[16] In Aristotle's theory of knowledge and sensation it is the activities of knowing and sensing which make the heretofore potential "what it is to be" the thing become actual or active. When these powers become activities in actual sensing and knowing Aristotle believes that the sense organ and mind become one with the form of the object. The sense organ or mind *as active* is "one and the same activity" or actuality as the object *as active* or actual, and "yet the distinction between their being remains."[17] This unity is located in what is acted-upon, the sensor-knower: "the actuality of the sensible object and that of the sensible subject are both realized in the latter."[18] What-it-means-to-be-the-object is identified with that activity which is what-it-means-to-be-the knower-sensor. Consequently, for Aristotle, "The thinking part of the soul must . . . be . . . capable of receiving the form of an object without being the object."[19] In this sense, mind is capable of "becoming all things."[20]

Because Aristotle and his medieval philosophical descendents distinguish between the being of a thing and the thing's form or actuality, they are able to claim that an object is known *not* merely through producing or serving as the occasion for the arising of an effect or representation in the mind, an effect or representation which is extrinsic to the independent being of the thing (the "thing-in-itself"). Rather, knowledge of the object involves an intrinsic relation between what the knower essentially is and what the independent thing essentially is, an actualization of the thing itself in the modality of form in the mind. The thing, in a sense, is one with the mind. Aristotle's important addition that "yet the distinction between their being remains" prevents his view from falling into idealism. Thus, while mind and thing remain distinct in their being, there is yet a real dimension (form) in which they exist in community, in an internal or intrinsic relation.

Subjectivism cannot admit this internal relation of mind and thing, this dimension within which they are one. A consistent subjectivism, asserting that the most fundamental and inviolable categorical distinction is that between mind (understood as individual subjectivity) and all other things, *prima facie* cannot admit any such internal relation or community. Descartes correctly argues against the doctrine of "substantial forms" as inconsistent with his fundamental subjectivist viewpoint. The Cartesian model disengages sensation from any obvious ontological and physical relation to natural or physical reality, and intellection is disengaged from any obvious access to a community of rational discourse previously provided it by the common recognition of universals.

Consequently, for Descartes, mind, consciousness, and soul comprise one uniform field of representations uniformly disengaged by the methodical doubt from whatever is not 'in' awareness, from whatever is represented. Descartes did not discover individual consciousness or invent it. He gave it a new and foundational role in philosophy, thereby diminishing the role of previously dominant distinctions and concepts, such as *aisthēsis* and *nous,* sensation and intellection.

The doctrine of *res cogitans* and *res extensa* is not the core of the Cartesian dualism. The primacy of consciousness and the dualism of personal consciousness and the rest of reality is already present, explicitly or implicitly, in Descartes' method and in his psychological notions. Even the so-called 'problem of knowledge' that stems from the problem of the relation of mind to the world (for which Descartes is generally criticized) antecedes Meditation Two, because the world of "body, figure, extension, movement and place" has been reduced to "fictions," whereas mind is never doubted and is subsequently declared to be indubitable.

This pre-givenness of the Cartesian dualism deserves emphasis because it implies that the rejection of Descartes' metaphysical doctrine of two substances is not tantamount to a rejection of his dualism in its methodological and psychological forms. Many contemporary philosophers have explicitly rejected the former while implicitly accepting the latter, thereby accepting a significant portion of the doctrine they wish to condemn.[21] As Randall argues:

> The revolution involved in Cartesian dualism is not merely the sharp denaturalization of mind; it is the wholly new fashion in which

"mind" as well as "body" were taken. The acceptance of Descartes' classification of processes far outlasted the acceptance of his "dualism."[22]

Descartes declares in Meditation Two, and repeats in the subsequent Meditations, that he is a thing which thinks and that the essence of a perceptible thing is to be an extended thing. There are two kinds of finite substances for Descartes, *res cogitans* and *res extensa*. The philosophical implications and problems associated with this view have been widely discussed, beginning in Descartes' time. It is unnecessary to recapitulate the entire discussion here; a few points, however, must be made.

By conceiving of everything that is finite and non-mental as extensional, devoid of teleology and subject to a purely mechanical analysis, Descartes has all but declared that natural entities can have no intrinsic value. *Res cogitans* is the sole realm of meaning and value. Matter is devoid of non-spatial qualities. Mind or soul is the only finite existence having intrinsic value. If, within Descartes' scheme, anything non-mental is to be regarded as having universal and unchanging value, a value that is not simply bestowed on it by contingent human purpose, it could only be so regarded in virtue of its being created by God.

The dualism requires us to think of human beings as composed of two absolutely distinct substances, mind and body. Descartes, like any sane person, insists that they are "very closely united" and "seem to compose . . . one whole." Nevertheless, despite his recognition of this fact and his attempt to account for their interaction, mind and body remain irreconcilable. This directly contradicts the Aristotelian-Scholastic conception of the unity of the person established by the definition of soul as the "act" or "form" of the body.[23] Especially problematic for subsequent theories of knowledge is the difficulty this dualism causes in trying to conceive the internal relation of the knower-experiencer and the known-experienced. For Aristotle, when knowledge occurs an internal relationship between the thing known and the knower is consummated.[24] The elimination of the possibility of such a relationship is intrinsic to the Cartesian starting point, not just to his metaphysical dualism.

An enumeration of these problems should not be taken as a blanket condemnation of the Cartesian philosophy, or even of the metaphysical doctrine of two substances. The segregation of mind from nature made possible the purely mechanical and quantitative-mathematical analysis of nature by eliminating all substantial forms, final causes, and occult qualities that were part of the prevailing medieval view of nature. Descartes' philosophy was extremely influential in this regard.[25] His dualism allowed him at the same time to affirm what he saw as the basis of the integrity of the human mind: namely, its certain knowledge of God and nature, and its immortality. Descartes' dualism is a coherent and plausible answer to what he considered to be the chief questions demanding philosophical response.

Yet the problem remains that Descartes founded his philosophy on a privatist basis. It did not *remain* privatist, because the privacy of the starting point of Meditations One and Two was overcome in the later Meditations. The system as a *whole* is not privatistic. But the *foundation* remains intrinsically private, and this has an effect on the finished system. The non-privatist elements are derivative, and are therefore in a weaker position within the system. The non-privatist, transcendental elements of Descartes' system stand as a late achievement of the system, as the solution to the privatism of his starting point.

Now, it may be objected that the foundations of the *Meditations* are not private precisely because we all can think them just as Descartes did. Descartes wrote a book, a fundamentally communicative instrument, hoping that it would be read by other thoughtful souls, and he rightly expected that any human would be able to think these same thoughts himself or herself and thereby share his reasoning. This is true; yet it is also true that this communicative vehicle, the *Meditations,* describes a metaphysical picture in which communication has no *natural* place. Its basic concepts and viewpoint militate against the possibility of there being communication in the world it describes and leave that possibility to be explained only through recourse to God. That two or more or an indefinitely large number of people can perform identical private thought experiments makes the thought experiments no less private. Identity and similarity are not equivalent to community.

Even if the phenomenon of reading itself were to make sense within the metaphysical picture of the *Meditations*, which is doubtful, it would in no way establish the possibility of a community among its readers, although it might be said to establish an indefinite number of dyadic communities involving each individual reader and Descartes. The fact that there is an actual community of shared ideas and actual or potential discussion among all Descartes' readers simply demonstrates that Descartes has created a metaphysical picture within which the intelligent assimilation of that very picture is difficult or impossible to explain. This is not unique to Descartes. The human activities of thinking, theorizing, and communicating have often produced theories that cannot account for their own possibility.

That the question of the existence of the material universe is addressed only at the end of the *Meditations* is itself significant. It rhetorically emphasizes a tenet of his subjectivism by presuming that Descartes and his reader could conduct a coherent philosophical discussion while the existence of the entire universe was in doubt. It is as if the contents of Descartes' mind would be left unchanged by either the existence or non-existence of the universe, so that when its existence is eventually affirmed in Meditation Six the contents of Descartes' mind are not altered but only confirmed or supplemented. The relation of world to mind is purely external. This externality was implicit in the method of doubt. That commentators can find this complete externality of the world and, indeed, the doubt itself philosophically plausible, is testimony to how thoroughly Descartes' subjectivist viewpoint has been adopted to this day.

To argue that the doubt is proposed solely for methodological purposes, that Descartes does not really doubt the existence of material bodies, while true, does not change the essential point. Descartes writes in the Synopsis of Meditation Six:

> finally all the reasons from which we may deduce the existence of material things are set forth. Not that I judge them to be very useful in establishing that which they prove, to wit, that there is in truth a world, that men possess bodies, and other such things which never have been doubted by anyone of sense . . . .[26]

The point is that Descartes is suggesting that true knowledge and the true practice of philosophy require us to think *as if* the material world were not a fact, to imagine that philosophical thinking could take place while the existence of the universe is in doubt and then to imagine what such thinking would be like.

The Transcendental Bridge

We have thus far been concerned mainly with themes that appear in the first two Meditations, with those Meditations in which Descartes proposes and begins to generate a philosophy founded on a subjectivist basis. If Descartes had not gone beyond the second Meditation his philosophy as a whole would indeed be subject to the charge of privatism. Descartes does, however, pass beyond the second Meditation to provide a theological justification for both the existence of non-mental finite things and the relatedness of mind to those things.

Descartes presents arguments for the existence of God in Meditations Three and Five. In both arguments "clarity and distinctness" as the criteria of truth and the concept of the "natural light" play a role, although this role is more explicit in Meditation Three. The following discussion is not intended to evaluate Descartes' proofs for God's existence, but rather to trace in them the function of certain key concepts and to explore the importance of the arguments as a whole for the relation of mind to nature in Descartes' system.

In Meditation Three Descartes derives the famous "clear and distinct" criteria for the truth of ideas from an inspection of the one truth he has thus far affirmed, his own existence. He asks himself what it is about the knowledge of his own existence as a thinking thing that makes it indubitable and answers that:

> there is nothing that assures me of its truth, excepting the clear and distinct perception of that which I state . . . and accordingly it seems to me that already I can establish as a general rule that all things which I perceive very clearly and very distinctly are true.[27]

A few paragraphs later he distinguishes what he is taught by "nature" from what he learns through the "natural light." Nature is a source of mere "spontaneous inclinations" and is not to be trusted regarding questions of truth. The natural light cannot be doubted, since:

> for example, it has been shown me that I am from the fact that I doubt . . . . And I possess no other faculty whereby to distinguish truth from falsehood, which can teach me that what this light shows me to be true is not really true, and no other faculty that is equally trustworthy.[28]

The natural light allows us to recognize what is clearly and distinctly true. Clarity and distinctness are the criteria of truth and the natural light is the faculty by which we recognize truth. Descartes will later prove that since we possess "no other faculty" for obtaining truth, whatever the natural light shows us to be true must be true.

The proof in the third Meditation depends heavily on the natural light. It is through it that we know both that there must be at least as much reality in a cause as in its effect, and that the objective reality of an idea must have as its ultimate cause some formal reality.[29] Given these principles, Descartes can claim that the only possible cause of the idea of a perfect being that he has in his mind is an actual perfect being existing outside of his mind.

In the fifth Meditation proof the natural light is not mentioned. Clarity and distinctness, however, appear twice: the idea of God is itself a "very" clear and distinct idea and Descartes says that we know clearly and distinctly that God's existence is necessarily entailed in the idea of God.

It is only after proving God's existence twice that Descartes can turn to the question of the existence of finite non-mental substances in the sixth Meditation. He has already asserted the principles on which his argument concerning this question will be based. At the close of the third Meditation he had reasoned that, since God "possesses all perfections," then, "from this it is manifest that He cannot be a deceiver, since the light of nature teaches us that fraud and deception necessarily proceed from some defect."[30] More precisely, this implies, as Descartes remarks later, that since God cannot be a deceiver and since He has given us a capacity for judgment, there must be a right way to use that capacity which will allow us to avoid error.[31] This right way, he concludes, is to accept as true only what is known clearly and distinctly.[32]

On this basis, Descartes is ready in the sixth and last Meditation to give us his proof of the existence of corporeal substance. It is a simple argument. He declares that he clearly has within himself a "passive faculty" that receives the impressions of sensible things. The question is, what is the "active faculty" or cause that is producing these impressions? Descartes concludes that the cause(s) could not be God Himself, or some other creature, or his own mind,[33] because since God:

> has given me no faculty to recognize that this is the case, but, on the other hand, a very great inclination to believe that . . . they [sensible ideas] are conveyed to me by corporeal objects, I do not see how He could be defended from the accusation of deceit if these ideas were produced by causes other than corporeal objects. Hence we must allow that corporeal things exist.[34]

Descartes' proof is theological and epistemological. Given the nature and content of our knowing faculty and the existence of a nondeceiving God, there must be material substance 'producing' some of the content of our minds. But, Descartes is quick to add, these corporeal things "are perhaps not exactly what we perceive by the senses . . . ." Only what the mind knows of the things "clearly and distinctly . . . that is to say, all things which, speaking generally, are comprehended in the object of pure mathematics, are truly to be recognized as external objects."[35]

Descartes' assertions of the existence of non-mental things and of the possibility of coming to know those things have two related justifications: the existence of God and the existence of transcendental reason. Transcendental reason is the mental faculty or activity (like the Greek *nous*) that can assert or recognize truths, truths that apply to the world in-itself as well as the world as we encounter it, and which are not the mere product of either sense experience or the logical consideration of a chain of reasons.[36] That is, beyond the capacity to draw true conclusions from already asserted true premises (logical reason) and the capacity to determine the practical means to accomplish already given ends (instrumental reason), Descartes presumes the existence of a mental faculty that has *content,* that intuits the first principles and values that form the basis of logical and technical reasoning. These principles and values hold true for non-mental, non-personal existence. There is a part of the individual mind that knows, or can know, the ultimate or intrinsic nature of reality beyond the individual mind's representations of that reality.

In Descartes' case this faculty is the natural light which shows us truths that hold for both personal consciousness and the world outside: for example, that the cause of an idea must have at least as much formal reality as the idea has objective reality. This truth explicitly compares extra-mental reality with the content of ideas. Descartes' natural light is not bound by the methodical doubt or by the dualism that the doubt embodies.

Descartes' version of the ontological argument presented in Meditation Five exhibits a slightly new wrinkle on this scheme. The proof runs as follows: since the idea of God includes "every sort of perfection" and since Descartes has "recognized that existence is a perfection," the idea of God necessarily entails the idea of existence, just as the idea of a mountain entails the idea of a valley. Thus, if one thinks of God, one must conclude that God exists. Here, Descartes attempts to prove the existence of an external entity without recourse to premises involving external realities. One could argue that, strictly speaking, this is not the case; that the idea of existence itself, by referring to all reality in general, itself refers to external reality since it is not restricted to consciousness. Nevertheless, Descartes has certainly not resorted to the kind of principles he employed in the third Meditation proof, principles that violate the dualism of his methodological presuppositions.

Kant's famous criticism of this argument will be that to think a concept is to think a possibility and that we cannot smuggle the idea of actuality or necessity into this thought.[37] For Kant, being cannot be a predicate, a content of a concept, but is rather the positing of that content as belonging to existence. For Kant, such positing occurs only in synthetic judgment. In a sense, Kant is here simply reapplying the medieval and Cartesian distinction more rigorously than Descartes did. The objective reality of an idea is strictly distinguished from its formal reality.

Taking a somewhat different slant from that of Kant's criticism, we can distinguish within Descartes' ontological argument two implicit claims. The first is that the idea of God implies the idea of God's non-mental existence. The second is that the *idea* of an entity's non-mental existence implies its *actual* non-mental existence: that is, thinking something as existing in reality implies that it must exist in reality.

In Descartes' time, the objection to the ontological argument that it leads to the absurd conclusion that whatever we think must exist, was already known. Descartes believed that he could defeat that objection by arguing—quite correctly, given his presuppositions—that the ontological argument works only for one idea, the idea of God. This is to say, the first claim is true only of the idea of God; the idea of God is the only idea which intrinsically implies the idea of non-mental existence, which forces us to think existence as implied within it.

But Descartes' disclaimer does not in fact defeat the attempt to reduce his argument to absurdity. For his argument still requires that the fact that we must think an entity as existing—in this case, God—implies that the entity actually does exist; this is the second claim. Descartes' disclaimer merely functions to deny the *necessity of thinking* a thing's non-mental existence in all cases where the thing being thought is not God; it does *not* disclaim the assertion that the idea of a thing's non-mental existence, once thought, must imply its actual non-mental existence. And Descartes clearly accepts this claim as part of his ontological argument. Thus, if I think of a unicorn, it is quite true that I am not *required* to think of the unicorn as existing non-mentally; only the idea of God would require this. Nevertheless, I *may* think the unicorn as existing non-mentally. There is nothing to prevent me from doing so. And once I do, the necessity of concluding from this thought of the unicorn as existing that the unicorn must exist *is as fully implied by the second claim of Descartes' argument* as the necessity of concluding from the thought of God as existing that God must exist outside of the mind.

The second claim of Descartes' argument clearly leads to absurdity. Independent of any considerations of subjectivism, it must be rejected as false, and within the boundaries of subjectivism itself it is inconsistent with the categorial distinction of subjectivity and non-mental existence.

The issue here, in both Kant's and my own critique of Descartes, is the nature of the bridge(s) that can be erected across the subjectivist gulf between thinking subject and non-subjective world. Descartes' third Meditation proof erects a transcendental bridge; we will see that Kant's own bridge belongs to the same general type, however different it is usually claimed to be. The ontological argument would have been a very different kind of bridge; but it not only fails, it is out of step with Descartes' own system.

With the notions of natural light and the related criteria of clarity and distinctness, Descartes established an avenue of access for personal consciousness to formal or external reality. Descartes has given a particular mode of thinking—the thinking of clear and distinct ideas, illumined by natural light—a privileged relation to non-mental reality. The epistemological validity of this special access and its metaphysical justification is given by the arguments for God.[38] As is well known, Descartes is here caught in a circle: the natural light and the clarity-distinctness criteria are employed to prove God's existence, but their validity can only be guaranteed by God's existence.

If one accepts the interpretation that Descartes is actually trying to build a philosophical system up from nothing, from the base of a total doubt, then this circle does represent a serious flaw. But Descartes is not attempting a creation *ex nihilo;* he is simply bringing together and harmonizing the religious ideas he wished to establish with the vicissitudes of the new standpoint he has adopted, namely subjectivism.[39] They fit together remarkably well. The problems of his subjectivism are answered by his theological views. God, along with the God-given faculty of natural light, makes the relation of personal consciousness and material world possible. The philosophical power of Descartes' system lies not in any presuppositionless logical argumentation, but in the working out of an innovative, profound, and yet simple viewpoint, demonstrating that the most crucial philosophical questions of his time could be answered from that viewpoint. A mathematical science of nature and a religious knowledge of God could both be "demonstrated," be generated out of an unaided, untutored private consciousness.

The circularity of Descartes' argument is nevertheless significant for what it reveals. It is a clue to what I referred to earlier as the deeper level at which the incompatibility of his system is manifest. The circle shows us that Descartes fails to generate God and the world out of privacy. He cannot prove God's existence or the existence of material substance if he adheres strictly to the subjectivist standpoint. To execute the proofs, to go beyond the subjectivist standpoint, he must introduce into personal consciousness a knowledge of truths that are relevant to realities outside that consciousness. That is, he must go beyond the subjectivist standpoint proper, into a transcendentalism which gives subjectivity a vehicle of access to non-subjectivity, which, by strict subjectivist standards, it cannot have.

In summary, Descartes has given us the classic formulation of early modern subjectivism, a formulation which, in its broadest outlines, remained canonical for 250 years. In that formulation the most fundamental distinction for all inquiry is the distinction of subjectivity or consciousness and the totality of its contents or what is internally related to it, on the one hand, and all other features and factors of what is, or objectivity, on the other. The two sides of this dichotomy are brought into relation with each other, or develop a relationship, through the idea of the ultimate transcendental being, God, and through that feature or capacity of the subject which most resembles God, and which itself transcends the subject-object dichotomy, transcendental reason. Leibniz and Spinoza accept these terms as fully as Descartes. And despite the different and dynamic formulations of Hegel's system, these points remain essentially true for him, and the concepts of subjectivity, objectivity, God, and reason stand as the cornerstones of his philosophy.

This is not to say that the subjectivist-transcendental synthesis was universally accepted or unchallenged. On the contrary, it was challenged from the outset. But, after Descartes' time, it was increasingly the transcendental elements which came under fire, and not the subjectivist categories, especially in the eighteenth century. Even the most thoroughgoing and radical critic of the transcendental, David Hume, launched his attacks on the transcendental synthesis—on the proofs of God, substance, and the notion of transcendental reason—from the basis of an *acceptance* of the primacy of the subjectivist categories. Hume thus became the first prominent figure in a long line of philosophers who critiqued the subjectivist-transcendental synthesis from within, who drew out the implications of the universal application of the subject-object dichotomy and the consequent de-legitimation of the transcendental components of the synthesis.

But Hume was a century ahead of his time and a chapter ahead of our present story. Before examining the historical de-legitimation of the transcendental, we must first confront the work of another philosopher, a man so disturbed by Hume's critical questions that he was driven to formulate a new version of the subjectivist-transcendental synthesis. That man is Kant, a philosopher who, in the process of struggling with the inherent problems of transcendental subjectivism, permanently changed the language in which any philosophical business would henceforth be conducted. His work would reveal the great theoretical difficulties entailed in trying to harmonize subjectivism and the transcendental. Yet Kant knew that given the assumptions of his time, such harmony was indispensable for making philosophical sense of the undeniable facts of scientific knowledge and everyday moral insight. Kant labored very hard to try to make subjectivism safe for reality.

3

Recasting the Synthesis: Kant

The 140 years that elapsed between the publication of the first edition of the *Meditations* and the first appearance of Kant's *Critique of Pure Reason* were years of great social, intellectual, and philosophical change. In that time philosophy had grown further from medieval ways of thought, and science was no longer inciting its revolution, but had fully installed a new regime under its universally acclaimed leader, Newton. The intellectual density of this period is reflected in Kant's text, wherein we find a systematic response to the major schools of thought active in philosophy during that period.

The ways in which Cartesian philosophy is subjectivist do not have clear parallels in Kant, despite superficial continuities. Where Kant adopts Cartesian notions and viewpoints he complicates them to deal with a more complex theoretical situation. Behind the superficial similarities, and the deeper discontinuities, we find yet deeper convergences. The ensuing discussion will focus on key areas of Kant's masterwork wherein the relevant problems can be seen. Indeed, we will see that the determination of Kant's project in the *Critique* is in some ways the most difficult question of all.

Among the variety of tasks the *Critique* undertakes, two in particular are of concern here. The first task explicitly and repeatedly claimed by Kant as his primary aim is to discover "what and how much can the understanding and reason know apart from all experience?"[1] This is the aim of the Kant who had been "awakened from [his] dogmatic slumbers" by Hume, the Kant concerned to legitimate an indubitable, demonstrative science of the natural world. His second aim, which extends beyond the proper task of the first *Critique* and in regard to which the latter serves as a kind of prolegomena, is first mentioned in the preface to the second edition. It is "to deny knowledge in order to make room for faith."[2] Human knowledge, when it illegitimately attempts to determine questions concerning the soul, God, freedom, and immortality, interferes with morality or practical reason. The limitation of the possibilities of knowledge is a morally inspired task. Kant believes that his *Critique:*

> removes an obstacle which stands in the way of the employment of practical reason, nay threatens to destroy it . . . . We are convinced that there is an absolutely necessary, *practical* employment of pure reason—the *moral*—in which it inevitably goes beyond the limits of sensibility . . . it must yet be assured against [speculative reason's] opposition, that reason may not be brought into conflict with itself.[3]

It is in the context of these two aims that Kant's Copernican Revolution, his so-called "transcendental turn," is introduced. This turn is Kant's distinctive methodological innovation and is specifically designed to enable him to achieve his two aims.

Kant proposes that:

> Hitherto it has been assumed that all our knowledge must conform to objects. But all attempts to extend our knowledge of objects by establishing something in regard to them *a priori,* by means of concepts, have, on this assumption, ended in failure. We must therefore make trial whether we may not have more success in the tasks of metaphysics, if we suppose that objects must conform to our knowledge.[4]

Along with this "supposition"[5] Kant proposes the distinction between "things in themselves," which he associates with the "unconditioned,"[6] and "appearances" and "phenomena," the determinate and indeterminate objects of experience, respectively. (The terms 'appearances' and 'phenomena' will refer interchangeably to the objects of experience, in opposition to things-in-themselves or noumena.) Things-in-themselves and appearances are the two senses in which objectivity is to be taken. This distinction, along with the statement of the transcendental turn, defines Kant's new approach to the twin problems of *a priori* knowledge of the world and the moral need to limit that knowledge.

A priori knowledge can only be had, Kant asserts, of objects as appearances, of objects as they "conform to our knowledge." There are universal and necessary requirements for anything to appear as an object for us, and these requirements are themselves all that can be known of objectivity *a priori*. What cannot be an object of experience, for example, the human soul and its allegedly free will, cannot be known and therefore cannot be determined by human knowledge. Such things can therefore be the objects of thought and faith without contradicting knowledge.

Now, the transcendental turn is often seen as definitive of the Kantian project in the first *Critique,* and it would seem to be an obvious move to subjectivism. Rorty's critique of modern philosophy treats Kant's significance in just this way, as orienting the attention of philosophy toward the subject and making the nature of the world as it appears to us dependent on the former.[7] It is not clear, however, that Rorty's critique applies as well to Kant as to Kant's legacy, to the various ways Kant has been interpreted and employed by others. While it is undeniable that a philosophy based on the transcendental turn is subjectivist in some sense, the precise meaning of this turn and its subjectivism is ambiguous in Kant's text.

The transcendental turn and the project to which it gives rise can be described either in subjective or objective terms. (The former term is not equivalent to my notion of subjectivism, although, as we will see, the subjective interpretation of the *Critique* will seem to be more susceptible to my criticism than the objective interpretation.) According to the subjective interpretation, the nature of the world we know, the object-world, is significantly determined by the inherent constitution of our faculty of knowledge or capacity to know. Simply put, the structure of the world as we experience and know it is significantly determined by our minds or mental activity. Kant often makes statements describing his project in just these terms. For example, he writes:

> The object must conform to the constitution of our faculty of intuition . . . .[8]
> We can know *a priori* of things only what we ourselves put into them . . . .[9]
> For it may well be that even our empirical knowledge is made up of what we receive through impressions and of what our own faculty of knowledge supplies from itself. If our faculty of knowledge makes any such *addition,* it may be that we are not in a position to distinguish it from the raw material . . . .[10] (my emphasis)

In the last statement we see a corollary to the subjective interpretation, namely, the notion that the objective world as we know and experience it is the product of two sources, one raw and unformed, which Kant calls "sensation," the other the formal imposition of the mind. The object-world is the result of an interaction which, to push the subjective interpretation to its psychologistic extremes, Kant sometimes describes as a simply additive composition, as when he declares in the "Transcendental Aesthetic" that he will first "isolate" sensibility by "taking away" the conceptual addition and then "separate off" sensation, "so that nothing may remain save pure intuition . . ." as if the object-world were the result of a purely arithmetical process and could be analyzed via a kind of epistemological subtraction.

The objective interpretation represents an attempt to avoid reference to "mind," "contributions of mind," "two sources of knowledge," "things in themselves," "matter of sensation," and "constitution of our faculty of knowledge." According to it Kant, at least in the "Transcendental Analytic," is concerned to delimit the necessary features of any objective world, or of all objective knowledge. The system of representations that constitute an object-world must exhibit certain forms of relation and organization, and it is these forms that Kant sought to discover. Where these forms do not obtain there is nothing that could be called an object or a world and no possibility of objective knowledge.[11]

The contrast between the two interpretations is parallel, although not equivalent to, the contrast between Kant's own "subjective" and "objective" deductions, two different tasks which, Kant says in the first edition, are performed by the "Transcendental Deduction." The subjective deduction asks, "How is the faculty of thought itself possible?" and explores the nature of the understanding,[12] whereas the objective deduction is concerned solely with the objective validity of the pure concepts of the understanding, with *quid juris,* the question of the inherent 'right' or necessity of the application of pure concepts to the intuition of objects.[13] The appeal of the objective interpretation is that it allows us to avoid, and thus to spare Kant, the difficulties involved in talking about things-in-themselves, interaction of mind with unformed sensation, and the constitution of mental faculties or capacities.

While the objective interpretation may appear to avoid the more obvious problems of the subjective interpretation, it is an inadequate reading of Kant's project. Some version of the subjective interpretation is inescapable if we want to make sense of the task of the Transcendental Analytic as a whole.

According to the objective interpretation, any objective world and all objective knowledge must conform to certain necessary conditions. One may then ask of this interpretation: what is an object, or an objective world, or objective knowledge? A possible answer is "representations ordered by the above-mentioned conditions." This is to say that the very meanings of objectivity and world are exhausted by the necessary conditions Kant sought to discover. But if so, then why is this particular ordering of representations of any special interest or importance? If objectivity has no meaning outside of Kant's system, then why is that particular way of ordering representations of any significance outside of the system?

The answer to why this order is important, Kant would reply, is that it is the order of the *real* world of experience and of Newtonian science, it is the world we actually live in. One of the purposes of the *Critique* is to justify universal and necessary knowledge of the actually experienced world, whose systematic expression is science. This project would have no meaning if the objective world described by science were only one possible ordering of representations among an indefinite number of other possible orderings—religious, poetic, etc. If it were merely one among an indefinite number of possible orders, then the scientific order would perhaps have a unique status due to its own internal, stylistic principles, and hence have some claim to an aesthetic superiority to other orders; but it could have no special claim on the real or the true, no cognitive superiority, which is what matters to Kant here.

The same problem occurs if we ask for a justification of Kant's project according to the objective interpretation. By what right are these particular conditions, the categories, constitutive of objective knowledge? This is essentially the question of Kant's objective deduction. Either these conditions hold by definition, in which case the objective world (as a *stipulated* ordering) again loses any claim to special status among possible orderings of representations, or there must be some process of analysis or demonstration through which an already given objectivity is shown necessarily to presume these conditions. If the latter is admitted then it is legitimate to ask how objectivity is given, which is precisely the question of the subjective deduction. As we know, Kant would not have allowed a merely analytic demonstration of the necessity of the categories. But even independently of Kant's reasoning it can be seen that such a demonstration would deny the *Critique* any significance, because, again, such an objectivity would only be one of an indefinite number of possible orderings of representations.

The point is that as soon as one attempts to understand the *Critique* through the objective interpretation, to locate it, to describe its meaning, one is forced to talk in the very terms that the interpretation was offered in order to avoid. One is forced to speak of human beings cognitively grasping an already given empirical world, of minds and sensations: one is forced into the subjective interpretation.

Kant himself felt the effects of this 'subjective force' in the Transcendental Deduction. Despite the fact that he explicitly privileged the objective deduction as the essential task of the deductions, he finds himself continually forced to discuss the subjective factors involved in the production of the objective world or objective ordering of representations.

In general, while the objective interpretation seems to avoid the problems of the subjective, it is able to do so only as long as we do not ask what it *means*. Its own terms can be defined in only two ways, either through the subjective interpretation or in a purely analytic way. The latter form of definition, which was rejected by Kant as purely formal, contentless, and therefore inadequate to his task, would have drained the *Critique* of the meaning its author clearly intended it to have. The *Critique*, whatever its problems, has meaning only within the bounds of the actual world, wherein human beings experience and attempt to know an already given reality, which is to say, a reality existentially independent of and prior to the act of knowing.[14] A purely objectivist *Critique* would be a bloodless, inhuman critique, an inquiry into knowledge devoid of reference to the knower. In short, it would not be Kant's *Critique*, which like all important works, suffers from inadequacies precisely because it addresses issues of human relevance.

The Two Orders of Knowing

Kant defined the project of the *Critique* as the discovery of *a priori* knowledge of appearances. Such knowledge, which is by definition "absolutely independent of all experience," is contrasted with empirical, *a posteriori* knowledge of appearances.[15] Kant also distinguishes between analytic and synthetic judgments. In the former the predicate of the judgment is derived from the subject via logical analysis, delivering necessary truths but without any new content, while in the latter the relation of predicate to subject requires an additional element, and is thus the product of a synthesis.[16] The contrast between these two sets of distinctions is crucial to Kant's project.

The analytic–synthetic distinction had already been employed by Hume and Leibniz, in different terms. Hume in fact had set the stage for the *Critique* by insisting on the absolute separation of the two orders.[17] This meant that analytic truths, or in Hume's language, truths derived from the "relations of ideas," could not demonstrate the existence of any "matter of fact," and no accumulation of contingent experiences of matters of fact could attain the necessity and universality of statements that owed their truth to the relations of ideas. This became a fundamental tenet of most empiricist philosophies, that there are two distinct orders of truth, one exhibiting necessity and certainty but by itself incapable of telling us anything about the actual world and the other providing information about the actual world, but always only probabilistically, never with necessity.

Kant's innovation was, while strictly maintaining the distinction between the analytic order and the order of actual appearances, to assert the existence of a third category of knowledge, synthetic *a priori* knowledge, universal and necessary conditions of objectivity that are not derived through logical analysis. Kant maintains the Humean distinction, but asserts that there is yet a third possibility in addition to the analytic and empirical-existential orders.[18]

The *a priori*–empirical distinction and Kant's innovative tripartite categorization, analytic–synthetic *a priori*–empirical, are related to a set of psychological concepts employed by Kant. He announces that:

> Our knowledge springs from two fundamental sources of the mind: the first is the capacity of receiving representations, the second is the power of knowing an object through these representations. Through the first an object is *given* to us, through the second the object is *thought* . . . . Intuitions and concepts constitute, therefore, the elements of all our knowledge . . . .
> If the *receptivity* of our mind . . . is to be entitled sensibility, then the mind's power of producing representations from itself, the *spontaneity* of knowledge, should be called the understanding.[19]

The intuitions of the receptive power, sensibility, relate to objects in two ways. For Kant, "the effect of an object upon the faculty of representation, so far as we are affected by it is *sensation*."[20] When an intuition is related to an object via sensation, which Kant says corresponds to the "matter" of the apparent object, then intuition is "empirical." When the intuition relates to the "form" of the apparent object, devoid of sensation, it is "pure" or "*a priori*."

What is received in sensation is the essence of the empirical for Kant. The form of the intuited object must, according to Kant's transcendental method, "lie ready for the sensations *a priori* in the mind, and so must allow of being considered apart from all sensation."[21] The matter of the object of sensation will turn out to be composed of qualities like color, hardness, softness, weight, and impenetrability.[22] The pure form of the intuition of objects will be extension and figure. Intuition in general, empirical and pure, constitutes our "immediate" relation to objects and "all thought must, directly or indirectly . . . relate ultimately to intuitions . . . ."[23]

Now, these notions do not make Kant, as some have criticized him, a "faculty psychologist." Epistemology and psychology are inevitably linked; it is impossible to explore the questions Kant raises without delineating different modes of human cognitive activity, at least implicitly.[24]

Kant clearly divides that activity, excluding for the moment the speculative employment of reason, into two modes; the immediate-receptive and the mediate-spontaneous. These psychological presumptions of Kant's are implicit in the epistemological doctrine of the analytic–synthetic distinction, endorsed by both Kant and the empiricists, and subsequently overcome by Kant with the notion of the synthetic *a priori*. Just as Kant affirms a third term intermediate between the analytic and the empirical, he will discover a third faculty intermediate between intuition and understanding, namely, imagination. But just as the analytic–synthetic distinction is open to criticism (for example, that of Quine), the picture of mentation implied in Kant's psychological distinctions is subject to the charge of subjectivism.[25]

Both the analytic-synthetic and the concept-intuition distinctions, as Kant defines them, rest on the notion that there is a fundamental dichotomy of function within the mind. It implies that there are two orders of mental representations. One is in immediate contact with things-in-themselves or reality and is more or less determined by the latter; these representations are what they are because of non-mental, non-subjective factors. This order is "receptive" in Kant's language. There is a second, mediate order which relates to objectivity only through the immediate order, is under-determined by objectivity, and instead expresses the determining character of mind itself. The former serves as content to the latter's form, the former is passive for the latter's active processes or structures.

This model is intrinsically subjectivist. It is an application of the subject–object distinction *within* the domain of mental representations, dividing representations according to their immediacy to objectivity. Its association of other qualities with the degree of immediacy is consistent with the subjectivist tradition: representations immediate to objectivity are marked by receptivity or passivity and determination by the object, while more mediate, "inner" representations are "spontaneous," are produced by the subject or mind itself. The former are the source of content, of all contact with objectivity, but lack the organization characteristic of the final product of knowledge. The latter provide organization and perhaps certainty, but by themselves are contentless, unrelated to objectivity.

Many thinkers besides Kant are concerned to distinguish between types or levels of knowledge and experience, one of which is designated as capable of obtaining certain and incorruptible knowledge, while the other or others are at best probabilistic or otherwise limited. These types are claimed to have their own specific object-types as well. Some objects can be known with certainty, others cannot. For Kant, for example, color, being part of the matter of the appearance, cannot be the occasion of *a priori* knowledge, whereas mass and shape can. This idea is at least as old as Plato. It becomes *subjectivist* in my sense of that word when the two (or more) types of knowledge or experience are claimed to have differential and determinate relations to subjectivity and objectivity. For Hume certainty is possible only in the knowledge of the relations of intra-mental objects, ideas, whereas all knowledge of objectivity, of matters of fact, comes thorough impressions and can be only probabilistic. It is the same for Kant; the certain is what is dictated by mind, what we "put into" the objects, whereas the effect of the object on the faculty of representation (sensation) can produce no certainty.

In general, subjectivism privileges those modes of the subject's knowing, experiencing, and interacting with the world in which the subject is in greater *control* over the product of this interaction, as opposed to those modes or situations in which the subject is more vulnerable to, affected, or determined by the object. As we will see shortly, this dualistic understanding of human cognitive activity, which in Kant gives privilege to the understanding and which serves his project of justifying the science of nature, will be contradicted by other theoretical requirements of the *Critique* equally essential to Kant's task.

Relating the Two Orders

The question of the relation of mind to what exists independently of mind is much more complex in the case of the *Critique* than in the *Meditations*. Unlike Descartes, Kant is not concerned to prove the existence of non-mental things, which he never doubts.[26] Indeed Kant does not doubt the existence of things-in-themselves, although they are in principle outside the bounds of possible knowledge. His concern in the Transcendental Analytic is solely with what Descartes called the "material" and the "objective" reality of representations. It must be emphasized that for Kant appearances or "objective realities" are entirely real and non-mental. While non-mental they are nevertheless, in some sense, products of the transcendental synthesis of the mind. The question of Kant's subjectivism, given that his Copernican Revolution dictates that objects must conform to knowledge, may seem superficially obvious, but the ambiguous status of appearances in relation to mind make this question much more difficult once one penetrates beneath the surface. The key to this ambiguity, and to many others in the *Critique,* lies in the status Kant accords to sensuous receptivity.

Kant writes in the preface to the second (or "B") edition that it would be "absurd" to claim that "there can be appearance without anything that appears."[27] He repeats in the section "Phenomena and Noumena," first (or "A") edition, that:

> Unless therefore we are to move constantly in a circle, the word
> appearance must be recognized as already indicating a relation to
> something, the immediate representation of which is, indeed, sensible,
> but which, even apart from the constitution of our sensibility . . .
> must be something in itself, that is, independent of sensibility.[28]

In that section, in both editions, Kant identifies things-in-themselves as noumena or purely intelligible, non-sensible entities. Kant vacillates in both editions between asserting that noumena must exist but cannot be known or determined in any way, and saying that the concept of noumena is a purely negative limiting concept, employed, "like an empty space," to limit the claims of appearances to reality. Keeping in mind the above-cited passages, however, this apparent vascillation does not seem to apply to the notion of thing-in-itself. Kant implies that the latter notion is logically required by way of distinction from the notion of appearance.

Appearances are necessarily sensible or empirical. The source of the sensible or empirical within the appearance is sensation, which is, "the effect of an object upon the faculty of representation, so far as we are affected by it . . . ."[29] Kant even gives a name to "that in the appearance which corresponds to sensation," namely matter, which he distinguishes from the form of the appearance whose source is transcendental (in Kant's sense).

The insidious and perplexing difficulty which Kant must face again and again in the *Critique* is this: if mind synthesizes, structures, or organizes what comes to be its objective world, does this mean that mind first passively receives *un*synthesized, *un*structured sensations and only subsequently works on them? Is it the case that a world independent of mind first impinges on mind, presumably producing some effect, and consciousness only then grasps or synthesizes the already mental effect of that world? Kant does in fact accept some version of this approach, in which the modes of synthesis are understood as synthesizing a manifold that in some sense is already given and already a possession of consciousness, that has already been received through sensuous receptivity. But this poses a serious problem, namely, how the mediate, synthetic work of thought can determine and be presupposed by immediate sensuous receptivity. The primacy of synthesis is in direct competition with the independence of receptivity. And Kant cannot allow sensational receptivity to be compromised because it is, in its way, the source of all experience and knowledge of reality.

Only what can be sensed can be known for Kant. His critique of dogmatic metaphysics absolutely requires this and he repeats it again and again. It is not the understanding which limits human knowledge, it is the range of sensation. What limits human knowledge in the way

Kant wants it limited is the fact that human receptivity (intuition) is always *sensuous*.

Sensation is relevant to only one of the categories, that of reality itself. In the "Anticipations of Perception" Kant sees that it is the degree of affectedness of sense by the appearing 'X' that makes reality itself possible. The concept of reality is the only category that relates to sensation alone, as distinct from intuition, and is the *a priori* condition of the affectedness of mind by what is outside mind. Reality for Kant is contacted sensationally: we cannot know *what* the real is via sensation, but only through sensation can we know *that* it is.

Especially striking in this regard is Kant's "Refutation of Idealism" and the emendation of it he inserted in the second edition introduction. There Kant laments that:

> it still remains a scandal to philosophy and to human reason in general that the existence of things outside us (from which we derive the whole material of knowledge, even for our inner sense) must be accepted merely on faith, and that if anyone thinks good to doubt their existence, we are unable to counter his doubts by satisfactory proof.[30]

Kant intends to offer such a proof. The crux of his argument is that the consciousness of one's own existence as determined in time presupposes the consciousness of something permanent outside of one's self, without which one's existence in time could not be known.[31] This argument hinges on the nature of the two consciousnesses in question, that of one's self and that of the external "permanent," which is clarified in the note to the second edition introduction.

In this footnote Kant takes the crucial position that the consciousness to which he referred in the preceding argument is *not* the "I think" of apperception. The latter is the "*intellectual consciousness* of my existence," which is a consciousness of self as "representation." Kant distinguishes this consciousness from the "*empirical consciousness* of my existence," which alone is the determinate consciousness of one's self as existing in time, and is had through inner sense. While, Kant admits, the "intellectual consciousness does indeed come first," it is the empirical consciousness of one's existence which presupposes the empirical consciousness of a something in "outer sense" and thus makes the refutation of idealism possible. The empirical consciousness is:

> bound up in the way of identity with the consciousness of a relation to something outside me, and it is therefore experience not invention, sense not imagination, which inseparably connects this outside something with my inner sense . . . . The reality of outer sense is

thus necessarily bound up with inner sense, if experience in general is
to be possible at all; that is, I am just as certainly conscious that
there are things outside me, which are in relation to my sense, as I
am conscious that I myself exist as determined in time.[32]

It is the receptive (intuitive) consciousness of the empirical reality
of the self—not the "I think" of apperception, the mere consciousness of
the belongingness of all representation to one consciousness—that allows
Kant to prove the existence of external reality. This external, outside
reality, because it is available to outer sense, must be appearance.

It is important to note that the certainty of the existence of outer
objects is not, for Kant, "inferential." He explicitly rejects idealism on
the grounds that it accepts outer things through an inference and declares that in his own proof "it has been shown that outer experience
is really immediate." Indeed, he goes as far as to claim that "inner
experience is itself possible only mediately, and only through outer experience."[33]

Sensuous receptivity establishes a dimension or mode of analysis
within which the Kantian subject does not have priority over the object.
Through empirical receptive consciousness I am conscious of my self as
belonging to the same empirical order as do "outer" objects of which I
am sensuously, receptively conscious. Within the order of empirical reality, self and object (the outside "permanent") are equally present to consciousness (empirical consciousness), are present with equal certainty,
are temporal and determinate, and each has its own specific mode of
receptivity (inner and outer).[34] Kant writes that the existence of external,
permanent things "must be included in the *determination* of my own
existence, constituting with it but a single experience such as would not
take place even inwardly if it were not also at the same time, in part,
outer."[35] It is as a sensuously receptive consciousness that the self shares
in empirical reality and is affected by it, and only through sensuous
receptivity and within its limits are the concept and knowledge of reality possible.

This priority of sensuous receptivity becomes problematic when
compared to the transcendental project of the Transcendental Deduction.
Kant interprets his whole project in the Transcendental Analytic as demanding proof that immediate receptive consciousness presupposes a
mediate act of synthesis involving the categories. The question then
arises of whether the empirical consciousness of outer objects, of an
outer permanency, presupposes transcendental synthesis. Such a presupposition is not in evidence in the previously cited footnote to the second
edition introduction, but it is made explicit in the Refutation of Idealism.[36] Given the task of the Deduction and the "First Analogy" of the

"Principles," the empirical consciousness of outer objects must presuppose a transcendental synthesis and the transcendental unity of apperception. If a transcendental-mental synthesis is presupposed, indeed, if the outer "permanent" required by the Refutation is itself, according to the First Analogy, a transcendental condition, then what in the "empirical consciousness of outer objects" is necessarily outside me, "distinct from all my representations"?

The only possible candidate is that ambiguous Kantian factor: sensation. That part of each intuition which is not the result of transcendental conditions is sensation, "the effect of an object upon the faculty of representation . . . ." Sensation, independent of the forms of intuition, yields no objective experience or knowledge for Kant. It manifests not "properties of things, but only changes in the subject . . . ." Kant argues that:

> the taste of a wine does not belong to the objective determinations of the wine, not even if by the wine as an object we mean the wine as appearance, but to the special constitution of sense in the subject that tastes it.[37]

Here we see the continuing paradox of Kantian sensation. Only what can be sensed can be objectively known. The affectedness of sense itself is the universal and necessary condition for the experience of an objective world, of reality. Yet what is sensed, or the affections of sense, are the result of purely subjective conditions giving no information about objective reality.

The problem cannot be solved by taking the position that while the Refutation proves *that* outer objects exist through intuition, we can only know these objects, know *what* they are, insofar as they are the product of a transcendental synthesis. Kant has claimed to prove, not that we have the right to *infer* the existence of outer objects, but that we are as immediately and empirically conscious of them as we are of ourselves. Simply put, we perceive them. Surely, such a consciousness necessarily involves consciousness of content, of a 'what' in some sense, and not the mere consciousness 'that' something exists. Yet the combined effect of the Aesthetic's account of sensation and the Deduction's account of transcendental synthesis is to dissolve this objective intuition into the joint product of transcendental conditions and the "subjective constitution of sense." What, then, can be "received"?

The tasks of the Refutation of Idealism and of the Transcendental Deduction are in competition. The former argues that we have an immediate sensible and receptive consciousness of external objects distinct from all our representations. The latter argues that all receptive consciousness of objects presupposes a transcendental imaginative synthesis based on the transcendental unity of all representations. The burning problem of the entire Analytic, as Kant poses it, is, how can the immediate givenness of objects (as appearances) presuppose the spontaneous, mediate synthesis of thought? It is in the torturous convolutions of the two versions of the Transcendental Deduction and the "Schematism," the murky boilerroom of the *Critique,* that Kant attempts to plug up this dangerous hole in his theoretical structure and keep the Transcendental Analytic afloat.

The ultimate condition of the unity of objective conditions is, for Kant, the transcendental or synthetic unity of apperception. The belongingness of all my representations to one consciousness must presuppose a synthesis, and the transcendental condition of this synthesis is the transcendental unity of apperception. It is represented by the word 'I' in the phrase "I think" which must in principle be able to accompany all my representations. It also allows me with certainty to say that "I am," as for Descartes; but unlike Descartes, Kant distinguishes the existence known thereby from that known through inner intuition. The strategic importance of the transcendental unity of apperception is that, having demonstrated its presupposition by the intuition of objects, Kant is able to claim that the categories of the understanding are its "modes," modes of transcendental unity, thereby obviating the task of demonstrating the necessity of the various categories individually.

As Kant states in the first edition preface, the objective task of the Deduction is to prove the necessary applicability of the categories to all experience. The subjective and allegedly non-essential task is the examination of the faculty of thought itself. But the problematic nature of the former task drives Kant again and again to the latter. How can a purely intellectual principle of spontaneous thought be presupposed by immediate sensory givenness? Kant tries to answer this difficulty by proposing a variety of acts of synthesis in the two versions of the Deduction and later with the doctrine of the Schematism. Most of these synthetic acts are founded in Kant's concept of the imagination.

For Kant, the imagination, *Einbildungskraft,* is in a sense the root of all objective knowledge, a claim it shares with the transcendental unity of apperception. Kant writes in the chapter on the categories that:

> synthesis in general . . . is the mere result of the power of
> imagination, a blind but indispensable function of the soul, without
> which we should have no knowledge whatsoever, but of which we are
> scarcely ever conscious.[38]

This obscure power of mind also produces the "schemata" which ultimately make the application of categories to intuitions possible by virtue of being homogeneous with both. The schema, or "third thing," is a temporal determination of the category, making the latter able to relate to already temporally determined intuitions. The activity of producing this ultimate synthesis is more than obscure:

> it is an art concealed in the depts of the human soul, whose real modes of activity nature is hardly likely ever to allow us to discover, and have open to our gaze.[39]

It is ironic and revealing that Kant refers to nature in this passage. Just a few pages earlier (in both the A and B Deductions) Kant had written that nature, insofar as it is lawful, is thoroughly dependent on the categories. Indeed, in the A Deduction he concluded, "thus the order and regularity in appearances, which we entitle *nature*, we ourselves introduce."[40] Yet, in this passage, nature escapes transcendental control: it is implied to be an independent factor involved even in the workings of the human soul, capable of withholding its "real modes" from the light of reason.[41]

The problem of the synthesis of understanding and receptivity is so difficult that Kant's only solution is to posit a power of synthesis whose origin is inexplicable and whose existence can only be inferred. This recourse to imagination is not illegitimate, but that the source and basis of this power cannot be explicated, described, or illuminated, that Kant himself feels he is at the limit of his explanatory powers, reveals something about the problem to which imagination is offered as a solution. In addition, the passage in question points back to the fundamental problem of receptivity, which reappears in this context as the dilemma of conceiving nature as an independently existing power affecting sensibility, or as a system of laws ultimately derived from transcendental unity.

The simple problem haunts Kant again and again: how can the immediate givenness of objects (as appearances) presuppose the spontaneous, mediate synthesis of thought? If the latter is presupposed by intuition, then in what sense are the objects given or received? And if they are not in any sense received, then how can Kant avoid speculative or dogmatic idealism?

It is not only the avoidance of idealism that is at stake. The roots of the problem can be traced back to the projects that determined Kant's adoption of the transcendental method itself. These projects are two: the moral and the scientific. The ways that Kant understands these two terms required him to distinguish what can be known, science, from what can be thought, morality.[42] Knowledge must be restricted to the objects received in sense experience in order to leave "transcendent" matters undetermined; this is required by the moral project. The limits of sensuous receptivity determine the limits of knowledge. The scientific knowledge which Kant wishes to justify with an *a priori* foundation is clearly of a different order than that of receptivity. The Newtonian world that Kant wishes to epistemically justify cannot be derived from receptivity as such. Kant must prove that highly intellectual conditions, the conditions of thought that determine scientific objectivity, are the preconditions for objective reality as received through intuition. These intellectual conditions, founded on the pure transcendental unity of consciousness, inevitably compromise or even undermine the integrity of sensuous receptivity. It is difficult to conceive how the immediate can be maintained as such if it is shown to presuppose the mediate. The status of sensuous receptivity here threatens to become nonsensical. If its integrity is compromised or undermined, which seems to be required by the task of the Deduction, then not only does Kant fall into idealism, but the "bounds of possible experience" would be effaced. If so, then nothing would prevent the application of pure concepts to anything which could be thought, including the moral subject.[43] And this would subvert Kant's most basic, far-reaching and dearly held intentions.

In Heidegger's *Being and Time* there are several relatively brief discussions of the *Critique*.[44] In each discussion Heidegger laments one point: that with the transcendental unity of apperception, the "I think," Kant adopted the notion of a "worldless subject" and gave it a central role in his system. In doing so, Heidegger claims, "Kant took over Descartes' position quite dogmatically," meaning that Kant derived the "I think" from the *Cogito*.[45] The result was that, "Kant did not see the phenomenon of the world" and "as a consequence the 'I' was again forced back to an *isolated* subject . . . ."[46] Heidegger writes of Kant's Refutation of Idealism and of any attempt to "prove" the existence of external reality, that:

> to *have faith* in the Reality of the 'external world', whether rightly or wrongly; to '*prove*' this Reality for it, whether adequately or inadequately; to *presuppose* it, whether explicitly or not—attempts such as these which have not mastered their own basis with full transparency, presuppose a subject which is proximally *worldless* or unsure of its world, and which must, at bottom, first assure itself of a world.[47]

Heidegger is largely right. Kant locates the governance of the world as we know it in the transcendental faculties and conditions of the subject, in the transcendental conditions of consciousness. In the Deduction he makes the mere unity of consciousness, in some sense, the ultimate condition of the world and of nature. Kant deprives external nature of any effect on empirical reality as we *know* it, making its regularity the product of transcendental subjectivity and its various phenomena the result of the subjective constitution of sense.[48]

But Heidegger's critique is only partially correct. Kant thwarts his own subjectivism in two different ways: he undermines it and he attempts to transcend it.

Kant undermines it by retaining sensuous receptivity, in some sense, as the foundation of the known world. This puts consciousness, as receptive, into the world where it can be affected by 'outer' objects and where its certainty of itself is no greater than, and is even dependent on, its certainty of the world of outer objects. Kant thus undermines his subjectivism with a retained naturalism which situates the subject within a natural world that affects it *in all of its being*. Kant's naturalism is not a thoroughgoing one, but it is an ineradicable element of certain of his doctrines, especially the Refutation.

Kant's aim in the Transcendental Analytic is to transcend forms of subjectivism that he inherits or presumes as a necessary starting point. Some of the vehicles of this attempted transcendence are effectively transcendental in *my* sense of the word: that is, they bridge subject and object, mitigating some of the problems of subjectivism. But others simply reassert subjectivism on another level of analysis. This is the effect of 'transcendental philosophy' in Kant's sense of the term. For example, Kant's search for synthetic *a priori* truths is an attempt to transcend the subjectivist analytic–synthetic model of cognition. However, his solution asserts a new subjectivism on another level of analysis; namely the necessary conformity of experience to the transcendental unity of consciousness and its various modes.

The transcendental determination of the world-as-known makes little sense without reference to the thinking subject. Transcendental philosophy dictates conditions to which objective experience must conform in order to be objective, and these conditions *must* in some sense belong to the thinking-experiencing subject. As such, transcendental philosophy in Kant's sense of that term is inevitably subjectivist.

Kant suggested in the preface to the second edition:

> Hitherto it has been assumed that all of our knowledge must conform to objects . . . . We must . . . make trial whether we may not have more success in the tasks of metaphysics, if we suppose that objects must conform to our knowledge.[49]

He does not here consider the possibility of mutual conformity, which is to say, interaction between knowledge and objects. He implies that either knowledge must determine or subsume objectivity or vice versa.[50]

As we have seen, this notion of the conformity of objects to knowledge is extremely difficult for Kant. He cannot reconcile the sense in which knowledge or mind must exist in a kind of empirical community with the non-mental, with consciousness' transcendental, subsumptive determination of objective experience. He cannot give up the former, but he must establish the latter. The latter often becomes a subjectivism in a strong sense; this is especially true in the Deductions.

Now, to talk of cognitive, experiential or imaginative synthesis is not inherently subjectivist.[51] Such synthesis becomes subjectivist only when it takes on a subjectivist function, as when it serves to make a subjectivist system workable. This is precisely the status of synthesis in key sections of the *Critique of Pure Reason*. It has this status because Kant adopts fundamentally subjectivist categorial distinctions at the outset of his project, distinctions embodied in the terminological opposition of concepts and intuitions and in the strict distinction of the order of receptivity and the order of spontaneity. Further, the opposition of things-in-themselves and appearances or phenomena itself grounds Kant's project in a subjectivist distinction, since appearances or phenomena can only be understood in Kant as intrinsically related to or standing within subjectivity. Things-in-themselves are excluded from any possible interaction with mind or subjectivity, and the processes of objective perception and knowledge of appearances are analyzed as functions of the transcendental activity of the subject. At multiple levels of analysis, Kant applies the distinction between the subjective and the non-subjective. However complex the Kantian system, however original and intricate its formulations, and despite Kant's aim to forge a way out of subjectivism's problems, his system remains pervasively subjectivist. It stands as a brilliant answer to a flawed question.

4

Philosophical Narcissism and the Radicalization of Subjectivism

Subjectivism served important functions for modern thought. But it contained within itself the seeds of a dilemma that could only be resolved by further radicalizing subjectivism. This chapter discusses the historical development of radicalized subjectivism and introduces the concept of philosophical narcissism to describe it. It will be seen that behind the historical radicalization of subjectivism lie the abstract but fascinating conceptual paradoxes or antinomies that had always been implicit in the subjectivist categories, but which only became explicit when the category of the transcendental was de-legitimated. These paradoxes are the result of a breakdown of the relations of subject and object, a breakdown that is analogous to the breakdown of the relations of self and object that has been the focus of attention for recent theories of psychopathological narcissism. For this reason, radicalized, non-transcendental subjectivism can be best understood through the notion of philosophical narcissism.

The Fortunes of Subjectivism

The value, success, and importance of subjectivism lay in its aptness both for addressing the problems it was proposed to solve and for understanding social and intellectual changes that were yet to come, changes to whose production subjectivism lent a hand. It proved to be adequate to the greatest social changes of the last three centuries, and its philosophical cogency and cultural power were thereby reinforced. It repeatedly helped to create the reality with which it was again and again found to correspond.

As a total system, including the transcendental elements that maintained it as a system, subjectivist philosophy exhibited three features that made it enormously valuable and influential: it cleared the metaphysical and, to some extent, epistemological ground for the development of modern science; it separated the domains of science and religion, making possible the simultaneous retention of religion and pursuit of science; and, it was remarkably compatible with Christian belief regarding the nature of the soul, especially in its Protestant versions. As such, subjectivism answered one of the burning questions of the seventeenth and eighteenth centuries, namely, how can the competing claims of religion and science be reconciled? Its answer was strictly to separate the spiritual and the natural and the realms of life to which each was to have immediate application, giving the spiritual ascendency.

The great intellectual power of subjectivism and the reason for its endurance lay beyond the religion-versus-science issue, in its interpretive adequacy for the dominant social changes of the ensuing two centuries. The subjectivist dualism of thinking subject and world repeatedly proved, from the seventeenth through the twentieth century, to be valuable in the interpretation of the momentous changes in the general conditions of European and American social life that have constituted the development of the modern world. Among these changes three in particular should be mentioned.

The decline of feudal social structures and the establishment of democracy. The decline of aristocracy, the growth of the middle or business class, democratic revolution and progressively widening suffrage, all served to erode the power of super-individual structures in determining the life of the individual. Society became more and more a community of politically and legally equal individuals or citizens. Economic position, class status, and career increasingly came to be interpreted as purely a matter of extrinsic conditions, rather than as a matter of an individual's intrinsic nature. As thinking subjects, individuals are understood as equal and free; it is as members of a system of objective economic power that they are contingently determined and unequal.

The decline of religion as a public force. While the decline in the number of persons with religious affiliation or interest is a very recent and limited phenomenon, the decline of religion as a force in the determination of the public conditions of life has been long-standing and undeniable. The separation of religion from political-legal determinations has been official policy in some Western nations for centuries and has been reinforced by the growth of a purely secular culture. In the West, religion is officially and generally regarded as a private, personal, hence, subjective matter. This fate has increasingly befallen other areas of culture as well, for example, aesthetics, certain ethical questions, sexual habits. Subjectivism provides the categorial scheme to which the social categories of private and public have been increasingly amalgamated in modern times.

The withdrawal of religion to the private or subjective sphere has special significance for the history of subjectivism, because subjectivist systems gave a crucial role to the Divine or the transcendent. Descartes, as we have seen, made God the basis for the transcendental mediation of subject and object.[1]

It is impossible to overestimate the tremendous significance of this religious withdrawal to the subjective. Despite the fact that the decline of religion in the West has been a theme since Nietzsche, its importance has still not been fully understood. The key notions of modern philosophy and of modern culture as a whole that were formulated in the seventeenth and, to some extent, in the eighteenth century, were almost universally formulated in an explicitly *religious* context. These key notions, when withdrawn from the philosophical context within which they were initially intended to function, can no longer retain the same meaning. This is a point which contemporary philosophy has failed to recognize: seventeenth-century metaphysics, epistemology, and methodology existed in a theological firmament, and are intrinsically altered when taken out of that firmament. To the extent that contemporary philosophy employs an inheritance of these early modern notions, it does not understand the implications of its own doctrines. In early modern thought, religious belief provided the primary, although not the sole, ground for the possibility of the interaction of the individual subjectivity and the social and natural world; this can be seen in Spinoza and Leibniz as well as Descartes. God alone could make the subjectivist world hang together. Without God or without concepts equally as transcendent, the definitively modern notion of the thinking subject tends to lose the grounds of its relation to the rest of reality. Further, the loss of grounds for relation to the world changes the *internal* nature of the subject; when the subject becomes literally worldless, its own internal nature is radically altered.

The growth of scientific, medical, technological, economic, and organizational mastery over the conditions of life, especially over natural conditions. Nature has become increasingly manipulable. This power over nature has been growing steadily since the sixteenth century, geometrically since the mid-nineteenth, astronomically since the mid-twentieth. Mastery over nature gives weight to the image or notion of the latter as mere stuff, devoid not only of spiritual qualities, but of any intrinsic value, integrity, or power of resistance. Correspondingly, the image and notion of the master of nature, human subjectivity, continually amplifies its claim to being the ultimate center of power in the finite world.

This mastery is economic and social as well as technological. Not only natural conditions, but all objective conditions of life (for example, social and economic) are increasingly shown to be contingent, not inevitable, and to be subject to human influence. This, of course, like mastery over nature, means control by *some* humans, by those with the requisite power. Nevertheless, the human community as a whole, both the powerful and powerless, is universally treated to the spectacle of human subjectivity rendering all objective, "external" realities manipulable, however ambiguous the invitation to participation in the spectacle that is extended to the powerless.

These three examples and a variety of other tendencies that have constituted modernization were readily interpretable in terms of the subjectivist dualism, and this interpretability seemed to verify the dualism itself. The rise of mastery over nature and the growth of democracy and liberalism transformed cultural and social reality in ways that are readily interpretable through the subjectivist dualism. In liberal-democratic society people are regarded most purely as individuals, just as subjectivism treats them. Each individual appears to confront a value-neutral natural-economic environment, a "non-subjective" environment. Liberal society treats human beings increasingly as private individuals whose beliefs and thoughts are their own, non-public business, and who confront a non-subjective, non-religious, mechanical-material world. These developments are not only readily interpretable by applying subjectivist categories to socio-cultural realities; their fittingness to these realities serves to legitimate these very categories. Thus, modern society develops in ways that make the subjectivist viewpoint seem more and more legitimate, applicable to more and more regions of inquiry and understanding, more and more pervasive and inescapably obvious.

But what conforms to the subjectivist dualism and the subjectivist viewpoint tends to de-legitimate the transcendental doctrines and images associated with it, which, while adopted by subjectivism, are nevertheless incompatible with it on a deeper level. The internal changes in subjectivist philosophy leading to the emergence of philosophical narcissism are conditioned by social trends that legitimate the specifically subjectivist and de-legitimate the non-subjectivist, transcendental factors. When a particular philosopher no longer feels the theoretical necessity of transcendental elements, or feels a dominant theoretical need for contrary doctrines, the former must take a theoretical back-seat.

The turn away from subjectivist-transcendental systems and toward philosophical narcissism was conditioned in part by the sheer quantitative advance in social-cultural activities and achievements that tended to legitimate subjectivism and de-legitimate the transcendental. Abstractly conceived, the shift takes place at the point when the transcendental mediating images and beliefs become less important that the progressively more influential and useful subjectivist dualism for the interpretation of social reality. When the latter finally overtakes the former, after two to three centuries of competition, its inherent incompatibility with the former asserts itself and the synthesis breaks down. Suddenly the irreconcilability of individual thinking subject and the communal-natural world becomes apparent, and the formerly synthesizing, transcendental factors are reconceived as factors *within* the thinking subject, rather than *between* subject and world.

Associated with this straightforwardly quantitative growth of the intellectual power of the subjectivist dualism is the extension of the subjectivist dualism and the drive to scientific mastery associated with it to new regions of reality. In particular, parts of the subject itself came to be included within nature, within determined objectivity, as a target for scientific explanation and instrumental manipulation. Since the second half of the nineteenth century the development of the new human sciences—sociology, psychology, comparative biology, and today, the explosive growth of bio-psychology and genetics—has tended to shift components of human subjectivity into the realm of the objective. But, as more and various features of human being became objects for the sciences, less and less seemed left in the self that could constitute the basis for all thought.

The subjectivist program of systematically differentiating what is a property of a thinking subject from what is not eventually had to focus on the so-called transcendental capacities and features of the subject. This focusing took place both through the advance of philosophical criticism which, after the death of Hegel, increasingly turned a critical eye on the ideas of God, state, and monarchical authority, the unity of the self, and ultimately the concept of transcendental reason, and through the development of the aforesaid human sciences and their increasing influence on philosophy in the second half of the nineteenth and in the early twentieth centuries.

In the early modern period, the transcendental capacities of the human mind were those intellectual capacities of the subject which were believed capable of overcoming the subjectivist dichotomy, capable of grasping truths about the world in itself. Chief among the capacities was transcendental reason, the notion that human rationality functioned not only in an instrumental or a logical way, but that it was also a source of true first principles, that it was able to see into what must be true of what exists beyond the individual mind. Descartes' "light of reason" and Kant's concept of reason are examples of this notion.

The result of the expansion and radicalization of subjectivism in the late nineteenth and twentieth centuries was that the transcendental capacities of the subject were gradually reinterpreted as either purely subjective factors, the product of wishes, illusions, perspectival limitations, or as the effect of objective determinations of the subject, the product of environment, conditioning, biological factors. What then, remains of the thinking subject on which subjectivism sought to found all knowledge? There remains only the contents of personal consciousnesses, regarded purely as such, which presumably exist within a material environment. The implications of the original subjectivist dualism are now fulfilled, no longer obstructed and mitigated by transcendental factors.

This development is not a product of what is often considered to be the central achievement of modern thought, namely, the triumphant march of skepticism, the victory of critical consciousness over myth, religion, onto-theology, and metaphysics. Skepticism, doubt, and criticism, like all philosophical movements, are enacted from definite *points of view.* That twentieth-century philosophy has generally rejected traditional metaphysics does not mean that it is more critical than the philosophy of earlier times. The groundlessness or unjustifiability of metaphysical or "onto-theological" claims is by no means obvious. That it may appear obvious is a testament to the thoroughness with which a viewpoint or set of categories incompatible with such claims has been adopted. Doubt is a method for reducing features of reality to a categorial scheme that one wishes to affirm: the perspective determines the doubt, not vice versa. Likewise, the critical rejection of transcendental notions is frequently determined by a prior commitment to subjectivist categories.

This gradual loss of the transcendental, the breakdown of the subjectivist-transcendental synthesis that had made subjectivism workable since the seventeenth century, initiated a profound alteration of the subjectivist categories themselves. The subject and object categories were thereby freed to be universally and radically applied, unencumbered by God or reason or any other trans-subjective-objective factor. But these categories also lacked any transcendental means of relation or mediation, any over-arching context to limit their respective applicability and harmonize their respective scope. Without such a context it becomes impossible to conceive of subjectivity and objectivity as being independent existences *and yet* as being interrelated, mutually involved.

With the transcendental support for their interrelation de-legitimated, subject and object can no longer be plausibly conceived as separate yet related. But further, this loss of relation changes the internal nature of each, because ultimately, neither subjectivity nor objectivity can make any sense without some relation to the other. Thus the loss of the transcendental not only disrupts the context in which subject and object subsist, the loss of context also disrupts the nature of each. This sets up paradoxical, dialectical problems for the concepts of subject and object.

I will call this de-transcendentalized, radicalized form of subjectivism, philosophical narcissism. The sense of applying this psychological term to a philosophical position will be discussed presently. First, a thought experiment will make clearer how this paradoxical dialectic of philosophical narcissism was already implicit in early modern or transcendental subjectivism.

For Descartes, the types of finite substances—thinking and extended—are absolutely distinct. It is God who serves to guarantee that the ideas which exist in my consciousness represent extended substances existing 'outside' of my consciousness. Now, let us imagine that God were removed from the *Meditations*. What epistemological and anthropological picture would Descartes be left with if God were removed from the system? In answering this question we can rule out the status of God as creator and metaphysical sustainer of the universe, and thus of the potential answer that the universe would never have been created in the first place, or would immediately cease to exist if God were eliminated.

Except for certain ideas which Descartes claims to have been actively imparted to our minds by God—for example, the ideas of God, perfection, infinity—one must say that the ideational content of any particular consciousness would be unchanged. My mind would have the same perceptions, feelings, and imaginings that I had in the theocratic universe. Descartes gives us no reason in the *Meditations* which would make it necessary that some change in mental contents take place, with the above exceptions noted; everything that I had previously called my world could be perceptually unchanged, and I could live in and respond to the world just as before God's disappearance.

Yet, there would be one enormous difference. Because the bridge mediating and relating the ideas inhering in my mental substance to entities existing independently of my mind had been burnt, I would *no longer* be able to *rationally, justifiably* believe that my perceptions and thoughts *represented something existing independent of my consciousness*. I would not be rationally bound to deny the existence of extended substance, but I could never assert that such substance was related to or was represented by any contents of my consciousness, for example, my perceptions. Nor could I ever be certain of the existence of extended substance.

What would conscious living be like in such a situation? I could still respond to, manipulate, be affected by, moved by, desirous of all the appearances, all the perceived phenomena with which I was previously involved. In a sense, nothing would be lost, nothing would have changed. Yet, I would feel within myself a confusing emptiness. I could never say with reasonable conviction that the objects of my deepest concern and desire were anything other than ideas within myself. While I could never rationally affirm the truth of solipsism, neither could I ever rationally deny, or have any reason for denying it. I could never rationally affirm within myself the felt conviction that the world with which I struggled existed independently of my mind. My mind, I, would have the world *as phenomena*, but not as independently existing realities, not as existential integrities.

Every percept would therefore excite within me a *double* experience: I would respond to it *as if* it represented an independent existence, and simultaneously fail rationally to believe in its independent existence. "Reality" would equal "phenomena" and all that I encountered would be experienced as a depth-less, substance-less surface.

The denial of transcendental factors, most notably transcendental reason, has important effects both within and outside of philosophy. This is because, especially during the late Enlightenment, transcendental factors seeped into intellectual and popular culture, becoming entrenched in modern social thought. For example, transcendental reason became an important component of Liberalism, and was therefore embedded in Western politics, jurisprudence, and economic theory. The notion that every individual mind is capable of perceiving both reality and universal, "self-evident" moral-political truths, and capable of rational discourse, was written into the American Constitution as well as the *Critique of Pure Reason*.

Philosophically, the loss of transcendental reason accomplished the transformation of subjectivism into philosophical narcissism. The philosophical narcissism of the twentieth century exhibits a host of problems which are in fact radicalized versions of the difficulties inherent in subjectivism.

Just as Descartes' critics had seen in the seventeenth century, subjectivity and the world outside of the subject have no conceivable bridge to connect them. They cannot conceivably interact or communicate. This is not solely because they represent different kinds of metaphysical substances; it is because the *categories* of subjectivism, which remain in effect, are wholly antithetical. 'Thinking subject and what belongs to it' and 'what does not belong to it' are simply logical opposites.

This creates a variety of difficulties in various sub-fields of philosophy, all related to the central problem of the inconceivability or unjustifiability of any kind of internal relation, interaction, communication, or community between a now thoroughly private, subjective field of thought and experience and other subjects, nature, and cultural arti-facts. Meaning and value, or any features of reality that cannot be re-duced to materiality, must be conceived as purely private.

But this stark opposition of subject and non-subject opens up a host of paradoxical consequences that were not anticipated by subjectiv-ism or its earlier critics. This host of paradoxes forms much of the theme of Adorno and Horkheimer's *Dialectic of Enlightenment*.[2] The absolute diremption of individual consciousness and world leaves consciousness with nothing that would distinguish it from the world. What obtains for philosophical narcissism is a field of phenomena which is *all there is* of consciousness and of the world. Personal consciousness is nothing other than this field. There can then be no rational, philosophical justification for claiming *either* that the subject is anything other than this phenome-nal field *or* that the world, reality, or objectivity is anything other than the same phenomenal field. Consequently, the strict implications of the complete diremption of thinking subject and objective world is that they become paradoxically equatable: they are both definable only as a single phenomenal field, or as regions or segments of such a field. This prob-lem impacts the conception of values as well. Given the elimination of transcendental factors, what are the only rationally, philosophically con-ceivable value-aims for the thinking subject? Without a moral "light of reason," without a transcendental practical reason to affirm universal moral laws, and where reason is a property of a private consciousness, all that could be of value to the subject is the material objectivity that has now been reduced to a phenomenal field. As Adorno and Hork-heimer wrote, "Every substantial goal which men might adduce as an alleged rational insight is, in the strict Enlightenment sense, delusion, lies, or 'rationalization' . . . ."[3] But this means that value-aims can only be conceived as purely personal and thus not subject to rational discus-sion, organization, or criticism.

This problematic was always implicit in subjectivism, which had made the individual thinking subject the center of value in the world and the ultimate court for truth and value-decisions. But the subsequent his-tory of subjectivism revealed the paradox inherent in this position. The progressive realization of the inherent integrity, value, and freedom of the subject was conceived to be based on the progressive criticism and elimination of external embodiments of value and moral authority. The so-called "de-mystification" of nature and the destruction of metaphysics and religious belief were understood, on the subjectivist model, as steps toward human liberation. The result, however, was that the progressive denial of the inherent value of anything outside the subject left the sub-ject with nothing to value except materiality. The subject has been de-nuded of all capacities except its 'natural' impulses toward material objectivity, its instrumental rational mastery, and mere consciousness of objectivity. If material things are the only reality, then they must be the only embodiment of value. Under subjectivism any other proposed value can be understood only as private wish or fantasy. This is the paradox which forms the heart of the *Dialectic of Enlightenment,* that the foundation of all thought and value in the subject, which seemed the gateway to the subject's freedom from and mastery over nature, ends by restricting the subject to an exclusive devotion to nature, indeed, makes the subject into a mere intention or vector directed at nature.

This means that the subject, in a sense, *is* nature, is identified with nature; or, more precisely, subject and not-subject are each indistinguishable from the same phenomenal field. Adorno and Horkheimer's "nature," the material objectivity at which the subject is exclusively directed, is indistinguishable from the phenomena appearing to private consciousness. The world becomes equatable with the contents of the self, and vice versa.

The Psycho-Dynamic Concept of Narcissism

The psychoanalytic study of narcissistic personality disorders has produced an intriguing picture of the relation of subject and object. This disorder has virtually nothing to do with the self-love or excessive egoism which many writers find so distasteful in contemporary America. Narcissism is not egoism. It is a complex disturbance of the relation and nature of the self and the world. The examination of the theory of this disturbance will give us a picture of the relations of subject and object that has application outside of the psychological realm, in culture and philosophy. This is not to say that culture and philosophy are generated by psychic disturbance, nor that the concepts of philosophical and cultural narcissism are logically dependent on psychological narcissism. What is important is that the psychiatrists have done some fascinating conceptual work in this field, work of which the rest of us ought to take liberal advantage.

Some philosophers are disturbed by philosophical projects which seem to take their lead from extra-philosophical theories and intellectual developments. Philosophy, they believe, is the most foundational inquiry, and so philosophical concepts must be logically prior to all other concepts. Taking the lead from a psychological concept like narcissism would seem to be methodologically backwards, or worse, a kind of psychologism.

I disagree. Philosophy does not found or ground other disciplines. Philosophy is the most general or comprehensive kind of inquiry, but this is very different from being foundational. Other disciplines do not need philosophy in order to have validity, but they do need philosophy in order to be understood beyond the context of their own perspective, in relation to other human activities, intellectual or otherwise. Philosophers have always responded to non-philosophical concepts, exploring and clarifying them, and making them philosophical. To claim that the philosophical exposition of a concept is logically prior to its non-philosophical version has little justification and holds little advantage. The philosopher handles ideas differently, elaborates and analyzes them differently, and most importantly, applies, relates, and employs them in a more general way, such that the ideas take on a function in their philosophical application that they cannot have in the hands of non-philosophers. Philosophy does not lose its logically prior, foundationalist role when it borrows from other fields of human thought, because it did not have that role in the first place.

Philosophical narcissism is a way of conceiving of subject and object, concepts that can be seen to be implicit in certain theories of psychopathology. Philosophy, as is its talent, can distill a philosophical conception of subject–object relations from the psychodynamic theories of self–object relations. The conception of philosophical narcissism used herein is simply the making-explicit and the making-general of ideas and relationships originally posited by theoreticians of human mental life and human behavior.

In his 1914 paper "On Narcissism: An Introduction,"[4] Freud introduced the idea of narcissism in connection with the preoccupation with self and loss of interest in the external world that are characteristic of paraphrenia (schizophrenia, we would say) and paranoia, as opposed to the transference neuroses. The latter, he claimed, are diseases of the libidinal object-cathexes; they are obsessions with the object, even if in fantasy, and their genetic origins lie in the resolution of the Oedipus-Electra complex. "As the transference neuroses have enabled us to trace the libidinal instinctual impulses," he wrote, "so dementia praecox and paranoia will give us insight into the psychology of the ego."[5] It is in the spirit of this statement that the contemporary psychoanalyst Heinz Kohut writes that the topic of narcissism concerns "half of the contents of the human mind," that is, the ego or self, versus object-cathexes.[6] The psychoses indicated to Freud a withdrawal of libido from the outer world and its redirection onto the ego itself, "giving rise to a state which we may call narcissism."[7] This state is, however, a "secondary" narcissism, because it is a regression to a state which has already existed at an earlier stage of development. The "primary" narcissism of the infant and of primitive peoples consists in an "original libidinal cathexis of the ego, part of which cathexis is later yielded up to objects . . . ."[8]

Whether or not Freud, in this essay, means to say that *all* libido is originally narcissistic or ego-libido, and thus that all object cathexes derive their energy from a reservoir of narcissistic libido, is problematic.[9] It is clear, however, that cathexis of the ego is at least equiprimordial with the original libidinal object-cathexis. There are thus two "original" sexual objects, oneself and one's primary parent, usually the mother.

Not only do we have a primary love of ourselves, according to Freud we can love ourselves *in* other people. Narcissistic libido can be invested in objects outside ourselves and in this way the love of the ego attains satisfaction through love of another. There are thus two kinds of object love, one based on the model of the primary love for the mother— "anaclitic" or "true" object-love—and one deriving from the love of the ego.

The multiplication of object-cathexes and the displacement of ego-libido onto external objects in the course of development lead, Freud says, to the libidinal impoverishment of the ego, a diminishing of self-regard. Nostalgia results: "The development of the ego consists in a departure from the primary narcissism and results in a *vigorous attempt to recover it.*"[10] The ego then devises ways to incorporate the recovery of narcissism into its very overcoming of narcissism. In being-loved, the state of primary narcissism is partially re-created through relations with the loved object, and thus ego-libido can receive satisfaction indirectly through anaclitic object libido, not to mention through narcissistic object choice. Freud also indicated a means by which primary ego-libido itself can receive non-pathological satisfaction without the mediation of object-love, and this gives the concept of narcissism a new significance. In normal development narcissistic libido is displaced onto the ego-ideal, the internal image of the ego as it should be. Infantile megalomania is thereby reinstated as the idea of a perfect self, which receives the love once given to the whole self in primary narcissism, at which time the infant was identical with its ideal.

Freud connects narcissistic libido not only to the ideal (and to the later concept of the "super-ego"), but to the censorial function of consciousness, to self- and parental criticism, to simple self-observation, and even to philosophy. "That activity of the mind," he claims, "which took over the function of conscience has also enlisted itself in the service of introspection, which furnishes philosophy with the material for its intellectual operations."[11] Ego-libido fuels the activity of self-observation. The pathological alternative, according to Freud, to the displacement of narcissistic libido onto the ego-ideal, and its consequent satisfaction through achievement of that ideal is homosexuality, the love of objects that resemble oneself.

Freud takes an important step in the understanding of the dynamics of secondary narcissism in an analysis of a disorder that appears to be the antithesis of self-love. In melancholia, Freud claims, the loss of a narcissistically loved object is compensated not by a displacement onto a new object, but by identification with the introjected image of the lost object.[12] This is a "regression . . . to the still narcissistic oral phase of the libido," in which the object is incorporated, 'eaten'. The melancholiac then vents the hatred that had been part of his or her ambivalent feelings for the object on his or her own self. This dynamic of incorporation and identification in response to loss will be central for later theories of secondary narcissism.

Heinz Hartmann redefined narcissism in a way that became determinative for the subsequent history of the concept. Hartmann defined narcissism as ". . . the libidinal cathexis not of the ego but of the self."[13] It remains ambiguous whether the self is for Hartmann "one's own person," that is, the actual person, or the person's intra-psychic self-representation, or both. Hartmann elsewhere implies that pathological narcissism, that is, the narcissism of the psychoses, can be understood as a "hypercathexis of the self."[14]

Under the impact of the object-relations theory of Melanie Klein and the "British School" of psychoanalysis—Fairbairn, Harry Guntrip, David Winnicott and others—and in the context of the growing body of research into "borderline conditions," a new and complex theory of secondary pathological narcissism, of certain adult personality disorders characterized by core narcissistic disturbances, was developed, most significantly by Heinz Kohut and Otto Kernberg. It is this conception of pathological secondary narcissism as worked out in recent psychoanalytic and psychodynamic theory that will serve as a model for the concept of philosophical narcissism.

Borderline conditions, among which Kernberg classes narcissistic personality disorders,[15] are personality disorders that occupy an intermediate level of pathology between neurosis and psychosis. In general, they are characterized by the existence of a stable ego, intact reality-testing and adaptive, even successful, functioning in the world (which differentiates these conditions from the psychoses) and yet involve archaic and severe disturbances of affect and self-regard (which makes these conditions less like the neuroses and more like psychosis). Psychoanalytic theory's developmental perspective finds those pathologies whose aetiology is characteristically earlier in the individual's development to be more severe. The transference neuroses have their root in the resolution of the Oedipus-Electra conflict, while borderline conditions and the psychoses have their original causation in the pre-Oedipal period.

It must be noted that the theory of secondary or pathological narcissism is a complex and controversial topic within psychoanalytic theory. Part of the controversy stems from the strategic position of this disorder in relation to the theoretical debate between so-called "drive-structure" theorists who wish to retain Freud's early emphasis on the centrality of drives in the determination of psychic life and the "relation-structure" theorists who see object-relations, independent of drives, at the center of psychic life.[16] Indeed, the very name of the constellation of symptoms and dynamics in question has been affected by this underlying controversy: thinkers loyal to drive theory employ the term narcissism; others, like Kernberg, prefer to speak of the "borderline" personality; and those most fully adopting an object-relations viewpoint, like Fairbairn, use the term "schizoid" personality. (For the sake of convenience and clarity I will use the term 'narcissism' to refer to the relevant disorder.)

The theory of secondary narcissism owes much to the work of Kernberg and Kohut. This is not to imply that they are in complete agreement; on the contrary, they differ in their theories of metapsychology, diagnosis, and treatment.[17] Despite these differences there is a less controversial core of agreement regarding the dynamics and symptoms of narcissism, and it is with this core that we will be concerned.

For Kernberg and Kohut, the narcissistic personality in particular and borderline conditions in general could be considered *pathologies of the self.* For them, the self is a concatenation of images of the person (child), a set of self-representations, existing as a content of the psyche, and coordinated with collected object-images (for example, images of the mother). The self is related to, but entirely distinct from, the ego, the latter being an intra-psychic agency not at all equivalent to what an individual means or refers to when saying "I" or "me." Within Freud's structural theory, the ego exists in conflictual relation with the id and super-ego; for Kernberg and Kohut, the self and object-images exist at a different level of analysis. A disturbance of self-image has a disturbing effect on the strength and organization of the ego, but a relatively intact ego can co-exist with severe deficits in the area of the self and its coordinated object-images.

For Kernberg and Kohut the central pathology of the narcissistic personality involves an inability to integrate good and bad images of both self and objects. The coordinated splitting of both self and object-images into good (omnipotent self, satisfying object) and bad (fragmented self, frustrating object) images was seen by Melanie Klein as a central feature of the normal process of the infant's gradual differentiation from the mother.[18] In the case of the developing narcissistic personality, some frustrating disturbance of the infant-mother relationship makes this splitting more severe; hence it is accompanied by a deeper than normal aggressiveness which is impossible to overcome at the appropriate phase. The result is an inability on the part of the child to integrate, on the one hand, its omnipotent or grandiose fantasy of itself with its experiences of frustration and abandonment, and, on the other hand, its image of the all-satisfying mother with its image of the denying or indifferent mother, cathected as the latter is with intense aggressive feelings.

The results of this are manifold. The adult narcissist's emotional life is characterized by a variety of dissociations or 'splits'. These splits serve to defend against the anxiety and destructive rage that would attend any integration of good and bad. The active maintenance of these dissociations as a response to anxiety is, Kernberg claims, the central dynamic of borderline conditions in general. Or, as David Winnicott says, the best way to conceive of these patients is to conceive of them as always on the brink of "unthinkable anxiety."[19]

There is first of all a dissociation between the level of everyday ego-functioning which may be devoid of emotional content, an "inability to feel," a "protective shallowness," on the one hand, and a deeper level dominated by unsatisfied infantile needs, archaic fantasies of omnipotence, and paranoid fears, on the other.

The dominant split is between good and bad, or the infantile fantasied realm of perfection and the infantile fear of utter devastation or fragmentation. This schism, in a sense, substitutes for the normal distinction between self and other at a deep emotional level. The latter distinction has never been clearly drawn because of a failure of integration. The good self and good object have a tendency to fuse, like the bad self and bad object. Thus, the narcissist's libidinally cathected objects are experienced as "more like a mature adult experiences his own body and mind."[20] Life experiences stimulate oscillatory swings of self-esteem and object-regard. While functioning realistically in daily life, emotionally the narcissist lacks a realistic and integrated sense of self, of others, and even of the world as a whole. The deepest feelings are fixated on the schizoid self and object-images of infancy, in which the only meaning- or value-possibilities are total, loved perfection and frustrated annihilation.

The narcissistic personality, while emotionally shallow on the surface, exhibits intense aggression toward others and the world at a deeper level. The split between the unthinkable anxiety and hatred in the depths of the psyche and the surface generates characteristic feelings of the unreality of the world and the emptiness of the self. These dissociations make for the seemingly paradoxical condition of the narcissist. The narcissist insatiably searches the environment for cues that would indicate the substantiality and perfection of the self, and yet distrusts the world, feels it to be unreal, and so evidence of worldly success can only have temporary and superficial effect on self-esteem. Intimate relations are intensely needed yet never trusted, and the objects of love are regarded and treated in a depersonalizing way. Ultimately, others can only be inadequate stand-ins for the disappointing, hated, and needed parent of infancy. Often superficially aloof and independent, the narcissist exists in a state of anxious search for self-definition from the approval and love of others, a search inevitably frustrated by the narcissist's hatred and mistrust of all objects of dependency. The self is an absence which the narcissist is driven to fill. The dissociation of surface functioning from core feelings, the avoidance of deep relationships, and protective shallowness all serve to defend against the full experience of that absence and its attendant rage, terror, and anxiety. As Kernberg writes:

> At the very bottom . . . [in the narcissistic psyche] . . . lies . . . the image of a hungry, enraged, empty self, full of impotent anger at being frustrated, and fearful of a world which seems as hateful and revengeful as the patient himself.[21]

Philosophical Narcissism

Since the mid-nineteenth century many philosophical systems have rejected the transcendental elements of the transcendental-subjectivist synthesis while retaining the subjectivist categories. These radical subjectivist systems can be best understood as types of philosophical narcissism.

The term "philosophical narcissism" has a definite meaning and relation to the psychopathological use of the term narcissism. Philosophical narcissism does not in any way refer to the personalities of individual philosophers. It refers to philosophical systems of ideas, specifically to those in which the nature of and relations between subjectivity and objectivity exhibit a structural parallel to the nature of and relations between the self or ego, on the one hand, and real others or object-images, on the other hand, characteristic of borderline conditions in general and narcissistic personalities in particular.

The unrecognized dilemma of this radical subjectivism is that it has no way to conceive of either subjectivity or the non-subjective as integral, as characterized by an independent existential integrity *and simultaneously* as internally related to, involved with, the other. This touches on a metaphysical problem which reaches beyond the discussion of philosophical narcissism and will be more fully explored in a later chapter.[22] In general, Western philosophy since the time of Parmenides has found it difficult to conceive of beings as having existential integrity *and* as being internally related to other beings with existential integrity. The tendency has been to regard a being's integrity and its internal relatedness to others as incompatible.

Existential integrity refers to that characteristic of an existing individual entity, factor, being, or process by which we can say that the individual has a degree of wholeness, a character, a "nature" in the broadest sense of the term, by which it is an irreducible, existing something. Existential integrity is not equivalent to the metaphysical concept of substance, although some of the value or function of that concept is meant to be captured by the term. The existential integrity of a thing does not refer to some "underlying subject" of predication, an imperceptible something lying beneath and behind the perceptible qualities of a thing. It refers to the thing's totality insofar as it must be considered an existing something, an existent in its own right, not reducible to a nexus of relations to or relata of more primitive elements or ideas.

A thing is internally related to some other thing if it is related to the latter in such a way that, without this relation, it would not be what it is. Internal relations to things are constitutive for the thing that is internally related. This does not necessarily mean that they *determine* the thing, however. External relations are non-constitutive relations; that is, relations whose absence does not make the related thing other than what it is.

The early modern subjectivists tried to solve the problem of how things can both have existential integrity and exhibit internal relations through positing transcendental factors which internally related subject and object while allowing them to retain their distinct existential integrities. God played this role in the Cartesian system by guaranteeing that the subject's clear and distinct ideas were true insights into the nature of non-subjective reality. The concept of God, and of God as performing this function, made it possible for Descartes to conceive of subject and material entities as independent existences and yet as internally related, so that the subject's ideas were true reflections of the natural entities *in themselves*. In other words, God made it possible for the internal nature of the subject and the internal nature of the object to reflect each other, despite their absolutely distinct and independent being.

Philosophical narcissism quite correctly rejected the transcendental factors of God and transcendental reason as inconsistent with the underlying subjectivist categories. It rejected the idea of transcendental vehicles of relatedness which are somehow exempt from division into subjective and objective spheres. Philosophical narcissism admits no Cartesian God, no light of reason, no Kantian "third thing", instead restricting philosophical analysis to the level of subject and object.

Consequently, philosophical narcissism has no access to that means by which earlier subjectivism solved, albeit inconsistently, the problem of integrity and relation. Nor does this radicalized subjectivism offer any new means for solving it. Indeed, it is characteristic of philosophical narcissism that it does not recognize the problem of integrity and relation as a problem at all.

But it is a problem. The result of failing to address it is that both the existential integrity and the relatedness of the subject and of the object become radically problematic. Each narcissistic philosophy is thereby impaled on the horns of a dilemma. If the philosophy in question attempts to conceive of subjectivity as having existential integrity, then for any objectivity to be conceived as related to the subject it must be conceived as *part of* the subject, as *in* it, as belonging to it as a constituent of itself. If, on the other hand, the philosophy thinks of the subject as related to and involved with objects, then the subject must be conceived as having no existential integrity, as being a *function* of or set of relations to objectivity. This dilemma holds for either the subject or the object. Given the lack of a means of combining integrity and relation, the conception of the integrity of one factor—subject or object—implicitly leads to the reduction or elimination of the integrity of the other; and the conception of one factor's relatedness leads to the reduction or elimination of its own integrity. Philosophical narcissism has put itself into a position in which its subjectivities and objectivities cannot have both integrity and relatedness. They can claim one or the other, but not both.

The dilemma becomes even deeper, however, at this point. For, as will be seen, neither of the subjectivist categories makes any sense *without an integral, independent other* to relate to. Subjectivity and objectivity can each have their own existential integrity only as long as there is an 'outside', another entity with existential integrity to relate to. When the existential integrity of one is reduced or eliminated, when it is implicitly transformed into a function of its opposite, then the opposite, the other, loses its existential integrity as well. The reduction of one leads to the reduction of the other.

Now, what does this complex theoretical situation have to do with psychopathological borderline conditions and narcissism? There is an interesting structural parallel between the depiction of self-image and other- or object-images in narcissism and borderline conditions, and the conception of subjectivity and objectivity in the philosophies that are philosophically narcissistic. In each case, a breakdown of the relationship of self or subject and object leads to a volatilization of the representations of each in which each loses its integrity and self/subject and object become paradoxically equatable.

This dialectic, which is quite complex, will be systematically described in the following section. At present we must explore the four general features of psychopathological narcissism and borderline conditions that are most relevant for philosophical narcissism.

1. The Mirror World, the Empty Self

For the narcissist the world is felt, at a deep level of experience, to be unreal and tends to have meaning only as a mirror of the self. There are two reasons for this.

First, because the deep structure of the self was never differentiated from parental images, and because the parents—at least, the primary parent—are for all infants the first representatives of external reality, the narcissistic child fails to differentiate the world as a whole from its own fantasies at a deep level of experience. As a result, the very substantiality of an adult narcissist's world is always involved with primary fantasies and urges, rather than being given as independent of the self.

Second, the ever present and most fundamental issue in the life of a narcissist is his or her self. Never having been established on a secure basis, the self must be constantly fed in a psychic sense. Having been unsure of parental love in infancy, the narcissistic self, which is based on fantasied infantile love, must constantly ask the world whether or not it is loveable, good, beautiful. The world consequently has the status of mirror, sign, or representation of the self. This is operative, of course, on an unconscious level; the adult narcissist does not consciously fail to believe in the reality of the world. But he or she typically will emotionally react to everyday events solely in terms of their meaning for whether the self is competent or incompetent, loved or unloved, and ultimately, grandiose or worthless. The world has the emotional status of a kind of depth-less surface.

At the same time, the narcissistic psyche, whose center is founded only on infantile fantasy images, is "thinly populated." The narcissist experiences his or her own self as shallow, tends to feel empty, emotionless—except for continual anxiety—and lacking in depth of feeling. The narcissist feels empty despite, or rather because of, an obsessive concern for the surface of things, for superficial approval and disapproval, for personal image and appearance. Again, the self is an absence which must be continually filled.

This is precisely the way philosophical narcissism conceives of the subject and the object-world. The subject is empty and the object-world is a mere system of signs or representations for the subject. Neither subject nor object-world is characterized by independent existence, existential integrity, substantiality, or reality. This is because the existential integrity of each is reduced or eliminated. The characteristic of philosophical narcissism that is parallel to the mirror world/empty self feature of pathological narcissism is its *reduction of the existential integrity of subject and object.*

Narcissistic philosophies do not perform the reductions of subject and object simultaneously, as we will see. Philosophical narcissism divides into two types: one initially reduces the integrity of the object-world to a function of the subject, the other initially reduces the subject to the object-world. The former more or less explicitly reduces the existential integrity of worldly objects to the status of a system of representations ("mirror of the self"), while the latter more or less explicitly reduces the subject to a set of intentions or impulses directed at the object-world (the "empty self"). The dialectical result of either of these one-way reductions is a *two-way* reduction; the negation of the integrity of the self necessarily implies a negation of the integrity of the object-world, and vice versa. As in the case of the narcissistic personality, where the failure to achieve an integrated and substantial self corresponds to and is conditioned by a failure to achieve integrated and substantial object-images, likewise in philosophical narcissism regarding the concept of subjectivity and the object-world.

2. Equatability of Self and Object

This feature is related to the last. Because both self and object-images are unstable and insubstantial, and because they are inherently related in all individuals, the narcissist's self and object-images are to some extent equatable. Self-esteem fluctuates due to changes in the evaluation of objects, which directly determines the value of the self; so, for example, any bad experience or bad object related to the self implies that the self is bad or worthless. In general, self and object-images are conflated, confused, over-involved with each other.

In philosophical narcissism, the loss of the existential integrity of subject and object makes them equatable. The subject, upon analysis, is seen to have no content or nature except the objectivities to which it is related. This is due to the fact that any object related to the subject must be conceived as actually constituting the subject, as part of it. The more one examines the subject, the more one finds only objectivities, viewed as content. The subject becomes a function of objectivity. The same is true of the conception of the non-subject or objectivity, which comes to be conceived as a property of the subject.

The categories of subject and object are not completely equated, however, because philosophical narcissism continues to insist on a strict application of the subjectivist dichotomy. Subject and object are claimed to be absolutely distinct at one level of analysis while each is reduced to the status of a function or property of the other at another level of analysis. The subject–object dichotomy therefore becomes a *dichotomy of indistinguishables*. This paradoxical situation, parallel to the relation of self and other in psychopathological narcissism, in which subject and object are absolutely distinct and yet indistinguishable, reveals the *asymptotic equatability* of subject and object in philosophical narcissism.

3. *Splitting*

This is perhaps the most fundamental and important feature of the dynamics of borderline conditions. Rather than distinguishing a whole and integrated self from holistic object-images, the borderline patient's psyche has made its basic distinction along a different axis: the distinction between good and bad, between ideal and fragmented images has supplanted the normal distinction of self and objects. The self and object-images are each split into an ideal, good self and a fragmented, worthless self on the one hand, and ideal, good object-images and fragmented, destructive object-images on the other. Self and object are split into antithetical components, the ideal components being associated with each other and the fragmented, bad components being linked together.

In philosophical narcissism, the loss of the existential integrity and relatedness of subject and object leads to the splitting of the integrity of each into the abstract components of an ideal, formal contentless unity and formless, fluctuating phenomenal content. The concept of subject and the concept of the object each oscillates between the idea of an abstract identity—which is what remains of the existential integrity of subject and object once all relation to the other has been eliminated—and the contents of consciousness, the fluctuating field or process of experience understood as pure phenomena—which is what remains of subject and object once both have lost their existential integrity.

It is this splitting which is at the basis of the preceding two characteristics of philosophical narcissism. If we ask about the nature of the subject, this splitting dictates that there are only two possible answers: the subject is an ideal 'X' with no relation to objectivity and no content; or, the subject is a name for, or function of, or state of phenomena. Likewise, if we examine objectivity we discover that all non-subjective reality is either: an ideal 'X' with no content, the mere concept of 'being' without any relation to appearing beings; or the phenomena. If the former, ideal answers are chosen (ideal subject, ideal object), then subject and object can be claimed to be distinct, thereby preserving the subjectivist dichotomy, yet they would have no content to distinguish them from each other or from nothing. If the latter answers are allowed, then subject and object are identified as the same field of formless, undefinable phenomena, and are thereby equated.

This characteristic of philosophical narcissism, which is parallel to the splitting of psychopathological narcissism, is its dialectical oscillation of terms, or simply, the *dialectics of philosophical narcissism*.

There is another manifestation of the phenomenon of splitting in psychopathological narcissism that is relevant here. It is the splitting between surface functioning or reality-testing and deeper emotional experience. Borderline patients are not psychotic; they function adequately in society, they can distinguish between themselves as social facts and others. It is at a deeper level of experience, at the level of the fundamental images that lie at the root of life-perspectives and emotional experience that they are severely impaired. This splitting of surface and depth is itself defensively motivated, for it keeps the tremendous rage and fear that dominate the depths from overwhelming everyday experience.

Likewise, philosophically narcissistic theories exhibit a schism between their affirmed doctrinal or conceptual content, and the values, aims, and realities that are presupposed by engagement in philosophical activity. Strictly speaking, what philosophical narcissism depicts makes no sense, or rather, if it does make sense, then human living and everyday reality make no sense. These theories are characterized by a remarkable indifference to socio-cultural and common sense realities, *realities which are presumed by philosophical activity itself,* for example, by attending seminars, writing, finding a publisher, communicating with others, etc. At its most extreme, or in its most consistent manifestations, philosophical narcissism implicitly repudiates the notion that philosophical theorizing is susceptible to criticism based on a recognition of common sense, of everyday realities. For this and other reasons, few philosophies are consistently or thoroughly narcissistic. Narcissistic philosophies in practice endorse, to a far greater degree than earlier subjectivism, a *divorce of philosophy from cultural life.* This theme will have special significance in the later chapters of this study.

4. Relation as Context for Integrity

British psychiatrist David Winnicott has argued that in borderline patients the very experience of being-an-entity-having-experiences, the experience of being an integrated entity, of being a something with existential integrity, has disintegrated or was never established.[23] It is interesting to note that in the development of the child this experience can only evolve through a relationship to a loving other. Winnicott emphasizes this by denying the maturational centrality of what is often called "separation" of the ego or self from the infantile sense of continuity with the parental environment. He claims that continuity or unity is never entirely lost in healthy children. Separation is always a limited phenomenon; it takes place at a certain dimension or level of experience, but this is possible only if there remains a deeper level at which continuity is maintained. Borderline patients are precisely those whose dimension of continuity was shattered by a failure of the parent-child relationship. The normal ego, for Winnicott, always nestles within a context of relatedness.

This feature of the aetiology of narcissism and borderline conditions is significant for understanding what is missing in narcissistic philosophies. What is missing is a recognition that a thing's existential integrity is not conceivable outside of a context of internal relations to other things with existential integrity. Integrity requires a context of relations; otherwise, it disintegrates into part-concepts, into ideal and fragmented or phenomenal aspects, as in the oscillatory dialectics of philosophical narcissism.

The existential integrity of things cannot be conceived within philosophical narcissism. This makes a subtle but crucial difference in such philosophies. The notion of existential integrity (as will be seen in Chapter 10) is essential to an adequate concept of reality itself. Narcissistic philosophies cover the *scope* of reality, but they deprive it of *depth;* they present a description of what is in which every thing can be studied, every thing has a name, but in which the fundamental existential integrity of each thing has no place.

This is precisely what is most tantalizing and disturbing in many of the new schools of twentieth-century philosophy: Husserlian and Heideggerian phenomenology, logical positivism, many of the philosophies of deconstruction and the text, and behaviorism. While the criticisms that these schools level at pre-twentieth-century philosophy are often undeniably valid, it is clear that something has been lost in these schools, something has gone out of philosophy with their ascendency, and with this loss philosophy's conception of itself and of its role in culture have been altered.

Of course, these schools have adopted views of inquiry within which the factors that have been lost do not count as factors at all, do not count as legitimate factors in philosophic inquiry. They thus perform the double feat of desiccating philosophy, of drying up its life, and then, like some overzealous taxidermist, declaring the formal purity of the corpse superior to the messiness of the living animal. They find it easy to trade importance for incorrigibility and meaning for formalism.

The Dialectic of Philosophical Narcissism

Dialectic refers to a process of self-negation by which a concept or assertion, upon analysis, can be seen to imply its opposite. This use of the term is, like Kant's, negative; the kind of dialectic referred to ought to be avoided. Unlike Kant's usage, however, the dialectic of philosophic narcissism is not an inevitable "logic of illusion," but is the consequence of an avoidable conceptual error. It will be seen that the dialectic of philosophical narcissism is analogous to a particular kind of dialectical inference in Kant's sense, the Antinomy of Pure Reason.

The dialectical antinomies at issue here have been noticed or suggested by a number of writers but have not been the subject of sustained investigation.

Wittgenstein remarks:

> Here it can be seen that solipsism, when its implications are followed
> out strictly, coincides with pure realism. The self of solipsism shrinks
> to a point without extension, and there remains the reality
> coordinated with it.[24]

Wittgenstein is claiming that two superficially antithetical doctrines, upon analysis of their implications, coincide due to the nature of
their claims about reality and the self. Something about the claims of
solipsism lead it to negate itself, to imply what seems to be its opposite,
namely, realism.

Hegel's phenomenology of the Skeptical and the Unhappy consciousness reflects a related problematic.[25] In the skeptical phase of the
development of spirit, consciousness has sought to overcome the contentlessness or abstraction of "Stoicism" by taking up determinate phenomena or appearances. It asserts its freedom in a new way: rather than
the Stoical aloofness from the apparent world, consciousness takes up
the determinate world and actively negates it in "Scepticism." But this
leaves consciousness with a dilemma because in negating all content,
consciousness makes itself aloof from all existence and life, it is literally
nothing. And yet its negation of content is *just another content*. These
facts tend to push consciousness back into an identification with its phenomenal content. This produces an internal schism that forms the basis
for Hegel's notion of the "Unhappy Consciousness," which Hippolyte
claims to be "the fundamental theme of the *Phenomenology*."[26]

The Skeptical Consciousness experiences itself as oscillating between a unitary, self-identical, but abstract consciousness over against
which all content is 'nothing', and a "medley of sensuous and intellectual
representations . . ." which constitutes the Skeptical appropriation of the
external world. Hegel describes this schism in strikingly pathological
terms:

> this consciousness, instead of being self-identical, is in fact nothing
> but a purely casual, confused medley, the dizziness of a perpetually
> self-engendered disorder. It is itself aware of this . . . it owns to
> being . . . a consciousness which is *empirical,* which takes its
> guidance from what has no reality for it, which obeys what is for it
> not an essential being, which does those things and brings to
> realization what it knows has no truth for it . . . it also, on the
> contrary, converts itself again into a consciousness that is universal
> and self-identical for it is the negativity of all singularity and all
> differences. From this self-identity, or within its own self, it falls back

again into the former contingency and confusion . . . . This consciousness is therefore the unconscious, thoughtless rambling which passes back and forth from the one extreme to the other extreme of the contingent consciousness that is both bewildered and bewildering. It does not itself bring these two thoughts of itself together.[27]

The examples from Wittgenstein and Hegel are conditioned by a common theoretical situation: the dialectics into which a radical or consistent subjectivism necessarily falls, creating philosophical narcissism.

Subjectivism declares subjectivity and the non-subjective to be the most fruitful categorial scheme for interpreting what is. Phenomena or appearances—necessarily including all content, all perceived entities, in other words, most of the population of reality for subjectivism—belong or are internally related to subjectivity. Transcendental factors are then posited by early subjectivism as mechanisms of relation, by which that-which-appeared to a consciousness could justifiably be claimed to represent something *not* belonging to subjectivity, something non-phenomenal.

Philosophical narcissism originates in that radicalization of subjectivism which denies the existence or even the sense of transcendental factors. Hence, the totality of what is must belong to the two antithetical subjectivist categories of subject and non-subject.

The dilemma of this radical subjectivism is that it is impossible for it to understand subjectivity and the non-subjective as related. Once transcendental and naturalistic means of relating the subjective and the non-subjective have been rejected, it becomes evident that either subjectivity must absorb the non-subjective or vice versa.[28] Once this reduction takes place the radical subjectivism in question can be considered a true philosophical narcissism.

There are two forms of philosophical narcissism. One begins by reducing the independently existing object-world to subjectivity; the other by reducing independently existing subjectivity to the object-world. "Reduction" here means that the independent existence or existential integrity of a factor is eliminated. The reduced factor continues to be recognized within the system in question, but only as a property, quality, aspect, or function of something else.

The dialectic inherent in any philosophical narcissism which ensues from this point consists of three logical stages. The first stage is the more or less explicit reduction of subjectivity to the non-subjective or vice versa, as just mentioned. We might use a shorthand symbolism to make these stages more understandable. Let us call the term which is reduced 'R' and the privileged term 'P'. R is the term whose integrity is being eliminated through R's reduction to the status of a trait or function of P, and P is that factor whose integrity is ostensibly being preserved. If we let the lower case letters 's' and 'n' indicate that the factor thus noted is subjectivity and the non-subjective, respectively, then the two forms of philosophical narcissism can be notated:

1. $Ps,(Rn)$

2. $Pn,(Rs)$

Notice that the totality of phenomena, including all of perceived reality now necessarily belongs to P, whether P is subjective or non-subjective. Notice further that the two forms of philosophical narcissism are mirror images of each other; that is, $Ps = Rs$ and $Rn = Pn$. What is reduced in the first form (n) is privileged in the second, and what is privileged in the first form (s) is reduced in the second.

In the second stage, the P term in both forms of philosophical narcissism *breaks down,* upon analysis, into two opposing elements. That is, its very integrity can be seen to be no longer justifiable, now that the R term has lost *its* integrity through the initial reduction. This is because P's integrity was always dependent upon P's relation to an R which also had integrity. Consequently, once R is reduced, P's integrity is also undermined.

P is then radically split into two antithetical components of its former integrity: the concept of an abstract, contentless, pure identity, on one hand, and fluctuating, indeterminate phenomena, on the other hand; or, abstract form (F) and formless content (C). Simply put, if we try to determine the nature of P, we are unable to come up with any such integrated nature. Instead, in answer to the question, "What is P?" we get two antithetical answers, two opposing factors which are *non-integrable within the bounds of the subjectivist-narcissistic system.* Insofar as we try to say that P is an existent with an identity, a formal integrity, we will find ourselves describing P as an existent with no specifiable content, nature, or character; that is, P will appear as a contentless formal abstraction, rather than as an existent. Insofar as we try to see in P a contentual nature, we will find ourselves confronting P as the totality of phenomena, devoid of form or distinction. Thus, in this stage the concept of the privileged term—be it subjectivity or non-subjectivity—has *disintegrated* into the antithetical terms of a purely formal identity and the totality of fluctuating phenomena.

It should be noted that the content, C, is identical for both types of philosophical narcissism. While the formal factors of the now-disintegrated P terms are antithetical, at least superficially, the content-factor is the same for both types. The formal-factor is either an abstract contentless subject or an abstract contentless non-subjectivity, whereas the content-factor is the same single field of subjective phenomena with which the subjectivist system began. Using the same lower case designations, this means that Cs = Cn. These complex relationships of stage two can be notated, for the two types of philosophical narcissism, as follows:

$$1. \quad Ps,(Rn) \rightarrow Fs,Cs(= Cn)$$
$$2. \quad Pn,(Rs) \rightarrow Fn,Cn(= Cs)$$

Now, in each type of philosophical narcissism, neither form nor content can pass minimal standards for being an existing something, an existent, a being, an entity. As pure content and pure form, neither factor can unambiguously be said to exist at all; each could be claimed with some justification to be nothing, non-being. As a result of this, the two factors subsist in a dialectical relation. If we analyze one, we are led to the concept of the other. If we analyze the form, form reduces to content, but then, upon analysis, the latter reveals itself to be equivalent to its antithesis, form. This is precisely the dialectic which Hegel described in the preceding passage, in which consciousness oscillates between identification with a contentless formal principle—that is, Ps (Rn) = Fs—and identification with fluctuating, indeterminate content—Fs[Ps (Rn)] = Cs. This is the dialectic or antinomy of each type of philosophical narcissism which occurs *within* a philosophy of that type, and it would be notated in this way:

$$1. \quad Fs,n \rightarrow Cs,n$$
$$2. \quad Cs,n \rightarrow Fs,n$$

There is, simultaneously, another dialectic or antinomy characteristic of philosophical narcissism which is a consequence of the fact, mentioned previously, that Cs = Cn. The identity of the content-factor brings the two different types of philosophical narcissism into a dialectical relationship. In particular, in those logical moments when the privileged term of each type has been reduced to its content-factor, the privileged terms of the two types *become equivalent.* That is, there is a moment of the dialectical oscillation within each of the two types of philosophical narcissism when both types have reduced the totality of what is to the same, identical realm of fluctuating, ontologically indeterminate phenomena. At this moment, the two types of philosophic narcissism become, in a sense, equivalent. Thus, the dialectic *within* each type has established a dialectic *between* the two types, so that each type of philosophical narcissism implies the other. This part of the third stage of the dialectic would be notated,

$$3. \quad Ps(Rn) = Cs = Cn = Pn(Rs)$$

This is precisely the significance of the passage from Wittgenstein. Wittgenstein suggested that solipsism—that is, Ps(Rn)—"when its implications are followed out strictly coincides with pure realism"—coincides with Pn(Rs). Wittgenstein's remark even delineated the way this coincidence comes about: "The self of solipsism [Ps] shrinks to a point without extension [Fs] and there remains the reality coordinated with it [Cs]." This "reality," which is to say, phenomena, Cs, is equivalent to the reality or content, Cn, of pure realism—that is, of Pn(Rs)—when the latter's "implications are followed out strictly" as well, thereby reducing Pn to Cn.

If we were to examine "pure realism," as Wittgenstein does not in the aforementioned passage, we would find the same internal dialectic, by which it would equate itself with solipsism. For any pure realism (for example, logical positivism) the attempt to deny and reduce subjectivity's role in objective knowing necessitates the rejection of all "objects" and all "unobservable entities" of scientific theorizing as "subjective positings." At this point the only remaining candidate for the role of the purely real is *sense-data,* which is to say, a property of *consciousness.* Thus, logical empiricism inevitably collapses reality into consciousness.

In the dialectic of philosophical narcissism, as schematically outlined above, the concepts of the integrity of the subject and the integrity of the non-subjective, or objectivity, each *fall apart,* disintegrate into part-concepts, into abstract ideas of form and content which cannot stand on their own. This disintegration is analagous to the dynamics of psychopathological narcissism. It is interesting to note Hippolyte's remark that, "Skepticism, as Hegel envisages it, is . . . a skepticism that leads human consciousness to the double feeling of its nothingness and its grandeur."[29] This statement also describes the condition of the self in pathological secondary narcissism. The dialectic of philosophical narcissism, embodied by the Skeptical Consciousness, exhibits a striking structural analogy to the oscillation of self and object-images in narcissistic personality disorders. This analogy can be illustrated by referring to a diagram of Kohut's (see Diagram A).[30] His diagram is accompanied by my own (see Diagram B), which translates Kohut's terms into those applicable to philosophical narcissism.

Kohut's diagram illustrates two lines of development and regression characteristic of psychological secondary narcissism: that of the self and that of the object-image. Each of these two lines exhibits a possible oscillation between a state of perfection or totality, a state of not being limited, bounded, or opposed by anything external, and a state of fragmentation or reduction to part-images.

Kohut's two lines of development-regression are parallel to the two forms of philosophical narcissism, namely; the reduction of world to subject, on the one hand, and the reduction of subject to the world, on the other, respectively. Each of these forms exhibits an oscillation between a state of ideal completeness, of perfectly independent existence, and a state of reduction to fragmentary phenomena. My diagram illustrates this dialectic *within* each of the forms of philosophical narcissism

DIAGRAM A*

Phases of Psychopathological Narcissism

Development and
Regression in Realm
of Grandiose Self

Development and
Regression in Realm
of Omnipotent Object

Solipsistic claims
for attention:
the grandiose self

Compelling need for
merger with powerful
object: stage of
idealized parent imago

Nuclei (fragments)
of the grandiose
self: hypochondria

Nuclei (fragments)
of idealized
omnipotent object:
mystical awe, vague
religious feelings

---

*modified from Heinz Kohut, The Analysis of Self (New York: IUP, 1971).

DIAGRAM B

Phases of Philosophical Narcissism

Oscillation of Subject—Concept	Oscillation of Object—Concept
Subject conceived as Abstract Independent Ideal	Object—world conceived as Abstract Independent Ideal
↓	↓
Subject equated to Fragmentary (objective) Phenomena	Object—world equated to Fragmentary (subjective) Phenomena

Fragmentary (objective) = Fragmentary (subjective)

and the dialectic *between* the two forms, in which antithetical reductive posits of subject and world are each reduced to the same realm of fragmentary phenomena.

Both pathological and philosophical narcissism involve a failure or inability to establish the self/subject as an entity with its own existential integrity *and* as internally related to, involved with, and dependent on other entities with existential integrity. Of course, in pathological narcissism this is a failure of emotional and personal being, while in philosophical narcissism it is a failure of conception. Nevertheless, in each case there is a failure to establish a system of entities which *both* fully exist in themselves and are fully interrelated and interdependent. This failure results, first, in a breakdown of the relation of self/subject to object/world and, second, a breakdown of the very possibility of being an integrated, fully existent, related, interdependent entity. The former leads to an alternating fusion and total diremption of self/subject and object/world; inner and outer become alternately fused and entirely unrelatable. The latter breakdown leads to the disintegration of the concept or experience of a being into the antithetical poles of an ideal formal Being with no content or relation to what we might wish to call 'reality', and a fragmented, fluctuating collection of elementary phenomena.

This complex interaction can be described in another way if we return to the basic categories of subjectivism, which philosophical narcissism retains. For subjectivism, the most fundamental distinction is that between what-is-or-belongs-to an individual subjectivity and what-is-not subjective. But 'what-is-or-belongs-to-subjectivity' has a dual meaning: it is both subjectivity conceived as an entity, substance, factor, or process *and* it is the contents of subjectivity, that is, the manifold thoughts, feelings, representations, or appearances which are subjective, which subjectivity *has.* Among these contents are appearances, representations, perceptions; in short, phenomena. Earlier subjectivism, for example, in Descartes and Kant, provided means and justifications for understanding some of these phenomena as properly representative of what-is-not-subjective, that is, of the object-world or reality.

Philosophical narcissism operates within these three terms: *subjectivity* (conceived as an existing entity or process); *phenomena;* and the non-subjective, non-phenomenal natural *world.* The two forms of philosophical narcissism reduce either the object-world to the subject or vice versa. In either case, phenomena are retained as the only possible *content* of the privileged term. Both forms of philosophical narcissism retain the phenomena, since all stripes of philosophical narcissism and subjectivism accept the Cartesian principle that it is impossible to question the existence of phenomena, of appearances *as* appearances. What can be questioned is whether these phenomena inhere in an existing subjectivity, and whether these phenomena indicate the existence of, or tell us anything about, realities existing independently of the subject and its phenomena. In the triad subject–phenomena–world, once either subject or world has been negated as an independently existing entity, has been absorbed by its antithesis, one is left with either one of two categorial dualities: subject–phenomena or world–phenomena. If one then asks about the nature of the subject or the world, the only answer is that they *are the phenomena*. The phenomena are the only possible content for the remaining term, be it subject or world. If one tries to differentiate the retained term (subject or world) from the fluctuating phenomenal appearances, from the only possible content, then that term must necessarily be conceived as an abstract, purely empty ideal.

The result is that in each of the two forms of philosophical narcissism there is an oscillation between the concept of a fluctuating field of phenomenal content and the concept of an empty abstract existence, either an abstract subject or an abstract world. Both of these terms lack what we, speaking independently of subjectivist terminology, could call reality. The phenomena of consciousness are ultimately an unnameable flux; while the abstract existent, like the concept of Being in Hegel's *Logic*, is equivalent to Nothing.[31]

Narcissistic philosophy, by virtue of its retained subjectivist categories, maintains the absolute distinction between subject and non-subject. Without transcendental mediation the narcissistic philosophy is split into a theoretical level at which the dialectical reduction of subject and object to phenomena occurs, and the level at which the now unmediated subjectivist dualism is more rigid than ever. Thus, the philosophy as a whole is characterized by a *dichotomy of indistinguishables*. While one level of the narcissistic philosophy maintains that they are absolutely distinct, the rest of the theory follows out a line of thought which progressively denudes them of anything which would distinguish them. Subject and non-subject approach each other to an infinitesimal closeness, a virtual identity, a practical indistinguishability, and yet they cannot be equated.

5

Subjectivism without the Object: Husserl

Edmund Husserl was born only fifty-five years after Kant's death, yet his philosophic system belongs, both chronologically and spiritually, not to Kant's century, nor to the nineteenth century of Hegel, Marx, and Darwin, but exclusively to the twentieth century. The initial volume of Husserl's first phenomenological work, *Logical Investigations,* was published in 1900, like another work that proved definitive of the twentieth-century West, Freud's *The Interpretation of Dreams.*[1] Husserl then turned his attention to a complex explication of temporality as the foundational stratum of the constitution of the experienced and known world, composing what would become his *The Phenomenology of Internal Time Consciousness* simultaneously with the appearance of Einstein's essay, "The Electrodynamics of Moving Bodies," a paper that marked the break of twentieth- from nineteenth-century physics and which accorded temporal concepts a new status in physical theory.[2]

In this chapter we will examine the project of Husserl's *Cartesian Meditations* in order to present a comprehensive picture of the nature of transcendental phenomenology in general and of Husserl's later conception of phenomenology in particular. The question of the precise nature of Husserl's project is controversial; it must clarified before proceeding to the analysis of a particular work. Husserl's conception of his philosophy changed frequently from 1900 until the time of his death in 1938: he wrote no less than four introductions to phenomenology, each of which either presented a new conception of phenomenology or gave a new point of departure for it.

In his *Logical Investigations* (1900–1901), Husserl attacked the psychologism which had influenced his earlier *Philosophy of Arithmetic* (1891), and presented for the first time his notion of a non-psychologistic phenomenological description and analysis.[3] It was not until 1913, with the publication of the first volume of *Ideas Toward a Pure Phenomenology and Phenomenological Philosophy*, that Husserl officially introduced both the concept of the '*epoché*', the strict methodological bracketing of the 'natural attitude', and the concept of 'transcendental phenomenology', an *a priori* science of reduced phenomena and the processes of their constitution.[4] A regressive analysis of the layers of intentional objects and intentional acts revealed them, according to *Ideas*, to be rooted in and derived from the 'transcendental ego.'

In 1929, at the age of seventy, Husserl delivered two lectures at the Sorbonne which he later elaborated and published in French in 1931 under the title, *Cartesian Meditations: An Introduction to Phenomenology*.[5] He then worked on yet another introduction from 1934 until the year before his death, which was published under the title, *The Crisis of European Sciences and Transcendental Phenomenology: An Introduction to Phenomenological Philosophy*.[6] These two works, together with a definitive essay by Eugene Fink published in 1933, form a coherent picture of the concept of transcendental phenomenology that Husserl held in the last nine years of his life, his mature conception of phenomenology.

The Project of Husserl's Late Work

Eugene Fink's paper, "The Phenomenological Philosophy of Edmund Husserl and Contemporary Criticism," was written during the years 1928–1938, while Fink worked as Husserl's assistant.[7] Husserl's preface to the paper indicates that he prompted the writing of the paper and is in total agreement with it.

> I have carefully read through this essay . . . and I am happy to be able to state that *it contains no sentence which I could not completely accept as my own* or openly acknowledge as my own conviction.[8]
> (my emphasis)

Fink's paper can be taken as one among several reliable representations of Husserl's mature conception of transcendental phenomenology as it evolved from 1929 to 1937. The Fink essay is especially valuable for its specific historical aim. It was an attempt to clarify the concept of transcendental philosophy by contrasting it with contemporary neo-Kantianism and defending it against neo-Kantian criticism. As a result, the paper defines transcendental phenomenology in a highly sophisticated and fundamental way.[9]

The conception of phenomenology common to the *Crisis*, the *Cartesian Meditations* and the Fink essay is defined by three simple points:

1. Phenomenology is not merely a method; it is a philosophical science. While it is based on a method and a set of principles chiefly concerning the nature of evidence, phenomenology evolves a system of definite conclusions about what is.

2. Only with the transcendental reduction and related concepts (for example, the transcendental ego) does phenomenology become complete and self-consistent. True phenomenology *is* transcendental phenomenology.

3. Lastly, all worldly beings are meaning-complexes and all meaning-complexes are constituted by transcendental subjectivity. The claim that worldly beings exist independently of constituted meaning-complexes is philosophically untenable.

According to this mature conception of phenomenology, the individual, mundane consciousness in everyday life, our normal psycho-physical ego, has as its true essence a pure, transcendental subjectivity. As Fink writes:

> Thus the intramundane psychical "life" is in fact none other than the transcendental world-preceding life, but is such in being *concealed* from itself in a form of "constitutedness."[10]

When our everyday consciousness is modified or purified via abstention from the naive acceptance of natural existence we can become aware of the purified or essential features and processes of this consciousness. Simultaneously, we become aware of how the various levels of objectivity come to be, or are constituted, within these purified conscious processes. This implies understanding the world as a complex of meanings, as a "constituted sense" which depends on transcendental consciousness.

If the conclusions drawn within phenomenological research are to have any meaning once we return to the naive acceptance of the world, we must maintain this understanding of the world as a constituted sense. In other words, the *epoché* is not an arbitrary or hypothetical method, a theoretical 'as if' aimed at drawing interesting conclusions about the world; the *epoché* reveals the true nature of the world as dependent on consciousness, a truth which is absolute and not relative to the performance of the phenomenological method. This is what Husserl must maintain if phenomenology is the ultimate science he clearly wants it to be.

Thus transcendental phenomenology is the theory that the totality of meanings or senses that comprise what *is* for the human consciousness, what we call the 'world', is the on-going product of something which is not itself a member of that world. That something is transcendental subjectivity, and whether this be understood as an ego-pole, an entity, a field, a process, or group of processes, or conceived otherwise, it is something whose mundane representative is the individual consciousness or thinking ego and which is itself the pure essence of the latter. The natural world depends on consciousness in a way that is not reciprocal.

Fink vigorously contrasts phenomenology with neo-Kantianism, or "criticism" as he calls it. For the neo-Kantians, meaning is distinguished from being; the former structures the latter. The task of neo-Kantian philosophy is to clarify the meaning-structures that lie immanently in transcendental subjectivity, and which are proved through a deduction to apply to experienced being. Phenomenology rejects this extrinsic relation of form and content, subjectivity and world, characteristic of "criticism." The world lies immanently within transcendental subjectivity: it is a meaning-complex, a system of constituted sense, as opposed to a system of natural-world being. That is, the world is a meaning.

It may appear that this view of transcendental phenomenology pushes it in the direction of ontology. Rather than shrinking from these implications, Fink embraces and defends them. Transcendental phenomenology is a theory of the "becoming of the world," of the "origin of the world"—the world understood as accepted meaning-complexes—within the flowing constitutive life of transcendental subjectivity, the "absolute ground."

> [The] transcendental noema is the world itself viewed as the unity of acceptances contained within the belief which belongs to transcendental subjectivity's flowing world-apperception.[11]

Phenomenology is therefore the science of the origin of all things, not of their "ontic" or "causal" origin, but of the originary transcendental-subjective processes within which all things become what they are. Fink writes:

> The true theme of phenomenology is neither the world on the one hand, nor a transcendental subjectivity which is to be set over and against the world on the other, but the *world's becoming in the constitution of transcendental* subjectivity . . . "phenomenology" . . . is essentially "*constitutive* phenomenology."[12]

Fink contrasts phenomenology with "dogmatic" metaphysics as well as with Kantian or neo-Kantian philosophy. Dogmatic metaphysics sought the origin of beings in *other beings,* thus remaining within ontic categories. Kantianism eschewed the question of origin and sought to interpret the meaning or form of beings, thus separating the ontic from the transcendental, the latter subsisting outside of the question of existence. Phenomenology seeks the origin of the entire world, of all beings and all meanings, in the non-ontic sphere of transcendental subjectivity.

In the *Cartesian Meditations* Husserl endorses essentially the same view, without using quite the same language. The "universe of true being" and the "universe of possible consciousness," Husserl writes:

> belong together essentially; and, as belonging together essentially, they are also concretely one, one in the only absolute concretion: transcendental subjectivity. If transcendental subjectivity is the universe of sense, then an outside is precisely—nonsense.[13]

And further:

> Precisely thereby, every sort of existent itself, real or ideal, becomes understandable as a "product" of transcendental subjectivity, a product constituted in . . . [its intentional] performance.[14]

Phenomenology is the fulfillment of the hope of idealism. It is the *a priori* determination of the world through the self-explication of the monad.[15] This view, which is pursued in the *Cartesian Meditations,* will be explored later.

The problem with this conception of phenomenology is that while it radically distinguishes the transcendental realm of reduced phenomena from ontic, natural world entities and events, thus avoiding the idealism of claiming that natural existence is itself constituted by consciousness, it nevertheless becomes more and more difficult to define just what it is which is left out of transcendental constitution, just what this "natural existence" is which is not constituted by consciousness. If what remains outside of constitution is mere existence, not definable beings but their mere existingness, then we can ask: just what is mere existence conceived apart from *what* exists? This is one manifestation of the problem posed by a theoretical dichotomy of indistinguishables; natural existence must be distinguished from the field of what is transcendentally constituted, yet the Husserlian logic gradually absorbs all that could characterize the former into the latter, making it impossible to indicate what distinguishes the two.

The *Cartesian Meditations* and the *Crisis* are usually seen as repre-

senting antithetical approaches to phenomenology, the former representing a "Cartesian" approach not dissimilar to that of *Ideas,* and the latter
representing a "teleological-historical" approach.[16] On this view, the *Crisis* forms a decisive break with earlier conceptions of phenomenology
and represents Husserl's attempt to move in a new direction, a direction
influenced by his desire to answer concerns expressed in the existentialism of Heidegger and others. The differences between the *Cartesian
Meditations* and the *Crisis* are, however, differences in *approach* to phenomenology, differences in the "way into" or mode of access to phenomenology. The system and nature of the phenomenology to which one
gains access remains fundamentally the same in both works.

The difference between these two ways into phenomenology is primarily that in the *Cartesian Meditations,* Husserl begins by positing the
ideal of a universal, apodictic science, which is then discovered to be
achievable only through phenomenology, while in the *Crisis* he attempts
to demonstrate the necessity of phenomenology by exploring the history
of philosophic and scientific thought about the "life-world" of experience and by explaining this history as the development of an intellectual
project of which phenomenology is both the historical product and the
sole theoretical fulfillment. The *Crisis* and the *Cartesian Meditations*
give us different conceptions of the *education* of the phenomenologist
(the process of moving from the natural attitude to transcendental-
phenomenological research) and the relation of phenomenology and
phenomenological consciousness to other sciences, the natural attitude
and the life-world.

The *Crisis* does break new ground for Husserl; it presents his first
systematic attempt at cultural-historical analysis. Facing the building historical and intellectual crisis of the 1920's and 1930's, Husserl intends to
rethink the entire philosophic character of "European humanity."[17] For
Husserl, the roots and the uniqueness of European culture lie in the
Renaissance development of the concept of a universal science. He re-
formulates the concept and the *praxis* of science through his notion of
the life-world (*Lebenswelt.*) It is this reinterpretation of science (and
eventually of his own phenomenological science as well) in terms of the
life-world that justifies the eminent place of the *Crisis* in twentieth-
century philosophy.

The "life-world" of the *Crisis* is a descendant of "the surrounding
world of life" and "the cultural world" of the *Cartesian Meditations.* In
the latter work, the meanings of these three concepts are intertwined in a
brief section concerning the constitution of spiritual, or "intersubjective
communities."[18] But it is in the *Crisis,* that the concept of the life-world
emerges with full clarity and significance.

The life-world is the pre-given, pre-scientific, pre-theoretical world
in which we live. It is the "straightforwardly intuited" world, a "merely

subjective-relative world" which is nevertheless, the "realm of original self-evidences," "prior to all theoretical-scientific praxis."[19] Husserl's claim is that all mathematics, logic, science, philosophy, and phenomenology itself are grounded in this life-world, depend upon it for their ultimate evidences and can never escape it or go outside of it.[20]

Within this context, phenomenology becomes the first and only *a priori* science of the life-world. Husserl writes:

> In opposition to all previously designed objective sciences, which are sciences on the ground of the world, this would be a science of the universal *how* of the pregivenness of the world, i.e. of what makes it a universal ground for any sort of objectivity.[21]

Phenomenology alone can derive and account for the constitution of the life-world.

Despite its novelty, the new approach of the *Crisis* is exactly what Husserl tells us it is: an *introduction* to phenomenology, an introduction to the same science to which the *Cartesian Meditations* was an introduction. The investigation of the life-world requires:

> a *total change* of the natural attitude, such that we no longer live . . . as human beings within natural existence, constantly effecting the validity of the pregiven world; rather we must constantly deny ourselves this.[22]

This "total change," here called a "denial" by Husserl, is the "transcendental *epoché*." From this flow the familiar features of transcendental phenomenology, features the *Crisis* shares with the *Cartesian Meditations*. The transcendental reduction discloses the nature of the world as a "*phenomenon*," as the "correlate" of an "absolute subjectivity" which "constitutes" the world's ontic meanings, a subjectivity "through whose validities the world 'is' at all."[23] The life-world remains, but as a system of meanings constituted by transcendental subjectivity. For the phenomenologist:

> the naive ontic meaning of the world . . . is transformed for him into the meaning 'system of poles for transcendental subjectivity', which 'has' a world and real entities by constituting them.[24]

In this way, phenomenology discovers "*how* . . . the coherent universal validity *world—the* world—comes into being for us . . . ."[25]

The phenomenologist of the *Crisis* is no less a "disinterested spectator"[26] than the phenomenologist of the *Cartesian Meditations*. Natural life and the natural attitude have been just as resolutely excluded in the former as in the latter; in each case "we take no part in all the interests which set any kind of human praxis in motion," and "we are . . . not concerned with what the world . . . actually is . . . ."[27] Most importantly, both works extol a "method of epochē . . . [by which] everything objective is transformed into something subjective."[28] In the *Crisis* no less than in the *Cartesian Meditations,* "the ego . . . [is] the *performer* . . . of *all validities.*"[29]

It is significant that in the only section of the central part of the *Crisis* devoted to developing the concept of the ego, Husserl refers to his own categories *"ego-cogitatio-cogitata"* as "Cartesian."[30] It is true that Husserl then goes on to say that the order of inquiry suggested by these three Cartesian categories must be opposite to that of the Cartesian approach. Inquiry must, for the Husserl of the *Crisis,* regress from the *cogitata* back to the *ego,* rather than proceeding from the ego to the object. The difference with Descartes that Husserl expresses here perfectly reflects the true relation between his own major late works, the *Cartesian Meditations* and the *Crisis.* It is the *order of inquiry* that differentiates the *Crisis* from the earlier Cartesian approach, while the core concepts *within* that order remain constant. Regardless of what road the would-be phenomenologist takes, the transcendental destination is the same.

That Husserlian transcendental phenomenology is subjectivist is undeniable. The *epochē* makes the distinction between the subjective and the non-subjective into a foundational principle. The subjective–non-subjective distinction appears at each level of Husserl's analysis. Indeed, it is Husserl's intention to develop a purely scientific, radically subjectivist philosophy. What is less obvious and certainly is not Husserl's intention is that the very radicalism and purity of his application of subjectivist categories reveals the inherent instability of those categories and their implicit narcissism.

The Failure of Intersubjectivity in the *Cartesian Meditations*

Husserl makes the close relationship of his phenomenology with Cartesianism clear from the outset of the *Cartesian Meditations.* In the very first paragraph of the book, he tells us not only that his research into Descartes' *Meditations* ". . . acted quite directly on the transformation of an already developing phenomenology into a new kind of transcendental phenomenology," but further, that "one might almost call transcendental phenomenology a neo-Cartesianism . . . ."[31] The reason for the qualification "almost" is that while Husserl is indebted to the Cartesian method and viewpoint, which he wishes to apply radically, he believes that this method is incompatible with "nearly all the well-known doctrinal content of the Cartesian philosophy."[32]

What Husserl finds essential in Descartes is the conviction that a "radical new beginning" is required in philosophy; the project of making philosophy a rigorous science by finding an apodictic foundation; and, most importantly, the view that such a foundation can only be had through a "necessary regress" to the "pure *ego cogito*."[33]

In his first Meditation, Husserl argues for the necessity of this last point in a characteristically different way than Descartes in the original *Meditations*. Descartes began by doubting, objecting to various forms of belief and knowledge on various grounds, and only formulated a criterion of knowledge (clarity and distinctness) *after* achieving the *ego cogito* as a first principle. Husserl first formulates a conception of evidence, science, and a methodology, and only through these explicit criteria does he arrive at his Archimedian point.

For Husserl, "evidence" is a "judicative having of" something,[34] an "*experiencing* of something,"[35] where that something is "present as the . . .[thing] 'itself' . . . ." Judgments are founded on evidences. Clearly, if we are to have a "genuine science" we must:

> neither make nor go on accepting any judgement . . . that [is] not derived from evidence, from "experiences" in which the affairs and affair-complexes in question are present [to us] as "they themselves."[36]

There is a hierarchy of evidences such that some "are recognizable as preceding all other imaginable evidences."[37] Although any evidence carries with it the "full certainty of its being" due to its being immediately 'had' by experience, only some evidences are "apodictic," which means that their non-being is absolutely unimaginable.[38] Consequently, a radically new and certain beginning of philosophy must first aim at unearthing evidence which "precede[s] all other imaginable evidences and, on the other hand, can be seen to be themselves apodictic."[39] Only then:

> it becomes manifest that our experiential evidence of the world lacks . . . the superiority of being the absolutely primary evidence . . . [it] is obviously not to be taken . . . as an apodictic evidence . . . . Not only can a particular experienced thing suffer devaluation as an illusion . . . the whole universally surveyable nexus . . . can prove to be an illusion, a coherent dream . . . . It follows that . . . the experienced world must . . . be deprived of its naive acceptance . . . . The being of the world . . . must be for us, henceforth only an acceptance-phenomenon.[40]

The transformation of naive acceptance into a withholding of acceptance is the phenomenological *epochē*. This modification of the acceptance of the world's existence, far from 'losing' something, is for Husserl the taking possession or revealing of something, namely:

> my pure being, with all the pure subjective processes making this up,
> and everything meant in them, *purely as* the universe of "phenomena"
> in the . . . phenomenological sense.[41]

What is gained is a clear light trained on the "positing processes of consciousness" and everything that is "*meant* in these processes."[42]

Husserl leaves no question that the inhibition of the acceptance of the existence of the world is not merely an interesting method for seeing the world as phenomenon and observing the subjective processes of consciousness in a new way. Rather it is the necessary condition for the apprehension of the essence of oneself, it is the only way "by which I apprehend myself purely." And this pure essence of consciousness has epistemic, evidential priority—and as we will see later, other kinds of priority—over the world whose naive acceptance has heretofore obscured it. He writes, still in the first Meditation:

> The world is for me absolutely nothing else but the world existing for
> and accepted by me in . . . a conscious *cogito* [as in Descartes]. It
> gets its whole sense . . . and its acceptance as existing, exclusively
> from such *cogitationes* . . . . If I put myself above this life [of
> experiencing, thinking, valuing and acting] and refrain from doing
> any believing that takes "the" world . . . as existing . . . I thereby
> acquire myself as the pure ego, with the pure stream of my
> cogitationes . . . . *Thus the being of the pure ego and his*
> *cogitationes . . . is antecedent to the natural being of the world . . .*
> [the latter] continually presupposes the realm of transcendental
> being.[43] (my emphasis)

In Hussérl's view, Descartes failed to achieve complete clarity regarding the possibilities of a science of this transcendental realm in that the latter's residual Scholasticism caused him to conceive of the *cogito* as a foundational principle or axiom for a deductive science of the existing natural world. Descartes conceived of the field of "reduced" consciousness as something ontologically akin to the natural world, as something subsceptible to an ontological characterization not unlike that of the world; that is as a *res cogitans,* standing in a definite, external and in some cases causal relation to *res extensa.* Descartes, having grounded philosophy in the notion of a pure subjectivity, mistakenly interpreted subjectivity through a concept which was appropriate to other entities within the world.[44] He did so, as we saw in Chapter 2, in order to develop a system of relations between pure subjectivity and the natural world; thus it was necessary for him to conceive them on the same level of ontological analysis. For Husserl, this kind of relation cannot hold between pure subjectivity and the world. They cannot as Fink argued, occupy the same level of analysis.

For Husserl, Descartes' error led him to become "the father of transcendental realism, an absurd position," and to fail to enter into a new science of "transcendental subjectivity."[45] This "unprecedented" science of transcendental subjectivity will be, in contrast to the "objective" sciences of subjectivity which take subjectivity as a phenomenon within the world, ". . . a science that is . . . absolutely subjective, whose thematic object exists *whether or not the world exists.*"[46]

In Meditations Two through Four Husserl elaborates the basic categories and insights of his new science. His aim in these Meditations is to sketch the outlines of his new science which, while it begins as an *a priori* investigation of the structures and dynamic processes constituting the phenomenologically reduced world in consciousness, gradually reveals itself as a theory of the actual genesis of the meant-world. In an addition to the text which he intended to be inserted in the second Meditation, Husserl writes:

> The first procedure in Meditations I–IV is to awaken the guiding thought: The world is a meaning, an accepted sense. When we go back to the ego, we can explicate the founding and founded strata with which that sense is built up . . . we can reach the absolute being and process in which the being of the world shares its ultimate truth and in which the ultimate problems of being reveal themselves . . . .[47]

Here again, we see that Husserl's understanding of transcendental phenomenology takes phenomenology beyond a descriptive or eidetic science and brings it into the realm of metaphysics.

Before proceeding to the central issue of the *Cartesian Meditations*—the analysis of intersubjectivity—a prefatory comment must be made. The present critique attacks Husserlian phenomenology at a theoretical level; it confronts phenomenology's basic categorial structure and orientation. What such a critique does not take into account is the *concrete work* of Husserlian phenomenology, a body of work whose value, insofar as it can be taken *independently* of the theoretical structure within which it is embedded, is not at issue. This distinction is parallel to Schutz's distinction between phenomenology as an explication and constitutional analysis of the "sense-structure" of conscious life, and phenomenology as a theory of the genesis and "foundation of the structure of being."[48]

Husserl is rightly credited as the major force behind the creation of a new form of inquiry; namely, the inquiry into the systematic, dynamic relations between acts of consciousness and their intentional objects, an inquiry which has unquestionably generated valuable work. This inquiry is founded on what Husserl made of Brentano's notion of "intentionality"—the notion that consciousness is essentially characterized as always a "consciousness of" something.[49] What Husserl saw in this principle was that every act of consciousness (*cogitatione* or noetic act) must be systematically and structurally correlated with its objects-in-consciousness, its phenomena (*cogitata* or noemata), and vice versa. This implies that conscious life is constituted by complex and—insofar as that life is coherent—lawful and systematic processes of *synthesis*. Husserl writes:

> Thus each passing cogito intends its cogitatum, not with an undifferentiated blankness, but as a cogito with a describable *structure of multiplicities,* a structure having a *quite definite* noetic-noematic composition, which, by virtue of its essential nature, pertains to just this cogitatum.[50]

The facts of correlation and synthesis make possible a rigorous inquiry into these *a priori* systematic processes of consciousness by which the world-phenomenon is constituted. Husserl remarks in passing in the *Crisis* that the recognition of this correlation of intending acts and intentional objects affected him ". . . so deeply that [his] whole subsequent life-work has been dominated by the task of systematically elaborating . . . [these correlations]."[51] In the *Cartesian Meditations* he writes that it is the elucidation of this dynamic synthetic structure of transcendental subjectivity which "makes fruitful . . . Franz Brentano's significant discovery that 'intentionality' is the fundamental characteristic of 'psychic phenomena'."[52]

This project of elucidating whatever structures or synthetic processes can be shown to be implicit in conscious life is not invalidated by my criticisms. The object of the present attack is rather the philosophical infrastructure, the context, within which such analyses function in Husserl's philosophy, and, hence, a certain interpretation of the meaning of such analyses. Of course, it is precisely this infrastructure which gives Husserl's analyses their philosophical significance. Husserl's philosophy is wrong, but it *is* a philosophy and not merely a technical analysis of conscious processes. Those interpreters who see the latter as the essence of Husserl's project may make Husserl more true, but they certainly make him less important, especially in comparison to his own expansive aims.

Early in the second Meditation Husserl mentions a possible difficulty that casts a shadow over his new science. It is the prospect of "solipsism." Husserl admits that:

> without doubt the sense of the transcendental reduction implies that, at the beginning, this science can posit nothing but the ego . . . .
> Without doubt [this science] must at first parenthesize the

distinction . . . between "me myself" . . . and others . . . and thus, in a certain sense, it begins accordingly as a pure egology and . . . apparently condemns us to a solipsism, albeit a transcendental one . . . . But, at this point in our meditations, we can make no definite decision about this matter . . . .[53]

It is in the fifth Meditation that Husserl turns to address the question of intersubjectivity and solipsism. That discussion stands as the most thorough and systematic attempt by Husserl to defend his phenomenological science from the charge of solipsism. This charge is a serious one, as Husserl admits. He had written in Meditation Four that:

> The attempt to conceive the universe of true being as something lying outside of the universe of possible consciousness . . . is nonsensical. They belong together essentially . . . they are also concretely one, one in the only absolute concretion: transcendental subjectivity. If transcendental subjectivity is the universe of possible sense, then an outside is precisely—nonsense.[54]

The problem addressed in the fifth Meditation is to show how it is possible that, within the "pure conscious processes" of my own ego, other egos can be constituted and, with them, the common world which always carries with it the sense that it is an intersubjective or shared world, a world that is "there-for-everyone."

Husserl sees that the problem of the constitution of the "objective world" hinges on the logically prior problem of the constitution of other egos I experience, with whom I have "empathy."[55] The problem of how transcendental subjectivity can constitute within itself *other* subjectivities becomes *the* most crucial issue for transcendental phenomenology.

Husserl's first step in addressing the issue is to reformulate it in terms appropriate to transcendental phenomenology. For this purpose, Husserl introduces a new *"peculiar kind of epochē"*[56] which must be applied *within* the already phenomenologically reduced transcendental realm. This new *epochē* excludes *"all constitutional effects of intentionality relating immediately or mediately to other subjectivity . . . ."*[57] What is excluded is everything "alien" (*Fremden*) or other, and what remains over is *"my transcendental sphere of peculiar ownness,"* what is peculiarly my own (*des Selbst-eigenen*) or the ego's "proper sphere" (*Eigenheit*).

This *epochē* excludes all noemata insofar as their sense is in some way dependent on the sense "there-for-others," in other words, dependent on the constitution of other egos. Consequently, the sphere of ownness (which Husserl names with the Leibnizian term "monad") includes my "every intentionality," and thus, every "intentionality . . . directed to what is other"—all the intending subjective processes of the transcendental ego.[58] Further, the entire noematic field insofar as its intentional objects are not dependent on other egos, belongs to the monad.

> In this manner it becomes clear that *the ego, taken concretely*, has a *universe of what is peculiarly his own*, which can be uncovered by an original explication of his apodictic "ego sum" . . . within this *"original sphere"* . . . we find also a "transcendent world" . . . belong[ing to] . . . what I am in myself as this monad.[59]

The full significance of the new *epochē* becomes apparent in Husserl's subsequent restatement of the problem of intersubjectivity. The new *epochē* divides the life of transcendental subjectivity into two parts: the "primordial" realm of "immanent transcendency" belonging to one's own monad, and the realm of "constitutionally secondary *Objective transcendency*."[60] Husserl's task is now to show that although the latter is constituted both within and by the former, it does *not* belong to the former as part of the former's "essence." It must be remembered that this distinction and the entire ensuing discussion takes place after and on the presumption of the phenomenological and transcendental reductions; "Objective transcendency" and "immanent transcendency" each refer to meaning-complexes constituted by the transcendental ego.

Husserl's argument to demonstrate that another ego can be constituted within one's own monad, and that these two monads nevertheless share a commonly constituted world, runs as follows. Husserl claims that:

1. The body of the other, as perceptually *originarily presented*, is included within one's sphere of peculiar ownness (monad).

2. Because of the presentational *similarity* of the other body with one's own presented body, a "pairing" or "association" of these two presentations takes place—verified through the on-going perception of the "harmonious behavior" of the other—whereby the characteristic 'sense' of one's own body as "governed by an ego" is "analogically transferred" to the other presented body.

3. Consequently, the ego has an *appresented* apprehension of another ego as governing the other *presented* body; that is, another ego is in fact appresentatively constituted in one's own monad.

4. Because all contents of one's monad carry the sense of being-'Here', and the presented other body carries the sense of being-'There'— "such as I should be if I were there"[61]—the other *cannot* belong to one's own monad. Thus, the appresented ego *cannot* be included within me, within my primordial sphere, but must be authentically *other*.

5. Because every appresentation stands in an intrinsic "functional community" with the presentation that is its necessary core, the presented body of the other, which is part of one's own intra-monadic

sphere of nature, is inseparable from the other ego, which, analogically, must have its own body as a presentation in its own monadic sphere. Thus, the *same content*—other's body, and by extension, all of nature— is *commonly presented in both monads,* although connected in each case with differing appearances.

With this argument, Husserl believes he has shown that one monad can constitute another, another that is truly separate in that "no really inherent connexion leads from their subjective processes to my subjective processes,"[62] and yet with whom there exists an "intentional communion." He goes on to describe the repetition of this process as establishing a "community of monads," which is the basis for that "transcendental intersubjectivity" presupposed by the constitution of the objective world.[63]

There are many criticisms that could be, and have been made of Husserl's argument in the fifth Meditation. A number of these have been presented by Schutz and Theunissen.[64] The problems with his argument are, however, deeper than many critics have indicated. It is not the argument alone which is flawed, but also the system which the argument attempts to protect. Essentially, Husserl's task is less to prove than to disprove something, namely, that:

> everything I, qua transcendental ego, *know as existing in consequence of myself,* and explicate as *constituted in myself,* must *belong to me as part of my own essence.*"[65]

Husserl must disprove that my intentional objects *are* me, belong to me. Not only has Husserl failed to disprove this, more importantly, he *had to* fail.

First, the concept of appresentation as applied in Husserl's argument is problematic, as Fink admits.[66] Husserl had defined appresentation in terms of the "anticipation" of a possible presentation which could in fact be brought about. For example, in the case of a perceptual object, the backside of the object is appresented in that the perceptual presentation of the front carries with it the sense of the backside as something which could be presented if I were to walk around the object. Fink calls this the "redeemableness" (*Einlösbarkeit*) of appresentation: the appresented must be intrinsically capable of fulfillment in a presentation.

This quality of redeemableness is clearly not present in the case of the appresentation of the other ego. Indeed, it cannot be, for the possible *presentation* of the other ego would mean that the other ego could be part of my primordial monadic world. This is precisely what Husserl is trying to disprove.

Husserl attempts to reassure us of the unextraordinary character of the appresentation of the other ego by likening it to the temporal synthesis of appresented past moments with presented present moments;[67] to the temporal synthesis by which multiple, separate intentional acts can intend "the same . . . *identical intentional object* . . . ;[68] and even to "every external perception" in which there is an appresented aspect.[69] But, no less than in the case of redeemable perceptual appresentations, these cases fail to sustain an analogy with the appresentation of the other ego. In the case of both perception and temporal synthesis, the applicability of the concept of appresentation is based on the idea of an "*intentional modification*" of presentations; that is, either a retention of a now-past presentation or an anticipation of a kinaesthetically achievable presentation. But, as Husserl knows, the other ego is in principle incapable of being presented. He has not shown that the appresentation of the other ego is conceivable at all given the central concepts of his phenomenology.

This problem leads to deeper and more far-reaching ones. There are serious difficulties not only with the application of appresentation, but with the differentiation of and relation between appresentation and presentation, and in general, between any "non-originary" and "originary" intentional modalities. There is an implicit problem here that strikes at the heart of what Husserl is trying to defend against in the fifth Meditation and is a dilemma for transcendental phenomenology.

The problem is this: Husserl wishes to distinguish (after the phenomenological *epoché* and within the reduced sphere) intentional modalities and the corresponding evidences which are prior, originary and "founding," and other strata of intentional acts and noemata that are derivative or "founded." There is no intrinsic problem with this distinction insofar as the present lines of criticism are concerned. The problem arises with the fundamental phenomenological method of distinguishing between the realm of natural existence and the realm of subjectivity and of "bracketing" the former. Husserl repeatedly associates the founding or originary stratum with whatever acts and objects can be said to dwell most fully and exclusively within individual conscious life and to *most fully exclude reference to what is not exclusively within subjective processes*. Thus, the founding acts and evidences, at each level of analysis, are those most exclusively "immanent" in transcendental subjectivity, and the founded are those which have a closer relation to objectivity. This is the consequence of conflating subjectivist categories with the distinction founding-founded, as described earlier.[70]

In Husserl's five-step argument against solipsism, the reader may notice an apparent inconsistency concerning the concepts 'Here' and 'There' in point number four. These concepts are a central part of Husserl's proof that the appresented other, as 'There', cannot belong to my peculiar ownness, within which every content has the sense Here. The inconsistency is not merely apparent, it is real. Husserl has declared that whatever is presented as an originary evidence must belong to my monadic sphere of ownness. He writes that,

> whatever can become presented, and evidently verified, *originally*—is something I am; or else it belongs to me as peculiarly my own.[71]

Consequently, the entire natural world of originary presentations, insofar as it is not dependent on intersubjectivity, is "something I am," in my monad. This necessarily includes the presented body of the other.

When Husserl introduces the opposition Here-There, he says repeatedly that one's own body has the meaning Here and the other's body has the meaning There, in accord with our common sense view. But the implications of the preceding paragraph force him to admit that, not only is my own body Here, but,

> Consequently my entire primordial ownness, proper to me as a monad, has the content of the Here . . .[72]

This 'Hereness' of the presented world of ownness is made necessary not only by the preceding paragraph, but also by the argument Husserl is making for the authentic otherness of the other ego. The latter presumes that the primordial world as a whole is Here, so that the other's being There will *exclude* the other from the primordial world. Husserl fails to explain or even to notice the contradiction in this. The entire presented world, and so the body of the other, must have the sense Here, and yet the other's body must also have the sense There if Husserl is to prove that the ego appresented with that body cannot be part of my primordial world, which is Here. (It should be noted that the Hereness of the other's body in question is constituted within one's own monad, just as is its 'Thereness'. That is, the Hereness in question is *not* the Hereness which the other would have *for itself* within its own monadic life.)

Husserl's difficulty cannot be solved by claiming that, since the Here and There in question are intended meanings, are an intended-as-Here and an intended-as-There, they are capable of coexisting without the contradiction that would hold for the same entity being here and there in the sense of natural existence. Even if their status as intentional made Hereness and Thereness compatible, which would be strange enough, the point is that Husserl needs them to be *in*compatible. His proof of intersubjectivity hinges on the other's body, as There, *not* being included within my own monadic sphere, which is Here. If Thereness and Hereness are compatible in such a way that the same intended complex, the other's body, can be intended as *both* There and as Here (and it must be Here because everything in my own sphere is Here), then how can the intended Thereness of the other's body *exclude* that body from any possible belongingness to my own monad? Husserl's real problem is that he needs Hereness and Thereness to be *both* compatible and incompatible to make his argument work.

This contradiction does more than discredit Husserl's argument against solipsism. It throws into question the whole strategy and project initiated by the new *epochē*.

Husserl's aim in the fifth Meditation was to establish an area within transcendental subjectivity within which are constituted those regions or levels of what is which do not have the sense of 'belonging to me as part of myself'. This area includes other egos, the natural world insofar as its meaning-complexes are dependent on the constitution of other egos, and "spiritual objectivities" or the cultural world. For this purpose, Husserl invented his new *epochē* to distinguish between this intersubjective, alien world, and the rest of the realm of transcendental subjectivity, the peculiar ownness of the monad.

Along with this distinction, Husserl continued in the fifth Meditation to act in accordance with an impulse which has been an essential part of transcendental phenomenology since *Ideas,* volume one. He derives all meaning, all sense, from the deepest possible stratum of the transcendental ego = I (regarded as the primordial constituting sphere), in relation to which all other intending acts and objects are founded or derivative. The intersubjective world had to be derived from and constituted *by* the "primordial" sphere of peculiar ownness, the "transcendental concrete I-myself" which contains the founding level of originary presentation. Husserl writes:

> This unitary stratum . . . [of ownness] is distinguished by being essentially the *founding* stratum . . . . I obviously cannot have the "alien" or "other" as experience, and therefore cannot have the sense "objective world" as an experiential sense, without having this stratum in actual experience; whereas the reverse is not the case.[73]

Husserl is simply repeating the transcendental reduction at a different level of analysis. Whereas the original reduction was meant to reveal all meaning-complexes as derivative from the transcendental subject, the new *epochē* of the fifth Meditation reveals all meaning-complexes within transcendental subjectivity to be derivative from primordial ownness.

But the new *epochē* also leaves the entire natural world, insofar as it is constituted independently of intersubjectivity, in the monad of primordial ownness. This is entirely necessary, since the *epochē* distinguishes ownness from otherness; ownness or the I must incorporate the sphere of originary evidences, and the body of the other, or indeed, nature in general must be given *originarily* if Husserl is ever to avoid solipsism.

Thus the irony of Husserl's position. If the founding stratum is to be identified with my monad, with what 'I am', then any attempt to assure the existence of and access to the natural world for the monad would seem to require that the experience or constitution of that world obtain at the founding, originary level. Given the prejudice of the system, the only apparently sound basis for overcoming solipsism would seem to be to constitute the world *within* the monad. But this is paradoxical. It not only appears to be the very definition of solipsism, but within Husserl's argument it proves to undo him by incorporating the body of the other into one's own monad, thereby making it 'Here' as well as 'There'.

Husserl is not unaware of the paradoxical situation set up by his new *epochē*. He recognizes, for example, that the monad constitutes its own psychophysical ego within its primordial natural world, and yet at the same time the entire "differentiation . . . into the systems that constitute what is included in my peculiar ownness and the systems that constitute what is other" all belong to the psychophysical ego.[74] The psychophysical ego is a member of the natural world, yet it contains all peculiar ownness and thus the natural world.[75] This paradoxical nature of the new *epochē* goes further than Husserl acknowledges. It is not simply that the psychophysical ego within the monadic world contains that world of which it is itself a member. The psychophysical ego includes within itself, as Husserl admits but does not fully explore, my monadic subjectivity, the alien world, and the differentiation of and, presumably, the relation between the former two spheres. Since the psychophysical ego is within my monad, my monadic subjectivity must paradoxically include within itself the alien world which had been excluded by the new *epochē*. The objective, there-for-everyone world *must* necessarily belong to my monadic sphere of originary presentations because it comprises part of my psychophysical ego. This is not to mention the infinite regress of paradoxes established by making several of these spheres or factors mutually inclusive.[76]

These paradoxes are not incidental nuisances at the periphery of Husserlian phenomenology. They are the symptoms of a deep categorical-logical problem that is inseparable from the aims of Husserl's mature conception of phenomenology. The consequence of instituting, at every level of the analysis of being, a program of systematically distinguishing the subjective from the objective, the "constitutive life-process of transcendental subjectivity" from the varying layers of objectivity that are related to them (natural world, reduced alien world, monadic noemata), is the discovery that in the very opposition of subject and object it becomes harder and harder to say which is subject and which is object. We begin to find objectivity in what was the essence of the subject, and subjectivity in what was the essence of the object-world or the other. The analysis of one leads to the discovery of the other within the one.

In the fifth Meditation Husserl fails to construct another ego that is independent of the monadic subject. This is perhaps not surprising, since the whole thrust of transcendental phenomenology is to ground the object in the subject. Husserl has thus succeeded in grounding the other in the monad, but has failed to prove that this constituted other has its own existential integrity independent of the monad. The implications of the failure rebound unexpectedly upon the perhaps solipsistic, but presumably irreducible and integral Husserlian monad. We will see that the effacement of the independent integrity of the other ego undermines the integrity of the monadic ego. The demonstration of this claim requires us to examine the manifold nature of the ego in Husserl's late philosophy.

The Uninhabited Ego

The essential problem concerning the Husserlian concept of the I or the ego is this: if the non-alien world dwells within the "sphere of peculiar ownness" of the monadic I or ego, how is the I or ego distinct from that world? Is there an ego distinct from the non-ego, or, has the concept of an ego been made identical to the reduced world-phenomena? Is there in Husserl's later work a concept of an ego, an I, a subject or a self which has existential integrity? Is there an ego or I for Husserl which is an *existing, discriminable something?* Let us examine the three meanings of the term 'ego' given in the fourth Meditation of the *Cartesian Meditations.*

Husserl describes the transcendental ego, the ego which is revealed by the transcendental reduction as constituting all meaning-complexes, as *"continuously constituting himself as existing."*[77] This self-constitution has three aspects. First, the transcendental ego is a "flowing *cogito,"* a continuous subjective temporal process. Second, it is a "centering ego," which is to say that the transcendental ego constitutes itself as an enduring, self-identical unity "who lives through" the flowing cogito. Last, the transcendental ego exists also in its "full concreteness," as the monad, which incorporates the flowing *cogito,* self-identity and the noemata which constitute the "surrounding world." Husserl clearly means this last to be the most important conception of the transcendental ego. He writes:

> The Ego can be concrete only in the flowing multiformity of his intentional life, along with the objects meant . . . in that life . . . .
> Since the monadically concrete ego includes . . . the whole of actual and potential conscious life . . . the problem of *explicating this*

monadic ego phenomonologically . . . must include *all constitutional problems without exception.* Consequently the phenomenology of this *self-constitution* coincides with *phenomonology* as a whole.[78]

The flowing *cogito in itself* cannot be described as having content or a character. It is the process or processes *within which* all intentional complexes and objects take form, and thus, the place where all contents and characters are formed, but in itself it has no content or character. It must have a temporal structure or form, but Husserl, in his contrasting descriptions of the next two conceptions of the ego as "non-empty" or "concrete," implicitly recognizes that the flowing *cogito* has no intrinsic content or character.

The "centering ego" is the way the ego "grasps himself," as incorporating within itself all *cogitationes* as members of a unity which is related "*through*" the *cogitationes* to objects.[79] Husserl claims that this centering ego "*is not an empty pole of identity,*" but rather generates a continually accumulating character or content because of the "abiding" property of all acts of consciousness.[80] All the ego's acts alter the ego by making it thereafter "the ego who did or decided such-and-such." Even when the act and its object are no longer present (and thus no longer presented) even if "I become passive and sink into a heavy sleep . . ." the ego is nevertheless "changed" and retains the character of the past act.[81] The centering ego is a "substrate of habitualities."

This process is not, Husserl says, a matter of memory, not a matter of the retention or presentification of the past act and object as part of the immanent conscious present. This "abidingness":

> manifestly is not a continuous filling of immanent time with subjective processes—just as the abiding ego himself, as the pole of abiding ego-properties, is not a process or continuity of processes . . . .[82]

Rather, Husserl describes this unusual quality of abidingness as simply characteristic of the way that the ego constitutes himself. That is, "the Ego constitutes himself as the *identical substrate of Ego-properties*" and thus as "a 'fixed and abiding' *personal Ego.*"[83]

These ideas are deeply problematic. Husserl does not explain how a content of pure consciousness can be "enduring" or "abiding" without being present or retained in the present *as* past. Such abiding properties must be transcendent. They cannot be properties of consciousness, since they endure without being present or appresented at all. To say, as Husserl does, that this abidingness is simply characteristic of the self-constitution of the transcendental ego is insufficient. The very possibility of abidingness is as questionable as the constitution of the other ego. In the case of the latter, Husserl correctly saw that his fundamental principles appeared to lead to solipsism, and that a proof of the possibility of intersubjectivity was necessary. It is also incumbent upon Husserl to justify the possibility of the abidingness of the transcendental ego, since it appears to be inconsistent with the principles he has laid down. But he gives no justification. Though the notion of the centering ego as the transcendental ego's principle of self-identity is plausible, Husserl's ascription to the centering ego a character or content which could possibly be construed as existential integrity is not.

The third formulation of the transcendental ego, the "fully concrete" ego, seems to be the most promising candidate for the role of an ego with existential integrity. The fully concrete ego includes the noematic objects of its intentional acts, as well as the flowing cogito and the self-identical ego which are two different ways of representing the source of those acts. The fully concrete ego as defined by Husserl in the fourth Meditation, is not yet the "monad" of the fifth Meditation. It includes "the whole of actual and potential conscious life," and so must include all objective transcendencies (for example, other egos). The *epochē* of the fifth Meditation serves to bracket, within the sphere of the fully concrete ego, the objective transcendencies from the immanent transcendencies.

The fully concrete ego contains within itself *the entire world,* given that the world has been phenomenologically reduced to a system of meanings. In the fifth Meditation, when Husserl creates the notion of a "peculiarly own" sphere *within* this fully concrete ego, he admits that it contains within itself both the "own-world" (all noematic objects insofar as they do not include the sense "there-for-everyone") and the psychophysical ego. Paradoxically the latter brings with it the objective, alien world.

Since the cogency of Husserl's proof of intersubjectivity is in doubt, this threatens to reincorporate the objective, intersubjective world back into the "peculiarly own" sphere. The concept of the monad as it is developed *after* Meditation Four does little or nothing to alter the situation current *in* Meditation Four, namely that the fully concrete ego or monad *contains the (reduced) world within itself.* Can there by anything like a concept of the I, ego, self, or subject that is *distinct from* the noematic world? Once the reduced objective world has been brought *into* the ego, into the "I myself" as Husserl refers to it, is there a possibility of an ego, an "I myself" that has existential integrity?

We find *only three possible* meanings for the ego in Husserl's late work. The ego or I can be transcendental subjectivity itself, conceived as the flowing processes of conscious life, as characterized by a principle of self-identity or, in Finkian terms, as the field in which all meaning-complexes become. It can be the contents of the monad, the contents of the fully concrete ego. In this case, the ego is *indistinguishable* from the noematic world. Lastly, the I or ego can be the psychophysical or mundane ego. In this case, the only possible meaning of ego is the human-personal ego of natural life, which, having been phenomeno-logically-transcendentally reduced, subsists as a *member of* the noematic world within the monad or fully concrete ego. Here, the ego is not indistinguishable from the noematic world as a whole, but is rather one of the noematic objects within that world.

Of these possible meanings of the ego, the first is contentless or empty in itself. The second merges the ego with the transcendentally reduced world so that there is no distinct 'ego.' The third makes the ego an object of transcendental subjectivity *with no special or more intimate* relationship to transcendental subjectivity than that of any other reduced noematic complex. There is thus no room in Husserl's scheme for an ego or I which retains something of the meaning we normally attach to these terms and which has the integrity of a distinct existent. Within the phe-nomenological sphere the ego is merely a *name* for either: the *contentless process* or *self-identity* of pure consciousness; the reduced *world;* or, an *object* in that world.

It might be argued that transcendental subjectivity does have an 'act-intentional' character, that it is a dynamic organization of inten-tional acts, and so has content. This does not work, however, because acts cannot be defined without reference to objects, if only generalized objects. For example, how could perception be defined without any ref-erence to perceptible objects? The notion of a pure, objectless activity makes little sense. Furthermore, the notion of pure act without reference to objects would seem to contradict Husserl's fundamental concept of intentionality.

The point is that transcendental subjectivity, insofar as it is con-ceived as *not* including objects or phenomena, is contentless. As a pure self-identical field or "flowing life" of acts within which the reduced world "becomes," it is devoid of intrinsic content.

Nor can the question of the existential integrity of the ego within the phenomenologically reduced sphere be defused by the claim that one cannot find a distinct ego within this sphere because the ego *is* that sphere. This would be to say that the ego in Husserlian phenomenology is distinct, but distinct from the *naturally existing world.* Indeed—this objection would continue—it is the whole point of transcendental phe-nomenology to ground the meaning-structure of the natural world in the ego; thus the *epoché* has already brought us within the egoic sphere. It is therefore unfair and nonsensical to look for another distinct ego within the phenomenologically reduced sphere.

This attempt to defend the Husserlian ego is fundamentally con-fused. Husserl does indeed wish to ground the natural world, or more exactly, the natural world as sense or meaning, in the essence, the core, the fundamental evidential layer of the conscious ego, properly reduced. Yet once within the phenomenologically reduced sphere (even if we call this sphere the "monadic ego") we are faced with a new problem: the reduced world has reappeared within that sphere. The *epoché* effectively *eliminates* the natural world distinction between inner and outer, ego and world. That distinction was part of the world whose existence has been bracketed, and it must be shown to have been transcendentally constituted. There must be a *new* distinction made between ego and world at the *reduced* level; otherwise, Husserl could not claim that the real natural-existential distinction between ego and world gains its meaning from transcendental constitution.

Let us explore one further defense of Husserl. Whatever the success or failure of the scheme presented in Meditations Four and Five, can transcendental phenomenology render a better account? It might proceed as follows. Transcendental subjectivity, in its flowing conscious life, constitutes within itself two different spheres: the ego, I or monad, and the (reduced) world. All presented noemata belong to this reduced world. The constituted ego-sphere is a domain of intentional acts, not objects. Here, the ego is not conceived as containing its perceptual (reduced) world within itself—which, after all, was the focus of much of the foregoing criticism. The perceived noemata of the world might then contain or be merged with the intersubjective world, or there might be some further layers of transcendental machination lying 'between' these levels.

Unfortunately, the separation of the presented world or perceptual noemata (the "immanent transcendencies" of the fifth Meditation) from the ego cannot begin to solve the problem. First, this separation would seem to contradict the very notion of intentionality on which phenomenology is based by segregating the intentional act and the intentional object to different systems of meaning, constituted in this case as separate spheres. More importantly, this separation would make the ego utterly contentless: the ego would be nothing other than a set of intentional vectors directed toward something outside of itself. This scheme would raise in even harsher terms the problem of solipsism, since there would now be no realm of "immanent transcendencies" from which to derive objectivity.

Husserl was trapped from the beginning. In attempting to fend off solipsism he built the object-world into the monad itself: the result is that he not only failed to disprove solipsism, but in the process eliminated the integrity of the ego. If he had instead purged the monad of noemata (thereby seemingly insuring the distinction of ego and object-world), he would have worsened his prospects of overcoming solipsism.

The scheme would have had a contentless ego whose distinction from objects would be paradoxical, since this seemingly distinct ego would have no content or character to distinguish it from the world.

Husserl and Sartre

These criticisms may seem reminiscent of Jean-Paul Sartre.[84] My claim that the concept of the transcendental ego necessarily develops into either a transcendental subjectivity which is contentless or characterless, or into a noematic-transcendent object for consciousness, is completely in accord with Sartre's criticism of Husserl. Nevertheless, Sartre's position exhibits many of the same conundrums as Husserl's. A brief examination of Sartre's view is revealing in regard to both of these phenomenologists, because each is stuck on one of the horns of the dilemma of philosophical narcissism.

The final section of the Sartre's early work, *The Transcendence of the Ego,* offers up a fascinating and rich discussion.[85] In it, Sartre summarizes his critique of Husserl, gives classic definition to the "anti-egology" movement that would later become increasingly important in continental philosophy, and gives us several hints of the conceptual foundation for the transition from Husserlian phenomenology to existentialism and historical materialism, both of which characterize Sartre's later works.

For Sartre, the "Transcendental Field," pure consciousness or transcendental subjectivity, is literally "a *nothing*,"[86] a pure transparency which reaches out to objects but cannot itself be conceived through any of the categories applied to objects. He writes:

> This transcendental sphere is a sphere of *absolute* existence . . . a sphere of pure spontaneities which are never objects and which determine their own existence.[87]

On the other hand, all psychic states, emotions, and the ego itself are *objects* of this spontaneous consciousness. The 'I' is an object of certain kinds of spontaneities, namely "reflected acts." The ego is "out in the world," along with all other objects, while "transcendental consciousness" is a purely "impersonal spontaneity."[88]

Here Sartre is drawing out some of the implications of Husserl's transcendental phenomenology. He is doing so for a specific reason. He writes that:

> This conception of the ego seems to us the only possible refutation of solipsism.[89]

Sartre has made 'my' ego an object as equally available to others as to 'myself'. Transcendental consciousness is, on the other hand, not so available; in fact it is *"radically* impenetrable."[90] It has no content, it is a pure transcendence. There remains, literally, *nothing* private; that which is private is, in a sense, "nothing." There can no longer be a private structure or content of consciousness.

Sartre goes on to trace a way into existentialism and other non-Husserlian movements. He paints an intriguing picture of the *epochē*. The *epochē* is not, according to Sartre, the exclusive methodological property of the phenomenologist, initiated by a decision to engage in phenomenological-scientific inquiry: it is not a "knowledgeable operation."[91] The *epochē* is human reflection on the transcendental, totally free and undetermined spontaneity of consciousness, a spontaneity which is wholly at odds with the objectified character of the ego. The *epochē* is enacted whenever a person suddenly envisions the abyss of the absolute freedom and the nothingness of his or her consciousness. The *epochē* is:

> an anxiety which is imposed on us and which we cannot avoid: it is both a pure event of transcendental origin and an ever possible accident of our daily life.[92]

This "existential" *epochē,* by which consciousness "tears itself away" from the I, reveals the ego to be a kind of falsification.

> Everything happens . . . as if consciousness constituted the ego as a false representation of itself . . . .[93]

This new awareness has catastrophic implications in that it implies an undermining or demystification of a whole structure of distinctions that were maintained by the ego.

> It is thanks to the ego, indeed, that a distinction can be made between the possible and the real, between appearance and being, between the willed and the undergone.[94]

(Interestingly, at almost precisely the same moment as these words of Sartre appeared, very similar ideas were being developed, in a psychoanalytic context, by another important French thinker, Jacques Lacan.)[95]

Sartre's antithetical definitions of consciousness and ego are precisely the first and third of the three possible meanings of the ego in Husserl's late work. Sartre's consciousness is Husserl's transcendental ego conceived as a flowing subjective process, or as a self-identity, as long as these are both understood to be *contentless*. Sartre's ego is Husserl's mundane or psychophysical ego conceived as a noematic object. Sartre is here affirming the problematic and paradoxical implications of Husserl's transcendental phenomenology.

Sartre has attacked one of the core doctrines of modern subjectivism: the equation of consciousness with the I or ego. But he has not thereby avoided subjectivism; he has radically affirmed it in its unmitigated, or narcissistic, form. Sartre denies the equation of consciousness and ego by throwing the ego into the object-world, not only retaining, but emphasizing the absolute distinction of consciousness from the world of objects.

Sartre believes he has defeated solipsism by severing the tie of the I to consciousness and throwing the former into the world. The I, he writes:

> Falls like other existences at the stroke of the *epochē;* and solipsism becomes unthinkable from the moment that the *I* no longer has a privileged status . . . . My I, in effect, is *no more certain for consciousness than the I of other men.* It is only more intimate.[96]

The qualification presented by Sartre's last sentence is a revealing residue of egology, inconsistent with the view Sartre is developing. If Sartre is to be consistent, my ego cannot be more "intimate" to consciousness than other egos. Why? Because there is no such thing as "*my* consciousness" at all to which my ego could be more intimately related than either other egos *or any other objects whatsoever.* Consciousness is entirely impersonal and the ego is simply an object, like any other object. There can be no special relationship whatsoever between the two.

But this causes us to ask, what is the meaning of the terms 'my ego', 'me', and 'I'? My ego must be understood as a misleading expression, for it implies possession. There is nothing, by virtue of its belonging to which, an ego could be called my or mine. The terms I and me both represent a kind of object, an ego which appears in certain intentional (reflective) acts. What is the justification for setting off this particular ego from all others by the label 'I' or 'me'? What does this label signify? Certainly it signifies some sense constituted by consciousness, by the transcendental field. All that we can possibly say of I and me within Sartre's framework is that they are shorthand labels for a number of conditions or qualities that belong to the constituted sense of one particular ego-object. There can be no explanation of why or how consciousness does constitute such an ego.

Sartre is not always faithful to the extreme and rigorous logic he has unleashed. He often refers to "my consciousness," and, as noted above, conceives of a special "intimate" relation between consciousness and the I. In this, Sartre lapses into a methodological error that seems to be the occupational hazard of phenomenology, namely, that of switching between the phenomenological *explanation* of the possibility of a thing's constitution, and the phenomenological *description* of that thing as it appears within reduced subjective life. It may well be true that, given the *epoché*, phenomena *appear* to me as related to a consciousness which is mine; but Sartre cannot appeal to this descriptive, apparent truth, since he has already denied its possibility.

The Sartrian position, which is simply the extension of tendencies inherent in the Husserlian position, leaves us in the end with no I or me at all, if these words are to have any legitimate meaning. Any ego is for Sartre an object, a synthetic unity of, for example, emotional states and dispositions. The I is one such object, its unique manner of appearance distinguishing it from other egos. But to say this is to deny the existence of an I *qua* I. Sartre's view totally amalgamates the first to the third person; for Sartre, the first person voice is intrinsically falsifying. It is certainly true that there are phases of experience and modes of its existence in which the I is, as Sartre says, "another," but the I is not *solely* composed of such phases and modes.

Not only is the Sartrian I problematic, but so is his notion of consciousness. Transcendental consciousness is a "sphere of absolute existence," which:

> determines its [own] existence at each instant, without our being able to conceive anything *before* it. Thus each instant of our conscious life reveals to us a creation *ex nihilo*.[97]

This consciousness is "radically impenetrable"; indeed, "a consciousness cannot *conceive* of a consciousness other than itself"[98] (my emphasis). At the same time, this absolute existence which literally creates the phenomenal world is a nothing, since all objects, truths, and values are outside it. Sartre understands that this is paradoxical, adding immediately:

> But this nothing is *all* since it is *consciousness of* all these objects.[99]

These two passages reveal the extreme ironies of Sartre's position.

The first expresses a conception of consciousness which is actually very close to Fink's conception of the transcendental ego, a conception which would ostensibly be anathema to Sartre, as it is tantamount to an ontologization of the transcendental ego. Sartre's consciousness is very like Fink's transcendental field within which all beings become what they are. It is an absolute existence, in which a "creation *ex nihilo*" of objectivity takes place. With Sartre, as with Fink, it would be legitimate to compare his concept of the transcendental field with the idea of God.

Each represents the absolute undeterminable source of all, the ground of being.

The second passage represents the opposite side of the transcendental (and, as we shall see, narcissistic) coin. Consciousness, simultaneous with being the absolute origin, is nothing; it contains nothing and has no character. It is a spontaneity, a vector directed at the world. In the space of two sentences Sartre makes exactly the point that must be made about his position: the concept of consciousness as a nothing directed toward the world leads implicitly to an equation of consciousness with the world or, as Sartre says, "this nothing is *all.* . . ."

Consciousness and world are not explicitly equated in either Sartre's or Husserl's work. Rather, all possible characteristics which would distinguish the two are undermined by the philosophical narcissism of their viewpoints. Sartre and Husserl insist that consciousness and world are not identical, yet their theoretical orientations and their programs make it harder and harder to distinguish them, to say or define what holds them apart as different. Their positions lead to a dichotomy of indistinguishables in which consciousness and world are implicitly, though paradoxically, identical.

This equatability with the object-world was the second of the three possible meanings of the Husserlian ego. Transcendental consciousness, which Husserl integrates with the ego or monad, but which Sartre radically separates from the latter, is for both Husserl and Sartre implicitly merged with, identified with, the very world of objects from which they had radically distinguished it. Sartre, like Husserl, declares transcendental consciousness to be the absolute origin and reduces the object-world to the spontaneous activity of consciousness. Having done so, Sartre finds that consciousness *is* that reduced object-world, that consciousness is "*all.*" Sartre's analysis in the *Transcendence of the Ego* emphasizes the reality of the object and the transcending, vectorial nature of consciousness, while Husserl's late work is aimed at maintaining the self-identity and constitutive activity of consciousness as against the dependent, reduced, constituted nature of objectivity. Each inevitably implies the other; in Sartre the things themselves, the world, come to be equated with the nothing of consciousness, while in Husserl we discover the nothingness of the transcendental ego. In both systems, we see the fundamental dynamic of philosophical narcissism: the consequence of radically distinguishing consciousness and the objective world ultimately devolves into an equation of the two.

The Enigmas of Phenomenology

In the *Crisis* Husserl discusses the emergence of certain "paradoxical enigmas" within his final reconception of transcendental phenomenology. The most important of these enigmas is "the paradox of human subjectivity," a "truly serious difficulty . . . which assails our whole undertaking and the sense of its results . . . ."[100]

The first problem is that, because of the *epoché,* "everything objective is transformed into something subjective,"[101] and "the world . . . becomes itself something subjective . . . ."[102] But all "ego-poles," as a group, are themselves "within" the world. How can these ego-poles, these subjectivities, be *both* the constituting agents of the world *and* members of the world? Husserl laments:

> Universal intersubjectivity, into which all objectivity, everything that exists at all, is resolved, can obviously be nothing other than mankind; and the latter is undeniably a component part of the world. *How can a component part of the world . . . constitute the whole world,* namely, constitute it . . . by the universal interconnection of intentionally accomplishing subjectivity, while . . . the subjects accomplishing in cooperation, are themselves only a partial formation of the total accomplishment? *The subjective part of the world swallows up, so to speak, the whole world and thus itself too.* What an absurdity![103] (my emphasis)

Husserl presents what he believes to be a resolution of the paradox. The alleged paradox, he tells us, was the product of a methodological error, of "jumping immediately" from the ego of the *epoché* to the membership of all egos within the objective-constituted world. This jumping neglected the intermediary step of explicating the constitution of transcendental intersubjectivity by the individual, solitary ego; this intersubjectivity then constitutes the objective world. My ego constitutes all other egos and it is only through the presentification of those egos that my ego finds itself as a member of an objective world. Thus, the ego:

> constitutes transcendental intersubjectivity, to which it then adds itself as a merely privileged member . . . .[104]

Husserl fails to see, however, that the dialectical problems of subjectivity go deeper than the reach of this resolution. Husserl sees the paradox by which "the subjective part of the world swallows up . . . the whole world and thus itself too" as hinging on the factor of intersubjectivity. He sees the apparent paradox as a product of the fact that, while the world is reduced to my subjectivity, that reduced world obviously contains a community of "ego-poles," which in turn co-constitute my world. What Husserl does not see is that the same dialectical problem, the "swallowing the world and thus itself too," obtains *regardless* of any reference to other egos. The transcendental ego becomes identified with, is swallowed by, the world it has itself swallowed. Whether or not Husserl's "resolution" is cogent, this "truly serious difficulty," this "absurdity," remains unsolved.

Before offering the resolution just described, there is a passage in which Husserl paints a poignant and almost tragic picture of his philosophical position. "The phenomonologist," he writes, "lives in the paradox of having to look upon the obvious as questionable, as enigmatic."[105] But, more than this, phenomenology appears to Husserl to be inescapably paradoxical.

> Its fate . . . is to become involved again and again in paradoxes, which, arising out of uninvestigated and even unnoticed horizons, remain functional and announce themselves as incomprehensibilities.[106]

This is a theme that Fink had already explored. In the rich discussions of his 1933 paper Fink wrote of the *"pathos"* of phenomenology and mentioned a series of paradoxes that appeared to be intrinsic to transcendental phenomenology. One of these he calls the *"paradox of the position from which statements are made."*[107] This paradox arises when, having performed the transcendental reduction, the "theorizing ego" attempts to communicate its knowledge to others. But how can the phenomenologist, without stepping outside of his reduction, communicate with the "dogmatist" of the natural attitude? Communication, Fink admits, presumes a "shared basis." But the reduction has removed the phenomenologist from the most fundamental basis shared by mankind. Therefore, he concludes, such communication, if there be any at all, must take on a special and limited meaning.

> Communication with the dogmatist thus has the meaning of a provisional transmission of phenomenological knowledge whose purpose is that of leading the other to the performance of the reduction on his own.[108]

One may ask whether this kind of intrinsically one-sided transmission can rightly be called communication at all.

There is another paradox Fink mentions which lies at the heart of the paradox of communication and which may be the most basic and disturbing of phenomenology's conundrums. The more deeply one thinks about the phenomenological *epochē,* and the other subsequent reductions, the more one sees how truly radical a self-consistent concept of the *epochē* must be. The *epochē* cannot be conceived as *something a human ego does.* Conceiving it thus would compromise the radical distinction between reduced conscious life and natural world conscious life because it would imply a *continuity* between the mundane ego, the ego-performing-the-*epochē* and the transcendental sphere revealed by the *epochē*. The radical discontinuity implicit in the *epochē* is the reason that Husserl and Fink both emphasize that the *epochē* leads us out of the "human" world and our "human selves." The *epochē* is not, Fink asserts a "human possibility" at all.[109]

One of the implications of the radical discontinuity represented by the *epochē* is that the latter is intrinsically "*unmotivated.*" There can in principle be no reason or motivation leading to its adoption; there is "no wordly problem which could serve as its real motive."[110] Nothing leads "up to" the *epochē;* it "is its own presupposition." Consequently:

> Unmotivated and unfamiliar with respect to its possibility, every exposition of the phenomenological reduction is in a unique way *false* . . . . Phenomenology's problem is not one which can be explained within the compass of the natural attitude.[111]

This paradox is a graphic reflection of one of the characteristics of philosophical narcissism described in Chapter 4; namely, the dichotomy between the meaning of philosophical statements or a philosophical system and the human world in which philosophy subsists. This characteristic is not tantamount to the usual charge of abstraction, irrelevance, or otherworldliness leveled at much of philosophic work. In philosophically narcissistic systems of thought, this dichotomy is a matter of *principle.* Such systems endorse a strict division between the motivations of life and the motivations of philosophic thought, and between everyday evidence and philosophic evidence. They implicitly accept a dichotomous situation: philosophic thinking and the thinking of life have no relationship. The latter does not, cannot, and ought not affect the former, except insofar as the latter ought to admit its evidential inferiority to and epistemic-metaphysical groundedness in the former. Husserl and Fink do not want to renounce such relationship, to endorse this radical break between philosophy and life, but the logic of their system forces it on them.

The method of Husserlian phenomenology is intrinsically paradoxical. No argument, no motive can demonstrate the necessity of adopting the *epochē*. Once we adopt it, we make observations, analyses, and conclusions. But the claim for the preeminent status of phenomenology, its claim of being more than an arbitrarily chosen, hypothetical exercise, requires it to make reference to the world that has been put out of play. Phenomenology must claim that the meaning-complexes of the truly existing natural world, the world of non-phenomenologists independent of the *epochē,* are generated by transcendental subjectivity, of which phenomenology is the theory and to which it is the only mode of access.

Husserl would not have been satisfied with the notion that his whole philosophical career had established only the hypothetical statement: "If we adopt the *epochē*, then the world appears as a meaning constituted by transcendental subjectivity." For Husserl, the world's true nature *is* a constituted meaning-complex. If this cannot be said, then there is no justification for claiming that the results of phenomenological investigation have any relevance or importance once we resume the natural attitude. Yet, to make this claim, without which Husserl's transcendental philosophy loses much of its meaning, requires precisely that reference to and continuity with the naturally existing world which was *disallowed* by the *epochē*.

This situation is not similar to that of Cartesian or Kantian subjectivism; indeed Husserl himself has emphasized the difference from these predecessors. Phenomenology does not wish, having plumbed the roots of subjectivity, to climb back 'out' of the subject in order to establish a correspondence with the naturally existing world. Phenomenology requires, unlike Kantian philosophy, no transcendental deduction; and Husserl, unlike Descartes, felt no need to include a sixth Meditation in his Cartesian lectures, which Descartes had needed to prove the existence of the non-subjective natural world. Phenomenology desires no mediation between subjectivity and an 'outside'.

Conclusion

To summarize, Husserl's mature philosophy is a systematic attempt to ground inquiry in the distinction of subjectivity and non-subjectivity or objectivity, rigorously applied. Husserl wishes to purge the naturalistic and transcendental factors of Descartes, Kant, and others from the subjectivist tradition, thereby purifying the original categorical impulse of that tradition. Nothing may remain between or beyond subject and object to relate them, either from above or from below. Subjectivity itself must be the only source of synthesis with and relation to objects, at each level of analysis. Only in this way, Husserl believed, can the original Cartesian, that is, subjectivist, project become consistent and scientific.

But this purification of subjectivism changed the relations and even the nature of subject and non-subject. Subject and object became paradoxically, asymptotically equatable at one level of analysis while remaining absolutely distinct at another level. Having rejected all transcendental means of relating subjectivity and objectivity, Husserl insisted on their absolute distinction, an insistence initially embodied in the *epochē* and re-enacted again and again at deeper levels of analysis. Because he wanted to give subjectivity the privileged position in this dichotomy as constituting the object, Husserl reduced objectivity to the status of a property of subjectivity, his attempts to prove otherwise notwithstanding.

The dialectic of philosophical narcissism led to an unexpected result. Not only did objectivity lose its independent existential integrity, but so did the subject. At each level of analysis, as Husserl discovered new layers of constituted objectivity within what was previously the subjective sphere, subjectivity was pushed back, reduced, shrunken until it became a contentless, characterless 'X', the infinitely small point of origin. This is the fulfillment of Wittgenstein's remark about solipsism, the reduction of reality to the subject: ". . . solipsism, when its implications are followed out strictly, coincides with pure realism. The self of solipsism shrinks to a point without extension and there remains the reality coordinated with it."[112] The fundamental subjectivist concepts of Husserl's system—subjectivity and objectivity—have been thrown into a dialectical, narcissistic oscillation. This oscillation can be described in terms of the triad: subjectivity–subjective phenomena–world (in itself). The Husserlian *epochē* explicitly puts the 'world in itself' out of play, reducing the triad to the dyad subjectivity–phenomena. Having reduced or eliminated one factor of the triad (the world) the question of the nature of subjectivity now has only two possible answers: subjectivity is either a contentless ideal or it is identical with the phenomena. Both possibilities imply the loss of any existential integrity on the part of subjectivity.

The problem lies in Husserl's simultaneous assertion of two propositions:

First, all consciousness is consciousness *of* something. This is an expression of the fundamental principle of intentionality, formulated by Brentano and taken over by Husserl. Some of its implications can be seen in Husserl's statement in the *Cartesian Meditations* that "the transcendental ego is what it is solely in relation to intentional objectivities."[113]

Second, the world—which is to say, all humanly encountered reality not composed solely of the primary founding evidences that lie immanent in pure consciousness—is a meaning-complex constituted by the founding principles or processes of pure consciousness. There is no sense or meaning which exists *for* consciousness that is not constituted *by* consciousness.

The first proposition defines consciousness in terms of its objects. The second proposition eliminates the independent, existential integrity of all worldly objects, reduces them to meaning-complexes and regressively derives the latter from deeper and deeper founding layers of pure consciousness. Taken together these propositions imply that 'pure' or 'essential' or 'true' subjectivity (pure consciousness, transcendental ego, etc.) is determined and defined by *that which it produces* (the world as meaning-complex). They also imply that the world is produced by something *it defines and determines*. The first implication alone, concerning subjectivity, makes it *logically impossible* to answer any question about the being, nature, or character of subjectivity. Subjectivity produces that which determines its own nature. As this production cannot be determined by any prior nature of subjectivity, how can it determine or produce anything at all?

As Sartre writes, "Thus each instant of our conscious life reveals to us a creation *ex nihilo*."[114] According to the two propositions given above, the world is indeed an *ex nihilo* creation in the strictest sense, an instantaneous creation devoid of any rational connection with anything that existed in the preceding instant. Subjectivity or consciousness has no nature, no content, no structure which determines, limits or leaves its mark on the world it creates.

Sartre's reference to the theological concept is apt. As mentioned previously, the function of transcendental subjectivity exhibits an undeniable resemblance to that of God, and Fink's paradoxes strongly suggest that the description of transcendental life must, if it goes far enough, adopt the mystical silence of negative theology. The God of transcendental subjectivity represents, however, a very austere God, one with no character or nature and no particular valuative predilictions or plans for his or her world.

It is often thought that the *Crisis* depicts a Husserlian phenomenology closer to the existential phenomenology of Heidegger, Sartre, and Merleau-Ponty, than are the conceptions of Husserl's transcendental-Cartesian works of 1913–1931. It is felt that the historical approach of the *Crisis* has certain commonalities with existentialism, while Husserl's commitment to an *a priori* science of the transcendental constitution of the world in *Ideas* and the *Cartesian Meditations* seems antithetical to existentialism.

This picture is simplistic and misleading. Existential phenomenology was certainly born in the critique of Husserl, but Husserl's transcendentalism is not incompatible with the existentialism of his follower-critics.

Sartre rejects some aspects of Husserl's conception of the ego-subject, as do Heidegger and others. But what is interesting is the extent to which the existentialist conclusions of Sartre are directly implied in some of Husserl's most essentialist and transcendentalist notions. Sartre, in existentialist fashion, speaks of the "dread" and "anxiety" of consciousness faced with its own absolute indeterminacy and freedom, a consequence of consciousness's utter diremption from the ego and the natural world of things. While Husserl does not use terms like anxiety and dread, these Sartrian qualities are the direct results of the radical discontinuity of phenomenological consciousness and natural or naive consciousness, a discontinuity that is at the basis of Husserl's thought. Husserl expresses his recognition of this discontinuity in terms of the phenomenologist's awareness of ever-recurrent paradoxes. Fink refers to these paradoxes and also speaks of the "pathos" of phenomenology. Sartre is deriving "existential" conclusions and insights, not from an abandonment of Husserl's radically transcendental, otherworldly standpoint, but from an elaboration and extension of the implications of that standpoint.

Another indication that those elements in Husserl's thought which seem least compatible with existentialism can actually be seen to lead to existentialist notions can be found in Fink. As recounted earlier, Fink presses Husserlian transcendentalism to the point of metaphysics. For Fink, transcendental subjectivity is the ground of the world's becoming. Phenomenology thus becomes the study of the coming-to-be of the world, a study of world-formation, of world-becoming.

When the concept of subjectivity is so transcendentally radicalized that it becomes both non-human and an absolute ground, as for Fink, then phenomenology could be described without reference to subjectivity at all. Transcendental subjectivity, absolutized beyond any resemblance to natural consciousness, becomes simply a name for the Origin, the ground of Being, not unlike Anaximander's "*apeiron*" or the Plotinian "One." Finkian phenomenology could be formulated purely as the study of the being of the world, or the coming-to-be of all beings; a study of being-in-itself, rather than of being-for a consciousness. The contentless nothingness of the transcendental ego makes Fink's transcendental subjectivity similar to Sartre's consciousness, which is a nothing that is identical to all of its objects. And in this indeterminate, ineffable, and yet absolute nature of the Finkian and Sartrian ground of all objectivities, one can hear the stirrings of the overriding Heideggerian question, the question of the meaning of Being.

6

Subjectivism without the Subject: Heidegger

Husserl's most famous disciple, Martin Heidegger, published *Being and Time* in 1927, two years before Husserl delivered the lectures which were to become the *Cartesian Meditations*. Few single works can claim as great an impact on philosophy. Few works strike the reader as so distinctive, as having broken so thoroughly with past viewpoints, as being so utterly original. And few philosophies would seem to be as refractory to the charges of subjectivism and philosophical narcissism as does Heidegger's.

Heidegger clearly has cast off the language of subjectivism. His project, the reopening of the question of the meaning of Being, appears wholly to undercut any division of what is into spheres of subjectivity and non-subjectivity. He specifically attacks what he calls "subjectivism" and rejects any construal of human being as "egological," or as centered in consciousness. Indeed, his project can be read as a reaction against the Cartesian-Kantian-Husserlian tradition which places the subject at the center of existence and epistemology at the center of philosophy.

This opposition to subjectivism, its language, and its tradition is, however, not as total as it may initially appear. Heidegger does not, for example, wish to reject Descartes and Kant wholesale, but rather to reinterpret them—this is especially true concerning Kant. And while

Heidegger is opposed to the doctrine of Husserl's transcendental "egology," he takes over Husserlian phenomenology as the basis for his own method. There are many ways in which Heidegger remains within the Cartesian-Kantian-Husserlian tradition. Though Heidegger disavows the language of that tradition, and rejects the egology of some versions of subjectivism, he retains the basic conceptual distinctions of subjectivism and his philosophy exhibits the antinomies of philosophical narcissism. In Heidegger we confront a non-egological subjectivism, a *subjectivism without the subject.*

Subjectivism and narcissism do not characterize all of Heidegger's philosophy, nor do they characterize all of his early work, which will be the focus of our attention. Just as with Kant, there are subjectivist and non-subjectivist elements in his philosophy. The subjectivist elements are, however, central to his thought and cause serious narcissistic difficulties for Heidegger's philosophy. And while his later works will not be examined here, it is not obvious that the charges of subjectivism and narcissism would fail to hold true of them as well. The disparity between Heidegger's early and late works, the discontinuity represented by the so-called "*Kehre*," or "Turn," may be exaggerated. No less a student of Heidegger than David Krell has maintained that *Being and Time,* ". . . provides the impetus for all the later investigations. Without exception."[1]

Other critics, especially devotees of Heidegger's late work, have attacked *Being and Time* as "subjectivist." However, their notions of subjectivism and their analyses of the early Heidegger are entirely different from mine. An example of this kind of criticism comes from Michael Zimmerman, who attacks the "anthropocentrism" and "voluntarism," both conceived as close relatives of subjectivism, which allegedly characterize Heidegger's early work.[2] First of all, my notion of subjectivism has little to do with anthropocentrism or voluntarism. More importantly, the fact that in *Being and Time* as opposed to the later work Heidegger conceives of the analysis of the structures of human existence as the proper first step in addressing the question of Being—which lies at the heart of Zimmerman's critique—is not decisive for my criticism of Heidegger. What Heidegger says about human being, or "Dasein" (Being-There) in his terminology, is central to my critique, but the mere fact that Heidegger approaches Being through Dasein is not definitive evidence of subjectivism. It would only be evidence of subjectivism if Dasein and Dasein's relation to other realities were interpreted in a subjectivist fashion. This *is* how Heidegger interprets these realities and it is this which needs critical analysis.

Heidegger does not eschew the terms 'subject' and 'subjectivity' *per se;* it is the manner in which those terms are often employed and understood that draws his criticism. That the subject is 'worldless', that it is a *res* or a thing, or that it stands in an antithetical relation to 'objects' which are purely 'outside' of itself—these are the notions which Heidegger attacks, and rightly so. But for Heidegger this signifies that the concept of the subject needs further analysis and review, not simple elimination. In 1927, in the lectures published as *Basic Problems of Phenomenology,* Heidegger wrote:

> Philosophy must perhaps start from the 'subject' and return to the 'subject' in its ultimate questions, and yet for all that it may not pose its questions in a one-sidedly subjectivistic manner.[3]

In the same work Heidegger writes, very revealingly, that what is required is "a radical interpretation of the subject."[4] Heidegger's central criticism of earlier philosophy of Dasein or human being is not that it employed the concept of subject at all, but that it failed to employ this concept *radically enough.* Philosophy has tended to interpret the subject in terms of categories that are appropriate for and are drawn from the interpretation of things, of non-human entities. In this sense, Heidegger's intention in *Being and Time* is to provide the first consistent and radically pure explication of the subject. An important element of this project is the need to conceive of the subject as including within itself essential relatedness to entities and the world. The Heideggerian subject is intrinsically non-insular. In *Basic Problems,* he writes:

> the relating belongs to the ontological constitution of the subject itself. To relate itself is implicit in the concept of the subject.[5]

It is worth noting that Heidegger identifies this essential "relating-itself-to" of the subject with intentionality. "Intentionality," he declares on the same page as the above, "belongs to the existence of Dasein." This is an example of Heidegger's desire to retain Husserlian concepts and even Husserlian terminology.

Heidegger is, in a sense, trapped by language. He wants to speak of something which has generally been called subjectivity, yet he wishes to avoid that term because of its connotations.[6] *Being and Time* is not anti-subject or anti-subjectivity; it does not in any sense attempt to demystify, debunk, or dispense with subjectivity. It attempts to dispense with the traditional *language* of subjectivity in order radically to implement the concept of that which has traditionally been called the subject.

Heidegger's attitude toward idealism is revealing in this connection. Idealism grants a privileged status to subjectivity, mind, and ideality. While Heidegger criticizes idealism and realism alike, he feels a special kinship with the former. He writes that:

It is not an already settled matter whether idealism does not in the end pose the problems of philosophy more radically than any realism ever can. But perhaps it is not tenable *in the form in which it has obtained up to now,* whereas of realism *it cannot even be said that it is untenable,* because it has not yet even pressed forward at all into the dimension of philosophical problems . . . the anxiety that prevails today in the face of idealism is an anxiety in the face of philosophy . . . .[7] (my emphasis)

While idealism may not be tenable, it is an attempt to struggle with the central philosophical problems, whereas, for Heidegger, realism fails to even enter into the project of philosophy. Idealism, however poorly formulated, has an inkling of the truth; it sought truth in the right place—in the subject—and it faced the utter questionability of reality. Heidegger links himself with the idealist tradition; he does not seek to destroy it but, as David Krell indicates, to "de-structure" it and thereby radicalize it.[8]

In this chapter, after discussing the extent to which Heidegger's methodology remains within the Cartesian-Kantian-Husserlian tradition, I will go on to search for the existential integrity of human being, Dasein, in *Being and Time,* and will show that there is none.[9] Dasein has no integrity; Dasein has been defined as disclosedness, its self dispersed into the world and the "they," of society, and its integrity undermined by temporality. Dasein is, at best, a set of relations to the world or a set of functions or tendencies directed toward the world. But this means that Dasein is indistinguishable from the world, worldly entities, and phenomena in general, and thus Dasein is paradoxically equatable with the latter.

After the concept of Dasein, we will move to examine Heidegger's concept of the world. The world into which Dasein has been dis-integratively "thrown" is essentially a subjective world, a world which has no existential integrity, no independent existence, a world not significantly different from a complex of Husserlian noema. Dasein is not related to an independent world; it is related to a world which is included within itself, projected by itself.

There results the ambiguous situation characteristic of philosophical narcissism in general. The distinction of Dasein from all other beings is absolutely fundamental for Heidegger. Yet, the implication of his analysis of Dasein on the one hand, and the world and worldly entities on the other, is that Dasein and worldly entities are increasingly indistinct, that they approach each other to a virtual sameness, like asymptotes. Dasein, as the arena for the appearance, the self-showing or disclosure of all other beings, is asymptotically equatable with the appearance, the self-showing of other beings. The paradox in Heidegger, common to philosophical narcissism in general, is that Dasein *cannot* be identical to other beings, Dasein must be absolutely distinct, and yet there is no set of characteristics, no nexus of traits, no content of either Dasein or worldly entities, beings, phenomena which can justify their distinct existences. Lacking an existential integrity which would distinguish them, Dasein and world, worldly entities, or phenomena represent a dichotomy of indistinguishables, and consequently the two factors become paradoxically or asymptotically equatable.

While eliminating nearly all of the language of subjectivism, Heidegger has in fact produced a radically subjectivist picture of human being-in-the-world, a picture not unlike Husserl's. Dasein is nothing in itself; it is the disclosing of the world, yet the world too is nothing in itself, but is rather a project of Dasein. This is essentially the same dialectic of philosophical narcissism that we saw in Husserl, albeit without the terms 'subject' and 'object'. Those who admire Heidegger's "destruction" of the post-Cartesian metaphysics of *res cogitans* and *res extensa* and the subject–object epistemology often fail to see that the same volatilization and "de-structuration" of the these categories was implicit, however unintended, in Husserl's transcendentalism. Unlike Husserl, Heidegger speaks not of the human consciousness which intends phenomena, but rather of the phenomena which are disclosed in human being. Yet, while Heidegger's language is, so to speak, on the side of the object or that which is disclosed, and not, like Husserl's on the side of the subject, the implicit dichotomy is still operative. The philosophical narcissism of *Being and Time* is the mirror image of the Husserlian position from which it is derived, and both are the product of the development of the modern subjectivist tradition.

The Project of *Being and Time*

Heidegger leaves no doubt as to the overriding question to be addressed by *Being and Time:* it is the "question of the meaning of Being (*Sein*)." Everything in his *magnum opus,* and all his later work as well, is bent toward thinking this question through.

Heidegger begins *Being and Time* by denying that this question is irrelevant, meaningless, has been already answered, or is intrinsically unanswerable. He asserts that, whatever our prospects of answering it, it is the most crucial and basic of questions and deserves our best efforts. He recognizes, however, that the subtlety and difficulty of the question requires that immense care be taken in the preliminary effort of determining the way the question should be approached.

Heidegger asserts that, "Being is always the Being of an entity,"[9] and yet the "Being of entities 'is' not itself an entity."[10] Being (*Sein*) "determines entities as entities," and is the "basis on which entities are already understood."[11] The only way of investigating *Sein* is to "interrogate" beings (*Seiendes*). To ask about Being, we must begin by selecting a being or beings to be interrogated.

The investigation of the meaning of Being must, like all inquiry, be guided by a pre-given understanding of the object of study. In this case, the inquiry into Being is necessarily guided by the "vague average understanding of Being" which we in "fact" have.[12] But this gives us an added guideline for the inquiry. For how are we to decide which of the innumerable types of entities to interrogate regarding their Being? Heidegger declares that the proper entity which will be interrogated regarding its *Sein* must be that entity which alone has an "average understanding" of Being, that entity "which we, the inquirers, are ourselves," which Heidegger names "Being-There," *Dasein*.[13]

Dasein is distinct from all other entities in that "in its very Being that Being is an *issue* for it."[14] This means that Dasein is "ontically distinctive in that it *is* ontological," which is to say, Dasein is distinctive as a being in that it has an understanding of Being (*Seinsverständnis*). Dasein is "pre-ontological" and has an "average understanding" of Being which is not yet an ontology proper.

The unique mode or way of Being characteristic of Dasein, the mode which is to be the central concern of *Being and Time,* is *Existenz,* existence. The analysis of the structures which "constitute" this mode of Being Heidegger terms "existential," and the "context" of the structures themselves are Dasein's "existentiality" (*Existenzialität*). In general, existentiality is the constitutive-Being (*Seinsverfassung*) of a being, the state-of-Being which is constitutive for an entity.[15] The structures and features of Dasein's existentiality will be called "existentialia." Existential analysis of the structural constituents of existing differs from the realm of the "existentiell," which refers to existence as it is articulated by the Dasein as it actually exists, as an "ontical affair" of Dasein.[16]

In that it is concerned to understand its own existence, Dasein possesses an "ontico-ontological" priority over other entities. But this fact of Dasein's *Seinsverständnis,* which determines Heidegger's inquiry by placing Dasein at its center, also introduces complexities and circularities into *Being and Time,* as Heidegger is well aware. Heidegger's book is not only an analysis *of* Dasein, but also an *instance* or a living-out of Dasein's own way of Being. As Heidegger writes in the final words of his first introduction:

> the question of Being is nothing other than the radicalization of an essential tendency-of-Being which belongs to Dasein itself . . . .[17]

In other words, *Being and Time* is a part of its own object of study.

In *Being and Time* Heidegger presents a "preparatory analysis" of

Dasein's *Existenz* in Division One, then reinterprets these results in Division Two in terms of "temporality" (*Zeitlichkeit*), leaving off at the end with the still open question of whether time, properly understood, is the "horizon" within which the meaning of Being must be interpreted. In the process he gives us an extraordinarily rich and seemingly systematic exposition of the existential-temporal constitution of Dasein's mode of Being.

Heidegger notes that not only does Dasein have an understanding of Being, but further, this pre-ontological understanding is simultaneously a *mis*understanding of Being. Dasein has only an "average everyday" (*durchschnittlich Alltäglichkeit*) understanding of Being as part of its own Being, an understanding which is not fully adequate. If this were not the case, *Being and Time* would not have to be written. Dasein is, in fact, ontologically "far" from its own Being; that is, it systematically misunderstands Being in general and its own *Existenz* in particular. This fact determines some of the intriguing complexity of *Being and Time,* in particular, the distinction between "authenticity" and "inauthenticity." Heidegger has chosen to explore the meaning of Being by explicating the Being of an entity which systematically, in its very Being, distorts the meaning of Being, while at the same time retaining an understanding of Being.

At the outset of the preparatory analysis of Dasein Heidegger presents two fundamental characteristics of Dasein: that Dasein's "essence" lies in its "existence," and that Dasein is in every case "mine," is essentially characterized by "mineness" (*Jemeinigkeit*). The latter is related to Dasein's understanding and misunderstanding of itself. *Jemeinigkeit* makes it possible that Dasein can be in two modes of Being: *Eigentlichkeit,* authenticity or realness, ("own-liness"); and *Uneigentlichkeit,* inauthenticity or unrealness ("non-own-liness"). These ways-of-being-Dasein correspond to Dasein's having a proper or authentic understanding of itself and an improper, inauthentic, or "fallen" (*verfallend*) misunderstanding of itself. An essential part of Dasein's peculiar way of existing is that it can (indeed, it ordinarily and systematically does) fail to be itself, to be its own; and an essential part of this everyday failure is an inauthentic self-understanding.

A further distinction, basic to Heidegger's whole project, is particularly relevant to the issue of authenticity. The mode of Being of Dasein, *Existenz,* is absolutely distinct from the modes of Being characteristic of other entities. Heidegger's most often used example is the case of entities which are not encountered as existing within a context of significance constituted by their "ready-to-hand" (*zuhanden*) character, which are thus merely "present-at-hand" (*vorhanden*). Nature, conceived scientifically or independently of ready-to-hand significance, has the Being of presence-at-hand (*Vorhandensein*). For Heidegger, the difference between *Existenz* and presence-at-hand cannot be overestimated. He writes in *Basic Problems of Phenomenology* that:

> The ontological difference between the constitution of the Dasein's being and that of nature proves to be so disparate that it seems at first as though [they] are incomparable . . . . *Existence* and *extantness* [*Vorhandensein*] are more disparate than, say, the determinations of God's being and man's being in traditional ontology.[18]

In inauthenticity, Dasein tends to understand itself and its own way of Being in terms of other entities and their characteristic modes of Being. This everyday misunderstanding of itself is mirrored in traditional ontology, which frequently interpreted Dasein's Being in terms of presence-at-hand. Thus, Descartes interpreted Dasein as *res cogitans,* a mental substance and literally a thinking thing, opposed to a world of extended things. Heidegger's main objective in the analysis of Dasein is to reject all terms and concepts (categories) which refer or even *could* refer to things, as in principle inappropriate for determining the Being of human being, and then to create a novel system of terms and concepts ("existentialia") for the latter which is entirely independent of the ontic description and account of things.

One of the most important introductory sections of *Being and Time* is Heidegger's discussion of phenomenological method (Introduction II, section seven). For Heidegger, phenomenology is a method, one which reveals the *Sachen selbst,* or "things themselves." This method is determined by two factors: phenomenon and *logos,* or, the nature of the evidence and the way of handling the evidence. Heidegger distinguishes between four types of evidence in phenomenological inquiry: "phenomenon" refers to "that which shows itself in itself," or the "manifest"; "semblance" or "seeming" is a kind of phenomenon which shows itself *as* something which it is not; "appearance" refers to something which does *not* show itself at all, but which "announces itself" through something which does show itself; lastly, "mere appearance" is that kind of appearance in which what appears, while "bringing-forth" the manifest that announces it, is never manifest.

All forms of evidence are based in and presuppose the phenomenon proper, that which shows-itself-in-itself. All appearances—an example would be the symptom of a disease—are founded on phenomena, without which the former would be impossible. Heidegger asserts that "all symbols" have the character of appearing.

Heidegger is here adopting, albeit in a new language, a dichotomy of originary and derivative types of evidence that is analogous to Husserl's distinction between the presentation and the presentification of "phenomena." All symbolic evidences, and hence all cultural realities, for example, are construed as derivative in this dichotomous system and as dependent upon a logically prior form of evidence, the "manifest." We will return to this important dichotomy later.

A corresponding dualism is evident in Heidegger's analysis of *logos*. *Logos* is a mode of discourse; it is a discourse which "make[s] manifest what one is talking about . . . ."[19] In other words, *logos* is a discourse which "lets something be seen," or uncovered or discovered. But this implies that *logos* is not the primary locus of truth or "unconcealedness." If *logos* is a discourse which lets something to be "seen," then seeing is "more primordial as the way in which truth comes to light." The *logos* of discourse can be true or false; this is not the case for mere perception (*aisthēsis*). For Heidegger:

[*Aisthesis*], the sheer sensory perception of something is 'true' in the Greek sense, and indeed more primordially than the [*logos*] which we have been discussing . . . . Pure [seeing] is the perception of the simplest determinative ways of Being which entities may possess, and it perceives them just by looking at them. This [seeing] is what is 'true' in the purest and most primordial sense . . . [it] can never cover up; it can never be false . . . .[20]

Thus the truth of all "letting-something-be-seen", which can be false, is founded in the necessary truth of seeing, or sheer *aisthēsis*, which is never false. The latter always uncovers the "simplest determinative ways of Being" of entities, their "[idea], such as colors or sounds."[21] Beyond merely "letting-something-be-seen" is the possibility of "letting-something-be-seen-*as* something," which is characterized by a "synthesis-structure," and which may actually "cover up" the things themselves. This is no longer the *logos,* however, whose function is to "merely" let something be "perceived."[22] This gives us a tripartite distinction: a founding mode, "seeing" or "perceiving," which is necessarily true; a founded mode which can be true or false and which is the mode of *logos,* namely, "letting-something-be-seen"; and another founded mode, which can cover up evidences, a "letting-something-be-seen-as something." Phenomenology is for Heidegger, the *logos* of phenomena, the attempt:

to let that which shows itself be seen from itself in the very way in which it shows itself from itself.[23]

Having defined phenomenology in a way that dispenses with most of the Husserlian terminology, if not with all of Husserl's conceptual distinctions, Heidegger proceeds to connect phenomenology with ontology and to give phenomenology precisely the preeminent position within philosophy and, indeed, within all inquiry in general, that Husserl had claimed for it.

Heidegger argues that the object of phenomenology must be that which does *not* show itself; otherwise, presumably, there would be no need to attempt to 'let something show itself', since it would already be showing itself. Thus, phenomenology directs itself toward:

> something that lies *hidden,* in contrast to that which proximally and for the most part does show itself; but at the same time it is something that belongs to what thus shows itself, and it belongs to it so essentially as to constitute its meaning and its ground.[24]

Heidegger then makes a crucial leap. That which "remains hidden in an egregious sense . . . is not just this entity or that but rather the *Being* of entities . . . .[25]" The ultimate, or true, or most natural, or inevitable, or intrinsic object of phenomenology is the *Being* of things. "Phenomenology," Heidegger writes:

> is our way of access to the theme of ontology . . . . *Only as phenomenology is ontology possible* . . . . 'Behind' the phenomena of phenomenology there is essentially nothing else . . . . Because phenomena, as understood phenomenologically, are never anything but what goes to make up Being . . . phenomenology is the science of the Being of entities—ontology.[26]

Since Being is the basic theme of philosophy for Heidegger, "Philosophy is universal phenomenological ontology . . . ."[27] Heidegger has united the terms 'philosophy', 'ontology', and 'phenomenology'; the three are inseparable, and we cannot properly engage in one without engaging in the other two. Despite Heidegger's radical divergence from Husserl in some respects, one cannot ignore the similarity between Heidegger's ontological interpretation of phenomenology and the claims of the transcendental phenomenology of Husserl and Fink. In each case the science of phenomena is interpreted as the science of Being.

Conceived in this way, phenomenology is inevitably the logical presupposition and foundation for all other sciences, just as Husserl had asserted. Anthropology, psychology, and biology, for example, must necessarily fail to give an adequate answer to the question of the kind of Being which characterizes their objects.[28] Empirical science, Heidegger tells us, cannot answer this question, which, while it is presupposed by empirical-scientific inquiry, is "basic" and "problematic in a more radical sense than any thesis of positive science can ever be."[29] In this context, Heidegger even refers to the kind of inquiry which is needed to address the question of Being as "*a priori*".[30]

Dasein and Disclosedness

Being and Time presents an archaeology of human being, a set of progressively more fundamental strata of the existential definition of human being.[31] These strata serve as definitions of human being because, after all, what *Dasein* refers to is human being, or more precisely, the entity which "each of us is himself," the class of possible readers of *Being and Time*.[32] The strata or basic stages in Heidegger's argument regarding Dasein can be reduced to two essential or key phases. The preliminary designation of the entity whose Being is to be interpreted as Dasein is the crucially important first step. The remainder of the preparatory existential analytic of Division One is the unfolding of a single theme implicit in the term Dasein, passing from characterization as Being-in-the-world to the ultimate concept of Care. This central theme of this phase is *Erschlossenheit* or disclosedness, the state of Dasein being its 'There' or *"Da."* The second phase of the definition of Dasein comprises the first four chapters in Division Two, in which the definition of authentic Dasein as anticipatory resoluteness or *vorflaufende Entschlossenheit*—clearly linked to the notion of *Erschlossenheit*—leads to the temporal interpretation of Dasein's existence.

These two phases form the core of Heidegger's argument concerning Dasein. We will examine the phases of this argument and see the ways in which they express subjectivist and narcissistic categories. My reconstruction of Heidegger's archeology of Dasein's existence is summarized in Diagram C.

Dasein is, first of all, an entity, a being. This entity has a distinctive mode of Being and this mode will be the object of analysis in Division One and of temporal interpretation in Division Two. Heidegger's preliminary designation of human being as Being-There and his early description of Dasein have two fundamental consequences for the whole of *Being and Time,* consequences which run throughout the entire book.[33]

With the very term Da-Sein Heidegger has defined the mode of Being of the being to be interpreted as disclosed, thrown Being-in-the-world. Heidegger makes it clear in the pivotal chapter 5 of Division One that the fact that Dasein *"is* itself in every case its 'There',"[34] that to be Dasein means *to be a 'Da'*, a 'There', implies that Dasein is existentially spatial, always located within a world of 'Here' versus 'Yonder'. Dasein is disclosedness, is a "place" or "clearing" (*Lichtung*) of unconcealedness, revealing both itself and the world of entities. Dasein is always already there, delivered-over-to its disclosure and its world, which is to say, Dasein is "factical" and "thrown." Consequently, as one discovers only in chapter 5, the very name Dasein indicates the Being of this entity in the most fundamental way. Being-There is its There, and its Being-its-There is the existential character of its "Being-In" (*In-Sein*). Being-in, Heidegger writes:

DIAGRAM C

Heidegger's Interpretation of Dasein

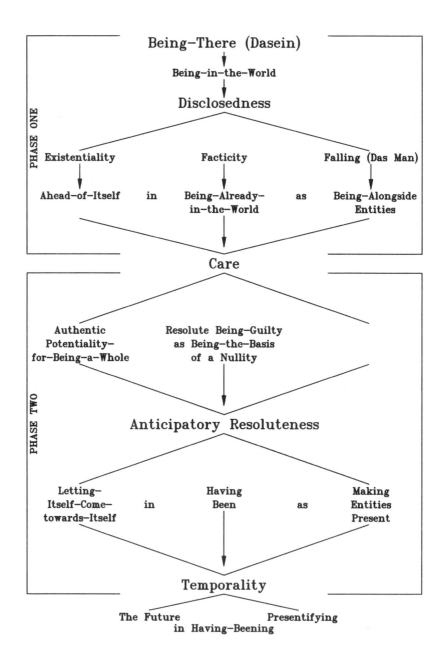

*is . . . the formal existential expression for the Being of Dasein, which
has Being-in-the-world as its essential state.*[35]

Being-its-There is the "formal existential expression for the Being
of" Being-There. What Heidegger regards as the most fundamental and
important existential structures given in Division One are all implicit in
the very name, Dasein.

The second important preliminary designation of Dasein is that
what makes Dasein "ontico-ontologically" distinctive and gives it priority in the inquiry into the meaning of Being is that Dasein's mode of
Being is characterized by an understanding of Being (*Seinsverständnis*),
as well as a misunderstanding of Being, and a corresponding understanding and misunderstanding of itself. *Verstehen* (understanding) is what
makes Dasein's Being distinctive. Despite the fact that Heidegger continually attempts to remove conceptual thought, assertive judgment and
epistēmē from a privileged status within the concept of the human, he
nevertheless gives understanding a special and privileged status within
his own existential analysis.

To be sure, Heidegger's 'understanding' is *not* tantamount to conceptual or analytic thought or knowledge; Heidegger attempts to interpret understanding in terms of Being-in-the-world. In chapter 5 of
Division One he presents understanding as one among four of the "constitutive ways of being the There," a part of disclosedness (*Erschlossenheit*), along with discourse, state-of-mind (*Befindlichkeit,* or, simply,
'state', the how-Dasein-is) and thrownness (*Geworfenheit*). Despite being
integrated into the overall existential structure of Dasein as only one of
several allegedly equiprimordial existentialia, understanding and the existentialia associated with it repeatedly take on a privileged status in the
interpretation of Dasein.

This accordance of a special status to understanding can be explained as the periodic reassertion of the special status given to understanding (*Verstehen*) at the outset of *Being and Time.* This special status
should not be minimized, since it is, after all, Dasein's understanding of
Being that is the primary justification for the existential analysis of
Dasein in the first place.

By designating Dasein as Being-in-the-world in chapter 2 of Division One Heidegger makes the world "a characteristic of Dasein itself."[36]

That wherein Dasein understands itself beforehand . . . is *that for
which* it has let entities be encountered beforehand. *The "wherein" of
an act of understanding . . . is that for which one lets entities be
encountered in the kind of Being that belongs to involvements; and
this "wherein" is the phenomenon of the world.*[37]

The world is the "wherein," the horizon projected by Dasein's understanding of entities with which it is involved, entities which have significance for it. Heidegger's concept of the world will be explored more fully in the following section; what is important to notice in the present context is that Dasein is the projector of a world which is a 'part' of itself, as essentially Being-in-the-world.

The world is, for Heidegger, the "relational totality" of "significance." As such,

> Dasein . . . is the ontical condition for the possibility of discovering entities which are . . . [ready-to-hand] . . . .[38]

Dasein is a condition for the possibility of the disclosedness of entities within the world. Dasein's existential spatiality, the condition for the possibility of its spatial relationship with entities is based, in part, in Dasein's "de-severence" (Ent-fernung, abolition of distance). De-severing is a "circumspective bringing-close."[39] "In Dasein," Heidegger writes, "there lies an essential tendency towards closeness."[40] It is in this de-severing that the world is revealed.[41] Heidegger goes as far as to assert that, "Dasein is essentially de-severance . . . ."[42] It is only because Dasein is its There that Dasein can have a world, intraworldly entities, and can be existentially spatial. Dasein's essential worldliness presumes its disclosedness and, as we will see, vice versa.

Disclosedness is the key to the preparatory existential analytic of Dasein. Heidegger tells us that it is the state of being the There—that is, disclosedness—which is the signification of the term 'Da-Sein'. It is the characteristic structure of Dasein's Being-In, which is the "formal existential expression for the Being of Dasein." Disclosedness is the essential existential character of Dasein as Being-in-the-world. Furthermore, it is the existential modes of disclosedness which prove to be the basis for the tripartite structure which constitutes the culminating definition of Dasein in Division One, Care (Sorge).

Care is the structure of Dasein's Existenz. Care, and thus the Being of Dasein, is "Ahead-of-itself-Being-already-in(the world)-as-Being-alongside (entities encountered within-the-world)." Dasein as Care is a fundamentally tripartite, although unified, structure of Being-ahead-of-itself, Being-already-in-the-world and Being-alongside-entities. Heidegger develops these three features of Dasein directly from the three existentialia of existentiality, facticity, and Being-fallen, respectively.[43] The latter are in turn existential derivatives of Dasein's essential disclosedness, the modalities of which are: understanding projection of Dasein's potentialities-for-Being; Being always already factically thrown into the world as revealed in states of mind; falling absorption in and understanding of one's factical existence in terms of entities within the world; and, discourse.

Disclosedness (*Erschlossenheit*) is the lynch-pin of the progression from Da-Sein to Care, and, as will be seen, three of its existentialia (understanding, state-of-mind, falling) structure the entire discussion from chapter 5 of Division One to chapter 4 of the temporal interpretation of Division Two.[44]

It is in chapter 5 of Division One that Heidegger explicitly introduces disclosedness and defines it. He does so in a very suggestive fashion. All "ontical" talk of the *"lumen naturale,"* he says, is in fact a reference to the existential structure of Dasein as being its There.[45] The "light" or "illumination" of Dasein refers to the fact that Dasein "is itself the *Lichtung,"* a term which evokes the senses of both a clearing in the woods and light.[46] The reference to the Cartesian "natural light" is a clue that what was for Descartes a mediating principle between subject and world will define for Heidegger the very *nature of* the 'subject', that is, of Dasein.

By defining Dasein as disclosedness, Heidegger indicates two fundamental existential traits of Dasein. First, Dasein is irrevocably always already 'in' a world, opened and delivered over to entities of the world. Second, Dasein is a *location* in which disclosing, revealing, appearing, take place.

For Heidegger, disclosedness means simultaneously already-there-as-being-delivered-over-to *and* disclosing or revealing. This is perhaps the most fundamental tenet and innovation of *Being and Time:* that appearing or disclosing necessarily presume 'being-already-there-as-delivered-over-to' worldly entities, and vice versa. To phrase this insight in a way more consonant with pre-Heideggerian terminology: perception, cognition, subjectivity, and truth are predicated upon concrete existence within and submissive vulnerability to a world of entities, *and* vice versa. Knowledge, insight, and truth are not the province of a detached, non-worldly mind; it is precisely the opposite. All disclosing occurs only in existing factically within a world, and all factical existence in a world discloses.

Given that this disclosedness is the dominant theme of Division One's definition of the existence of Dasein, we can ask, within the bounds of Division One, what or who *is* Dasein? Clearly, Dasein is disclosing-in-being-delivered-over-to. But what is disclosed in or by Dasein and to what is Dasein delivered over? The answer is twofold: worldly entities and itself.

Dasein is, firstly, the disclosing-of-the-world-in-submission-to-the-world. Dasein is the clearing within which the world appears. Indeed, Dasein is indistinguishable from phenomena as they show themselves, from what is as it appears. While Heidegger maintains, and needs to maintain, the distinctiveness of Dasein from all else that shows itself, it becomes impossible for him to provide a satisfactory answer to the question of what constitutes this distinctiveness. Heidegger's distinction becomes a dichotomy of indistinguishables. Dasein becomes paradoxically identical to the appearing world of entities.

Dasein is also the disclosing of itself. But what is this Dasein who is disclosed, what is Dasein's 'self'? For Heidegger, the everyday self or 'who' of Dasein is the they or the anonymous 'One' (*Das Man*).[47] As he writes, in what is one of the most striking passages in *Being and Time:*

> Dasein, as everyday Being-with-one-another, stands in *subjection* to
> Others. It itself *is* not; its Being has been taken away by [indefinite]
> Others . . . . Everyone is the Other, and no one is himself. The 'they'
> which supplies the answer to the question of the "who" of everyday
> Dasein, is the "nobody" to whom every Dasein has already
> surrendered itself . . . . The Self of everyday Dasein is the *they-self*
> [*das Man-selbst*] . . . . As the they-self, the particular Dasein has
> been *dispersed* into the "they", and must first find itself.[48]

Division One presents us with a perplexing circularity, a circularity which is not that of the "hermeneutic circle." Dasein's Being is defined by disclosedness-of the world, worldly entities, and itself in being-delivered-over-to the world, worldly entities, and itself. Dasein's self is merely a component of Dasein's existential structure (Care), and, in everydayness, this component has the meaning 'Others'. In Division One, Dasein is disclosedness of worldly entities and others in being delivered over to worldly entities and others. Even Dasein's state-of-mind, its mood, is itself a mode of disclosing the world. If we ask who or what Dasein is, the answer is that Dasein is the disclosure of itself and its world (here including entities); yet, if we ask what Dasein is 'itself', we must answer that it is in one sense others, and in another sense, it is again the disclosure of itself, the world, and entities. Consequently, Dasein is the revelation of what it putatively is not, that is, world, other, and entities. This means that, in some sense, Dasein is the appearance of what it is not.

In Division Two Heidegger proceeds to interpret Dasein's existence in its "authentic potentiality for Being-a-whole." Division One had, by concerning itself with Dasein's average everydayness, failed to achieve "primordiality" in its analysis of Dasein's existence. Dasein's everydayness is characterized by its projected possibilities, its being always not-yet, and its being not itself, but being others. Heidegger believes that he must discover Dasein's totality and authenticity before his analysis of Dasein can be considered primordial, for only then can it suggest a horizon for the question of the meaning of Being in general. Despite Heidegger's emphasis on finitude and the nullity of Dasein, he is here seeking the totality and the authenticity (*Eigentlichkeit*) or reality or ownness of Dasein, as the horizon of primordiality for the analysis of Dasein. Everyday Dasein is not-yet and not-itself. These two conditions must be analytically superseded, there must be a totality and an authenticity at their base, which must be uncovered for the analysis to be primordial. This is not to imply that authenticity is more essential to Dasein than everydayness; that would be a misreading of Heidegger. But while totality and authenticity are not more primordial *for* Dasein, they are more primordial in the existential analysis *of* Dasein. Here as elsewhere, Heidegger has not completely broken with the motivations of modern philosophy. He exhibits the same drive to conceive of human being as a totality, as a fully individuated *eigentlich* existence. This characterizes not only much of Western moral philosophizing, but also modern subjectivism in general, which seeks constantly to find the essence of the human and to rigorously distinguish what is man's "own" from what belongs to the non-human.

Heidegger accomplishes his interpretation of Dasein's authenticity and potentiality-for-being-a-whole in three steps. First, he shows that Dasein carries within its own existence the potentiality for Being-a-whole in its anticipation (*vorlaufen*) of death. Death is Dasein's "ownmost non-relational potentiality-for-Being which cannot be outstripped." In anticipation, Dasein opens itself to this ultimate potentiality, to its attendant anxiety, and is thereby "individualized," "wrenched from the they," and made "free" from all other concerns.[49] Indeed, this anxious anticipation of death reveals to Dasein for the first time "the responsibility of being itself."[50]

Second, Heidegger reasons that there must be some existentielle-ontical occurrence within Dasein that brings Dasein to "demand" authentic potentiality for Being-a-whole of itself, as an ontical possibility. Something must "call" Dasein to, in a sense, put this possibility in practice. Heidegger shows that it is conscience (*Gewissen*), a mode of disclosive discourse, which calls Dasein to recognize its own Being-guilty (*sein-Schulden:* Being-indebted, responsible, guilty). Being-guilty is Being-the-basis of a "nullity" or "not-ness" (*Nichtigkeit*). That is, Dasein, as always already thrown, does not have power over its own Being-there as what-it-is; and Dasein is "not" many things. The call of conscience proceeds from the "self" of the "they-self," calling itself away from the "they" toward its own anxious, not-at-home (*unheimlich*) Being-guilty. If Dasein "chooses to choose" this call, if it "reticently projects itself" upon its Being-guilty, then Dasein is characterized by resoluteness (*Entschlossenheit*). Anticipation of death is a mode of this resoluteness.[51] It is in "anticipatory resoluteness" (*vorlaufende Entschlossenheit*) that Dasein becomes its authentic self, exhibits its own authentic potentiality for Being-a-whole and thereby reveals "the primordial truth of existence."[52]

Third, the ontological meaning of authentic, primordial Care, revealed in anticipatory resoluteness, turns out to be ecstatico-horizonal temporality (*Zeitlichkeit*). Temporality, in its tripartite ecstatic unity, is the condition of the possibility of Dasein, and the modes of time constitute the existential modes of Dasein's disclosedness.

These developments do not constitute a break with the central theme of Division One. Heidegger asserts that "Resoluteness [*Entschlossenheit*] is a distinctive mode of Dasein's disclosedness [*Erschlossenheit*]."[53] Indeed, resoluteness is "authentic disclosedness."[54] Since resoluteness is authentic Care, and temporality is the ontological meaning of the latter, temporality is also the ontological meaning of disclosedness. Temporality is "the condition for the possibility that there can be an entity which exists as its 'there'," which is to say, temporality is the condition for the possibility of disclosedness. As Heidegger writes, "*Ecstatical temporality clears the 'there' primordially.*"[55] The essential structure of Dasein as disclosing-in-being-delivered-over-to is grounded in the horizon of temporality, the latter being the "primordial 'outside-of-itself' in and for itself", temporality.[56]

Anticipatory resoluteness is the key to the revelation of the truth of Dasein's existence. Anticipatory resoluteness is a running ahead (anticipating) of one's own non-Being in projecting oneself upon one's own Being-the-basis of what one is not. Anticipatory resoluteness reveals that the truth of Dasein's existence, the true self of Dasein, is grounded in a double nullity or nothingness. First, Dasein's "ownmost non-relational" possibility for Being, that possibility which radically individuates and brings Dasein to itself, is the possibility of non-Being. Only in running ahead and bringing the possibility of death understandingly close does Dasein become itself. The most essential potentiality of Being-There is non-Being. Second, in resoluteness Dasein projects itself upon its own Being-the-basis of a *Nichtigkeit*, "not-ness" or nullity. Dasein *is not*, essentially. Dasein is limited to Being what it is, and what it is is constituted by its thrownness, over which the Dasein has no control. Thus Dasein is not this, not that; its very existence is pervaded by 'Being-not', by nullity. Dasein's existence is constituted not only by the ultimate nullity of death, but by the pervasive nullity of its indefinitely many existentielle "nots." In resoluteness Dasein affirms, accepts, projects itself upon this not-ness, and upon its own Being-responsible.

As previously seen, resoluteness is a response to a "call." The authentic self of Dasein, the self buried in the They-self is both the caller and the called. The call calls Dasein to itself. The caller is "primordial thrown Being-in-the-world as not-at-home in the nothingness of the world."[57]

Whereas the everyday self flees in the face of itself into the They, becoming a "fugitive," in anticipatory resoluteness, Dasein comes face to face with itself and becomes its authentic self. In this, Dasein attains "self-constancy" or "stability" (*Standigkeit des Selbst*). Heidegger writes of the latter:

> The constancy of the Self, in the double sense of steadiness and steadfastness, is the *authentic* counter-possibility to the non-Self-constancy which is characteristic of irresolute falling.[58]

But what exactly is "Self-constancy," and what is the authentic self of Dasein? Heidegger describes self-constancy as "the sense of its having achieved some sort of position (*Standgewonnenhabens*)."[59] Yet this achievement of position "signifies nothing other than anticipatory resoluteness," which signifies nothing other than authentic Care.[60] Just as was the case with everyday Care, the self in authenticity is an element *of* Care. Heidegger writes:

> Care *does not need to be founded in a Self* . . . . When fully conceived, the Care-structure includes the phenomenon of Selfhood.[61]

Here we may ask the same questions that we asked of Division One: who or what is Dasein? Authentically and primordially, Dasein is thrown, not-at-home disclosing-in-being-delivered-over-to the world, which anticipates its own non-Being in projecting itself upon its own Being-the-basis of not-ness. Who is this Dasein and what is Dasein's authentic self? Who is Dasein insofar as Dasein has freed itself of its absorption in the 'they' and entities?

Heidegger does not give us an answer to who Dasein is. He tells us what Dasein does, or the existentiell-existential possibilities which bring Dasein to itself; for example, Dasein "anticipates" and "is resolved." But to the question of *who* anticipates and is resolved, Heidegger gives no answer. The only sense in which Heidegger does address authentic Dasein and Dasein's self is in terms of *what they are not* (others) and *the "not" which they are* (as null Being-towards non-Being.)

Finally in Division Two, Heidegger proceeds to interpret the existentialia of Care, now revealed in their primordial authenticity by resoluteness, in terms of temporality. Temporality, or primordial time, is the meaning of authentic Care, which is to say, it is that "upon-which" Care is projected and thereby "conceived in its possibility as that which it is."[62] Temporality is the primordial unity of authentic Care and the condition for the possibility of Dasein's existence. Dasein's temporality is constituted by the three "ecstases" of the future (letting-itself-come-towards-itself), having-Been, and making-present. These ecstases correspond to three of the existentialia that constitute Care, namely, existentiality as understanding, facticity as state-of-mind, and falling, respectively.

The future, and hence existentiality and understanding, has a unique and primary status in the formulation of temporality. Heidegger's German expression for temporality, *gewesend-gegenwärtigende Zu-kunft*, "a future which makes present in the process of having been," makes the future the active agent in temporality.[63] Heidegger writes that:

> the future has a priority in the ecstatical unity of primordial and authentic temporality . . . . *The primary phenomenon of primordial and authentic temporality is the future.*[64]

Temporality temporalizes itself *through* the future. This is consistent with the priority that Heidegger gives to understanding in *Being and Time,* since there is a direct line of progression from understanding (as an existential mode of disclosedness), to existentiality and the "Ahead-of-itself" (as a component of the Care-structure), and on to the future (as an ecstasy of the temporal horizon of authentic Care).

What is this temporality which has turned out to be the meaning of the Being of Dasein, the condition for the possibility of Dasein's existence, and the ground of Dasein's existential unity? Heidegger writes:

> Temporality 'is' not an *entity* at all. It *is* not, but it *temporalizes* itself . . . temporality [is] manifest as the [*ekstatikon*] pure and simple. *Temporality is the primordial 'outside-of-itself' in and for itself.*[65]

Temporality is not an entity. But, since "Being is always the Being of an entity," it is not clear that temporality has Being, or *is,* at all. Temporality, as the primordial "outside-of-itself," cannot be described in the language of entities or even of the Being of entities. Temporality temporalizes; it cannot be said unambiguously that it "is," and certainly not that it "is some*thing.*" Temporality is directly connected with the phenomenon of disclosedness. Ecstatical temporality is:

> the condition for the possibility that there can be an entity which exists as its 'There'. The entity which bears the title "Being-there" is one that has been '*cleared*' . . . . *Ecstatical temporality clears the "There" primordially.*[66]

Dasein's existential unity is grounded in the primordial ecstatical outside-of-itself, and the modes of being outside-of-itself are constitutive for the structure of Dasein as Care. Heidegger has here joined together two of his most innovative ideas: disclosedness and the *ekstatikon*. The unitary phenomenon of disclosing-in-being-delivered-over-to, the fact that disclosing can only occur in factical submission to a world, is here grounded by Heidegger in the phenomenon of the self-transcendence of an ecstatic being-outside-of-itself. Being outside-of-itself implicitly means being what-it-is-not, being something and yet not being that thing, since for a thing to be *ecstatic* is to transgress the limits of the thing that it is. Division Two asserts that disclosedness, and thus Dasein, is only possible on the basis of this paradoxical self-transcendence.

At the outset of the present study it was noted that the term 'consciousness' has a notoriously dual meaning; it is both a totality of contents or events of which we are said to be conscious, and it is the vehicle, receptacle, or process to which such contents or events are said to belong, by virtue of being conscious. Consciousness is both a something and what belongs to or gains status as a function of this something.

A subjectivist philosophy may employ either or both of these senses of the word consciousness. It may talk of consciousness as an entity or it may talk only of conscious events or 'consciousings'. In the latter case it may dispense with all talk of a mental substance and even with any mention of consciousness or subjectivity at all, speaking only of the objects of consciousness, of what *is* conscious or what is disclosed, what appears as phenomena to the human individual. Consciousness here is a predicate of entities; it is something which *happens to* things, which makes them present, disclosed, apparent. For a thing to be conscious is to be in such a relation to a human being that is becomes apparent to that human being. Consciousness is the condition for the possibility of things showing themselves, the condition for the possibility of phenomena.

Subjectivism without reference to consciousness is characterized by two familiar subjectivist notions, terminologically reformulated so as to eliminate any reference to consciousness as an entity. These characteristic notions are:

a) Human being is primarily characterized by, or is essentially, a making-apparent of things. This is to say, the essential human activity is consciousing, intending, or disclosing things.

b) The most fundamental distinction for inquiry is the distinction between, on the one hand, the activity or process of making-apparent, the entity which makes-entities-apparent, and the state of being apparent, and, on the other hand, the state of not-being apparent, and that which does not make entities apparent.

It cannot be denied that Heidegger has ingeniously dispensed with the language of subjectivity and consciousness. But it is also undeniable that in *Being and Time* human being is systematically interpreted as disclosedness, as making-apparent, as a clearing, a 'place' in which what is comes to light. And the distinction between disclosedness and non-disclosedness is central for Heidegger in a variety of ways.

Levinas and the Emptiness of Dasein

Heidegger's definition of phenomenology, his preliminary designation of what is, what constitutes Being, and his typology of the kinds of evidences available for inquiry are all founded on "that which shows itself in itself," that is, on phenomena. What is, for Heidegger, is essentially phenomena, the manifest. Phenomena are "what goes to make up Being," behind which there is "nothing else."

For Heidegger, phenomenology, ontology, what we can know of the Being of entities, and the whole of *Being and Time* are evidentially based on the pure perception of what shows itself. Phenomena constitute not only all that we can know, but *all that there is* as well. For Heidegger, what does not show itself in any sense, *cannot be*. Appearances occupy a unique status insofar as they do not show themselves, yet announce themselves in what does show itself.

This is nothing other than subjectivism, radically applied, albeit with the terms 'consciousness' and 'subject' systematically replaced by a terminology oriented around the *objects* of consciousness. Heidegger defines human being in terms of the showing or disclosing of entities, others, and the world. Heidegger's language drops out the first and modifies the second term of the Husserlian triad "ego–noesis–noema." Yet his remains a philosophy of the third term, the "noema" or phenomena, and the reinterpreted second term, the noeses, in which phenomena are revealed. The phenomena show themselves in and to that which lets them show themselves, the Clearing. Dasein is defined by that which it allows to become manifest. Heidegger writes in regard to ready-to-hand entities (but it is applicable to all disclosed beings) that:

> Dasein . . . is the ontical condition for the possibility of discovering entities which are encountered in a world . . . .[67]

This subjectivism can also be seen in the distinction Heidegger makes between the Being of the entity whose existence is disclosive and all other modes of Being. Dasein is disclosedness, the showing of whatever shows itself, the clearing for phenomena. *Being and Time* is predicated upon an absolute distinction between Dasein (and whatever participates *in* Dasein's *Existenz*, for example intraworldly entities) and all other ways of Beings. As seen above, Heidegger believes that the ontological difference between Dasein's and nature's being is "so disparate" as to make them seem "incomparable," more disparate in fact than "God's being and man's being in traditional ontology."[68]

This point exhibits the most basic feature of subjectivism, and is common to Descartes, Kant, and Husserl. Human being is absolutely distinct from all of nature and all natural entities. Its distinctness is constituted by its status and function as *an arena or state for the appearance or disclosure of* all other entities. That which discloses, human being, is utterly distinct from that which does not (for example, nature); this is the most fundamental ontological fact for subjectivism. All inquiry which aims at systematic knowledge of what is, be it science or philosophy, must be logically grounded in and presuppose a more foundational, *a priori* analysis of this arena of appearing, this *"Lichtung,"* the "within-which" of all phenomena and knowledge of phenomena. A foundational philosophical inquiry, a "first" or "critical" philosophy, can accept as evidence *only that which belongs to this clearing,* only what shows itself in human being, on the lighted stage of what some call consciousness, and what Heidegger calls 'that which discloses'.

The French philosopher Emmanuel Levinas makes a similar attack on Heidegger and on phenomenology in general. Levinas criticizes Heidegger on two related counts: the priority that Heidegger grants to Being and ontology over beings or entities; and Heidegger's interpretation of Being through the existentiale of understanding.

Levinas sharply contrasts ontology with metaphysics. The former reduces the Other to the Same (the Subject); it interprets Being as a 'light' within which extistents become intelligible. The latter, based in a respect for exteriority, questions or criticizes the Same through a recognition of the Other and the Other's nature. This is why, for Levinas, metaphysics achieves its fulfillment only in ethics. Even the simple affirmation that all beings must presuppose and be determined by Being is illegitimate in this sense for Levinas. He writes that:

> To affirm the priority of *Being* over the existent is to already decide the essence of philosophy . . . .[69]

Levinas claims that Western philosophy, which has displayed a penchant for this ontological reduction, tends to interpret this reduction as freedom, that is, to understand freedom as the condition of not being limited by anything external. The abolition of the Other's "alterity" brings freedom to the same, the ego. This abolition or reduction is accomplished through "mediation"; an element of the subject, like a concept or category, is taken to subsume or represent the Other. Thus, the Other, as a mere instance of the concept which belongs to me, loses his or her alterity.

For Levinas, Heidegger's ontological reduction of the Other is consistent with the method of Husserlian phenomenology. Phenomenology's "ontological imperialism" is, according to Levinas, even more visible than that of most of Western philosophy. Phenomenology makes the Being of the existent into a mediating factor which in its intelligibility belongs to the subject:

It is the Being of the existent that is the *medium* of truth; truth
regarding the existent presupposes the prior openness of Being.[70]

Levinas argues that:

Since Husserl the whole of phenomenology is the promotion of the
idea of *horizon,* which for it plays a role equivalent to that of the
concept in classical idealism; the existent arises upon a ground that
extends beyond it, as the individual arises from the concept . . . the
Being of the existent, which guarantees the independence of the
existent—is a phosphorescence, a luminosity, a generous effulgence.
The existing of the existent is converted into intelligibility, its
independence is a surrender in radiation.[71]

Regarding Heidegger, Levinas boldly asserts that *"Being and Time*
has argued perhaps but one sole thesis: Being is inseparable from the
comprehension of Being (which unfolds as time); *Being is already an
appeal to subjectivity"*[72] (my emphasis).

Along with this interpretation of Being through the concept of horizonal intelligibility, Heidegger subordinates the existent to its Being. As
Levinas argues, this "is to subordinate the relations with *someone . . .*
(the ethical relation) . . . to a relation with the *Being of the existent,*
which, impersonal, permits the apprehension, the domination of the
existent (a relationship of knowing)."[73] Heidegger's ontology privileges
epistemology over ethics and freedom over justice. This freedom of Dasein is not, to be sure, a freedom of the will, for in *Being and Time:*

Freedom comes from an obedience to Being: it is not man who
possesses freedom; it is freedom that possesses man.[74]

Levinas rightly sees in Heidegger a "dialectic" which "reconciles
freedom and obedience" through the concept of truth, and asserts that
this reconciliation presupposes the "primacy of the same."[75] This presupposition places Heidegger firmly within the subjectivist tradition in modern philosophy. It provides further support for viewing Heidegger as
attempting to radicalize that tradition from within, rather than as attempting to destroy it from without. Heidegger grounds all entities in
Sein, and having done so, declares that the understanding of *Sein* is
determinative of *Sein* itself. If the understanding of Being is determinative of phenomena, of the showing of what shows itself, then Dasein's
Seinsverständnis must be determinative for the Being of all entities.
Heidegger writes that:

All ontical experience of entities . . . is based upon projections of the
Being of the corresponding entities . . . . If we say that entities 'have

meaning' this signifies that they have become accessible *in their Being* . . . .[76]

The very concept of meaning for Heidegger is that of a *horizon for conceptualization.* "Meaning," Heidegger writes:

> signifies the "upon-which" of a primary projection in terms of which something can be conceived in its possibility as that which it is.[77]

By construing that which constitutes the *meaning* of authentic Care (namely, time) as the ground and condition for the possibility of Dasein's existence, Heidegger shows his willingness to construe meaning as the *constitution* of Being, or existence. Likewise, ". . . Being is dependent upon the understanding of Being; that is to say, Reality is dependent upon Care."[78]

In general, Heidegger gives the concepts of horizon, meaning, and understanding—and therefore, intelligibility—a privileged place in the heart of Being itself. Heidegger has made intelligibility, in whatever modes in which it occurs, constitutive for Being.

The problems with *Being and Time* are deeper and more paradoxical, however. They are the problems not merely of subjectivism, but of radicalized subjectivism, of philosophical narcissism.

Heidegger's Dasein has no existential integrity. Dasein is a place where something happens, where disclosing takes place. Dasein is a set of relations to worldly entities and others. Dasein does not have the character of a something (or someone) which exists. If we ask about the nature of Dasein, we find ourselves moving in a circle, as previously described. Dasein is the disclosing of itself and the world, but 'itself' is either others and the world again, or can be redefined as Dasein, and thus as disclosedness, and so the circle begins once more.

This circle is conditioned by the fact that Dasein ultimately has two possible significations in *Being and Time.* Dasein is either disclosedness, openness, 'light' itself—which is to say that Dasein is in effect nothing, is not a something at all—or Dasein is in effect everything, that is, Dasein is the appearance of all other entities, is a *possibility of* all worldly entities (that is, the possibility of Being-uncovered). Dasein is a possible *state* that entities may enter.

These two possible significations form an antimony. If we ask about Dasein's nature we run into one of them, and if we try to define that signification further, it leads to its opposite. If Dasein is a mere openness, a "condition for the possibility of discovering entities," then Dasein is all entities in the sense that Dasein is indistinguishable from all entities as they appear. Yet, if Dasein is indistinguishable from all things in their disclosure, then Dasein is, in itself, literally "nothing," like

Sartre's description of consciousness as a "wind blowing toward" entities. This antinomy is none other than the dialectic of philosophical narcissism.

The dialectical nature of Dasein is borne out as much by the resoluteness and temporality of Division Two as it is by the disclosedness and Care of Division One. Authentic, resolved Dasein is a "Being-the-basis of a nullity in anticipating its non-Being." There is, in effect, *no authentic self of Dasein*. Rather, authentic Dasein is Dasein that has ceased to construe itself as the 'they' and instead projects itself on its own nullity with resolve while bringing its own non-Being towards itself (existentially, that is). Heidegger only defines the authentic self in two ways: he tells us what it is not (that is, it is not the 'they') and he tells us that it is constituted by nothingness (by the non-Being of death and the nullity of Being-guilty). Resolute, authentic Dasein accepts, affirms, and lives its own nullity. But this is only to say that Heidegger, in emptying Dasein of any possible character or integrity, in making Dasein's essence disclosedness, is here trying to define *that very emptiness as authentic selfhood*. Dasein's contentlessness, its "not-at-homeness" (*Unheimlichkeit*), its resolute uncharacterizability are held up as the true self of Dasein. The only definable, characterizable self which Heidegger allows Dasein is the 'they-self'. For Heidegger, true selfhood, authentic Dasein, is precisely the *lack* of anything we could call integrity, character, being-something. Heidegger endorses a kind of negative theology of the self; any characterization of Dasein's self is a violation of Dasein, whose authenticity is its resolute emptiness. In this respect, Heideggerian authenticity resembles Sartrian freedom.

By interpreting Dasein in terms of time, Heidegger has asserted that the unity of Dasein and the ground of Dasein's existence is a flowing self-transcendence which may be beyond the very categories of Being and non-Being. This final stratum in the archaeology of Dasein may indeed have unity, but does it have content? Is not the idea of content, character, nature, the status of being-something precisely what Heidegger means to get beyond and to deny entirely in the concept of temporality, the primordial "outside-of-itself"? It appears that Heidegger here wishes to ground Dasein exactly in that which is absolutely without a character, nature, a that-it-is, a being-something-or-other.

It may appear that Division One is promising in offering a possible own-content, character, or integrity for Dasein, particularly Heidegger's discussion of state-of-mind (*Befindlichkeit*) and *Stimmung* ("mood") in section twenty-nine. Upon examination, however, this proves not to be the case. Because Dasein has been defined primarily by the fundamental category of disclosive-submission, and all of the existentialia of Dasein interpreted in terms of disclosive-submission, these existentialia fail to provide anything like a character or an integrity for Dasein.

For Heidegger, state-of-mind is a mode or manifestation of Dasein's Being-its-There. Mood is a mode or manifestation of state-of-mind. Dasein is, for Heidegger, always in or characterized by a definite 'state' or mood.

State-of-mind and its moods are a "species" or mode of Dasein's disclosive-submission. Moods are a kind of disclosedness. Heidegger asserts that state-of-mind and mood reveal or disclose in three ways.

First, they reveal Dasein's *Geworfenheit* or thrownness, the "facticity of Dasein's being-delivered-over-to its There." Heidegger writes that the first essential characteristic of states-of-mind is that *"they disclose Dasein in its thrownness,* and, proximally and for the most part, in the manner of an evasive turning-away."[79] State-of-mind and mood reveal Dasein as factically submitted to its There, and Dasein typically evades or turns away from what is thereby revealed.

Second, they disclose Dasein as Being-in-the-world as a whole. That is, they "equiprimordially" disclose the world, Dasein-with and existence.

Third, they disclose the world. Heidegger argues that, since state-of-mind is that disclosive-submission to a world out of which we encounter something which "matters" to us, the "primary discovery of the world" is attributable to "bare mood," or mood in general.[80] It is in this mattering of the world to us, which mood "lets" happen, that Dasein "somehow evades its very self."[81] In a particular mood, Dasein attends to the disclosed world to which it is submitted, rather than to the disclosing-submission of itself, which mood simultaneously discloses.

In this original and intriguing existential analysis of a phenomenon that has been neglected by many philosophers, Heidegger gives mood a profound and unexpected philosophic status. He does this, however, by amalgamating mood to the function or activity of disclosedness. State-of-mind and mood are modes of disclosedness. They disclose two things—the world and the disclosing-in-being-delivered-over-to-the-world of Being-in-the-world. Thus, once again, we are trapped in the circle of disclosure where all that can be disclosed is disclosedness and disclosingness. State-of-mind and mood do not disclose anything which is Dasein's *own* except insofar as Dasein's own is restricted to revealing and Being-subjected-to and dispersed-in the world of entities. State-of-mind and mood, like Dasein itself, are defined in terms of disclosure. What is disclosed in disclosure can only be either what is *not* Dasein or further modes of the disclosingness of Dasein. State-of-mind and mood, modes of Dasein's disclosive-submission, serve to disclose Dasein's disclosive-submission.

Because Dasein is fundamentally disclosedness, every time we discover an existential characteristic of Dasein which might reveal the integrity or character of Dasein, that existentiale turns out to reveal the character of Dasein *as revelatory of* something (for example, entities). The Care-structure does not in any way contravene this lack of an integral content in the existence of Dasein. Dasein's Care-structure is "Ahead-of-itself-in-Being-already-in-the World-as-Being-alongside" entities. This structure represents Dasein as a set, albeit an integrated set, of relations to what it-is-not, to entities, others, and the world as a whole. Insofar as Care defines Dasein as "Being-already-in-(the world)-as-Being-alongside-(entities)" this is fairly obvious; Dasein as factical and fallen is simply defined as Being-in and Being-alongside.

Care defines Dasein as purely relational-functional, which is to say, everything which Dasein is is a relation to or a function of something. Although Heidegger understands the concept of Dasein as Care as totalizing or unifying Dasein's existentialia, this unification does not give existential integrity to Dasein. Unity *per se* does not imply existential integrity. The unity provided by Care remains purely relational-functional; Dasein is wholly constituted by relations or functions.

It is only in "Being-ahead-of-itself," in Dasein's understanding, projective existentiality that there might appear to be a possible characterization of *Dasein* as something other than a relation to entities and the world. It may seem that here, in the projection of itself upon its own potentialities, Dasein is something of its own.

Yet, this is not the case. Understanding is *"the existential Being of Dasein's own potentiality-for-Being."*[82] Dasein is always Being-possible (*Sein-können*) or Being-able-to, and understanding is the mode of disclosure of such essential possibility; understanding is the modality which makes what Dasein may be essential to what Dasein is. But what is the nature of these possibilities for Dasein? In Division One they can only be, again, possibilities of disclosedness. Dasein's possibilities are possibilities of *further disclosing* entities and others. In Division Two, we at last discover Dasein's "ownmost, non-relation" possibility: it is non-Being, death. Authentic Dasein projects itself most essentially upon its own non-Being. Finally, in the temporal interpretation of authentic Care, the future is formulated as Dasein's "letting-itself-come-towards-itself." Dasein's nature or self, like the uroboros-motif of Jungian psychology exemplified in the image of the snake swallowing its own tail, progressively swallows itself in the process of definition.

It cannot be objected that my criterion of existential integrity is an ontic criterion, here illegitimately imposed on Heidegger's ontological analysis of the mode of Being of Dasein. Heidegger has inextricably linked the ontic and ontological levels of analysis in Dasein's case. First, what-it-is-to-be Dasein, Dasein's essence or nature *is existence*. Thus the analysis of Dasein's existence should reveal what or who Dasein is, or the nature or character of Dasein, insofar as such can be claimed to exist at all. Whatever is true of Dasein must be grounded in the existential analytic, to use Heidegger's own terms. If Dasein the entity is to have individual integrity, then this integrity must be grounded in Dasein's *Existenz*. Second, Dasein *is* always *as* an entity, since "Being is always the Being of an entity"[83] and the *Existenz* of this entity is "in each case mine." Dasein's existence is always the existence of an individual entity. Consequently, the structure of the existence of Dasein must ground all that Dasein is. If this structure makes Dasein so purely relational that it has no contentual, integral self, then this excludes the possibility of such a self from Dasein the entity. And this is precisely what Heidegger's analysis does.

The Collapse of Heidegger's Concept of World

It might appear to some that, if Heidegger too radically de-insulated the subject and thereby mistakenly eliminated its integrity, he nevertheless succeeded in invigorating the concept of the world, in rescuing the world from the reductive, materialistic treatment to which it has been all too often subjected. Heidegger's most lasting contribution may lie in his revolutionizing the concepts of the world, nature, and intra-worldly entities. Heidegger himself wrote that:

> Elucidation of the world-concept is one of the most central tasks of philosophy. The concept of world, or the phenomenon thus designated, is what has hitherto not yet been recognized in philosophy . . . . In the end it is precisely the phenomenon of the world that forces us to a more radical formulation of the subject concept![84]

Thus, some might say that if Heidegger mistakenly reduced human being to the world, at least he formulated, perhaps for the first time, a philosophical vision of the concrete world of entities as having its own existential integrity, as irreducible to a transcendental subject or to the abstractly conceived movements of matter.

Unfortunately, this is not the case. As in Husserl and in philosophical narcissism in general, the effacing of the mediating mechanisms standing between subject and object, and the reduction of one side of this dichotomy, paradoxically implies the reduction of the other side of the dichotomy. Heidegger's world lacks existential integrity, like Dasein itself.

The question that must be asked of Heidegger's system is: is Dasein related to, does Dasein encounter, entities that have an existential integrity which obtains independently of Dasein? If the answer is negative, then either there are no entities with existential integrity, or there are but they are not encountered in their independent existence by human beings. If there are no such entities, then Heidegger's system is a form of idealism. If such entities exist but are never encountered in their independent existence, then they have the same status as Kantian things-in-themselves.

Readiness-to-hand (*Zuhandenheit*) is a mode of the Being of entities. Such entities, understood as equipment (*das Zeug*), are encountered as things of use, entities to be manipulated, whose very Being includes a "reference" or "assignment" to an implicit end, an "in order to" and a "towards-which." Dasein's relation to *Zuhanden* entities is the most primordial of Dasein's relations to things.[85] For Heidegger, "*Readiness-to-hand is the way in which entities as they are 'in themselves' are defined ontologico-categorically.*"[86] In our usual, "circumspective" dealings with the ready-to-hand, its referential character is not encountered thematically, not made an explicit object of understanding. In this mode, the ready-to-hand "holds itself in," that is, it does not go out of itself to "announce" its reference. Readiness-to-hand is the true "Being-in-itself" (*An-sich-sein*) of an entity.

A different mode of Being is "presence-at-hand" (*Vorhandensein*), or (as rendered by Albert Hofstadter) "extantness." Present-at-hand entities lack the referential, instrumental character of equipment; they are encountered as simply a "Thing," or as simply "there," not to be confused with the disclosive There of Dasein. If, for example, the usual manipulability of a ready-to-hand entity becomes blocked or obscured, then the presence-at-hand of that entity may emerge. The entity becomes "conspicuous," becomes discovered as a present-at-hand entity and as having already been present-at-hand in its very readiness-to-hand. A thing may have both modes of Being; Heidegger writes as if there were a kind of continuum from the circumspectively manipulated ready-to-hand, to the "conspicuous" "unready-to-hand" discovered to have always been present-at-hand, to what he calls the "limiting case of the Being of possible entities within-the-world," nature.[87]

'Nature', like 'Reality', refers to the Being of purely present-at-hand entities within-the-world. (Heidegger does use the term 'nature' in a second sense when he refers to *die Umweltnatur,* or "environing nature" insofar as it has the character of the ready-to-hand. In general, however, Nature for Heidegger is purely *vorhanden*).[88] Presence-at-hand is encountered primarily in cognition, the latter being a derivative or "founded mode of Being-in-the-world" for Heidegger.[89] Heidegger's analysis of the relation between presence-at-hand and readiness-to-hand is a subtle one; present-at-hand Nature is always already there, and without it there could be no ready-to-hand entities, yet readiness-to-hand is more primordial and is encountered in a more originary way by Dasein. He remarks:

> To lay bare what is just present-at-hand and no more, cognition must first penetrate *beyond* what is ready-to-hand in our concern.[90]

The linchpin of the differentiation between the ready-to-hand and the present-at-hand is Heidegger's concept of the world. Without even beginning to read the chapter concerning "The Worldhood of the World" in *Being and Time,* we already know the most crucial fact about the world: it is an element or dimension of *Dasein's* existence. Dasein is Being-in-the-world; consequently worldhood for Heidegger:

> stands for the structure of one of the constitutive items of Being-in-the-world . . . . Thus worldhood itself is an *existentiale* . . . . Ontologically, 'world' is . . . a characteristic of Dasein itself.[91]

Heidegger defines the world and the worldhood of the world through an explication of the ready-to-hand and the emergence of the present-at-hand from the former. It is only when the assignment of the ready-to-hand is disturbed that the assignment becomes explicit.[92] This disturbance coincides (as noted above) with the emergence of the present-at-hand. In this disturbance, "The context of equipment is lit up . . ." and "the world announces itself."[93] The world is exhibited in the revelation of the context of equipmentality. Yet, equipment (*Zuhandenheit*) alone does not comprise the world. Heidegger writes:

> That the world does not 'consist' of the ready-to-hand shows itself in the fact . . . that whenever the world is lit up . . . the ready-to-hand becomes deprived of its worldhood so that Being-just-present-at-hand comes to the fore.[94]

The transformation of readiness-to-hand into some mode of present-at-hand and finally into the pure *Vorhandensein* of Nature, is a progressive deprivation of worldhood. The cognition of entities "as Nature . . . has the character of depriving the world of its worldhood."[95] Yet, the world and its worldhood can only be discovered or "lit up" if some measure of such deprivation takes place. When the world is lit up presence-at-hand automatically comes to the fore.

The "involvement-character" of the ready-to-hand includes complex references to a totality of equipment. There is, however, always an "ultimate" referent. Heidegger writes:

> But the totality of involvements itself goes back ultimately to a
> "towards-which" in which there is *no* further involvement: this
> "towards-which" . . . is Being-in-the-world . . . .[96]

The ultimate "towards-which" and "for-the-sake-of-which" of all ready-to-hand equipment is Dasein.

The discovery of an entity as ready-to-hand implicitly presumes a disclosure of Dasein itself and of Dasein's Being, since Dasein is the ultimate for-the-sake-of-which of the ready-to-hand.[97] A disclosive understanding of Dasein necessarily implies an understanding of the world, since Dasein, as Being-in-the-world, "always" comports itself towards the world.[98] Dasein thus has its own "towards-which" and "in order to," which partially constitute its world. All of Dasein's "letting" something be involved or encountered as ready-to-hand ". . . is grounded in . . . [Dasein's] understanding such things as letting something be involved, and such things as the 'with-which' and the 'in-which' of involvements."[99] The world, for Heidegger, is *both* that which Dasein understands as the environment towards which it comports or assigns itself, *and* that for which Dasein directs its own letting entities be encountered as ready-to-hand.

> *That wherein* Dasein understands itself beforehand in the mode of
> assigning itself is *that for which* it has let entities be encountered
> beforehand. *The "wherein" of an act of understanding which assigns
> or refers itself, is that for which one lets entities be encountered in the
> kind of Being that belongs to involvements; and this "wherein" is the
> phenomenon of the world. And the structure of that to which Dasein
> assigns itself is what makes up the worldhood of the world.*[100]

The world is that horizon of Dasein's self-understanding which lets entities be encountered as involved, significant, and ready-to-hand. The structure of this horizon is constituted by "significance" itself, that is, by "the relational totality of this signifying" of entities.[101]

In order to answer the question of the existential integrity of the world, entities, and what is not-Dasein in general in *Being and Time*, two different cases must be considered. The first is the case of what is *not* "intraworldly," of those entities which are not within *Dasein's* world (if such can be said to exist at all).[102] The second is the case of the world and all intraworldly entities.

Regarding the first case, in the works under consideration Heidegger is unclear as to whether anything non-worldly exists at all. He wavers between saying that nothing is outside Dasein's world and saying that the question cannot be answered.

In *Being and Time,* section 43, Heidegger writes:

> Of course only as long as Dasein *is* 'is there' Being. When Dasein does not exist, 'independence' 'is' not either, nor 'is' the 'in-itself' . . . . *In such a case* [as the non-existence of *Dasein*] it cannot be said that entities are, nor can it be said that they are not.[103]

In *Basic Problems of Phenomenology,* however, Heidegger asserts that Nature

> is, even if we do not uncover it, without our encountering it within our world . . . . World is only, if, and as long as a *Dasein* exists. Nature can also be when no *Dasein* exists.[104]

As this last passage indicates, intraworldliness implies uncoveredness. What is within the world is uncovered by *Dasein,* disclosed in *Dasein.* The question of the ontological status of the non-worldly, the entirely uncovered, is thoroughly unclear. It is unclear in part because the status of non-worldly Being, beings, and Nature need not be the same. Thus, while in the first passage above Heidegger feels that it is obvious that Being is not if Dasein is not ("Of course . . ."), it is not at all certain that entities are not in this circumstance. In the second passage, Heidegger tells us that Nature can be if *Dasein* is not. But does this mean Nature *would* be? The question is left unanswered.

That Heidegger fails to answer this question unambiguously is not evidence of subjectivism. It is not subjectivist to say that we are unable to decide the ontological status of a reality that lacks human beings. The point is that even if entirely undisclosed entities did exist in the Heideggerian system they would resemble the Kantian things-in-themselves of the first *Critique* insofar as they could not have any knowable or experienceable relation to that which is disclosed within the world. For Heidegger there can be no internal or intrinsic relation between the disclosing/disclosed and the undisclosed, between the "clearing" of Dasein and Nature which, if it is at all, stands outside of possible disclosure. On this point Heidegger is in complete harmony with earlier subjectivism. Insofar as Heidegger does admit the existence of undisclosed natural entities, such entities would have a purely abstract, theoretical existence—a most un-Heideggerian existence.

Furthermore, Heidegger's own methodological prescriptions would seem to exclude the possibility of the Being of that which is not disclosed in any way, since there is "nothing else" behind or beyond "that which shows itself in itself." As a phenomenologist Heidegger cannot claim that a thing which does not show itself in any sense has Being. Consequently, the non-worldly, in being not-uncovered cannot be said to have Being.

There is a possible mode of Being which lies half-way between the two cases mentioned, that is, between the nonworldly and the worldly. Heidegger mentions in *Basic Problems of Phenomenology* that Nature as "extant" (*Vorhandensein*) is not intraworldly "in its Being" but can *become* intraworldly.[105] Nature's Being is characterized by the *possibility* of intraworldliness. What is most significant in this passage, however, is that it is here that Heidegger makes the statement, previously quoted, that the "ontological difference between" Dasein and Nature, or between *Existenz* and *Vorhandensein,* is "more disparate than . . . the determinations of God's being and man's being in traditional ontology."[106]

Now, the status of that which is non-worldly, either accidentally or intrinsically, remains unclear in Heidegger. But the preceding statement makes one fact very clear: that mode of Being which is not intrinsically intraworldly (extantness or *Vorhandensein*) is absolutely distinct from *Existenz,* the Being of Dasein. Heidegger makes explicit a fundamental assumption of *Being and Time,* namely, an absolutely rigid ontological dualism. Heidegger's diremption of extantness and existence is quite literally more dichotomous than the dualism of *res extensa* and *res cogitans* in Descartes, for the latter are both substances and both finite in contrast to the infinite substance of God. Heidegger makes the extraordinary statement that the disparity of extant and existent is more extreme than the disparity of God and man, the infinite and the finite!

This Heideggerian dualism makes highly unlikely any possibility of an interactive relationship between Dasein and entities whose mode of Being is not intrinsically intraworldly. To argue otherwise one would have to overcome the kind of objections levelled at the Cartesian dualism, for example, that ontologically antithetical substances could not conceivably interact. In Heidegger's case the antithesis is greater, so such objections would seem to apply with even greater strength. Consequently, whatever can be said about what is not intrinsically intraworldly (whether or not it has Being or exists at all) such entities cannot interact with, relate to, or have an effect on Dasein in Dasein's Being. Heidegger's "opening up" Dasein, his throwing Dasein into disclosive-submission to entities, does *not* apply to that which is not intrinsically intraworldly. The latter remains truly 'outside' of Dasein's Being and Dasein's world, not unlike the "thing-in-itself" and the "formal reality" of earlier forms of subjectivism.

The real burden of the question of existential integrity devolves upon the second case mentioned above, the case of the world and intraworldly entities.

Regarding the world itself it is incontrovertible that the world does not have existential integrity or independent 'own-being' for Heidegger. Heidegger's world literally *is* Dasein, that is, is an element of Being-in-the-world's existence. It is a "project" of Dasein, a horizon for Dasein's self-understanding, the "wherein of an act of understanding." The worldhood of the world is "significance," and significance is founded on Dasein's projection for understanding. For Heidegger the world completely belongs to Dasein and, in particular, belongs to Dasein's self-understanding. This is quite consistent with what we have learned thusfar. For, if what is is the manifest and Dasein is the location of all disclosure and the intraworldly is uncovered, then the world is the boundary of the disclosure of what-shows-itself, that is, the world is the boundary of Dasein. If Dasein is the stage on which Being and beings show themselves, then the world is Dasein's proscenium. The world *is* Dasein in a paradoxical sense; that is, it is indistinguishable from Dasein.

There is a second sense in which the world is denied any existential integrity by Heidegger. In Division Two, he reinterprets the phenomenon of the world as a manifestation of the temporalizing of temporality. To each of the ecstases of temporality there belongs a "whither," a "horizonal schema." These horizonal schemata are unified by the ecstatical unity of temporality, thereby determining the "whereupon" Dasein is disclosed.[107]

> This implies that on the basis of the horizonal constitution of the ecstatical unity of temporality, there belongs to that entity which is in each case its own "there," something like a world . . . .[108]

World, like Dasein, is constituted by that which *least* resembles something with independent integrity; that is, it is constituted by the "primordial outside-of-itself," temporality.

Whether intraworldly entities also lack existential integrity in Heidegger is a more complex question and the answer is less clear. It is less clear because Heidegger, in both *Being and Time* and *Basic Problems of Phenomenology,* fails to fully explicate the nature of extant entities and their relation to the ready-to-hand.

Ready-to-hand entities are clearly dependent in their very Being upon worldhood; it is the deprivation of worldhood which makes them un-ready-to-hand and causes their presence-at-hand to emerge. It is precisely from the phenomenon of the ready-to-hand that Heidegger derives the concept of world, through the referential and signifying character of ready-to-hand entities. It is the encounter with the ready-to-hand which is clearly, for Heidegger, the most primordial mode of Dasein's essential relatedness to entities. In addition, the purely ready-to-hand, in holding itself in, is "Being-in-itself." Heidegger clearly wishes to give that mode of the Being of entities which is most dependent upon or constituted by worldhood a priority over entities with other modes of Being.

Heidegger's account of the specific character of present-at-hand entities leaves it less clear as to the specific manner in which and extent to which their Being is dependent upon the world. On the one hand, in *Basic Problems of Phenomenology* presence-at-hand is clearly defined as the mode of Being which is not intrinsically worldly; on the other hand, Heidegger firmly roots all uncovered entities, *zuhanden* or *vorhanden*, in the phenomenon of the world. Heidegger does not reconcile the fact that present-at-hand entities have been deprived of worldhood to some unknown degree or in some way, with the fact that they remain intraworldly, nor does he explain the relationship of readiness-to-hand, presence-at-hand, and worldhood in a satisfactory way. *Vorhandensein,* while *not* intrinsically worldly, comes to be constituted by the world when within the world. While Heidegger fails to explain the details of this situation, he is clear in regard to the general relation of intraworldly entities and the world. He asserts in *Being and Time* that:

> *all* the modes of Being of entities within-the-world are founded
> ontologically upon the worldhood of the world . . . .[109]

For the present-at-hand as well as the ready-to-hand, the world is constitutive. Heidegger says:

> *The world is already presupposed* in one's Being alongside the
> ready-to-hand . . . in one's thematizing of the present-at-hand, and in
> one's discovering of this latter entity by Objectification . . . .[110]

In *Being and Time* Heidegger allows the term 'Reality' to be taken in two different ways: as intraworldly entities in general, or as purely present-at-hand things. Reality always refers to the present-at-hand, but it may refer to the ready-to-hand as well. Having defined reality in this way, Heidegger goes on to tell us that ". . . Reality is ontologically grounded in the Being of Dasein . . . Reality is dependent upon Care."[111] Whatever the ambiguities concerning the status of the present-at-hand, the Being of the present-at-hand entities within the world is, no less than the Being of ready-to-hand entities, clearly founded in and dependent upon Dasein's projected world.

Heidegger's account of the world and its entities is both subjectivistic and philosophically narcissistic.

It is subjectivistic because it adopts as the fundamental distinction for its inquiry the distinction between what is included within (or within the horizon of) the agent or arena of disclosure and what is not so included. Given this dichotomous categorization, Being is equated with what shows itself (phenomena), with what is included within disclosure. Of what is not uncovered nothing can be said. This scheme divides the totality of evidence, or of what is, into three classes: the undisclosed, the disclosed, and the disclosing. Dasein is disclosing and disclosed; entities are only disclosed.

Heidegger's view is narcissistic because, while retaining this tripartite distinction, he acknowledges that neither the disclosing nor the disclosed can be conceived without the other. Thus, the disclosing and the disclosed merge: the integrity of each is lost and each can only be defined as the other. The world becomes asymptotically, paradoxically equivalent to Dasein. All that Dasein encounters, all that Dasein knows, all that is manifest for Dasein is constituted by a project of Dasein. The Heideggerian world, and the entities within it, have no independent integrity; Dasein's Being casts them forth as the horizon for its understanding. Heidegger makes the narcissism of this position complete by recognizing that this understanding whose horizon is the world is actually a "self-understanding." The wherein of Dasein's self-understanding and that for which Dasein lets entities be encountered are the same: they are the world. Dasein lets entities be encountered as involved with itself within the horizon of its own self-understanding. The world constitutes Dasein's self-understanding. The picture is quasi-theological: Dasein, whose Being is as different from the extant as God from man, comes to understand itself through a world of its own projection, as if the purpose of worldly Being were the self-understanding of the Creator achieved through God's creative positing of a 'not-me', opposed to His Divine Being.

What differentiates Heidegger's view from that of Plotinian theology (and also differentiates philosophical narcissism from metaphysical idealism) is indicated by a passage in *Basic Problems of Phenomenology* in which Heidegger aims to refute any charges of "subjectivism" and idealism that may be leveled against his concept of world.

Heidegger has at this point[112] announced that the world is:

> a determination of Being-in-the-world, a moment in the structure of the Dasein's mode of being. The world is, so to speak Dasein-ish.[113]

Heidegger admits that this may appear to make the world something "subjective," generating a "most extreme subjective idealism." He sets out to defend his view against this appearance.

The core of his defense is as follows. For the world to be subjective presumes that it belongs to a "subjectivity" which " 'projects [it] outward', as it were, from within itself,"[114] from within an 'inner' sphere. Yet, Dasein is nothing like such a subjectivity: "Instead *Dasein* itself is as such already projected."[115] Heidegger argues:

In this projection [of a world] the Dasein has always already *stepped out beyond itself,* ex-sistere, it *is in* a world. Consequently, it is never anything like a subjective inner sphere.[116]

Heidegger's defense is entirely inadequate to refute the present critique, since the definition of subjectivism employed in the present study does not hinge on the concept of an "inner," insular sphere at the core of subjectivity. Heidegger defends himself against a narrow, egological subjectivism, but egology is not the *sine qua non* of subjectivism. Heidegger does not even attempt to show that the world has not been absorbed by or reduced to Dasein; he merely asserts that Dasein is no originary egopole, but is likewise projected. It is ironic that Heidegger thereby emphasizes precisely the philosophical narcissism of his view. The fact that Dasein itself is projected does not make his analysis of the world any less subjectivistic or narcissistic; it merely announces that Dasein is as lacking in existential integrity as is the world, that there is *no* independent existential integrity in the Heideggerian system. His defense does not disprove his subjectivism; rather, it emphasizes the radical nature of his subjectivism. It exhibits Heidegger's radicalization of subjectivism into philosophical narcissism.

Heidegger does not reduce the world to a projection of an adamantine subject; he reduces the world to a subject which itself has already been reduced to that which is disclosed in it. Heidegger's defense against subjectivism illustrates the antinomy of philosophical narcissism, the oscillatory definition of world in terms of subject and of subject in terms of world. It also illustrates the historical and logical origination of philosophical narcissism, which generally develops through the critique of classical subjectivism (for example, idealism). In seeking to avoid the latter, Heidegger develops a narcissistic alternative.

Conclusion

Martin Heidegger is an influential thinker, and for good reason. Many of his central notions are provocative and valuable even when considered independently of the overall project and context in which he locates them. Heidegger's analysis of the meaning of death, mood and "the they" are highly suggestive for our understanding of human being. His idea of disclosive-submission, that disclosure occurs only in submissive, vulnerable involvement in the world, is right, and is an admirable correction to much of the Western tradition. His attempt to bring the concept of the world to the center of philosophical attention is insightful and opportune. And his use of the primordial outside-of-itself, ecstatic Temporality, is tantamount to a much needed recognition that our fundamental conception of things needs radical revision, that a thing is somehow more that what it is, that it is the nature of things to be "outside" of themselves (I would say, things are internally related to other entities.)

But Heidegger elaborates these fascinating ideas within the context of a theory that conceals deep conceptual schisms. While Heidegger wants his interpretation of Dasein as Being-in-the-world to counteract the dichotomy of subject and object that has been the hallmark of so much of modern philosophy, he accepts this dichotomy at another level by asserting the absolute distinction of the Being of the being who understands, and the Being of all other entities. The former's Being is initially interpreted as disclosedness. Whatever is not intrinsically related to Dasein, what does not intrinsically share in Dasein's Being, is absolutely distinct from Dasein's Being and can have no conceivable relationship to Dasein within the bounds of phenomenology.

That which shows itself in and to Dasein (the phenomena) constitutes both the totality of evidences available for inquiry and all of Being. There is nothing else. That which is not manifest does not exist, or cannot be said to exist, or can have no relation to Dasein's existence. This generates three categories: the undisclosed, the disclosed, the disclosing. The undisclosed may not exist, and even if it does, it cannot be related to the latter two categories. Dasein is that which is both disclosed and disclosing. All else is disclosed. This tripartite categorization is definitive of subjectivism. It is common to Descartes, Kant, and Husserl, albeit without the egological connotations of the terms 'noesis–noema–natural world' or 'subject–phenomena–noumena'.

But here a paradoxical situation develops within the subjectivism of Husserl and Heidegger. Disclosing-*Sein* (Dasein) is distinct from both the merely disclosed and the undisclosed, yet all of whatever *is* can only be if it is disclosed in disclosing-*Sein*. Dasein is distinct from other existences, yet Dasein is the condition for all possible existence. The undisclosed is out-of-bounds (bracketed, reduced) and the disclosed is ontologically rooted in the disclosing (Dasein). What is paradoxical is that the distinction between the disclosed, disclosing, and undisclosed is affirmed and yet simultaneously undermined by the elimination of the undisclosed and the dependence of the disclosed on the disclosing. It is this simultaneous affirming and undermining of subjectivist categories that is characteristic of philosophical narcissism and of both Husserl's and Heidegger's conceptual schemes. Their approaches diverge in that Husserl describes the disclosing as an active process carried out be an entity with what appears to be unquestionable existential integrity—a transcendental ego—whereas Heidegger describes disclosing as a function of the disclosed, in relation to which that-which-discloses is a clearing that is delivered over to the disclosed. Husserl and Heidegger initially reduce either the disclosed or the disclosing to the other; Husserl reduces the former to the latter, Heidegger the latter to the former. In this reduction, one of the factors—the disclosed or the disclosing—loses its existential integrity and is declared to be a function of or set of relations to the other factor.

But, as the dialectic of philosophical narcissism dictates, the single reduction leads to a two-way reduction. For Husserl, not only is the world (that is, the other) reduced to the ego, but the ego becomes simply a name for the appearing of the world (that is, the other), or a set of intentions directed toward the world. For Heidegger, the reduction of Dasein to a locus for the disclosure of entities and others leads to a conception of entities and others as constituted by this locus for disclosure.

In both Husserl and Heidegger, the possibility of the existential integrity of a thing has been eliminated, and split into two parts: fluctuating content (or phenomena), and the abstract, contentless form of the thing. For Heidegger, Dasein and worldly entities are constituted by two antithetical factors: the formless content of "that-which-shows-itself" to pure "seeing," and the contentless outside-of-itself of temporality. The phenomena are said to constitute Being; behind them there is "nothing else." Yet these constituents of Being only 'are' by virtue of Dasein, the subject. Then, does Dasein show itself? No, it does not.

Heidegger has not escaped from the Humean dilemma of the phenomenal self: that self which is claimed to be the condition for the possibility of all that can be said to be, *never shows itself,* and therefore cannot be claimed to be. In *Being and Time* Dasein discloses only its own entities and others, or it discloses only its own disclosedness and its temporal 'outside-of-itself-ness'. We only know what shows itself, but the condition for the possibility of anything showing itself—Dasein, the subject—never shows itself. How, then, can we claim that Dasein or subjectivity exists? The assertion of the subject as the ground of Being is no less speculative than the assertion of God as the ground of Being.

This is the ultimate paradox of the subjectivist position, which becomes explicit only in the radical subjectivism of philosophical narcissism. What is claimed to exist must appear to a subject, yet the subject never appears. The subject, within the bounds of subjectivist doctrine, is the ultimate ground, yet it must be either identical to what appears, or literally nothing. But if this ground is nothing, then what of the world which appears only by virtue of this non-existent ground? The narcissistic categories set up a dialectical oscillation between the asymptotes of Being and Non-Being; whatever appears, whatever can be spoken of, can with equal legitimacy be claimed to be something and nothing.

PART TWO

The Theory
of Modernity

Introduction to Part Two

Philosophy is a part of culture, a dimension of cultural activity. Philosophy makes explicit the patterns of interpretation implicit in the cultural life of society and interprets, criticizes, promotes, and inhibits them. Philosophy is both a barometer of social change and an instrument of such change. The writings of philosophers "trickle down" (or "up" depending on one's point of view) into culture, often through scientific, literary, religious, and political circles, to affect the ideas which are already being formulated at other levels of society—reinforcing them, opposing them, or skewing them in various directions. At the same time, historical and social events and the ideas suggested by them set—or at least influence—the agenda for philosophers. The degree of directness of this mutual influence, of the tightness of the philosophy–culture relationship, varies with the kind of philosophy being done and the force of the social movements in question. There is a rolling, sliding scale of degree of involvement; some philosophers being less affected by social events—especially the more narrowly focused and technical—and others being more affected. Sometimes the social tidal waves are powerful enough to wash into virtually every philosopher's study, while at other times they merely lap against the doors of the few philosophers who live in the vicinity; for example, political philosophers in the case of a political event, philosophers of science in the case of a new scientific theory. In general, the culture of a society is the context for its philosophy.

The dynamics of philosophical subjectivism and narcissism as analyzed in Part One illustrate the strong involvement of philosophy in culture. The reason that philosophical subjectivism has been so influential since the seventeenth century is that it expressed, gave explicit form to, and thereby encouraged, what was a general cultural and social movement. Philosophical subjectivism was the explicitly conceptual, philosophical form given to a general interpretive perspective that was evolving in the educated culture of the time, in response to and in an

177

attempt to influence historical and social events. Eventually this perspective became sufficiently widespread that it became official social doctrine.

This evolving cultural perspective was the conviction that the individual human subject, the individual conceived as a thinking, perceiving, valuing mind, is the ultimate locus of all judgments of truth, value, and political authority. This perspective was implicit in the methodology of the new seventeenth-century science, which rejected scriptural authority in favor of the conceptually analyzed perceptions of individual researchers. It was implicit in the economic individualism of the gradually growing capitalist class. It was a component of the Protestantism prevalent in most of the modernized areas of Europe, in the distinction between the individual's inner faith and the outer forms of worship and ritual. Most of all, it formed the explicit basis of liberal republican ideology and thus of the political and social reforms that eventually came to define much of modern Western life.

Philosophers were important participants in pre–twentieth-century cultural movements, partly because the field of philosophy was defined differently in the seventeenth and eighteenth centuries than it is today. For example, in the late seventeenth century Isaac Newton could entitle his classic work in physics *Mathematical Principles of Natural Philosophy*. The great seventeenth-century philosophers, like Descartes, were scientists as well as philosophers. In the field of politics, the modern conception of democracy was forged in the philosophic furnaces of Locke, Rousseau, and others. It was not until later that physical inquiry and eventually, in the second half of the nineteenth century, psychological and social inquiry split off from philosophy, thereby narrowing the effective scope of philosophy and its role within society.

For these and other reasons, the theory developed in Part One to explain the dominant theme of philosophical modernity can illuminate the development of modern culture in general. Certain trends in modern culture described by Theodor Adorno, Max Horkheimer, Richard Sennett, Christopher Lasch, and others can be better understood through the model gained from the analysis of modern philosophy. My argument concerning modernity, while based on theirs, reinterprets the dialectic they see in modernity through the idea of the dynamics of subjectivism. I will argue that cultural modernity reveals a dominant strain of interpretation in which an early phase characterized by a subjectivist interpretive scheme synthesized by transcendental ideas develops into a later phase in which the transcendental elements have been de-legitimated and the increasingly hegemonistic subjectivist categories undergo a narcissistic transformation.

A philosophy does not simply and straightforwardly represent its culture. Any culture is too diverse for that. Further, all cultural elements are in a process of interaction, such that the tension or conflict between several cultural themes may reveal the most characteristic feature of a culture, rather than any of those themes taken in isolation. The elephant's tail does not straightforwardly represent the entire beast, but it does say something about the elephant as a whole, especially when its relations to other parts of the animal are taken into account. The dynamics of subjectivism, when seen in historical and intellectual context, can tell us much about the development of cultural modernity as a whole, but it cannot tell us everything. It is a hypothesis for understanding important features of modernity that have been neglected or misunderstood.

Chapters 7 and 8 develop this hypothesis by applying the theory of philosophical modernity of Part One to culture in general. Chapter 7 lays the groundwork by discussing and criticizing the dialectical theory of modernity. Chapter 8 then shows that the work of Part One can be used to change the dialectical theory, and proposes an original view, the *cultural theory* of modernity. This theory introduces a new viewpoint and a new concept into the analysis of modernity. The radicalized subjectivism of late modern culture, the "mass culture" of Adorno and Horkheimer, the "narcissistic culture" of Christopher Lasch, the "intimate society" of Richard Sennett, are characterized by a change in the interpretation of culture itself, by the prevalence of an *anti-culture*. An anti-culture is a cultural strain which interprets culture itself as possessing no inherent meaning or value. By introducing this concept and by focusing attention on this reflexivity of culture, the analysis of subjectivism and narcissism are reinterpreted in terms of their implicit interpretations of culture.

Important strains within the modern tradition have undermined themselves by bursting and de-legitimating the context within which they had functioned. In early modernity, the cultural interpretation of human communication, public discourse, and the cultural appropriation of non-human things served as the thread which wove otherwise separate subjectivities into a meaningful public realm. The view that these cultural processes are intrinsically valuable and meaningful provided the context by which subjectivity and objectivity could be conceived as related instead of disparate. But the subjectivist categories proved too strong; to be applied and utilized to the fullest, they had to burst that context. The often unnoticed result is that the loss of context and mediation changed the meaning of the categories themselves.

Modernity, late modernity included, has its glorious and sublime features as well as its devitalizing and ignoble ones; there is no intent to provide a blanket condemnation of modernity. The most influential theories of modernity, even those nuanced enough to see that there is both good and bad in their subject, consistently fail to recognize one of the most insidious tendencies of late modern culture. This is because such theories share that tendency, the tendency to de-value and reduce cultural artifacts and processes to the status of epiphenomena, of window-dressing for other, non-cultural processes, for example, the economic, the political and the psychological. Of all the multifarious critics of late modern culture who lambast the contemporary world from the left and from the right—as being unfree or too free, too monolithic or too pluralistic, too violent or not violent enough—few have recognized the underlying current running beneath our society's complex ambiguities as a continuing erosion of the felt value of communicative, shareable, cultural production and interpretation, and the profound effect of this erosion on intellectual, economic, political, and personal life.

7

Enlightenment and Narcissism: Adorno, Horkheimer, and Lasch

Nearly everyone admits that modernity in the broad sense—the related economic, social, scientific, political, and cultural programs of the Western world since the Renaissance—has had its costs as well as its benefits. As Freud remarked in his *Civilization and its Discontents,* modernity has given us the telephone with which I can now call up my son who has moved far from home, but modernity also gave us the train, which is what took him far from home in the first place. Beyond this homely example, even the staunchest supporters of modernity recognize that there are bitter pills to be swallowed along with the freedom and high standards of living that modernity has generally brought.

The dialectical theory does not merely assert that modernity has costs, that the achievements of modernity (for example, mobility) often cause undesired outcomes in a related facet of life (a lessened sense of family and community) so that modernity involves a trade-off of one value against another. The dialectical theory makes a much stronger claim. It asserts that the very achievements of modernity undermine and negate *themselves;* that the attempt to rationalize life ends in greater irrationality, that the goal of personal freedom ends in collective compulsion, etc. Modernity is not a trade-off of one goal or value for another; it is a paradoxical process in which that very goal or value which seems to be achieved, in the moment of its apparent achievement, is undermined, transformed into a hollow parody of itself.

This is a powerful claim. It is also an insightful one. There do seem to be certain modern tendencies and projects that exhibit self-negating aspects. The questions are how much of modernity and what features of modernity are self-negating, and why?

The Dialectical Theory

The critical theorists Theodor Adorno and Max Horkheimer developed their comprehensive dialectical theory of modern Western civilization in the 1940s during their stay in America. The chief presentations of the theory are their collaborative *Dialectic of Enlightenment* and Horkheimer's *Eclipse of Reason.*[1]

The *Dialectic of Enlightenment* attempts to explain how, at the height of the development of democratic European culture, the most barbarous and primitively destructive of social movements, fascism, could become dominant. In more personal terms, how could much of Europe, having attained freedom, willingly relinquish it? The authors' answer is that the spirit and principles embodied in the institutions of modern Western civilization, the "spirit of Enlightenment," which is responsible for the social, intellectual, and material progress of the West, has always had within it the seeds of a regression to primitive, unenlightened forms. There is a "dialectic" of enlightenment by which the Enlightenment reverses itself through following out its own logical implications and turns into a new barbarism.

Adorno and Horkheimer define the concept of enlightenment in various ways, but these coalesce around a single idea: enlightenment is the progressive liberation of the human self from a series of impositions and restrictions which come under the headings of "myth" and "nature." Myth is the submergence of self-consciousness and reason in what is natural or necessary. At each step in enlightenment the self asserts itself as independent of forces and conditions that were previously considered natural, inevitable, fateful, divinely imposed—all understood as forms of necessity. This independence is predicated upon and produces mastery over nature, over others, or over one's own emotional and bodily nature. Adorno and Horkheimer assert that freedom from natural forces is inseparable from mastery and control of those forces. They trace the history of this gradual process of enlightenment far beyond the modern period to the beginnings of Western culture, in fact, to Homer's *Odyssey.* However, the process of enlightenment enters into its final and most self-conscious phase in the eighteenth century, the "official" Enlightenment.

In *Dialectic of Enlightenment,* Adorno and Horkheimer argue that the project of enlightenment is implicitly paradoxical, and that at the height of its development, which has become more and more evident in various regions of European culture since the mid-nineteenth century, this paradox becomes explicit and manifest.

The problematic nature of enlightenment had already been examined by Hegel. Enlightenment for Adorno and Horkheimer, as for Hegel, is a process of the negation of necessity. Hegel's dialectic of the lord and the slave is a model for Adorno and Horkheimer's notion of how enlightenment proceeds, and of its costs. For Hegel, the master, in attaining mastery over the slave, suffers an alienation from his own existence in the name of attaining a higher, although abstract, freedom. For Adorno and Horkheimer, this alienation is intensified in that every civilized person must have the same relation to his or her own natural impulses that Hegel's lord has to the bondsman. Mastery over external nature and the organization of social and sexual life in civilized society requires progressively greater instinctual renunciations, as Freud had argued in *Civilization and Its Discontents.*[2] The freedom of the self from want, from fear of the violence of others, from various forms of authority, are all purchased through the denial of parts of the self: ". . . self-assertion—as in all epics [i.e., the *Odyssey*], as in civilization as a whole—is self-denial."[3]

Enlightenment reverses itself when the rational self succeeds in negating *all* natural necessity, all givens including the givens that had constituted its own nature *as a rational self,* for example, natural reason, *res cogitans,* the very concept of self or ego. The project of negation succeeds in negating everything except the project of negation itself. The progressive negation of necessity eventually negates all that served to justify the substantiality or reality of the self. The result is an emptied self or emptied subject, a self or subject with no necessary, given, natural content or form. Adorno and Horkheimer write:

> world domination over nature turns against the thinking subject himself; nothing is left of him but that eternally same *I think* that must accompany all my ideas. Subject and object are both rendered ineffectual. The abstract self, which justifies record-making and systematization, has nothing set over against it but the abstract material which possess no other quality than to be a substrate of such possession.[4]

The project of negation, which had previously succeeded in negating or demystifying the mythic power of fate, natural forces, the divine right of kings, the sanctity of a hierarchic social order, belief in God and religious values, now succeeds in negating the notions of natural reason, metaphysics, a universal moral conscience, a fixed transpersonal reality and human nature. All values and beliefs are negated as myths.

> Every substantial goal which men might adduce as an alleged rational insight is, in the strict Enlightenment sense, delusion, lies or 'rationalization' . . . .[5]

More and more, reality is regarded as void of inherent meaning, as a mere manipulable substrate for human control, while the human self, lacking a given and universal nature and any intrinsic ends or values, must be seen to be a mere consciousness engaged in rational manipulation of the material substrate. The result is a paradoxical resubmergence of the self in natural necessity, or an "equation of spirit and world," because the enlightened self has denied itself, has negated as illusory, any projects or hopes other than the knowledge and manipulation of the given. This is the reversal, the dialectic, of enlightenment:

> What appears to be the triumph of subjective rationality, the subjection of all reality to logical formalism, is paid for by the obedient subjection of reason to what is directly given.[6]

The Enlightenment reverses itself when, in accordance with its initial program, it rejects, as mythical obstacles to freedom, the values and beliefs which had constituted the positive support for its freedom. Adorno and Horkheimer argue that this reversal, which finds its most virulent and active demonstration in fascism, is also seen in an intellectual form in positivism, and in various institutions of mass culture. The banishing of all metaphysics and all questions of value from the domain of rational thought, to use the example of positivism, has two results: the unquestioning worship of the only remaining content, namely, the "facts," the "given"; and, the relegation of those questions which are not reducible to fact-questions to the domain of the non-rational, so that they can only be addressed at a non-rational and non-discursive level.

The chapter of *Dialectic of Enlightenment* entitled "The Culture Industry: Enlightenment as Mass Deception" can be seen as a neo-Marxist prelude to the more recent social critiques which employ the concept of narcissism. The major themes of Adorno and Horkheimer's work can be seen in the contemporary writings of Philip Rieff, Russell Jacoby, Christopher Lasch, and Richard Sennett. For example, in *The Culture of Narcissism* and its sequel, *The Minimal Self*, Lasch works out in historical detail the self-negation of early American, bourgeois culture and the arising of a late-modern culture of narcissism. Sennett's *Fall of Public Man* presents the historical stages through which the public culture of the *ancien regime* was transformed into the present day "intimate society" in which public, impersonal life is regarded with indifference at best, and meaning and value are increasingly withdrawn into the realm of privacy. The themes common to these theorists are, first, the self-negation of liberal, enlightened, bourgeois culture; and, second, their turning to the psychological theory of secondary narcissism for concepts that can bring order to the ambiguities and seeming paradoxes of late-modern, twentieth-century culture.

The following discussion will focus on what is perhaps the most controversial and widely criticized of the works employing this view, Lasch's *Culture of Narcissism.*[7] Commentators have failed to come to terms with the most important and interesting features of Lasch's work, preferring to reject Lasch's thesis wholesale on the basis of its least defensible passages. This skewed criticism fails to see that the two central notions of Lasch's book, the reversal of bourgeois principles and the social application of the concept of narcissism, had both been proposed earlier by Adorno himself. It also reflects a failure to face the real challenge in Lasch's book, a challenge which, as in *Dialectic of Enlightenment,* cannot be amalgamated to the stereotypical political categories of 'right' and 'left'.

Lasch attempts to show how narcissistic traits (feelings of unreality and emptiness, increased repressed hostility, sexualization of nonsexual activity, oscillation of self-esteem, emotional shallowness, and manipulation of personal image and personal relations) have progressively come to be embodied on a grand scale in many spheres of American life. He argues that this is a result of political and economic changes, namely, the development of monopolistic capitalism, the shift from a production- to a consumption-oriented, service economy, and the growth of the ideology of welfare liberalism. The cumulative effect of these trends has been the transformation of one kind of social control into another. The earlier bourgeois culture, with its "old paternalism," is giving way to the "new paternalism" of narcissistic culture:

> which has risen from the ruins of the old paternalism of kings, priests, authoritarian fathers, slavemasters and landed overlords. Capitalism has severed the ties of personal dependence only to revive dependency under cover of bureaucratic rationality . . . . It has evolved new modes of social control, which deal with the deviant as a patient and substitute medical rehabilitation for punishment. It has given rise to a new culture, the narcissistic culture of our time . . . .[8]

The development of cultural narcissism signifies not an excessive individualism or decadent hedonism, but rather a new and more insidious domination of the individual. In the culture of narcissism both community *and* private life are transformed into superficial self-parodies. Lasch's book, like the work of Sennett, is not a communitarian critique of decadent late-modern individuals. Cultural narcissism signifies not only the erosion of community standards, of the recognition of the inherent value and meaning of public life, and of morality and a sense of realism, but also the erosion of the integrity of the individual. Lasch claims that in an era characterized by the mass advertising of consumption-oriented capitalism, the intrusion of bureaucratic rationality into personal life under welfare liberalism, and the perceived necessity for daily performance and the diligent management of personal image resulting from the definition of success as celebrity, capitalist thinking has invaded private life to an unprecedented degree. In late capitalism, every aspect of life has been absorbed into the market. Lasch writes that:

> privatism no longer provides a haven from a heartless world. On the
> contrary, private life takes on the very qualities of the anarchic social
> order from which it is supposed to provide a refuge. It is the
> devastation of personal life, not the retreat into privatism, that needs
> to be criticized and condemned.[9]

The dialectical view of modernity thematized in *Dialectic of Enlightenment* is the most striking feature of Lasch's critique of American society in the 1970s. For Lasch, the liberal impulses characteristic of bourgeois, capitalist America in the late eighteenth and nineteenth centuries, precisely in their twentieth-century success, have led to their own negation. He writes:

> The bourgeois defense of privacy culminates . . . in the most
> thoroughgoing attack on privacy; the glorification of the individual in
> his annihilation.[10]

As democratic society progressively subjected itself more and more thoroughly to the ideals of "revolutionary individualism," as it cleared away what were perceived as barriers to the autonomy of the individual, it also de-legitimated all value-commitments and all beliefs that could serve as the *content* of the individual. All reality external to the individual subject came to be seen as inherently value-neutral, as manipulable commodities, as subject to the criticism and control of the individual; thus, there was little left for the individual to value. If all non-material commitments have been eliminated as mystifications, the individual is left in thrall to a material world which, at a deeper level, it does not value. The subject, in turn, becomes a mere knower-manipulator of this world, having no other source of interest, concern, value, or belief.

In this context, Lasch remarks that the development of a narcissistic culture signifies not the ascendency of imagination, playfulness, and fantasy over the "reality principle," but, on the contrary, an inability to take imagination, play and even representation seriously. Lasch suggests, for example, that the radical effacement of artistic conventions or even of the concept of art itself as distinct from non-artistic reality evident in some quarters reveals not a greater imaginative and creative freedom but rather an unwillingness or inability imaginatively to place oneself within the artificial universe of the art work and to take the internal laws, the truths or point of view embodied in that work seriously. Most importantly, this inability to take illusion seriously, disrupts the ability to encounter reality. Lasch very perceptively writes that:

> The illusion of reality dissolves, not in a heightened sense of reality as we might expect, but in a remarkable indifference to reality. Our sense of reality appears to rest, curiously enough, on our willingness to be taken in by the staged illusion of reality . . . a complete indifference even to the mechanics of illusion announces the collapse of the very idea of reality, dependent at every point on the distinction between nature and artifice, reality and illusion.[11]

Lasch is correct, except that, as we will see, what he refers to here with the term "illusion" is in fact "culture." Our selves and the reality we encounter, although not the product of culture, are only meaningfully, which is to say humanly, experienced and elaborated within culture, within the totality of shareable meanings embodied in human creations. This inability to "get outside" of culture in no sense leads us into some kind of "cultural relativism." Culture does not limit and obscure the truth; rather, it is truth's only vehicle, it is the way human beings know and understand. To attempt to "get outside" of culture and contact reality independently of everything humanly created is first of all nonsensical, and, if it were possible, once one had gotten "outside" of culture there would be no reality to encounter meaningfully. Reality, insofar as it is available to human beings, is found within culture.

A Flaw in the Theory

The dialectical theories of modernity exhibit a serious flaw. While they insightfully grasp an important contemporary process, they misinterpret it by placing it in the wrong context. Simply put, the foregoing analyses ought to be considered analyses of culture, not of society. This distinction will be described more fully in the following chapter; its present application can be seen in three areas.

The first is methodological. When Lasch cites certain phenomena which he then explains as narcissistic, the phenomena to which he refers are generally not demographics or statistical studies of mass behavior or inferred mass psychological characteristics, but rather books, public events, newspaper editorials, government policy statements, movies, television programming, etc.; in short, *cultural* artifacts and events. This is certainly true of Adorno and Horkheimer's discussion of mass culture, of Jacoby's and Philip Rieff's related works, and of Sennett's, despite Sennett's less impressionistic approach to the modern past. These studies are, at best, interpretations of certain strains of cultural expression; they cannot claim to be comprehensive and they cannot claim to be studies of mass social psychology.

It simply a *non sequitur* directly to infer global statements about the dominant social forms of personality organization, for example, about the structure of the 'bourgeois' and 'post-bourgeois' ego, from some of the meanings carried by cultural artifacts, or from some of the meanings implied in contemporary social roles and activities. The reason is not simply that the analysis of cultural trends is interpretive, uncertain, and always incomplete. The deeper problem is that any cultural artifact can participate in the experience of its producers and its audience in an indefinite variety of ways. There are layers of possible meanings present in the encounter with the artifact. The characteristics or implicit world view embodied in the artifact cannot be attributed to the personalities of producers and audience because the way the artifact is received and the spirit in which it is produced are not directly perceivable in the artifact itself. In particular, one of the key variant meanings that comes into play in the experience of the artifact, but is not necessarily apparent *in* the artifact, is the prevalent attitude toward cultural artifacts themselves.

For example, the fact that people spend many hours watching aesthetically valueless television programming need not mean that they have lost all sense of aesthetic value. It may instead indicate that they simply do not consider aesthetic values and standards relevant to television programming. The fact that a television writer composes a script portraying a human situation in which characters behave narcissistically need not mean that the scriptwriter is narcissistic; it may be that the writer simply knows that such a script will be well received and will generate income. The resulting narcissistic program will not mirror the personality traits of the writer, nor necessarily those of the audience. But, it should be noted, the resulting program does indicate the attitudes of both writer and viewers toward the nature and value of television programming, toward the meaning and value of this species of *cultural* artifact. This principle also applies to participation in socio-economic activity. One cannot automatically read off the personality traits of individuals from their socio-economic role. Personality and role are related, but they are not equivalent, nor do they exist in a one-to-one correspondence. One cannot claim that an eighteenth-century merchant is 'more' of an individual, by virtue of participation in capitalist modernity, than a medieval knight.

This does not imply that individual personality is an unknowable quantity, incapable of study. It is rather that personality cannot be known through declaring an undemonstrable association between certain personality traits, socio-economic activities and cultural themes, and then interpolating the existence of the personality traits from the observance of the latter two factors.

In the second area of application, the dialectical theories of modernity, by theoretically subjecting the actual personality structures of modern people to the determinative logic of self-negation, undermine the very values they wish to defend: the humanistic bases for democratic politics and morality. If the concepts of the rational ego, of the enlightened and self-interested individual, of the human person as an organized and rationally self-directed entity are in fact at the heart of modernity, and if we accept the contention that these ideas lead to their own barbarous self-negation, then on what basis ought modern society be organized? If liberalism, individualism, humanism, and rationality are all implicated in the dialectic, then on what basis can democracy and its attendant moral values be affirmed? This remains an unanswered—and tragically unanswerable—question for Adorno and Horkheimer, as we will see later.

There is one more difficulty with the dialectical theory which lies at the very heart of Adorno and Horkheimer's psycho-historical approach. The *Dialectic of Enlightenment* is founded on a simple although profound principle; namely, that all self-preservation is achieved through self-surrender. Primitive cultures, it is claimed, obeyed a primitive version of this principle through the notion of sacrifice, by which personal survival was bought through magical sacrifice. Western civilization and modernity obey a different, non-mythical form of the same principle: the assertion of the ego is bought through the renunciation of natural impulses and of continuity with nature.

For Adorno and Horkheimer this renunciation is linked to the domination of nature. It is the domination or control of nature within the human self that makes possible the domination of nature outside of the self. In the mid-1940s Horkheimer wrote:

> The disease of reason is that reason was born from man's urge to dominate nature . . . . One might say that the collective madness that

ranges today, from the concentration camps to the seemingly most
harmless mass-culture reactions, was already present in germ in
primitive objectivization, in the first man's calculating contemplation
of the world as a prey.[12]

Philosophically, Horkheimer criticizes what he calls monistic iden-
tifications of spirit or mind with nature, on the one hand, and, on the
other hand, rigid dualisms of spirit and nature, both of which express
and lend themselves to this legacy of domination. He stresses instead the
importance of maintaining the theoretical tension between subjective and
natural factors in existence, between the ideal and the real, without allowing this dialectical differentiation to become a hypostatization of
metaphysical opposites. This tension is essential to the "critical spirit"
itself, which "prepare[s] in the intellectual realm the reconciliation of the
two in reality," a reconciliation whose actualization can only take place
through some future transformation of social conditions.[13]

The problem here is that the principle that every self-preservation
or self-assertion is a renunciation is simply wrong. It is an unwarranted
simplification to claim that the universal human need to master *some
features* of the world is tantamount to an urge to dominate nature as a
whole. It would be difficult to imagine any person, including the capitalist entrepreneur, regarding the entire world as prey. To make this the
universal requirement of individuation, as the principle does, is a gross
simplification of personality development, in which renunciation plays a
part but not the dominant part.

The equation of self-development and renunciation would make
sense only if the 'self' which was being asserted had *already been conceived by those who propose the principle, as antithetical to nature.* One
may ask, in analyzing any given case of self-assertion through renunciation, how the psycho-historian could decide that what had been renounced was in fact 'nature' and what had been preserved or asserted
was 'self'? For example, in what sense is the control or repression of
emotionality tantamount to a renunciation of nature? In what sense is
that which remains in the person after such a repressive exclusion the self
or ego? It may be true that, in the modern Western intellectual tradition,
emotionality has been conceived as that part of the human *psychē* which
is more tied to nature, which is more natural, than for example, conceptual thought, and is therefore less internal, less essential to the self. It
may be true that, within this tradition, the human self has tended to
become progressively identified with theoretical reason and bare consciousness. But, even if this were true *of the tradition,* why do Adorno
and Horkheimer use that very language *as their own?* They are, in fact,
drawing conclusions not only about the cultural-philosophical tradition,
but about the actual self-development of Western humanity as well. The

fact is that Adorno and Horkheimer *accept* the intellectual tradition as a valid reflection of the general development of Western personality within its modern socio-economic history.

Thus, Adorno and Horkheimer evaluate Western history against a pre-conceived notion of the self or ego as antithetical to nature, to the body, to community, and to necessity, a notion which they have adopted from the history of modern philosophy. This notion is in fact the subjectivist conception of the self. For Adorno and Horkheimer, the 'core' self toward which the Western history of self-preservation and renunciation moves is the thinking subject, personal consciousness, to which material and biological nature indeed seem antithetical. It is precisely this conception of the self which allows them to link the assertion and development of the self to the renunciation of nature, myth, and inherent values. Adorno and Horkheimer have read the subjectivist concept of self and nature into all of Western history as the goal and principle of that history.

Their own philosophical ideal is consistent with the subjectivist conception that underlies their historical analysis. As noted, they oppose a monistic reduction of subject to object, ideal to real, and vice versa. Their critical ideal, according to which criticism is dependent upon maintaining the "tension" of subject and object, presumes an acceptance of the subjectivist dualism. Wary of any metaphysical dualism, they nevertheless accept a heuristic or methodological dualism of spirit and nature an necessary if their criticism—or any criticism—is to have normative implications. They see modernity as trapped within a blind alley because they are themselves caught in that same alley, and are unable to see strains of modernity that may have escaped the dead end.

Adorno and Horkheimer assert repeatedly that enlightenment never escapes myth, that it is shot through with the mythical impulse. There is a truth in this, but only a half-truth. If enlightenment is shot through with myth, why should we retain the dualistic and dialectical opposition of the two? Might we not instead see the two complexes of related ideas that these authors call "enlightenment" on the one hand, and "myth" on the other, as simply two complexes of related ideas? In particular, I am concerned with those alleged "myths" that are a part of modern philosophy: metaphysics, ethics, and systematic philosophy.

As we saw with respect to Descartes in Chapter 2, the critical Enlightenment impulse, the impulse to clear away all forms of necessity and necessary belief, the skeptical impulse, is itself a positive position, an assertion of the philosophic value, cogency, and importance of a particular viewpoint and set of interpretive categories. Whereas Adorno and Horkheimer portray how "criticism [is metamorphosed] into affirmation," it is my view that criticism is *always* an implicit affirmation; it does not need to be "determinately negated" in order to express an affirmation.[14] Adorno and Horkheimer are left at the end of the *Dialectic of Enlightenment,* it has been argued by some, in a position sufficiently pessimistic that the only hope for humanistic and politically concerned theorists is to try to insure the purity of the critical spirit.[15] This would be a delusion, because the critical spirit can never be and never has been pure, untainted by prior positional and valuative determinations, implicit positive implications, and socio-cultural predilections.

This recognition of criticism's impurity does not amount to a debunking of criticism, to an attempt to discount the value of criticism by equating it with generally descredited metaphysical or constructive forms of thought. Criticism and metaphysics are both legitimate aspects of philosophical activity; they are both legitimate pieces of what any philosopher may feel is important to say.

The conception of the spirit of enlightenment, of critical rationality, which considers the former to be opposed to all metaphysical and ethical position-taking and thereby to be characteristic of the spirit of modern philosophy or modernity in general (a conception which implies a monolithic characterization of modern intellectual history as a progressive skeptical or critical elimination of 'myths'), obscures and makes insoluable the fundamental problem with which Adorno and Horkheimer are themselves struggling. They are, they admit:

> wholly convinced—and therein lies our *petitio princippi*—that social freedom is inseparable from enlightened thought.[16]

Yet it is the whole point of their collaborative effort to argue that enlightened thought contains the seeds of "reversal universally apparent today," a reversal most virulently embodied in fascism.

The crucial question is, can that dimension of enlightenment which founds human freedom and dignity be critically separated from that dimension which founds authoritarianism, domination, and neo-primitivism, that is, unfreedom? Any possible separation of the progressive from the regressive would require us to conceive of the modern spirit as neither monolithic nor dialectical, but rather as a pluralistic complex of related tendencies undergoing dynamic change, so that those tendencies leading to "reversal" could be critically isolated from the rest of the context of the modern. This has been one of the motivations for the present study. It is not humanism, individualism, egoism, rationalism, skepticism, or instrumentalism that is to blame. These notions, which in various senses do define modernity, have been unnecessarily interpreted through the categories of subjectivism, which connects them all to the concept of a personal consciousness confronting an alien world. "Barbarism" and "cultural narcissism," insofar as they are products of ideas or ideologies at all, are not the logical result of the implications of humanism or individualism, but rather of the notion that the individual's true essence is *consciousness,* a non-interactive, private field of givenness taken *sui generis,* for which all encountered reality can only be thematized as intentional, representational objects, for which nature, objectivity, society, and culture are extrinsic factors, devoid of inherent meaning and intrinsic value.

8

The Cultural Theory and the Rise of Anti–Culture

This chapter presents an original theory of the development of modern culture. This theory, the "cultural theory," attempts to advance beyond the dialectical theory by applying the structure of the development of philosophical subjectivism and narcissism to modern culture in general, thereby preserving the insights of the dialectical theory while locating them in a new, non-dialectical context. This generates a theory of modernity which is not itself subjectivist, which does not fall into the trap of attacking the subject–object dichotomy in modern culture while employing that very dichotomy. This is important, for it makes possible a novel recognition of the role, value, and interpretation of culture itself *within* cultural life. The cultural theory claims that the key to the developments of late-modern or contemporary culture is the loss of the recognition of the inherent value and meaning of culture *per se* and the increasing prevalence of the view that cultural artifacts, events, and activities have value and meaning only insofar as they serve either economic or psychological ends.

It will be shown that the dialectical theory is in fact a theory of modern cultural subjectivism. What the dialectical theory explains through the idea of a dialectic of the rationalist, Enlightenment project can be better explained through the idea of the de-legitimation of the transcendental and consequent transformation of early subjectivism into radical subjectivism or narcissism.

In particular, it will be shown that the dialectical theory is *itself subjectivist* in its conception of culture. The dialectical theory implicitly conceives of culture as a mediator standing between public social necessity and private individual experience. This is precisely the way that modern subjectivist culture has conceived of itself. The dialectical theorists criticize the dynamic or dialectic of subjectivist modernity *from within* subjectivist categories, and this is why they find it so difficult to conceive of alternatives to the antinomies of modernity. What is needed is ultimately to criticize subjectivist modernity *from without,* thereby gaining a more adequate vision of this tradition and of alternative lines of development.

The dialectical theory, like so many contemporary theories of modern culture, tends to interpret cultural processes through either economic or psychological categories, or through a world-historical process which is a fusion of economics and psychology. But culture *cannot* be adequately understood through such categories. To interpret modern culture in this way is to reduce cultural processes to non-cultural categories. And because human being is essentially cultural, the reduction does theoretical violence to human nature itself, and particularly to the cogency of modern humanism. What is needed is a theory which interprets the development of modern culture in terms adequate to culture itself, and therefore adequate to the pluralistic complexity of human being. The fruit of the critique of subjectivist modernity and of the dialectical theory will be just that—a *cultural* theory of modernity.

Some restrictions on the scope of the theory to be proposed should be kept in mind. It is, like all theories, hypothetical, a tool proposed in order to enhance our understanding of the world, in this case, our understanding of modernity. Further, it is a philosophical theory and, as such, receives its justification on conceptual grounds. This means that one will find no statistical studies of contemporary culture herein. Rather, the theory seeks its justification in answering problems inherent in other theories of modernity, based on general observations and conceptual analysis. Lastly, the theory makes no pretense of comprehensiveness; it is not a comprehensive theory of everything of importance that is going on in the modern world. The cultural theory is a hypothesis that seeks to understand and explain only certain important and dominant cultural trends and themes, which is all any theory of the diverse cultural life of a complex society can hope to accomplish.

Cultural versus Dialectical Perspectives

The culture of a social group is the totality of its interpretive products, created or inherited, by which the group understands itself and its world. Interpretive products are humanly produced, publicly available words, ideas, events, or artifacts which express and provoke interpretations of the group's life and world. No culture is monolithic; it is made up of indefinitely complex and conflicting meanings. It is comprised of a variety of media, discursive, artistic, and otherwise: works of philosophy, manners, acts of congressional legislation, television situation comedies, and stylistic wall moldings are all shareable interpretive human products that express a style of understanding humankind and the world, and which subsequently become part of the given world which must be interpretively appropriated by future community members.

Culture and society are distinct and yet are in continual interaction. The distinction between culture and society is akin to the distinction between meaning and being. Meaning and being are never separate in reality, but appear as distinct phases of the real within our attempt to understand whatever we encounter. Their distinction is intellectually necessary and useful, despite the fact that they are thoroughly involved with each other: meaning *is* and therefore is part of being; being is normally encountered only within a horizon of meanings, it invokes and provokes meanings, and, through the agency of interpretive creatures, meanings are efficacious, they can create, alter, and destroy beings. Culture is a matter of meanings in this sense, whereas society is a matter of being, of what is. A social fact is not in itself a cultural fact; it becomes cultural when it acquires shareable meaning.

For example, while lead poisoning was a determining factor, a social reality, in the life of ancient Roman society, it was not at all a part of Roman culture. The Romans knew nothing of lead poisoning, lead did not have a poisonous signification for them, and so lead poisoning did not figure in their various shareable self- and world-interpretations. Perhaps ironically, lead poisoning would instead be a factor in our contemporary culture, even if it were eliminated as a *fact,* because it is now and will remain a part of our understanding of the world and of human living, regardless of whether or not it continues to exist in fact.

Culture is not co-extensive with nature. There are human processes and factors that, at some level of description, are not cultural, but would have to be called 'natural.' For example, while eating is certainly natural, it is not necessarily a cultural activity in itself. However, it can become cultural. The way one eats—for example, preparation of food in various biologically unnecessary ways, the use of certain kinds of utensils, the time and place of eating—can display varying understandings of eating and of *what is human,* that is, of what a human way of eating is.

Culture is thus a matter of things, that is, of products, which are publicly accessible and express or provoke shareable meanings, meanings which are related to the whole of human living and the world, that are trans-contextual, rather than functioning only in single, specific contexts. Thus a woman's dress, which expresses the life-interpretation and style of the wearer, is a cultural product whereas the placing of a light in a window as a pre-agreed signal that one is not home is not cultural, since it does not carry or provoke an interpretation of human living and the world, but has a meaning restricted to the specific context of its occurrence. But, the placing of a candle in the window to signify absence could *become* cultural, could come to function in a cultural way, if, for example, the light in the window is perceived by the community as a sign of a family member missing in action in a war.

Things can also cease to be cultural. When an artifact or activity ceases to be encountered or engaged in as having shareable meaning, when participation in it becomes purely mechanical and non-interpretive, it falls out of the cultural domain. It is even possible to imagine human social groups which have little or no culture at all, in which the natural or social facts of life are encountered as 'mere' facts, 'brute' facts that demand mechanical, non-interpretive response and have no meaning beyond that very demand. Such situations are rightfully called "primitive," which is not meant to indicate primarily tribal, aboriginal societies. In my terms, only the most 'primitive'—using the word now in its more usual sense—of such groups are legitimately called primitive; myth and tribal ritual are certainly forms of culture and are not less cultured than more contemporary forms. Ironically, the technologically advanced societies of the twentieth century have produced examples of social circumstances far more primitive than those obtaining in tribal societies; for example, the Nazi extermination camps, in which it is quite possible to imagine groups of people who had lost all sense of the mediate significance of human acts and the meaningfulness of human products.

Culture is a reservoir of meaningful products, more or less continually in the process of creation and assimilation, which provides the medium and the context for human communication and for the interpretive life of the individual. It is pluralistic, with an indefinite number of traditions, currents, and strains. Just how central culture is to a philosophical conception of human being will be explored later.

The distinction between culture and social-physical reality has important consequences for the theory of modernity. A number of critics have suggested that ours is a "culture of narcissism," that our culture is characterized by a de-vitalization of self or ego, that it reflects the symptoms of pathological narcissism on a grand scale. Employing the distinction between culture and social reality, I will argue that this critique is insightfully correct regarding the *culture* of contemporary America, but it cannot be true insofar as it is meant to apply to American *society*, to the mass psychology of Americans. Simply, it is the culture that is narcissistic, not the individual human beings.

For example, suppose that a 'narcissistic artifact' is a cultural product expressing a narcissistic view of things. It must be recognized that a non-narcissistic individual can produce and enjoy a narcissistic artifact. There is a distinction between the dominant meanings carried by a product and the actual personality traits of the creator and the audience; the former need *not* be a straightforward expression of the latter. Indeed, any product takes on different meanings depending on the context in which it is experienced; a particular product may take on narcissistic meanings only within a specific system of publication and distribution.

This is not to say that the theory of cultural narcissism is false or trivial. It is importantly insightful, but only as a critique of *culture per se* and of the status and style of cultural activities and artifacts within contemporary society, *not* as a critique of mass psychology. Thus, while contemporary culture is narcissistic, contemporary society is *not*. Now, culture, in turn, changes society; that is, the dominant views a society holds of itself as expressed in its culture are certainly significant for both individual and group life in that society, significant as a guide for future action and for the self-interpretation which is an intrinsic part of experience itself. Nevertheless, the distinction between culture and society must be maintained. Again, they are related and mutually influential, but not identical.

Without this distinction the theory of cultural narcissism and the most valuable of the theories of modernity, the dialectical theory, are at least wildly speculative and at most simply and grossly false. It would be bizarre to claim that an entire society, especially a large, national society, could be afflicted with a personality disorder. To be sure, none of the theorists in question argues this literally. Christopher Lasch, for example, claims that narcissistic traits, and not the full-blown personality disorder, are present in "milder" forms throughout American society. But even this qualified statement, if it implies that the average American embodies narcissistic traits, could never be empirically supported.

To take another example, Adorno and Horkheimer's critical theory demands an analysis of individual personality as a socio-economic product. Late capitalism, according to this view, determines individual personality in its most intimate dimensions. But this view must be rejected on moral and political, as well as conceptual, grounds. The dialectical theories of modernity, often motivated by a humanistic concern to defend the individual against socio-economic determination, have tended to treat human being as wholly determined, thus defeating their own purpose. In the name of revealing victimization they have produced a theory that itself expresses a general lack of respect for the integrity of the individual. In the name of combating "objectification," they have unwittingly produced yet another expression of objectification. To treat culture and cultural artifacts, symbols, and activities as psychologically, economically, or politically determined, as illusions, self-deceptions or epiphenomena, is to make culture meaningless and thereby deny human beings the capacity for meaningful interpretation and meaningful creation. This is, from the viewpoint of a specifically *cultural* philosophy, precisely to deny the essential features of human being, to undermine the integrity of the human process.

Today there is an important philosophic and cultural need for forms of social criticism that find no contradiction between respect for the integrity of the human individual and his or her products, and the recognition of social, economic, and political forces that affect and shape human possibilities. The key to the development of this kind of criticism is the recognition that both the individual and these super-individual forces exist within a larger context, namely, the humanly created interpretive web of culture. In light of this concern, the dialectical theories of modernity reveal qualitative changes within culture itself, namely, the development of an "anti-culture," a culture that is hostile to itself, a culture which denies the possibility and value of cultural processes and artifacts. To deny cogency, meaning, and value to cultural phenomena insofar as they are independent of, for example, economic vicissitudes is to deny humanity itself. It is to deny that human beings have the capacities to find or create value, to communicate and share, and to meaningfully interpret reality. A human being devoid of such capacities would indeed be, as British psychiatrist David Winnicott claims, pathological in an extreme and debilitating sense.[1] If important cultural media are dominated by this anti-cultural message, then culture ceases to perform its human and social functions and individual members of society are denied the shared symbols by which they would normally interpret their lives. It is this possibility, that the status of culture itself can change, that culture can evolve in such a way that it systematically undercuts the adequate interpretation and appreciation of itself, that is the key to understanding the culture of late modernity, a culture of which contemporary philosophy is but one expression.

The dialectic of enlightenment is the story of the development of a way of understanding human being and the world, *not* an account of the development of modern Western human being and society. It is an analysis of an important strain of modern culture, *not* a history of modern social reality. Adorno and Horkheimer do present a specifically social history, an analysis of modern economic and social institutions and activities, but they merge this analysis with a historical account of philosophical ideas and with claims about personality development. The social, cultural, and psychological realities of a historical period are, to be sure, related; but they are not equatable, reducible one to the other, nor are they merely different aspects of the development of a single formula. It is not the 'modern ego' or personality structure that has undergone a dialectical self-negation; it is the *literature* of the modern ego, the intellectual-philosophical-cultural tradition that has negated itself. The real egos of the world do indeed have their own characteristically modern problems; but dialectical self-negation is not one of them.

The ideals of the enlightenment were philosophical and cultural ideals, humanly created world understandings embodied in cultural artifacts, which could influence the course of social life to the extent that people came into contact, direct or mediated, with those artifacts and found their meaning convincing, compelling, or valuable. Adorno and Horkheimer show how these ideals, in interaction with certain changing historical and social conditions, undergo a dynamic self-negation. This self-negation or reversion to barbarism is a fact or process of *cultural* history, of human self-understandings embodied in cultural media and artifacts, which is indeed related to and influenced by socio-economic, historical conditions, but is *not* inevitably and essentially determined by those conditions. Socio-economic conditions may in fact be barbaric in some sense, but this is not equivalent to cultural or psychological barbarism.

What determines this cultural dialectic of enlightenment is in fact subjectivism. The categories and implicit world view of philosophical subjectivism have been a force, not only in modern philosophy, but in modern cultural history in general as well. The ideological and intellectual core of Adorno and Horkheimer's notion of enlightenment, and of Lasch's concept of bourgeois man, is defined by the principle that: *all reality is or ought to be subject to the authority, criticism, and judgment of the individual human subject.* This principle can be seen to be a version of philosophical subjectivism as long as "individual human subject" is conceived along the lines of a thinking-experiencing-willing subject which stands in an external relationship to other parts of reality (such as nature and society); that is, is conceived as a subjectivity or individual consciousness. The "dialectic of enlightenment," the "fall of public man," and the rise of the "culture of narcissism" involve a development of the subjectivist strain of modern culture in which the problematic implications of subjectivism became an important force or theme in culture.

In fact, the dialectical theories of culture can be seen to employ a common developmental scheme that is analagous to that of modern philosophical subjectivism. Despite their differences, they describe the early modern period as characterized by a particular conception of and set of relations between individual personality, the socio-economic-administrative system, and the cultural system, the last referring to important religious and philosophical beliefs, artistic styles, social manners, etc., that are characteristic of the period in question. The dialectical theories ascribe a mediating role to the *cultural* system in the early modern period that is analagous to the mediating role of transcendental factors in philosophical subjectivism. Culture is seen to mediate between individuals and the novel socio-economic-administrative system characteristic of modernity.

For instance, the "enlightened" and "bourgeois" socio-economic systems that the writers in question consider to be characteristic of the early, post-revolutionary modern period are republican, capitalist, and increasingly secular. In accordance with these conditions, individuals are presumed to be politically free, the economic life of the nation is understood to be constituted by the sum of contractual agreements between free individuals, and no official religious beliefs are adopted by the national community. This condition, the condition of a modern society, could be entered into without an overwhelming fear of political, economic, and moral anarchy only insofar as it was presumed that all free individuals shared certain common guiding capacities; for example, "enlightened" self-interest or "natural reason." Such beliefs were embodied, in a variety of media, in the modern *cultural* system. The newly developing concepts of individuality and freedom, concepts which had epistemological and religious as well as ethical and political impact, could be accepted only because cultural beliefs and activities remained significant, beliefs and activities which, for one thing, tied together, into a community, individuals who increasingly understood themselves as separate. In general, the early modern period was characterized by the growing importance and prevalence of such beliefs, and by the conviction that the activities of culture (for example, art, literature, sport, religious and social ritual) had special value, independent of economic values, on the one hand, and purely personal interests on the other.

In these terms, the negation of early modernity, which the dialectical theories assert, occurs when the development of the socio-economic-administrative system, which is taken by the dialectical theorists to be the driving force in modernity, renders the cultural system incapable of performing its mediating function. For the writers in question the expansion and development of the socio-economic-administrative sector certainly has direct impact on individuals independent of its impact on culture. Nevertheless, the turning point between the early modern, enlightened, or bourgeois phase and the late modern, post-bourgeois phase in these accounts occurs when culture loses its mediating function. It loses this function when its independence is seemingly absorbed and negated by the ever expanding and more consistent application of the powerful interpretive dualism of subjectivity and the non-subjective. The more culturally dominant and pervasive this dualism becomes, the more culture itself must be amalgamated to, interpreted in terms of, categories which are inadequate for its interpretation. Cultural activities and phenomena then cease to be thought of as having their own special meaning and value; all value has been reduced to one of two kinds: economic value, on the one hand, and individual or personal value, which is to say, whatever is valuable to an individual in any way that it is valuable, on the other hand. Thus, within the culture there is no legitimation for any communal non-economic values.

The reduction of mediating, transcendental factors is an explicit theme for Adorno and Horkheimer. For them, "substantive reason," a posited universal human faculty capable of grasping substantive universal truths and values, while a part of bourgeois enlightenment ideology, was nevertheless a humanizing factor. They see the recent philosophical critique of substantive reason as according with the developments of the late capitalist economy. These developments have served to deny the legitimacy of any interpretive category, any mediating principle, that could stand between the private feelings and fantasies of individuals and the objective, universal necessity of a seemingly unalterable and anonymous economic-administrative system.

Lasch's remark about the perception of reality depending on the experience of illusion, the implications of which Lasch himself does not fully explore, suggests a similar point. It implies that an operative distinction between subjectivity and the 'objective' world in a given society is dependent upon the existence of cultural artifacts and meanings which themselves cannot be categorized as properties of the subject nor of the objective world. The realm of "serious illusions," as Lasch calls them, mediates the private subject and the material world. If this mediation is disturbed, then the private and the material worlds lose their status as independent yet related spheres.

In Lasch's more recent work, *The Minimal Self,* he recognizes somewhat more clearly that the argument about cultural narcissism entails the notion that culture as a mediating force is losing its integrity. Referring to British psychiatrist David Winnicott's interpretation of culture as the adult form of childhood's "transitional objects"—which I will describe later—Lasch writes that:

> The culture of narcissism is not necessarily a culture in which moral constraints . . . have collapsed . . . . What has weakened is not so much the structure of moral obligations and commandments as the belief in a world that survives its inhabitants . . . . Culture mediates between the inner world and the outer world . . . . It is the

intermediate realm of man-made objects, then, that threatens to disappear in societies based on mass production and mass consumption.[2]

In this book, however, Lasch still fails to make the further step of recasting his whole critique in terms of this change in the status and function of culture itself.

From the viewpoint of the cultural reinterpretation of the development of narcissistic trends in various sectors of contemporary culture (art, literature, sports, education, family life, etc.), it is clear that this development involves the progressive reduction of the possible *meanings* of cultural activities and artifacts to two paradoxically related interpretive categories: the sphere of purely private experience and enjoyment, and the marketplace, the realm of objective, economic survival. In this context it becomes less and less possible to interpret any social or cultural activities and artifacts as having shared, communal, public meanings and values. And it was precisely the embodiments of shareable, non-personal values in cultural activities and artifacts that had provided, in early capitalist America, the limitations on competition and exploitation that, according to Lasch, today no longer exist.

Cultural Subjectivism and Anti-Culture

For the purpose of analysis, we can describe a given society in terms of three factors: a) the socio-economic-administrative system; b) the cultural system; and c) the individual personalities that constitute the society. "Administrative" refers to the system of law and governmental-political authority. The "cultural system" refers to the totality of cultural artifacts, meanings, and the activities of producing and interpreting them, which obtain in a given society. "Personality" or "individual personalities" refer to the actual living and breathing members of the society, in all their particularity and diversity. The three factors are, of course, in continual interaction in any society.

Within the cultural system, groupings of cultural products lend themselves to consistent, similar interpretations, which can be described as "themes." The cultural system may exhibit a small set of dominant and pervasive themes.

The interpretations, ideas, and themes present in the cultural system are representations or interpretations of nature, of socio-economic-administrative realities, of traits of personalities, and of *the cultural system itself* in whole or part. Within the cultural system, one finds shareable interpretations of natural existence, of economic life, of what it means to be a human individual, *and* of what are the values and meanings of various kinds of cultural artifacts and activities. This reflexivity of culture, by which the cultural system represents and interprets itself, is often neglected in discussions of culture. A cultural artifact implicitly or explicitly presents an understanding of what a cultural artifact is, what it does, what its value is, along with a correlative understanding of the activities of producing and interpreting such artifacts.

To talk of cultural subjectivism is to claim that the theme or themes of subjectivism is or are significant or dominant in a society's cultural system. It is to claim, first of all, that the characteristic pattern of the initial phase of subjectivism is exhibited by the cultural system in question. This means, according to my analysis of subjectivism, that the representations and interpretations of individual persons as thinking-experiencing-willing subjects, and of socio-economic-administrative realities as non-subjective, mechanical, and impersonal, are significant or dominant themes. But further, in a subjectivist cultural system this system's representations and interpretations *of itself* play a mediating, bridging, "transcendental" role *within* the cultural system. It is an analysis of this change in culture's representations and interpretations of itself which is the key to the cultural theory of modernity, and which is undeveloped in the dialectical theory.

In the initial phase of modern cultural subjectivism the notion that various public and institutional activities and artifacts carried transpersonal meaning and value was a powerful theme within the cultural system. Culture represented itself as important. This theme of the integrity and significance of cultural artifacts and activities was integrated with cultural representations and interpretations of socio-economic-administrative realities and individual personality as integrally related to cultural values.

For example, as Lasch recounts, it was a significant theme in early-modern culture that economic activity had religious and cultural meaning, and had implications for the moral character of the individual. It is true that the subjectivist element in modern, capitalist culture tended to make the socio-economic sphere seem a value-neutral realm open to the instrumental manipulation of the entrepreneurial subject, but the transcendental or mediating elements in the earlier phase of modern culture wove an integrative web of spiritual, communal, and characteriological meanings around that instrumental activity.

The dynamic or dialectic of cultural subjectivism, and thus the "dialectic of enlightenment," is a development of the *cultural system*. Society has certainly undergone colossal changes in the modern period, but these changes do not constitute a dialectical self-negation. The process of self-negation is characteristic of the cultural system of modern society, and not of the other systems of modern life, for example, economic and psychological.

To say that the dialectic of modernity is a development of the modern cultural system is to say that it is a development of the *cultural representations and interpretations of* the socio-economic-administrative system, personality, and culture itself. This development was related to and conditioned by the simultaneous development of the modern socio-economic-administrative system; not of its cultural representation, but a development of the system itself. This development and its effect on the development of culture are undeniably significant, yet they cannot be equated, nor can a one-to-one correspondence be drawn between socio-economic-administrative and cultural developments.

For example, Karl Marx to the contrary, the capitalist system has not today negated itself; it is a system of activities and materials, not a statement or thesis, and it therefore can have no definable "antithesis." Even if the system were to expire completely it would not be clear that we could call this expiration a self-negation, unless every ending of a historical movement is held to be a self-negation. The capitalist system may contain tendencies or factors that will contribute to its own demise, but so do virtually all existing things. At any rate, the system has certainly not yet expired.[3] What *can* be said to have undergone a reversal or self-negation, however, is the *ideology* of early capitalism, the set of beliefs about economic and social life that were held by the proponents of capitalism and by many others. In other words, it is a set or theme of *cultural* representations and interpretations *of* the early capitalist economic system that has been reversed, not the system itself, despite the fact that the reversal of the cultural theme has been conditioned by real changes in the economic system itself, and in turn has a real effect on that system.

Diagram D depicts this overall scheme. The three systems, in continual interaction, constitute the social reality of a given society during a given historical period. The socio-economic-administrative system and the cultural system develop along independent, although related, lines. They develop, so to speak, in related direction, but are not parallel.[4] Personality does not exhibit a historical development springing from itself; it changes insofar as its character is conditioned by the other two systems, and the depth of such changes is severely limited. While the description of modernity must take all three systems into account, it is the socio-economic-administrative and the cultural systems together that form the driving force of the modern, that create the modern world. The dialectic of enlightenment, the dynamic of modern subjectivism, that is, the self-negating tendency within modernity as a whole, belongs to the cultural system *alone*.

The so-called dialectic of modernity from the seventeenth through the twentieth century is the dynamic self-negation of cultural subjectivism. Similar to the development of subjectivism in that part of culture

DIAGRAM D

The Cultural Theory of Modernity

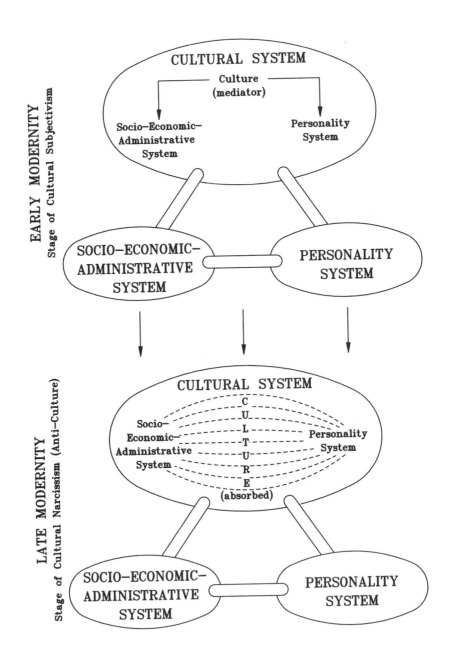

called philosophy, the dynamic of cultural subjectivism involves the progressive de-legitimation of subjectivist culture's: a) transcendental or mediating representations and interpretations *of itself,* that is, of its culture; and b) the cultural representations and interpretations of the socio-economic-administrative realities and individual personality that cohered with the former (a). In the history of subjectivist culture the opposed, culturally represented categories of subject and object (the belief that all reality, social and natural, devolves into these two categories), became a sufficiently dominant force in the cultural system to de-legitimate the transcendental or mediating cultural themes that had previously helped to integrate the opposed categories into a coherent system. The result was that, within the scope of these thematic tendencies, all meaning- and value-possibilities tended to be reduced to two categories: the intentions—instrumental, perceptual, emotive, cognitive—of individual subjects; and the objects of those intentions, understood as being value-neutral and non-meaningful in themselves. This resulting condition defines the dominant theme in the late modern cultural system which has been called narcissistic. Consequently, insofar as these cultural themes hold sway, cultural artifacts, activities and processes are interpretively reduced to and interpreted in terms of these two categories.

For example, in early-modern culture religion was regarded as a transpersonal reality that provided the context for individual and social life. In the Declaration of Independence, the only justification Thomas Jefferson offered for the existence of inalienable individual rights was a reference to their Divine origin (they are "endowed by their Creator"). Religion was interpreted as transcendental, as neither a matter of private belief nor public necessity, but as the legitimating context for the integrity and relation of both.

As the subjectivist categories become increasingly hegemonous in the late nineteenth century and began to de-legitimate the independent status of the transcendental, the interpretation of religion changed. Religion gradually withdrew to the sphere of privacy; religious conviction came to be regarded as a subjective matter, not appropriate for the determination of public life. The dominant categorical structure for interpretation changed: the transcendental was absorbed by the subject and object categories. For example, the assertion that a particular religious belief is true of reality and ought to determine communal behavior (an assertion which would have seemed obvious during the thousand years preceding the nineteenth century) would today be unacceptable to all but a small minority of late-modern Americans. For late modernity, religious belief, formerly transcendental, is now a private, subjective matter.

Culture is *not* in fact a mediating force standing somehow between individual personality and impersonal social and natural necessity. But this is precisely how subjectivist culture interprets culture. Early-modern culture understood cultural artifacts and activities as a transcendental mediating bridge between the personal and the impersonal, between the individual and the social and natural, which were regarded as antithetical. In late modernity that subjectivist culture evolves into narcissistic culture, in which the possibility of mediation is eliminated due to the now unrestricted hegemony of the categories of subjectivity and objectivity.

A crucial point here is that this interpretive categorical scheme of narcissistic culture is *antithetical to the very concept of culture.* If all physical objects, and thus all physical cultural artifacts—books, buildings, art objects, etc.—are held or felt to be intrinsically value-neutral, non-meaningful, and of value only insofar as they are appropriated by the private intentions or wishes of individual subjects, then the very notion of 'cultural artifact' no longer makes any sense. If meaning and value are present only in the intentions of individual and ultimately private subjects, then there can be no human products embodying publicly accessible meanings. Furthermore, the human processes and activities essential to the production, experience, and assimilation of culture become incomprehensible. Meaningful discourse, communal interaction, interpretation of symbols and of artifacts, and inheritance of cultural traditions cannot find a basis in the interpretive categories of narcissistic culture.

Richard Sennett makes a similar point in his *The Fall of Public Man.*[5] Sennett argues that contemporary America and Western society in general exhibit a loss of the sense of the inherent meaning and value of public life, a loss of the sense of a *res publica,* the notion that community life outside the intimate realm of the family is a *res* or substance or reality in its own right. Instead, the public sphere is interpreted as a value-neutral arena in which individuals participate only in order to compete for goods and then return to the private or familial sphere. This is a degenerate view, for the public realm is not a simple aggregation of individuals, nor a means for private ends, but a context for the meaningful existence of individuals with its own unique values and satisfactions. Sennett sees the contemporary scene as dominated by an "intimate vision of society" in which only intimate relations are felt to be meaningful and the non-intimate world of strangers, emotional distance, and everyday role-playing is experienced as meaningless and threatening. Like Lasch, Sennett defines this tyranny of the intimate as socialized narcissism.

Sennett's decline of the public realm is better understood as a degeneration of the interpretation of culture. The common opposition of the terms 'public' and 'private' may give the impression that the realm of privacy remains unaffected by the de-legitimation of the public. This impression would allow Sennett's analysis to be mistakenly lumped together with often-heard conservative and communitarian critiques of late modernity as excessively individualistic and hedonistic. Sennett recognized that the issue is not a conflict between the public and the private spheres, for the decay of the *res publica* undermines the integrity of the self as well. Something crucial goes out of private life when it no longer measures itself against and participates in a non-intimate public world. It is preferable, then, to focus on culture, which is not caught up in the assumed opposition of public and private, and which is crucial to the fabric of both public and private life.

Furthermore, Sennett's usage of narcissism (like Lasch's) must be understood as a reference to the cultural sphere and not as a massive generalization about contemporary personality characteristics. To interpret his work as a psychological generalization would amalgamate it to the very problem it is trying to describe, to the focus on personality as the most important factor in community life. What is "falling" in the late-modern world is less the image of "public man" than the cultural representation of culture, communication, and the meaningfulness of human creations as irreducible and inherently valuable.

For this reason, what has been called narcissistic culture is better understood as an "anti-culture," which is to say, a cultural system or dominant theme within that system, which conveys the meaning that cultural activities and artifacts have no inherent meaning or value. An anti-culture interprets culture itself as having only non-cultural meaning or value; for example, economic-administrative or private psychological meaning or value. An anti-culture is a culture which represents cultural objects and activities as being intrinsically meaningless, as having no intrinsic value *as cultural,* as valuable only insofar as they subserve a non-cultural function.

Cultural artifacts and events can convey this anti-cultural sense implicitly or explicitly. Explicit anti-cultural meanings are encountered in books that communicate the message that there can be no communication or rational discussion of interpretations, or in art objects which efface the distinction between art and non-aesthetic phenomena, which convey the sense that there is no such thing as an art object at all. Lasch produces a number of such examples prevalent in avant-garde movements in literature, plastic and visual art, music, and theater.[6] Within philosophy, thinkers as diverse as Wittgenstein and Heidegger have written philosophical works which announce that philosophy is at or should come to an "end." Post-structuralism is marked, as Levinas says, by a kind of "sensitivity for a certain apocalyptic poetry,"[7] which declares human theoretical culture to have exhausted itself.

It is, however, the implicitly anti-cultural messages and beliefs which are more pervasive and socially significant than these esoteric movements. In contemporary political discourse, in public beliefs about athletics, in general attitudes toward inherited social rituals and public manners, and in the educational practices of colleges and universities, one can see again and again the de-legitimation of one kind of belief and discourse, and the legitimation of another. What is being de-legitimated is the sense that public, external realities and activities embody communal meanings and values, in regard to which individuals participate and are thereby related to each other. What is being legitimated is the sense that social life and reality are exclusively divided into the opposed regions of privacy and impersonal necessity, that all public, social life is something foreign to the individual, and hence devoid of inherent meaning, and that meaning and value lie only in the personal wishes, intentions, and projects of the individual.

Thus, for example, professional athletics has come to be regarded by many less as arena for the communal celebration of excellence through competition and more as either an entertainment, a mere diversion from everyday stress, or as a business. Politics is increasingly viewed as either the mechanical, impersonal preservation of the status quo, which cannot be affected by the individual, or as the expression of the personal greed or fanatical impulses of a few private individuals. In higher education, the "liberal" ideal of becoming an educated person (the cultural ideal *par excellence*) seems to play almost no role at all. Rather, the goals of higher education are increasingly divided into either the economic and vocational, or the personal and psychological. Communal judgments, group agreement regarding course requirements and educational goals, are felt to be possible in the area of economic and technical necessity alone, while non-economic and non-technical decisions are widely considered to be the exclusive realm of taste, of merely personal opinion, of subjective preference and desire. In popular culture it has become common practice for everyday people, and the media which are concerned to communicate to them, to evaluate all art objects, all cultural products (for example, films, records) in terms of their economic value (for example, ticket sales). Except for personal preference, there are felt to be no other legitimate evaluative criteria.

One last example may be particularly telling. Anyone in contact with the mass media is daily exposed to a bombardment of messages, especially advertising messages. This level of exposure to novel images and talk is certainly unprecedented in human history. The net result in the cases of most people is not, as some critics have claimed, tantamount to a kind of "brainwashing." The effect on most people is both less catastrophic and more insidious. Brainwashing implies the internalization of meanings and either implicit or explicit belief. What is striking is that such brainwashing does *not* in fact generally occur. On the contrary, the bombardment of meanings makes it necessary for most contemporary people to contrive to encounter a large portion of their daily experience as *non-meaningful,* to develop the capacity *not* to experience images and talk as inherently meaningful. Extremely vivid, novel, and powerful images and hyperbolic discourse must be discounted, must be regarded superficially as 'mere' images and 'only' talk, which is to say, as non-meaningful, if one is to survive psychically. This is not difficult for most people.

The danger in this situation is that contemporary people, to an unprecedented degree, may inevitably come to regard more and more of public communication and public life in general as non-meaningful. The bombardment of advertising does not turn people into believing automatons; it makes them accustomed to inhibiting their judgment, to encountering public events as non-meaningful, to regarding what should be meaningful, communicative, cultural sectors of reality as appropriate neither for belief nor disbelief nor interpretation nor empathetic feeling, but only for passive, unthinking, unfeeling observation and endurance.

Contemporary writers tend to criticize modernity from one of two opposing viewpoints. Either they see in late modernity an excessive individualism (the hedonism of the "me generation," the erosion of community values and moral standards, the triumph of fantasy over realism) or a dissolving of individual freedom in the face of growing institutional power (the rise of "organizational man," bureaucratization, militarism, repression of minorities). The former tend to regard the culture of late modernity as a regression from the classical ideals of earlier modernity, while the latter view late-modern culture as the extension of early modernity's commitment to freedom, an extension that has been continually opposed by the powerful.

Each of these positions expresses a half-truth. The dialectical theorists have taken an important step beyond these opposing viewpoints, recognizing that late-modern culture is characterized by both an individualist withdrawal from community and by the rise of a "new paternalism" of bureaucratic power, and that both aspects of late modernity are the product of the development of the projects of early modernity.

The dialectical theorists, however, fail to see or make explicit the precise nature of this cultural process, which they often mistake as primarily economic or psychological or logical. The paradoxes and dilemmas of late-modern culture are a product of the *self-undermining* of an important strain of modern culture. This self-undermining is not due to a dialectic of subject and object, private and public, internality and externality. It is due to the *de-contextualization* of these categories. The interpretive categories of personal subjectivity and public objectivity became so effective, so universal, that they de-legitimated the interpretation of human culture as valuable and meaningful in itself. This undermined the context which had mediated and related the dichotomous subject and object, private and public categories and had made them workable. The loss of context radically changed the nature and significance of these categories, throwing them into a dialectical relationship in which they became paradoxically alien and equatable.

PART THREE

The Cultural Dimension

Introduction to Part Three

The preceding chapter introduced a new focus of attention into our discussion of modernity, a focus on the *cultural dimension* of human life. Late-modern culture, to the extent that its employs subjectivist categories, exhibits a de-legitimation of this cultural dimension as a primary, independently valuable dimension of reality. The cultural dimension of human individuality and social life, and the associated processes of communication, of community, of public, shareable meaning, and of the inherent significance and value of human products, have all been interpretively reduced to the categories of subject and object, categories which cannot adequately interpret culture and its related processes.

Theorists of modernity have generally passed over this change in the interpretation of culture in favor of explanations focusing on specific cultural areas or on social, economic, and psychological factors. Modernity is certainly predicated upon vast and on-going socio-economic change, but alterations in the status of the cultural and intellectual principles on which modernity based itself are not the product of such changes *in themselves*. The cultural system has its own integrity and momentum, albeit in continuous relationship with socio-economic and psychological processes. Whatever the colossal changes in the contemporary technical and economic spheres, the cultural theory of modernity asserts that late modernity exhibits a radicalization of the interpretive categories of modern cultural subjectivism, a radicalization which de-legitimates whatever is not readily interpretable as either the property of a private subject or a matter of impersonal, public necessity.

The modern subject–object dichotomy is inadequate for understanding reality in general, but inadequacy is a matter of degree and some features of life fare far worse than others at the hands of this dualistic scheme. Human cultural life fares worse than many others; its reduction to subject–object categories eliminates its independent integrity and value, and makes it incapable of performing its normal functions in human society. The subjectivist anti-culture cannot understand that human beings create, think, and become individuated, independent

215

creatures only within and through a context of meaningful relations to other human beings and to non-human things. It cannot understand that human beings and material entities can be independent and internally related at the same time, because its radicalized subjectivism dictates that for something to be related to an individual subjectivity it must actually belong to, must be a part or function of, that subjectivity. That these failures are fatal to the understanding of culture will be seen in Chapter 10.

Philosophy, as part of culture, has not been exempt from anti-cultural tendencies. Philosophical narcissism is fundamentally anti-cultural in that its basic interpretive categories leave no room for an understanding of culture as having integrity and inherent value. This charge is not restricted to the work of Husserl and Heidegger, the two cases of philosophical narcissism studied herein. The radical application of subject and object categories, which crowds out a cogent and meaningful understanding of culture, can be seen in logical positivism and in much of the Anglo-American philosophical tradition. Likewise, Marxism, structuralism, and post-structuralism commonly reduce cultural artifacts and processes to economic epiphenomena and to formal linguistic structures, respectively, in which the human aims of communication and reference to the world have little or no place.

The anti-culturalism of twentieth-century philosophy has, as will be seen in the following chapter, an unexpected effect. Anti-cultural philosophies make explicit what is already implicit in the anti-culture of late modernity as a whole: that the representational and interpretive processes of human 'subjects' can have no claim on knowledge of reality and that cultural products are mere material objects which in themselves possess no more inherent meaning or value than an undiscovered stone on the dark side of the moon. For, within the radicalized subjectivism of the anti-culture, characteristics of subjective processes can bear no internal relation to non-subjective realities.

What, then, of philosophy itself? Philosophy is a representational, interpretive human creation, a part of culture. Whatever reduction is visited upon culture must in some form, implicitly or explicitly, be visited upon philosophy as well. The de-legitimation of culture means the *de-legitimation of philosophy.* The anti-culturalism of late-modern philosophy is one of the driving forces behind the alleged "end" or "death" of philosophy that has been proclaimed by twentieth-century philosophers of so many diverse stripes, from Wittgenstein to Heidegger.

9

Anti-Culture and the Alleged Death of Philosophy

Modern philosophical subjectivism has always been characterized by an inadequate interpretation of culture. It systematically misconceived culture and refused to give culture its rightful place in an understanding of human being and the world. It tended to view culture as an obstacle to philosophy rather than as a fellow-traveller. Philosophical narcissism brings this bias to fruition by regarding non-philosophic culture as something about which questions of truth, validity, and philosophical value cannot sensibly be asked at all. In our age of philosophical narcissism, the criteria of philosophical truth and value have been so totally divorced from the criteria appropriate to other cultural domains that the former cannot be applied to the latter, nor vice versa.

The Limits of Subjectivism

Subjectivism, like any theoretical structure, is and was more adequate, fruitful, and valuable in the interpretation or understanding of some features of reality, some domains of what we encounter, than others. No important philosophical theory is uniformly inadequate; if it were, it would not be important. Each philosophical viewpoint is originally proposed by living thinkers to address certain intellectual problems rather than others, however extensively or comprehensively the viewpoint may subsequently be applied. Each philosophy is designed to address a limited set of problems, and it becomes a living part of the public tradition of philosophic thought or of cultural writing in general only if it appears reasonably successful in dealing with those problems. The public life of a philosophy then involves a process of expansion and testing whereby the original viewpoint is successively applied to diverse problems increasingly distant from the issues that had occasioned its initial formulation. The importance or influence of a philosophy, its hold on the collective imagination of philosophers or of the public in general, hinges both on its perceived adequacy for dealing with a large set of problems *and* the felt importance of those problems to which the philosophy appears to be most relevant.

Subjectivism had a degree of adequacy and fruitfulness in its application to what have been felt to be very important modern issues—for example, the reconciliation of the competing claims of scientific materialism and Christian spiritualism—issues that made it a dominant force in modern philosophy and culture. Subjectivism is, however, much less adequate for the interpretation of certain other domains of reality; in particular, those events or existences which *prima facie* involve an interweaving of subjectivity, mentality, and meaning, on the one hand, and objectivity, materiality, and factuality, on the other. In the subjectivist system, whatever is *not* merely and solely subjective, nor merely and solely non-subjective or objective, must be understood as a derivative product of some kind of synthesis of subjectivity and non-subjectivity.

Subjectivism as a philosophical viewpoint was, and still is, rooted in two powerful and undeniable perceptions. The first is the perception of the difference between the human and the non-human, particularly in reference to the uniquely human activity of inquiry. Subjectivism attempted to deal with the epistemic problems of the relation of appearance and reality, falsity and truth, and the ineradicable recurrence of error by turning attention toward the inquirer as a unique, potential Archimedean point for thought. It was in the nature of the inquirer and the essential distinction of that nature from all non-inquiring nature that the fundamental categorial orientation of inquiry was to be set up.

The second basic intuition was the reflexive perception of consciousness, as a flowing field of givenness, as associated with all inquirers. Consciousness seemed to be an essential characteristic of all inquirers—actual or potential—and to be impossible for non-inquiring nature, as well as being presupposed by the activity of inquiry and seeming to form the ground or context within which all objects and evidences of any possible inquiry obtain. Consciousness seemed to be that in which all evidence must appear in order to be evidence at all. For subjectivism, all this signified that consciousness constituted the essence of the inquirer, that is, of human being, as well as the presupposition of all knowledge and experience. Thus, the distinction between the conscious and the non-conscious would be the most fundamental distinction for philosophic inquiry.

Given this view, any cultural artifact, be it a work of art, a religious icon, the design of a woman's dress, or a sporting event, must be seen as basically dichotomous, ambiguous, or ambivalent, inherently suited to be a mediating link between the two realms, if it is to make sense at all. A cultural artifact is a non-subjective thing, like any material or natural object, yet it is created by a subject and subjects appraise it differently than they do other material objects.

In fact, the essence of a cultural thing includes *meanings;* that is, if we attempt to understand the cultural thing without reference to meanings, human uses and significances, then we no longer understand it as a cultural thing at all. Cultural artifacts are non-human things, objects, to whose essential being, to whose existential integrity, *meanings intrinsically belong.* The artifact is a meaningful thing; it is a material object which, once created, has an existence independent of any individual human being and yet meanings are inseparable from its being, such that without those meanings the thing would no longer be what it is.

Subjectivism cannot understand cultural artifacts in this way. The only ways that subjectivism can understand a cultural artifact is as either a complex of meanings intended by a subjectivity or subjectivities (and thus not as an independently existing material thing) or as a material thing to which 'subjective' meanings have somehow become attached. These explanations cannot do justice to the integrity of the artifact as an inherently meaningful thing. The artifact is, in subjectivist language, essentially both external–internal, factual–meaningful, objective–subjective. But the task of formulating an adequate theory of culture and cultural artifacts requires us to describe the artifact in non-dichotomous, coherent terms. This requires us to step outside of subjectivist categories.

The cultural artifact is the embodiment of public meanings, whereas subjectivism understands meanings as the possessions of private subjectivities. It is precisely in the realm of culture that we confront and share in public, non-subjective meaning, that we confront the fact that ideas, images, and systems of interpretations can be objective, quasi-material realities which we come to participate in and which constitute a world of social life and a system for the manipulation of material resources. If we are to conceive of culture as a primary phenomenon, rather than as derived from consciousness or matter or both, then we must theoretically recognize the existence of a realm of public meaning. We cannot derive or constitute the public realm from some kind of amalgamation of individual private subjectivities. A recognition of culture *sui generis,* of culture as a primary reality, requires us to deny that the public realm is derived from the private, derived either existentially or logically. On the contrary, it shows us that the human individual becomes itself, emerges as an individual, only within a cultural, publicly accessible order of existence. This is not an argument for communitarianism against individualism, nor for determinism against freedom, because culture is never monolithic, and is itself the creation of human individuals. Thus the primacy of culture does not make human individuals less free or less individual. Indeed, it is only through culture that human individuals attain personality, become fully human, and thus gain the possibility and the motivation to express their individuality and to oppose prevailing cultural traditions with their own interpretations, thus creating new cultural strains. The cultural community is prior only in the sense that it is the medium in which the human individual becomes, just as the atmosphere is the medium for the development of those flowering plants which not only use carbon dioxide for their nourishment and survival, but also pass on their seed and procreate through the wind.

Subjectivism tended to conceive of culture as a second-order mediating factor standing between subject and object. But this interpretation of culture as a mediating factor is by no means the most negative conception of culture extant in modern philosophy. A more negative, and yet common, view is that culture is actually an obstacle to two of the most fundamental projects of modernity, the attempt to know natural reality as it is in itself, with certainty, and the attempt to know oneself as a free individual, to attain the state of pure, intellectual self-determination, free of influence from tradition and collectivity. In this context, the word 'cultural' has for many philosophers mainly signified a justification for relativism.

For such philosophers, culture cloaks and obscures reality by providing a context of implicit beliefs and interpretive models, imbibed by the individual as if 'with his mother's milk,' which, once the individual becomes an adult 'inquirer,' must be thematized and critically suspended if the unsullied perception of naked reality is to be achieved. Likewise in the domain of action, the mere fact of culture seems to mitigate the possibility of universal ethical norms. In both epistemic and ethical terms, if culture is an inescapable condition of human existence, how can I ever be in absolute *possession* of myself, and hence, how can I ever contact pre-cultural or non-cultural reality?

Modern subjectivism has consistently exhibited a tendency to misconceive culture. This tendency is a natural and inevitable consequence of subjectivist modernity's aims and interests, and the categories through which it hoped to accomplish those aims. The goal of Descartes and other seventeenth- and eighteenth-century philosophers was to cut through medieval culture, to make a new beginning, a new science of nature unobscured by what many intellectuals had come to perceive as a decaying cultural tradition. The task of reforming inquiry was necessarily conceived as a radical one in reaction to the tremendous intellectual weight of a thousand years of medieval tradition. Thus the creators of modernity saw their project not merely as the organization of more adequate themes within culture, but as an attempt to cut beneath all cultural tradition, to found inquiry on *pre-* and *non-*cultural features of reality. Of course, they did not escape from culture; they instigated a new cultural tradition. But that new tradition conceived of itself as piercing through the veil of humanly created tradition to a bedrock of Divinely-made and mathematically-conceived reality.

Subjectivism feared the realm of diverse human customs and creativity as a distorting lens which obscured the simple reflection of what is, of nature, the soul, God, and the Good in the presuppositionless 'mirror of nature.' Any increase in the philosophical attention paid to the pervasiveness of culture threatened to make the individual mind seem an intrinsically social phenomenon, and to root all knowing and perceiving ineluctably in the contexts of particular human communities. This contextualization would belie the very essence of the subjectivist project.

The implicit hostility of subjectivism to culture constitutes one of the paradoxes or ironies of modernity: subjectivism became in the modern period almost synonomous with humanism, became the chief defender of the uniqueness and nobility of the human; yet subjectivism viewed the whole diverse range of human creative and interpretive activity, which is to say culture, as an obstacle to the human search for truth.

Philosophy since Descartes and until recently has with fair consistency clung to various epistemological fantasies criticized by Sellars, Quine, Rorty, and others: the "myth" of the given, the distinction between the order of thought or higher truth and the order of receptivity or empirical truth, and the metaphor of mind as a mirror of nature.[1] These ideas reveal a persistent dream: if only I, the enquirer into truth, could get *outside of* the totality of human interests, beliefs, constructions, interpretations, projects, inherited traditions of thought, and perspectival limitations dictated by birth, family, status, religion, social role, history, and those contrived by myself, then and only then could I know reality *in itself,* as it is, independently of human bias and limitation.

This dream is precisely what Rorty attacks in *Philosophy and the Mirror of Nature.* Not only is this fantasied escape impossible, as many twentieth-century philosophers have argued, but it is also wholly *undesirable,* for in such an 'emancipated' condition, there would not only be no knowledge but also no experience, insofar as experience involves meaning. Furthermore, this fantasy exhibits a dubious ideal for the aspiration of human thinking, according to which the highest state of human mentation is that of a mere register, a passive mirror for the given. For, according to this ideal, all intrinsic activity and content of the mind can only obscure the recognition of the independent nature of the things-themselves.

In fact, culture does not hide the truth; culture is truth's only vehicle. Not only can we not escape culture, we *ought* not, for we would find no meaning, and hence no truth, outside of it. Culture, and culturality (the human capacities for producing and interpreting culture) are essential to human being. Without them there is no human living, only a pre-human existence. Human being must be defined in terms of culture. It is through the revivification of the concept of culture that we can construct a more fruitful alternative perspective to subjectivism, and more fully understand the development of modernity in general.

Anti-Cultural Philosophy

To understand how early subjectivism and philosophical narcissism are anti-cultural, we must answer the following question: given the categories available to philosophical subjectivism and philosophical narcissism, how does each interpret culture and cultural activities?

Subjectivism interpreted culture ambivalently. On the one hand, it reduced culture to the status of either private, subjective meanings and feelings or purely objective artifacts devoid of inherent meaning. That is, subjectivism interpreted cultural events, activities and artifacts through its fundamental dichotomy of subject and object.

On the other hand, early subjectivism had available to it another way of viewing culture, namely, through its conception of transcendental mediating factors. Subjectivist philosophy could view culture and cultural activities as transcending the dichotomy of subject and object through the use of the criterion of rationality.

The conception of transcendental reason, as was seen in Descartes and Kant, provided subjectivism with a means of relating subject and object, of guaranteeing the validity of the subject's inquiry and insight into the nature of non-subjective things. Consequently, wherever subjectivism could consider a cultural theme or activity or artifact rational in execution or content, the latter could participate in transcendental reason and thereby escape reduction to the subject and object categories. Early subjectivist philosophy was therefore justified, on its own terms, in interpreting rational culture as inherently valuable, meaningful, and *true*. Cultural artifacts and activities which do not display a rational structure and content are merely subjective and objective; that is, they are both objective artifacts whose structure and thematic content represent the subjective ideas of their creator and audience, ideas which do not tell us anything about non-subjective reality, and material entities which, in their material being, have no inherent meaning. Rational culture, however, satisfies early subjectivist philosophy's epistemic criteria and reveals truths about the objective world.

The transcendental idea of reason in early subjectivism also made is possible to interpret philosophy as capable of transcending subject and object categories. Philosophy from the seventeenth century through the time of Hegel frequently viewed itself as reason's most complete expression. Philosophy was that cultural product, that form of communicable thought, which made reason explicit, which worked out the implications of transcendental reason, thereby providing explicit justification for the subject's cognitive relationship with the world. This function implied that philosophy had a priority over all other cultural activities. Philosophy lays bare that which is the foundation of all forms of inquiry and the basis of any hope for truth in human cultural activity, be it in art, science, or public discourse. Philosophy exposes the *source* of truth, while other activities (if rational) expose truths.

There is a fine line which needs to be drawn here. Richard Rorty, in his *Philosophy and the Mirror of Nature,* attacks philosophy's claim to priority. His critique is well founded, but it should be stressed that there is a difference between the claim that philosophy *provides* the epistemological justification without which the rest of culture would be epistemically unjustifiable, and the claim that philosophy merely *lays bare* and systematizes a pre-existing epistemological basis that justifies culture regardless of whether philosophy makes it explicit or not. Both claims give philosophy a kind of priority, and one can easily slide into the other. They are, however, different. Early-modern philosophy tended to view Reason itself, not philosophy, as providing the basis of truth and knowledge; philosophy's role is to show us what reason implies. Kant, for example, presumes the truth of Newtonian science; he believes that he is exposing and systematizing and interpreting the nature and limits of that truth. Kant does not believe that science would have no legitimacy without the *Critique.* It is only later in the modern period, most noticeably since the late nineteenth century, that philosophy increasingly conceives of itself as providing the basis for truth. Husserl and Heidegger are at pains to point out that the natural and social sciences are epistemically groundless by themselves and that they require a phenomenological philosophy to give them a foundation in the sphere of primary evidence, a sphere accessible only to philosophy. The Logicist project of early twentieth-century analytic philosophy, which attempted to ground the truth of mathematics, and thus of modern science, in logic, is another example of this tendency.

Philosophical narcissism, by rejecting the transcendental relatedness of subject and object embodied in the earlier concept of transcendental reason, restricts the possible interpretation of culture to its subject
and object categories.

Husserl and Heidegger discuss culture, communication, community, and the meaningfulness of human products, in a number of places.
In his account of transcendental intersubjectivity Husserl speaks of the
"community of monads" and the "spiritual Objectivities" they create,
which forms the "surrounding world of culture."[2] Heidegger discusses
Dasein's "Being-with" others, the encountering of entities as valuable
(the "ready-to-hand") and the world-historical "co-historizing" of communities of Dasein.[3]

These passages reveal that Husserl and Heidegger make the meaning of cultural artifacts and communication a function of the subject's
intentional structure or Dasein's projected world, respectively. Since Dasein's world is a phase of Dasein, Heidegger's interpretation makes the
meaning of artifacts and events a property of Dasein, just as Husserl's
view makes their meaning a property of the subject. For Husserl and
Heidegger such meanings can have no internal relation to artifacts or
events in themselves. Artifacts and events in themselves are intrinsically
non-meaningful, merely "extant" (Heidegger) and must be rigorously
"bracketed," separated from the realm of meaning (Husserl). The meanings of cultural artifacts and activities can reveal only the intentional or
projected world, not a natural world existing independently of the subject since, as Heidegger says, the Being of such a natural world is utterly
disparate from the Being of Dasein's projected world.

The historical embeddedness, community, and communication
that both phenomenologists attempt to establish are misleading. As has
been shown, Husserl's transcendental subjectivity cannot stand, and his
notions of spiritual objectivities, intentional community, and the surrounding world of culture fall with it. Heidegger's Being-with and his
notion of Dasein's involvement in world-historicity may initially appear
more promising, but these ideas suffer from inclusion in his overall conception of world as a characteristic project of Dasein.

The concepts of community and communication necessarily imply
that independent existing individuals do *not* project the world they live
in, that each human being lives in a world that is not structured solely by
his or her existence. The world of my existence is the joint product of an
infinite number of human and non-human entities that exist independently of whatever is projected by the existence I call mine. As Levinas
tells us, these entities are irreducibly "Other." The fact of community and
communication reveals that these irreducibly Other entities share something, affect each other, encounter each other in such a way as to set up a
constantly shifting context for the existence of each. It is impossible for

Husserl and Heidegger to conceive of community, communication, and cultural processes as a primary source of meaning and value, as the primary context for disclosedness, and as a vehicle for truth and understanding. They identify disclosedness, meaning, and understanding with the individual subject or Dasein ("which is in each case mine," says Heidegger). Transindividual processes are logically derivative, since individual subjectivity and individual disclosedness are the context for all phenomena, all philosophical evidence, all reality. Culture, as both communal and subjective–objective and meaningful–material, is inevitably dichotomized by the fundamental dualism of intentionality and nature in Husserl and the division of *Existenz* and *Vorhandensein* in Heidegger.

Philosophical narcissism is by no means restricted to the phenomenological tradition; its anti-culturalism can be seen in diverse schools of philosophy. Logical positivism attempted a radical application of the distinction of the subjective and the non-subjective, and the associated distinction (discussed earlier in connection with Hume and Kant) between the order of subjective receptivity (the empirical) and the order of the subject's spontaneous manipulation of symbols (the analytic). The implication of this view for culture is evident in the positivists' theory of value. Values are an ineradicable part of cultural processes; cultural artifacts and communicative events cannot be value-neutral without ceasing to be cultural. The positivists denied that values and meanings have any non-subjective existence, that the empirical world can be meaningful or valuable, and that values could be anything other than emotions.[4] Wittgenstein declared in his early *Tractatus Logico-Philosophicus* that:

> The sense of the world must lie outside the world . . . *in* it no value exists . . . . Any value . . . must lie outside the whole sphere of what happens and is the case . . . . So too it is impossible for there to be propositions of ethics. Propositions can express nothing that is higher . . . . (Ethics and aesthetics are one and the same.)[5]

It is striking to compare Wittgenstein's comment to a passage from Husserl's *Ideas* (volume one), a work usually considered antithetical to positivism. Husserl wrote:

> Absurdity first arises when one . . . fails to notice that the whole being of the world consists in a certain "meaning" which presupposes absolute consciousness as the field from which the meaning is derived.[6]

Meaning is derived solely from consciousness and the attempt to derive it from the world can only bring absurdity. Even more striking is Heidegger's remark on values in his later *Letter On Humanism* (1947): "Every valuing is a subjectivizing . . . thinking in values is the *greatest blasphemy imaginable* against Being."[7] (my emphasis)

These comments suggest that the whole world of cultural artifacts and cultural discourse is irrelevant to what philosophers could regard to be true. They imply that the criteria of philosophical truth find no application in non-philosophic culture, that culture contains no truth as far as the philosophers in question can see. This view is not atypical; many contemporary philosophers write as if the whole history of human culture, the cultural testimony of our entire species, has nothing to say to the project of philosophy, has no truths to tell. Such thinkers endorse epistemic and methodological criteria which make other cultural activities and products irrelevant to the philosophical quest. For example, positivism made the rational discussion of political values nonsensical and phenomenology makes the physical constitution of the universe seem irrelevant. According to this view, philosophy is a non-empirical, value-neutral, meta-critique primarily concerned with problems of language, logic, and signification. Philosophy's goal is not to enhance our understanding of the world, of nature, art, and human being, but to enhance our understanding of the tools of understanding (language, logic, texts, etc.) This view divorces philosophy from the rest of the culture, making philosophy epistemically superior or simply irrelevant to whatever non-philosophical human beings do, say, or think.

Just as the anti-culture of late modernity involves culture's delegitimation of itself, some of the most influential philosophical schools of this century have declared philosophy to be dead. Wittgenstein claimed that philosophy's only remaining legitimate task is to wait until someone utters a linguistically misleading statement, and then to point out the error. "The correct method in philosophy," he wrote, would be:

> to say nothing except what can be said, i.e., propositions of natural science—i.e., *something that has nothing to do with philosophy*—and then, whenever someone else wanted to say something metaphysical, to demonstrate to him that he had failed to give a meaning to certain signs in his propositions.[8]

Beyond this, according to Wittgenstein's famous phrase, "What we cannot speak about we must pass over in silence."[9]

Heidegger proclaimed the death of philosophy in his "The End of Philosophy and the Task of Thinking" (1966).[10] He argued that philosophy has emptied itself out into the scientific disciplines of the contemporary Western world. The latter are the proper fulfillment of the project by which philosophy has defined itself since Plato. How can this be? Because Heidegger identifies philosophy with the metaphysics of subjectivity, a metaphysics that is the foundation of and is realized in modern science. This makes the scientific-technological domination of the world the fulfillment of the essential project of Western philosophy. Heidegger distinguishes philosophy from thinking, of which we have continued need. But philosophy, which is a history of the working-out of an obstacle to thinking, is justifiably interred.

Many of the intellectual heirs of Wittgenstein agree with many of the heirs of Heidegger that philosophy ought to be resolved into an analysis of language, spoken or written. The former see their discipline as the clarification of the meanings and syntax of science or ordinary language, while the latter favor the dissolution of philosophy into a kind of literary criticism. In either case, the philosophical task of improving our understanding or appreciation of the world is de-legitimated.

The anti-culturalism of late-modern culture is apparent not only in philosophy, but in much of contemporary intellectual culture. Movements as seemingly antithetical as liberal capitalist ideology and Marxist-socialist theory share a common orientation: the subordination of communal-symbolic processes and socio-cultural activities to economic processes.[1] Both systems see socio-cultural phenomena as determined by economy, by the means and relations of production. Indeed, the subordination of society and culture to economy could justifiably be considered one of the hallmarks of modern culture in general, in both its capitalist and Marxist versions, and stands in sharp contrast to ideas characteristic of pre-modern or traditional societies. In the latter, social organization and cultural phenomena are believed to have a foundation and a stability independent of the economic order; economics was subordinated, subsumed and restricted by socio-cultural values. In contrast, the logic of both capitalist and Marxist ideology asserts that social life is founded on economic life, and that social progress, since it will inevitably be constituted by economic progress, requires that socio-cultural values and activities be made fluid and ever adaptable to changing modes of production and administration. The technical-productive-administrative sector is the determining sector, and the source of all benefit and value within society.

Recently, Marshall Berman has argued persuasively that Western avant-garde cultural movements since the late nineteenth century, despite their persistent attack on bourgeois values and concepts, were not only generated by bourgeois-capitalist development, but have actually shared much of the latter's view of life.[12] They shared the view that all cultural and traditional values and concepts are relative in the face of the fundamentally volatile and dynamic character of human social existence. This volatility and dynamism is the product of capitalist economic activity and must be, if capitalism is intellectually honest with itself, the essence of the capitalist view of human reality. Berman suggest that the avant-garde's critique of traditional values and its enshrinement of fluidity, dynamism, revolution, or even nihilism expressed a view of reality and of culture which implicitly accepted the modern economy's exclusive right to define reality. In this view, culture *reacts* to a reality which is created elsewhere; culture itself is fluid and determined by the non-cultural.

Post-Modernism

Subjectivism has run its course. Its liabilities now outweigh its possible contributions. Its paradoxes and difficulties make it unable to help us out of our present intellectual dilemmas. Most philosophers recognize this in some sense, but fail to see just how pervasive the subjectivist categories are, particularly when they are dressed up in the form of philosophical narcissism. The latter is thought by many to be an alternative to subjectivism. It is not an alternative; it is a more problematic stage of subjectivism itself.

The transformation of subjectivism into narcissism is part of what makes many contemporary philosophers believe that philosophy is at an end, or that the age of modernity is over, that we have entered a post-modern and post-philosophic epoch. Subjectivism has been so dominant and pervasive within modernity that many writers cannot distinguish between modernity and subjectivism, or between subjectivism and philosophy. The self-negation of subjectivism has led philosophers and other intellectuals to think that there are no possibilities left for philosophy or for intellectual culture in general, that, just as Spengler claimed, Western philosophic culture has exhausted itself.

Philosophy is not at its end. It is not at an end because it is not wedded for life to ideas like certainty, substance, consciousness, presence, absolute truth, God, subject, and object. Neither is modernity at an end, although it has certainly passed beyond its early or classical phase. Subjectivist modernity has exhausted itself in the sense that it has negated itself, but modernity was never synonomous with subjectivism. In the first place subjectivism was only a part, a phase, a strain of interpretation within intellectual modernity, although it was the most dominant and pervasive of modernity's traditions of interpretation. But further, modernity is not solely or even primarily a philosophical or intellectual movement. Social and economic modernity can continue with minimal cooperation from philosophy and other cultural activities. Modernity may have changed its course, but there is not sufficient reason to consider the most recent trends post-modern. Modernity has still more cards to play.

In *Philosophy and the Mirror of Nature*,[13] Richard Rorty has produced an important critique of philosophical modernity. Rorty's attack on the Cartesian-Lockean-Kantian epistemological tradition, and his perception that early twentieth-century analytic philosophy and phenomenology retain, rather than reject, the fundamental tendencies of that tradition is insightful and correct. His criticism of the conception of philosophy as providing the epistemological scaffolding and *Grund* for all of culture, a conception which Rorty correctly sees to be a common presupposition of diverse post-Kantian philosophical schools, is a necessary step in the revision of our notion of philosophy and of philosophy's role within culture. In the end, Rorty clearly wishes to move in the direction of the late Dewey, toward a generally pragmatic conception of philosophy. With all of this I have the greatest sympathy.

Yet, like so many of the critics of modern philosophy and advocates of post-modernity, Rorty's imagination of what is now left for philosophy to do seems ambiguous and limited. Rorty does not believe that philosophy is at an end, but he does believe that the traditional aims and goals of philosophy must be given up in favor of a philosophy which will accept its place within the "conversation" of culture as an "edifying" rather than a "systematic" endeavor. Rorty, like so many other contemporary thinkers, claims that there is a chasm, a great rift between most of the history of philosophy and the twentieth-century writers who have finally put philosophy on the right track; in Rorty's case, these writers are Dewey, Wittgenstein and Heidegger, each in their later works.

It is true that philosophy must be understood in cultural terms as part of the on-going "conversation of mankind." But this does not mean rejecting systematic philosophy, philosophy whose aim is to grasp truth, goodness, and beauty. To conceive of the quest for truth as a merely systematic notion, which is somehow opposed to the idea of philosophy as an edifying, non-systematic discipline, is to employ restricted notions of truth, system, and construction. If we accept as given that inquiry is hypothetical and never finished, never certain and never unimprovable, that it is a practical activity, that inquiry or the attempt to improve our understanding of things is a legitimate and virtually eternal aspect of human culture, and that it is only within and through cultural activities and products that understanding and truth *occur at all,* then systematic construction and non-systematic edification become simply different aspects and phases of the same cultural-philosophic process.

In this light, Plato, Descartes, and Kant are not cut off from us by a conceptual moat and we do not finally have it right, having rejected their falsely non-edifying notion of philosophy. They forged concepts to better understand the most problematic features of their world and we will continue to do the same.

Some contemporary writers, however, go far beyond Rorty's ambiguous hopes for philosophy's future to a straightforward rejection of the notion of philosophy as an independently valuable kind of inquiry. The philosophers of deconstruction often conceive of philosophy as the deconstruction of literary and past philosophical texts; while many Anglo-

American writers see philosophy as conceptual therapy for ordinary civilians and for those philistine philosophers who persist in their systematic ways. Both groups implicitly favor philosophy's dissolution into some form of critical social or natural science or literary criticism. Thus, philosophy's function becomes that of either a starving animal cannibalizing itself or a parasite living off of the still vital bodies of other disciplines.

These writers seem to have lost any notion of the intellectual life as having a social role, as being concerned with extra-textual reality and, in particular, concerned with the fate of human society and culture. Their work represents, as Emmanuel Levinas remarks, the "primacy of theoretical reason," of formal structures over human content. They seem especially unconscious (except for their "strange sensitivity for a certain apocalyptic poetry," as Levinas calls it) of the fact that modern civilization has run into a few difficulties lately, chief among which is our unparalleled capacity and propensity for the destruction of human individuals.[14] I refer not only to the possibility of nuclear destruction, but to the manifold technical innovations of modern warfare and of social control, as well as to the organizational advances which make the use of these new technologies possible, and to the frightening adaptability of our moral values and democratic ideals to these practices.

Other contemporary thinkers do employ structuralist, post-structuralist, and deconstructionist methods towards social and political ends. Michel Foucault and Giles Deleuze, for example, dissect the conceptual structures (like penal and psychiatric conceptions) used by power-centers for the repressive organization of society and personality. The logic of these methods, however, undermines all the positive conceptions of modernity, particularly those of modern humanism. They leave no room for positive conceptions of human nature and thus for the positive political conceptions essential to social reform. According to Foucault, "man is only a recent invention," because human nature is indistinguishable from the systems of representation of humanity embodied by modern human sciences.[15] For Deleuze, bourgeois repression can only be combatted by an analysis of human beings as "desiring-machines."[16] These and other "anti-egologists," despite the value of their attack on subjectivism, reject the understanding of human being as integral or substantial on political and epistemological grounds.[17] They fail to notice two problems with this approach. First, although they are apparently concerned to discredit the repressive forces militating against human freedom, their methods lead to the discrediting of the beings they wish to liberate from those forces. As Levinas writes, they have produced an "effacing of the living man," a reductive definition of human individuals in terms of the sociological and linguistic structures that work themselves out in them.[18] Second, the sweeping nature of their criticism can be used indiscriminately to attack any positive notion, any proposed reconstruction of society and human life. This is why Jurgen Habermas has labelled the proponents of post-structuralism and deconstruction the "young conservatives."[19] For purely negative criticism implicitly promotes the view that any potential rationale for social action is equally invalid. If all are equally invalid, then all are equally valid. Programs of social action are excused from the need to demonstrate a rationale, and, if they make no pretension of rationality or justifiability, are immune from rational criticism. The choice of one program over another is admitted to be irrational, thereby legitimating the self-serving, aggressive, and paranoiac tendencies of any political community.[20]

The philosophers who reject the notion of philosophy as inquiry, those whose devotion to formal analysis leads them to de-legitimate human integrity and those whose criticism is designed to sweep aside any potential positive claim about human being and the world, all implicitly accept philosophy's irrelevance to human choice and thus to human existence. They accept criteria for conceptual legitimacy that price their work out of the marketplace of human concerns. For humans are condemned to choose, and to interpret the world so as to choose better. Humans do not have the luxury of not choosing, the luxury of being purely negative or abstaining from judging the relative merits of problematic alternatives. Many philosophers, even many who see their work as politically relevant, implicitly consign their work to irrelevance by undermining the very notions of political community and the bases of value decisions that are presumed by social debate and choice. Such writers fulfill the diagnosis of the self-negation of the Enlightenment offered by Adorno and Horkheimer, that "Every substantial goal which men might adduce as an alleged rational insight is . . . delusion, lies or 'rationalization'."[21] They embody, perhaps unintentionally, Wittgenstein's proscription on the function of philosophy: philosophers may reveal the problematic nature of any pronouncement on human affairs and reality, but in response to the question, how then ought we understand reality and human affairs and what should we do about them?, philosophers must remain silent.

The post-modernists who call for a radical rejection of modernity often forget that we have a stake in the preservation of some aspects of modernity, a stake which reaches outside of philosophy. There are aspects of our modern social life and culture, the erosion of which is apparent today, about which we ought to think several times before abandoning. Humanism is one of these aspects and democracy is another. These ideas are not intellectual toys or chains of signifiers; they are cultural achievements with tremendous practical meaning (a theme to which I will return in the epilogue).

In his later years, after being forced into exile by the Nazis, Ernst Cassirer offered an indictment of the professional philosophy of his time which should be remembered as a warning to future philosophers. He contrasted the "scholastic" conception of philosophy with that of a philosophy immersed in the world. To this end, Cassirer echoed the words of Albert Schweitzer, who had said in 1922 that philosophy at that time had exempted itself from the struggle over the values of modern culture precisely at the moment when that culture was confronted with its greatest crisis, with a potential "self-annihilation of culture." Cassirer lamented in 1935, on the eve of events whose catastrophic impact no one could forsee:

> I believe that all of us who have worked in the area of theoretical philosophy in the last decades deserve . . . this reproach of Schweitzer; I do not exclude myself . . . . While endeavoring on behalf of the scholastic conception of philosophy, immersed in its difficulties as if caught in its subtle problems, we have all too frequently lost sight of the true connection of philosophy with the world. But today we can no longer keep our eyes closed to the menacing danger . . . .[22]

It is not necessary to believe that we are today on the brink of destruction in order to embrace a notion of philosophy as immersed in worldly matters. We need only see that the whole history of philosophy is a testament of its involvement in the cultural and social life of mankind. To believe otherwise is to accept an eviscerated conception of philosophy.

10

The Metaphysics of Culture: A Pluralist-Naturalist View

This chapter is a prolegomena to a systematic non-subjectivist philosophy rooted in an adequate understanding of culture. It is a prolegomena because its aim is to attack certain obstacles to such a philosophy and to suggest theoretical points on which the latter can be built.

When raising a tent, stakes are often used to pin key points of the tent to the ground. The stakes are not a foundation for the tent; they are fixed nodal points that orient the tent, determine its parameters, and help to give the established structure its shape. If the terrain is rocky, the ground has to be cleared of potential obstacles before planting the stakes.

This chapter will clear away conceptual obstacles that lie in the way of the stakes of a more adequate philosophical tent. The conceptual obstacles in question are three pernicious dichotomies which have had a great—although often unnoticed—effect on contemporary ways of thinking.

The first is the by now familiar subject–object dichotomy, along with the host of dualisms it has either spawned or made more intractable: the realm of meaning versus the realm of fact; mind versus body; inner (that is, within the subject) versus outer; conceptual spontaneity versus sensuous receptivity; theoretical language versus observation language; the subject matter and methods of the humanities versus the subject and methods of the sciences, etc.

The second dichotomy is the presumed incompatability of the existential integrity of things and the internal relatedness of things. The third is the common antithesis of culture and nature, the assumed unbridgeable qualitative distinction between the realm of human cultural life and natural, bio-physical processes.

After showing that these dichotomies are unnecessary, I will replace them with hypotheses that serve to stake out the basic points of a systematic philosophical perspective that would avoid the interminable and unprofitable problems entailed by these dichotomies.

A systematic philosophy, to paraphrase Robert Neville, is a philosophical perspective intended to be sufficiently general that everything can be addressed from it.[1] A systematic philosophy in this sense need not work out a system or an elaborated architectonic of categories. Rather, it is the articulation of a perspective which can potentially address all matters of import, and which concerns our fundamental interpretive approaches to the world. Another way of saying this is that a systematic philosophy is one which in principle renounces the possibility of responding to a counterexample by denying the counterexample's relevance to its own concerns.

The fundamental assumptions of a theory cannot be proven within the context of that theory. A systematic philosophical theory cannot be proven at all, since it aspires to being so general that it cannot be incorporated into a more general context (as, for example, a chemical theory might claim to have its assumptions validated by a theory of microphysics). It can, however, be shown to be inconsistent or inadequate to the interpretation of some area of reality.

Systematic philosophies are unavoidably *hypothetical*. They can be justified on only two grounds: that they are conceptually plausible or consistent; and, that they reveal or illuminate previously obscure features of reality, thereby enhancing our understanding or appreciation of what is. A systematic philosophical perspective is the assertion that, given its perspective, the world or some important aspect of the world makes more sense, or can be seen more fully, or understood more completely, or interpreted more fruitfully than is possible given other perspectives.

All philosophies, whether systematic or not, are oriented around or rooted in a particular set of problems or phenomena that arise in the face of particular intellectual traditions. The mind of the philosopher is fortunately no more a *tabula rasa* than the mind of any other human being. Every act of philosophy begins with the recognition of the inadequacy of a particular tradition of interpretation in the face of particular realities, giving rise to particular questions in regard to which the philosopher has an intuitive belief about the direction that will lead to a better interpretation.

Philosophies exhibit characteristic centers of gravity, concepts which seem to the philosopher in question to promise a better perspective for addressing the problem at hand. Once the problem at hand has been addressed to some degree of satisfaction, these core concepts or centers of gravity will affect the philosopher's subsequent investigations of new areas.

I am suggesting that philosophy will be better able to handle the most important problems it has now to face, to produce valuable work at this point in history, if philosophy orients itself around a particular center of gravity: the recognition of the centrality of culture to human being and the world that human beings encounter. It is not necessary for all philosophers to do so, but there is a crucial need for enough philosophers to turn in this direction so that the cultural dimension of the human process regains legitimacy within philosophy as a whole. The aim of this chapter is to open up new possibilities for philosophy by bridging some of the conceptual difficulties that make these possibilities seem too problematic to draw serious attention.

This chapter contains four sections. The first addresses the dichotomy of existential integrity and internal relatedness and proposes a hypothetical alternative that serves as the basis for the rest of chapter. The second section elaborates the concept of culture and its philosophically important features. The third section presents the implications of a cultural perspective for our notions of mind and knowledge. Lastly, section 4 argues that a pluralistic account of nature would defuse the dichotomy of culture and nature.

Integrity and Relation

The world will make more sense, and a number of philosophical conundrums will be defused, if the following hypothesis is accepted: the idea of reality requires that there be existences characterized by individual integrity—existential integrities—which are internally related. The individual existential integrity and internal relation of beings presume and imply each other, insofar as each is equally essential to the concept of reality or of any real entity. If we do not accept this principle, then the world makes no sense; or better, we cannot appreciate the world.

An individual existential integrity is an existing thing, entity, process, factor, or quality which has a degree of wholeness, a character or nature in the broadest sense, which makes it irreducible to and distinct from other existences. Reality must be conceived as populated, at least in part, by entities with existential integrity, such that the integrity of such individuals cannot be said to be entirely derived from or reducible to other individuals or relations to other individuals.

"Internally related" means that every individual with integrity must also be conceived as being related to at least some others in such a way that these relations, and consequently the related entities themselves (relata) are constituents of the individual integrity in question. That is, the individual would not be *what it is* without these relations to other individuals. The individual integrity and the internal relatedness of existences are mutually implicating and reciprocal; one cannot obtain without the other. An entity cannot have its own-being, its own individual character or integrity, cannot be an existing something without being dependent on and involved with other entities, without being constituted by relations, and vice versa. Reality makes no sense, cannot be adequately interpreted, if this principle is denied.

It should be noted that the principle of the necessary inclusion of relations in the integrity of an existent necessarily implies the inclusions of the *objects* of those relations (the relata) as well. It implies that that-to-which a thing is internally related is essentially reciprocal with and necessary for the thing's existential integrity. A thing's relata are part of it, are essential to it, along with its relations. (Henceforth the term "relation" is meant to include the corresponding relata, unless otherwise stated.)

The crucial import of this principle is the following. The *very idea of the real* collapses if either: all individual existents are thoroughly analyzed into relations to or functions of others, so that there can be no individual integrity; or, it is asserted that relations to others are irrelevant to what each individual is.

The import of the principle is that, however we approach the task of understanding our world, the conjunction of individual integrity and internal relatedness is a minimal condition for an adequate beginning. We must hold together two thoughts which are often treated as antithetical or incompatible: that existing things are *both* individual integrities and essentially related to other things.

The principle of the reciprocity of individual integrity and internal relatedness, and the spirit of the entire discussion of the present section, is inspired in part by the unique and profound work of Justus Buchler. Of concern here in particular is Buchler's concept of "integrity" and "identity." While Buchler employs a very different language from that used here, the issue at hand is one to which central notions of Buchler's philosophy speak directly.

For Buchler, whatever can be discriminated is a "natural complex."[2] Every complex is analyzable into an indefinite number of "traits," which are themselves "subaltern complexes" and constitute the given complex.

Every complex is also "located" within an "order" or "orders," themselves complexes, within which the complex in question "prevails" and exhibits relations to other complexes. Relations are traits, and a complex is related if it affects or conditions the complex in question. Buchler uses the term 'integrity' in a way that is *not* synonomous with my use of the term, to refer to what a complex is in a given order, which is distinct from its scope or comprehensiveness within a given order.

Every natural complex, since it prevails in an indefinite number of orders, has an indefinite number of integrities. The totality of its integrities is its "contour" or "gross integrity." Buchler defines the identity of a complex as "the continuous relation that obtains between the contour of a complex and any of its integrities."[3] For Buchler every entity is a society or a plurality; nothing is simple. Furthermore, every thing is unfinished or yet-to-be-fully-defined in that its future functioning or location in novel orders will give it ever new integrities, just as our future analysis of it will disclose in it new traits or complexes. It is Buchler's notion of "contour" or "gross integrity" which is roughly equivalent to what I mean by "integrity."

What is important for the present circumstance is that Buchler conceives of each entity as being at least partially constituted by its relations to other entities (traits) and by those other entities in relation to which the entity in question functions or stands as something or other (orders). The result is that the identity, contour, and integrities of a natural complex are unthinkable without relations and vice versa. Buchler has made the concept of integrity and the idea of identity necessary for the concept of relatedness and vice versa.

The failure to conjoin individual integrity and internal relatedness on the same theoretical level, the inability to see these two features of reality as co-constituting and mutually necessary, has been a pervasive characteristic of Western philosophy. (It is this failure which lies at the heart of Levinas' critique of the history of "ontology" as a history of the reduction of the Other to the Same.)[4]

There are many examples throughout the history of philosophy of systems of thought which have attempted to isolate certain existences or realms or types of existences from internal relatedness, such relatedness being then allowed to pervade the rest of existence. Certain existences have been claimed to have a non-related and hence non-dependent and non-changing integrity, thereby insuring that there be an absolute independency, an absolute being, in whatever order of things was being discussed.

The Aristotelian *ousia* or substance is only one, albeit one of the most influential and important, of the instances of this pervasive tendency of thought. In Aristotle's *Categories* substance is defined as *hypokeimenon,* the "underlying," that of which other factors are predicated but which is itself never predicated of anything else. Although Aristotle may have intended *ousia* to be understood in a way more consonant with the meaning it has in his physical and metaphysical theory, the concept was interpreted in medieval times and in much of modern philosophy in terms of that underlying, non-predicable subject of all predicates defined by his logic.[5] As *hypokeimenon,* substance is an essentially unchanging something, not essentially related to any other thing; that is, it is non-predicable. That which is a substance is not dependent upon relations to other existences for its own being. It is the other nine categories of existences defined by Aristotle which are dependent on substance for their being.

This notion is prototypical of much of the subsequent Western philosophical tradition, asserting that there must be an ultimate or foundational type of being, and that the criterion of its ultimacy or primacy is *independence* (non-dependence on other beings), which necessarily implies an absence of internal relations. For whatever is internally related must be intrinsically dependent.

The various Western philosophical and theological notions of God reflect the difficulties of attempting to conceive of an essentially non-dependent, non-related being, a being whose existence and character does not depend on relations to any other existences. To be sure, God has not always been conceived in this way in the Western tradition, nor have all non-relational conceptions of God been identical. Nevertheless, since ancient times Western thinkers have wrestled with the on-going problem of how to reconcile two seemingly opposing aspects of Divinity: God as essentially related to other beings (God as creator and preserver); and God as essentially unrelated to others (God as the primary, independent, ideal Being). If God is the ideal Being who needs nothing, why then did He act, why did He create, and what conceivable on-going interest could He have in the created universe? Interest would seem to indicate something like desire, yet if God has desires regarding creation then according to the tradition which identifies desire with need or incompleteness and lack of desire with self-sufficiency, must not God be thought of as *in*complete and *non*-self-sufficient?

Aristotle's Unmoved Mover was a brilliant resolution of this problem, within certain limits.[6] The Unmoved Mover can be both self-sufficient and the cause of all motion in the universe because it is a *final* cause, it moves other beings by itself being the ultimate object of desire. Yet this solution can only work within the Aristotelian system, because for Aristotle matter is eternal and uncreated, and so the Unmoved Mover did not have to create matter. Consequently, Aristotle could resolve the problem of the perfect integrity of self-sufficiency versus the essentially related-creative aspects of Divinity only because he had already accepted a limited divinity, a divinity which was not the only eternal, primary being.

The medieval and modern Christian tradition could not avail itself of this Aristotelian solution, given that it was committed to an absolute and unlimited notion of Divinity. The difficulty of reconciling God's self-sufficiency and creativity can be seen to run throughout Christian philosophy, reflected in arguments over the relation of God to creation. In the debate between voluntarists and rationalists, for example, the former claimed that creation was not necessary or logically required by God's nature, that the world is not essential to God, and the latter claimed that creation is the rational and necessary effluence of God's nature.[7] In short, the problems attendant upon the attempt to conceive of a self-sufficient, essentially unrelated and non-dependent being have been particularly evident in the field concerned with the ultimate being, theology.

The Cartesian concept of the essence of the human as *res cogitans* serves as another illustration of the attempt to conceive of a category of existences as essentially unrelated to others in order to conceive of it as integral, as having its own-being. The human being is essentially a 'thinking thing', *res cogitans,* a mental substance in which ideas inhere as attributes. This thinking substance is the logically and existentially primary being; it is, initially at least, the only being whose existence cannot be doubted. Descartes makes it clear that the existence of thinking substance, of 'I', *in no way* depends upon other finite entities. At the end of the *Meditations* he allows that mind and matter (the body) are closely related, yet this relation is clearly external. That is, the nature of the I, what the mind is essentially, is not constituted by nor dependent upon the body or any other finite substance. Descartes made it clear from the outset that one of his aims was to prove the immortality of the soul. This immortality requires that the soul or mind be independent of and essentially unrelated to that region of being which is subject to decay and disintegration, that is, *res extensa.* Minds cannot disintegrate or change their form; material objects, like bodies, can and do. Again, in Descartes' anthropology, as in much of Western theology and in Aristotle's metaphysics, the integrity of a being is inversely related to its internal relatedness to other beings.

There is a counter-tradition in Western philosophic history which finds internal relations beneath and behind every case of individual integrity. This tradition begins with Heraclitus; in modern and contemporary thought it has been radically emphasized by Hume and, recently, by structuralists and post-structuralists. This tradition acknowledges that each individual entity is what it is only because of its relations with other entities, processes, or factors. The more one looks for such relations or relata, the more one finds them, and ultimately it may appear, as it does to the theorists in question, that each individual is *nothing but* a nexus of relations and relata, that there is no existential integrity, no 'own-ness' belonging to the existing individual logically distinct from such relations.

This can be seen in David Hume's *Inquiry Concerning Human Understanding*. He rejects the Aristotelian-Scholastic concept of substance which had been a cornerstone of seventeenth-century thought. Hume reduces entities to collections of sense impressions; that is, a thing is the sum of impressions belonging to a mind which associates them as constituting the entity in question. There is no *hypokeimenon,* no underlying substance supporting these impressions, no non-predicable subject of all impressional predicates.

This analysis applies to human being, to mind or the self, as well as to non-human substance. There is no mental substance for Hume, no substantial self. The 'self' is a name for a collection of impressions and ideas, literally a "bundle" of perceptions,[8] as Hume writes in his *Treatise on Human Nature.* Impressions are relata; that is, they obtain in the individual by virtue of the individual's coming into certain kinds of relation (for example, the relation of 'perception') to other entities. Consequently, the self, mind, or 'I' is what it is solely by virtue of its relations to other things, so much so that it is literally a collection of the effects (impressions) of its relations or contacts with other entities. There is no own-being of the human self, no integral character; there are only the effects produced by its manifold and shifting relations to other entities.

These two apparently antithetical traditions of thought, one subordinating relatedness to integrity and one analyzing all integrity into relations and relata, are in fact both aspects of *one* overarching tradition which conceives of individual integrity and internal relatedness as somehow incompatible. The conception is common and pervasive that the more thoroughly an entity is internally related to others, the less fully it *is* in itself, and, on the other hand, the more an entity is characterized by a distinct identity or integrity, the less it is 'involved' in the world, in relations, in changing multiplicity.

In fact, these two lines of thought are almost always intertwined to some degree. That is, a philosophy may, on its surface, emphasize either integrity or relation, yet almost always smuggles the opposing principle into its system at some point or at some theoretical level. This is because no philosophy which claims to be aimed at furthering our understanding of the world can wholly dispense with either individual integrity or relatedness. The idea of the real would collapse without them. Yet, few philosophies explicitly admit the principle of their reciprocity. Lacking this explicit admission, a philosophical system must adopt one of two strategies. It may renounce the concern for and the aim of understanding reality, deny the connection of philosophic thought with reality. Or it may make room for both individual integrities and internal relations through various ultimately inadequate theoretical mechanisms, still without recognizing their intrinsic reciprocity; in particular, it may relegate them to different levels of analysis.

The end of Hume's *Inquiry* furnishes us with one of the few examples of the former.[9] By the final sections of the *Inquiry*, self and substance have been analyzed into complexes of impressions. As already mentioned, Hume has denied the existence of any existential integrities, coherences, and stabilities for the philosophic mind to know. He denies that we can know with certainty that there are natural entities which correspond to our manifold and changing impressions. At this point, with remarkable honesty and courage, Hume admits that while this is the end of what philosophy can tell us, it is also true that this skeptical conclusion of philosophy must necessarily fade in the daylight of living concerns. Life dictates that we must act *as if* we know what philosophic inquiry tells us we can never know. We must admit that philosophy, whatever its internal beauty and consistency, has *nothing* to do with living reality. Philosophic inquiry is a closed system, segregated from life, which it can make no claim to either understand or control. Philosophy reaches an absolute limit in its attempt to understand life and world, but life does not respect this limit, life forces us to live beyond what we can know in a rational, philosophic sense. Hume recognizes that given his analysis there is a chasm between inquiry and life, recognizes that he is at the limit of his philosophy, and does not attempt to obscure the fact.[10]

Most philosophers, unlike Hume, adopt the second strategy. That is, those who assert the existence of individual existential integrities generally do not fail to recognize the existence of relatedness, nor vice versa. To do so would lead to absurdities. Their strategy is rather to *segregate* the dimension, theoretical level, or region of reality within which the existence of integrity is recognized from the dimension within which relation is admitted to be prevalent. Thus it has often been claimed that the 'essence' of an entity is non-related, is independent and unchanging, while it is by virtue of the entity's 'accidental' qualities that it is related to other things. For example, in the seventeenth century essential or primary qualities of a material object were claimed to belong to it by virtue of its own nature and not to be dependent on its relations to other things, whereas its 'secondary' qualities belong to it only by virtue of its relations to sense organs and minds. The 'true' or real object of knowledge is then usually claimed to be the independent, unrelated entity of primary qualities, whereas its relational 'appearances', what it is by virtue of relations, is not the real or true thing, the thing-in-itself, the thing accessible to mathematical treatment and hence scientific knowledge.

This traditional problem of the seeming incompatibility of existential integrity and internal relation has great significance for the analysis of modern subjectivism. Modern subjectivism shares this pervasive inability to think individual integrity and internal relatedness together. Modern subjectivism brings this conceptual inability, which in itself is not peculiar to modern thought, to bear on its innovative grounding of philosophy in subjectivity. The dynamic self-negation of subjectivism and the subsequent dialectics of philosophical narcissism are *direct* results of this more general conceptual inability. The founding of philosophic inquiry on the dichotomous categories of subjectivity and objectivity is problematic in a variety of ways, but the dialectical and paradoxical difficulties that we have seen in modern subjectivism and narcissism are in particular the product of the *combination* of the subjectivist viewpoint and the tradition which views relation and integrity as antithetical. The latter pre-dates the former; the dialectical problems of modern subjectivism result from the long-standing dichotomy of integrity and relation being applied to the new, modern categories of subjectivity and objectivity.

Subjectivism necessarily understands individual subjectivity and what belongs to it as an individual entity, process, or field. It is incumbent upon subjectivism then to describe or present a theory of the relations of the subject and the subjective to what is not a part of the individual subjectivity; that is, to the rest of the world. This incumbency obtains regardless of whether a particular version of subjectivism does or does not ascribe to subjectivity the metaphysical status of a substance, as in Descartes. Once the distinction between the subjective and what-is-not-subjective is adopted as fundamental, then the field of subjectivity has been discriminated as an identifiable logical individual, and the question as to the way(s) in which its properties relate to other features and entities of the world becomes crucial.

And here, the old problem of integrity and relation comes into play. What subjectivism cannot allow is an *internal* or intrinsic relation between the subject and entities existing independently of subjectivity. Unable to admit internal relations between the independently existing integrities of the subject and of non-subjective entities, subjectivism sought other strategies for relating them. Early-modern subjectivism, as in the cases of Descartes and Kant, introduced specific faculties and principles to account for the possibility of relatedness to the world. The transcendental mediating factors referred to in the analysis of subjectivism are in fact mechanisms of relation by which the experiences and ideas, the contents or constituents of individual subjectivity can be said to characterize the nature or integrity of entities that do not belong to subjectivity. Thus subjectivism, unable to conceive each subjectivity as internally related to other individual integrities, including other subjectivities, posited mechanisms of relation that allowed the field of the subjective, the modern Archimedean point, to be regarded *sui generis,* as itself an individual existential integrity.

Philosophical narcissism criticized earlier subjectivism. It quite correctly recognized that the transcendental mechanisms of relation characteristic of earlier subjectivism are unjustifiable on subjectivism's own internal grounds. There can be no transcendental vehicle of relatedness split off from the level at which subject and object are conceived; and if such a means of relatedness cannot 'transcend' the level of analysis in which subject and non-subject stand as opposites, then it must stand within that level and therefore belong to either subject or object. There can be no "third thing."

As a result of this criticism (insofar as the fundamental subjectivist categories are still in force either explicitly or implicitly) the problem of individual integrity and relatedness becomes acute. Still unable to think individual integrity and relatedness together, and having rejected transcendental mechanisms of relation, the integrity of the subject and the objective integrities cannot be conceived as being internally related. In particular, the integrity of the subjective cannot be reconciled with its seemingly intrinsic relatedness to the object-world. The result: one or the other of these seemingly opposed factors must be denied or reduced to the other. *Either* the subject's integrity must absorb its relations and its relata *or* its relations and relata must absorb its integrity. Given that the tradition cannot think integrity and relation together without its now-defunct transcendentalism, one of the two factors must be eliminated.

Only two conceptual possibilities exist for a philosophy that retains subjectivist categories and eliminates their transcendental mechanisms of relation. If subjectivity is to continue to be conceived as having existential integrity then anything to which the subject is said to be internally related must belong to, must actually be part of, the subject itself. Subjectivity cannot be internally related to anything 'outside' of itself. All relata, all *cogitata,* all things-which-appear must be purely 'internal' to the subject. This is the path that Husserl's philosophy takes. If, on the other hand, subjectivity is to continue to be conceived as related to manifold elements of the world, then subjectivity must be nothing other than such relations. Here, subjectivity becomes a set of relations to or a function of the world or entities within the world. No integrity, identity, or 'nature' characterizes subjectivity other than its relation to or function for worldly entities or subjectivity's relata. This is the direction of Heidegger's analysis of Dasein.

Now, as we have seen, each of these philosophically narcissistic possibilities eventually negates itself and implies its opposite. That is, not only is each of these positions objectionable in itself, for example, as reductive, each is also dialectical in the sense that Kant's "antinomies" are dialectical. Upon inspection the privileged term, that to which the reduced term has been reduced, has also been reduced; that is, its originally asserted character turns out to be implicitly denied. This dialectic is generated because of philosophical narcissism's negation of either existential integrity or internal relatedness, through the reduction of subject to non-subject or vice versa. Once all relations and all relata are reduced to the subject, the subject's integrity is split apart: the subject can be conceived only as either an abstract contentless "ground of Being" for its relations-relata, or, as simply a name for or function of those relations-relata. Likewise, if the subject is conceived as that-in-which worldly entities become disclosed and attain their Being, then the entities can no longer be distinguished, be claimed to have an existential integrity distinct from the relata of the subject, from the phenomena which exist *in* the subject or subjective process.

The principle of the reciprocity of integrity and relation has application outside of philosophy as well. To adopt it is to reject that language, common in a variety of cultural fields today, according to which independence and vulnerability, individuality and mutuality, completeness and dependence, are felt to be opposing tendencies. This language is particularly pernicious when applied to human being, as it often is. The metapsychological view which treats individuation and sociality, relatedness and dependence as opposing tendencies, according to which strong or full individuation or individual integrity implies decreasing social involvement, decreasing vulnerability or openness, and vice versa, is frequently met in contemporary psycho-cultural criticism and in contemporary cultural-political work. For example, recent debates over gender identity and politics involving feminists, Marxists, and conservatives in which theorists typically associate femininity with relatedness, and hence vulnerability and openness, and masculinity with independence, and hence invulnerability and asocial, domineering impulses, betray a misunderstanding of the nature of the ego itself, the principle of personal individualization, as an anti-relational principle.[11]

The study of narcissistic and borderline personality disorders clearly shows this simplistic metapsychology to be false. This study demonstrates that, at the psychological level at least, only a full, whole, individuated character can be involved with, dependent on, vulnerable, and open to real others, as opposed to fantasied others. Indeed, it is the lesson of psychoanalysis in general that the psychic integrity of the person, ego, or self is a *social* product; that is, it can only develop through the appropriate and sustained interaction of child and parent. The healthy child and adult need and are dependent upon others and experience such needs as an intrinsic part of themselves. As David Winnicott has expressed it, even the capacity to be alone, in effect, the capacity to relax in a feeling of unarticulated personal existence, can only develop through the experience of "being along in the presence of someone else."[12] It is the borderline patient who cannot accept such needs and fails to develop such capacities, who experiences a non-specific anxiety and rage, and constructs a defensive structure that superficially apes a total, humanly impossible independence, while simultaneously feeling a lack of integrity and a complete dependence upon others at a deeper level of experience.

In conclusion, there are only two philosophical options available that will avoid the dialectical oscillation implicit in subjectivism. One is to reject the use of the categories of subjectivism as foundational for inquiry; that is, no longer to use the distinction between what is-or-belongs-to subjectivity and what-does-not as foundational for inquiry. Or one can, while retaining subjectivist categories, reject instead the very conception of philosophy as inquiry, as aimed at the improvement of our understanding of what is. Here, the dialectic of philosophical narcissism is avoided by simply ceasing to ask the kinds of questions which cause it to be generated by our fundamental categories, or by whatever terms or concepts predominate in our discourse. Philosophical narcissism itself does *not* reject the notion of philosophy as inquiry, or the terms "real," "unreal," "truth," "untruth," "ground," which frequently accompany the former. If it did there would be no dialectical oscillation of terms, no internal schism characteristic of the narcissistic position.

This latter option has been increasingly chosen by certain philosophical schools in recent years. Many contemporary philosophers throw up their hands in the face of the difficulties of the tradition from which, they fear, there is no escape, and claim that we are witnessing the "end," the "death" of philosophy. Philosophy becomes an analysis of itself, a form of literary criticism, a *reaction* to any positive, constructive gesture made elsewhere, which philosophy can only hope to "deconstruct."[13] Philosophy then lives a parasitic existence, able to comment but never create. It is ironic that practitioners of this brand of philosophy often try to claim Nietzsche as a forebear; Nietzsche, who reserved his most vitriolic criticism for merely reactive cultural forms.

The Concept of Culture

Culture has been conceived and misconceived in a variety of ways by philosophers and non-philosophers. The manifold misconceptions must be cleared out of the way before we can begin to forge a more adequate and non-subjectivist notion of culture.

Culture is not a mediator, a third thing standing between subjectivity and objectivity. Culture is not "objective mind," the derivative externalization of an inner mental life. It is not a veil cloaking an otherwise purely objective reality with subjective bias. It is not a deterministic force, imposing on otherwise free-thinking minds a set of customs and beliefs that merely enforce social conformity and stifle individual freedom. It is not antithetical to everything represented by the word 'nature', such that the sources of all human behavior can be divided into a purely physical, innate natural inheritance and a fund of learned, non-natural environmentally acquired cultural conventions. Culture is not spiritual or ideal. Culture is not that which insuperably divides human beings into local groups, making any conception of a universal human nature and universal human values impossible.

Culture cannot be adequately conceived as determined by or reducible to psychological or economic categories. Culture is not the sum of the psychological attitudes of private individuals. A culture is not a collective personality. Neither is culture a mere economic epiphenomenon, the subjective ideological response of groups or classes to their objective economic conditions.

There are two non-philosophical notions of culture between which we must steer to create an adequate philosophical concept of culture; namely, the aesthetic and the anthropological.

Dewey calls the aesthetic conception the "Matthew Arnold" idea of culture. According to it, 'culture' refers to art, literature, music, oratory, etc. While such activities do constitute 'high culture', they cannot by held to be synonomous with culture as a whole. Not only is it virtually impossible to distinguish between 'high' or aesthetic culture and 'lower' forms, the philosophical promise of the idea of culture, and its importance for human living, is lost if we adopt this definition.

While the aesthetic concept of culture is too narrow, the anthropological notion is too broad. Anthropologist Ruth Benedict defines culture as social custom, custom being the learned patterns of behavior and belief characteristic of a society that are transmitted from generation to generation.[14] Although this definition is common in the social sciences it has a very important shortcoming; it fails to distinguish culture from society, cultural activities and artifacts from the totality of social behavior. This common failure causes definite interpretive problems.

While social reality and culture are intimately related, they ought not to be conflated. A society is a type of grouping of human beings. A culture is the totality of a society's interpretations of itself and the world, embodied in public or shareable human products. The distinction between culture and society is analagous and related to the distinction between the way a person understands himself or herself, his or her self-interpretation, and what the person actually is. Of course, for both the individual and for society, self-interpretation not only reflects the self but is a constituent of the self; nevertheless, it is not identical to the self.

Culture is the totality of a social group's interpretive products, created or inherited, by which the group understands itself and its world. It is the publicly accessible words, ideas, and physical artifacts carrying shareable meanings that constitute the on-going interpretation of human life and the world. There are three features of this notion of culture which need to be explored in order to see what a more central philosophical role for culture would mean.

First, culture is a matter of *pre-dichotomous* meaningful things. By 'pre-dichotomous' I mean that cultural artifacts and activities are logically prior to and cannot be legitimately derived from the dichotomy of subject and object. To paraphrase D. W. Winnicott, cultural phenomena are things about which we cannot properly ask whether they are subjective or objective. Culture cannot be adequately understood unless it is acknowledged that a cultural event or artifact is a physical, perceivable thing to which meanings belong as part of the thing's existential integrity. This claim of the intrinsic meaningfulness of a cultural thing is a direct contradiction of subjectivism, since the latter cannot accept not-subjective entities as intrinsically meaningful. Subjectivism eliminates the specifically cultural nature of cultural things by viewing them as intrinsically meaningless objects onto which the subject somehow projects meanings, or by divorcing the meaning of the things (interpreted as intentional or 'subjective' objects) from the physical existence of the things.

A *cultural* interpretation of cultural artifacts, an interpretation that is adequate to culture, would assert that a public statue, a woman's dress, a child's toy, the setting of a table, and the bricks of a home would not be what they are without their meanings. Their meanings are part of their respective existential integrities as things.

This point takes us further. The meanings of cultural artifacts and events obtain by virtue of their relation to human beings. The artifacts and events would certainly not have their meanings except for their relations to their human creators and interpreters, and their meanings change over time as those relations change.

Second, culture is a communal, public, *communicative* phenomenon. Cultural activities, events, and artifacts are intrinsically publicly accessible and communicable. An artifact need not be public to be cultural, but it must be capable of being public. An idea, word, artifact, or event that is intrinsically private and incapable of being communicated to others is not a cultural entity—if such things exist at all. A private experience or idea, once interpreted by the experiencer in a common language, automatically becomes shareable, communicable, potentially public, and so, in its linguistic existence, becomes a part of culture.

Much of culture is inherited, that is, not created by a present individual but by past individuals and subsequently reinterpreted by others who thereby reconstruct their inheritance. The inheritance provides a context of cultural activities, events, artifacts, and meanings which serve as an interpretive reservoir on which each individual draws both in order to create his or her own interpretive patterns and in order to communicate and share meanings with others. Since language is itself a part of this cultural inheritance, it is clear that communication virtually would not exist without culture.

From the perspective of culture, the existential integrity of the human individual cannot exist without the context of relations to others and to the myriad meanings and meaningful objects provided by culture. As will be seen in the next section, individuality is not established solely through a process of division, of separation of the 'inner' from the 'outer'. Such a separation, if it were as straightforward and as absolute as much of psychoanalysis implies, would render the most important features of human living absurd. The degree of separation that does take place is possible only because a dimension of continuity is established and maintained through cultural objects and communication with others, a dimension which remains unaffected by the subsequent separation.

Whereas subjectivism understood human individuals as private subjects connected to an outside via a transcendental bridge, in a cultural perspective human individuals establish their existential integrity out of a context of relations to other people and things, a context which, although in continual transformation, remains the backdrop for the individual's integrity.

The communal-communicative-cultural matrix of relations is not the antithesis of individuality, it is the field of becoming for the individual, the pluralistic context in which individuality is located and on which it feeds and draws meanings and raw material for its own meaning-construction and interpretation. Culture is not on the side of the community and against the individual; it is the matrix for both. The individual cannot develop without culture, communication, and community. The extreme individualist, the revolutionary, and the iconoclast all use the cultural materials of their community, reinterpreting some strains and rejecting others, building their protest out of that very thing against which they protest. Communication, community, and the inheritance of a culture have little to do with agreement or shared belief; they have to do with a shared language.

Lastly, culture is the *pluralistic, contingent* creation of *historical* human acts of interpretation and construction. Culture is not monolithic and not *a priori;* it is an ever-changing plurality of activities, events, and artifacts, each involving multiple meanings, continually being reinterpreted and reconstructed. These acts of interpretation and construction are the contingent acts of masses of individuals living under particular, changing historical conditions. Culture does not have to exist, it must be created. Nor is it the product of an elite; it is the cumulative product of vast interlocking groups of individuals.

This has far-reaching consequences for any philosophy which views culture as a fundamental, irreducible phenomenon at the heart of human being. Unlike the concepts of God, subjectivity, matter, logic, and mind, the possible types and meanings of culture cannot be determined or limited *a priori*. We cannot determine the bounds of possible culture or cultural experience because history continues to reveal new types of cultural media and cultural themes. Painting, science, and written language each came into existence at specific historical or pre-historical times. We cannot know what new cultural forms will appear in the future, nor what new turns existing forms will take.

Culture, properly understood, cannot abide the first two dichotomies mentioned at the outset of this chapter. Culture spans the dichotomy of subject and object and of existential integrity and relatedness. As pre-dichotomous, as the context of community and individuality, and as historical, cultural phenomena cannot be adequately understood through these dualities. In a later section of this chapter, it will be seen that culture need not be understood as antithetical to natural processes.

Culture and Mind: Winnicott, Cassirer, and Dewey

What would it mean to go beyond the subjectivist interpretation of human being, to cease to allow philosophical anthropology to be determined by subjectivist categories?

It would mean asserting that human beings are not subjects, not consciousnesses. Nor are they objects. Nor are they synthetic unities of subjectivity and objectivity. Nor are they syntheses of antithetical traits and predicates usually associated with subjectivity and objectivity, like freedom and compulsion, mind and nature, individual and society, consciousness and things, activity and passivity. Human beings are not the kind of being which can properly be understood through the polarity of subject and object or through a proposed synthesis of such a logically prior antithesis.

Human beings are entities to whom subjectivity, consciousness or disclosedness essentially belong; whether there are any other beings with this characteristic or function is a matter of dispute. The fact that subjectivity is essential to human being does not mean that it is the essence of human being. It means that subjectivity is one among many features constituting what it means to be a living human being. Subjectivity or disclosedness is no more or less essential to human being than calcium, water, communication, or love.

Philosophers and to a significant extent the general public are, due to the influence of subjectivism, still in the habit of approaching human being as a two-sided, bifurcated phenomenon. They continue to think as if the distinction between private inner experiences, intentions, and meanings on the one hand, and public objects and events on the other, is the most fundamental, natural, and inevitable distinction; as if its necessity naturally outweighs that of any other countervailing distinctions. Despite the seeming defeat of Cartesianism within philosophy, the dualistic and subjectivist approach remains dominant.

A cultural perspective suggests that the nature of human being will be better understood and appreciated through a focus on the *cultural dimension* of human being; that is, on human participation in culture and on the capacities of the individual that make this participation possible, human *culturality*.

Two twentieth-century writers, one from the perspective of psychiatry and one engaged in philosophical anthropology, have given culture and culturality a central place in their theories of human being. They are D. W. Winnicott and Ernst Cassirer.

British psychiatrist David Winnicott, in a paper entitled, "The Location of Cultural Experience," criticizes Freud and the psychoanalytic tradition for failing to give culture an adequate place in psychoanalytic theory.[15] Psychoanalysts have tended to conceive of psychic health in terms of the achievement of a realistic differentiation of inner experience from outer reality, of impulse and fantasy from perceived necessity. This precluded an adequate theory of culture because culture, Winnicott says, is intrinsically *not* differentiable into subjective and objective categories.

For Winnicott, adult culture, symbolism, and play derive from the infant's experience of "transitional objects and transitional phenomena."[16] These phenomena first become significant for the infant at the time when it has begun to differentiate itself from the mother, to distinguish inner from outer. They are objects in the infant's experience—". . . perhaps a bundle of wool or the corner of a blanket . . . or a word or tune . . ."—regarding which we do not ask the child whether the object is "created" or "found," whether it is the product of the child's creativity or a realistically perceived external object. The "intermediate zone" of experience established by such objects is essential for the development of the child's sense of itself as an "entity having experiences," which sense is the basis of the infant's ego. Without this region of "experiencing" which is *not* recognized by the child as either inner or outer the child cannot endure separation from the mother, and the adult cannot experience living as meaningful and valuable.[17] This "region" of experiencing is, in adult experience, constituted by what we call "culture."

For Winnicott, culture is "the place where we live," it is the location where human living takes place.[18]

> You may cure your patient and not know what it is that makes him or her go on living. It is of first importance for us to acknowledge openly that absence of psychoneurotic illness may be health, but it is not life. Psychotic patients who are all the time hovering between living and not living force us to look at this problem, one that really

belongs *not to psychoneurotics but to all human beings.* I am claiming that these same phenomena that are life and death to our schizoid or borderline patients appear in our cultural experiences. It is these cultural experiences that provide the continuity in the human race that transcends personal existence.[19]

If what is the human "entity having experiences" is insuperably differentiated from what is *not* that entity, from what is 'outside', then the outside must inevitably be experienced as *dead,* as inert and lifeless matter, while the inside must be experienced as wholly cut-off from and incapable of contacting in a vital or intimate way anything outside of itself, of extending itself into the world that is not itself. For Winnicott the realistic and necessary distinction between inner and outer can only be viable if it is superseded by a level of experience in which there is no such distinction, in which creation and discovery are indistinguishable. This is the primary sphere of human living, the sphere from which all meaning and value devolves, and it is populated for adults by what we call culture. The inability to experience this sphere of reality is pathogenic at the individual, psychological level, and is an outstanding feature of the experience of borderline patients.

In Winnicott we see the radical implications of the move to a cultural perspective. This perspective requires that the dichotomy of self and other/object be removed from its determinative position in inquiry and that a pluralistic, changeable field of meaningful artifacts and the activities of creating and interpreting them be considered *prior* to the determination of self and non-self, consciousness and materiality, the created and the discovered. Moreover, it is not enough to merely posit such a pre-differentiated state as characteristic of the child or the psychological primitive, as developmental psychologies, like psychoanalysis, have done. Rather, we, the theorists, must *ourselves* adopt this perspective as our own.

Development theorists of mind in both philosophy and psychology, from Hegel to Freud, Piaget, Heinz Werner, and Kurt Goldstein, have conceived of the child, the primitive and the pathological individual as un-, pre-, or de-differentiated, as lacking the stable distinction of inner and outer, self and other, subject and object characteristic of mature adulthood. They have taken this distinction as real, even if, like Hegel, they wish eventually to transcend it. The undifferentiated state indicates an immature, pre-realistic state of mind. While the developmentalists have created fascinating systems, and have drawn valuable attention to the continuities between the various undifferentiated states, they have failed to see that the primacy of the undifferentiated is not merely temporal, not merely characteristic of less mature forms, but is a logical and existential presupposition of mental life in *all* phases of development.

The development of the differentiation of inner and outer cannot eclipse and supplant the undifferentiated state, because the former is unworkable without the latter. The undifferentiated state is supplemented and altered, but never supplanted or negated. The "meaning of life," the aim of human living, and the fullness of integrated experiencing for the adult, as for the child, resides, according to Winnicott, in the psychic region which escapes differentiation. The most fundamental and the most enduringly deep level of experience and reality escapes the subject–object distinction. The latter thus becomes a secondary, a derivative distinction in inquiry, which is applicable to some features of reality, but certainly not to all.

Among twentieth-century philosophers, no one has worked out a philosophy of culture and of culture's role in the development and definition of human being in as thorough and systematic a fashion as Ernst Cassirer. In *An Essay On Man* Cassirer argues that human being is essentially cultural and that all philosophy of human being and its various products—science, art religion, and philosophy itself—is inevitably and basically philosophy of culture. In a chapter entitled "The Definition of Man in Terms of Human Culture," Cassirer describes his philosophy of symbolic forms as a new and syncretic approach to an "anthropological philosophy." Cassirer writes:

> The philosophy of symbolic forms starts from the presupposition
> that, if there is any definition of the nature or "essence" of man, this
> definition can only be understood as a functional one, not a
> substantial one. We cannot define man by any inherent principle
> which constitutes his metaphysical essence—nor can we define him by
> any inborn faculty or instinct . . . . Man's outstanding
> characteristic . . . is not his metaphysical or physical nature—but his
> work. It is this work, it is the system of human activities which
> defines and determines the circle of 'humanity'. Language, myth,
> religion, art, science, history are . . . the various sectors of this
> circle . . . .[20]

Cassirer's systematic philosophy, expressed most fully in his monumental *The Philosophy of Symbolic Forms,*[21] is essentially a critical reformulation of Kant's three *Critiques* hinging on the replacement of the unchanging *a priori* concepts of the understanding, forms of judgment, and imperatives of reason, which belong to each rational creature for Kant, with historically changing forms of culture. It is through these cultural forms that reality and the self are articulated. Furthermore, for Cassirer, there is no pre-cultural thing-in-itself which lies outside of cultural articulation and in comparison to which culturally articulated knowledge could be judged to be merely phenomenal or somehow intrinsically inadequate.

In this connection, it is striking to consider a passage from John Dewey's unfinished "Re-Introduction" to his seminal metaphysical work, *Experience and Nature,* originally published in 1925.[22] On the suggestion of Beacon Press, Dewey composed and sent to his editor a substantial draft of an entirely new introduction in 1948–1949, which was to be included in a new edition. After various interruptions he returned to the project in 1951, adding several pages to the yet unfinished new introduction. The addition begins:

> Were I to write (or rewrite) *Experience and Nature* today I would entitle the book *Culture and Nature* and the treatment of specific subject-matters would be correspondingly modified. I would abandon the term "experience" because of my growing realization that the historical obstacles which prevented understanding of my use of "experience" are, for all practical purposes, insurmountable. I would substitute the term "culture" because with its meanings as now firmly established it can fully carry my philosophy of experience.[23]

Dewey goes on to say that the "thoroughly wholesome" appeal to experience of earlier modern philosophy has since been "corrupted," resulting in the identification of experience with private, psychological experienc*ing.* Dewey felt that his own "insistence that 'experience' also designates *what* is experienced" had been overpowered by the psychologistic, privatistic, and subjectivistic meanings with which the term had come to be almost exclusively identified. This is a crucial point for Dewey because it had been the central point of *Experience and Nature* to assert the continuity of what is experienced with the *way(s)* it is experienced, with the process of experienc*ing.* Dewey then suggests:

> The name "culture" in its anthropological (not its Matthew Arnold) sense designates the vast range of things experienced in an indefinite variety of ways. It possesses as a name just that body of substantial references which "experience" as a name has lost. It names artifacts which rank as "material" and operations upon and with material things . . . . It is a prime philosophical consideration that "culture" includes the material and the ideal in their reciprocal interrelationships . . . . What "experience" now fails to do and "culture" can successfully do for philosophy is of utmost importance if philosophy is to be comprehensive without becoming stagnant.[24]

Two features of human being come to the fore if the cultural views of Winnicott, Cassirer, and Dewey are taken seriously. First, the process of experiencing, assimilating, interpreting, and creating meaningful things is a fundamental, specifically human activity. Whereas subjectivism regarded the experience of things as meaningful as an improbable conundrum whose validity required either denial or elaborate justification, this experience is the most basic fact of the human process, a fact to be explicated and understood, not explained or justified. Human beings happen to be the kind of beings for whom sound waves, ink on paper, the movements of facial muscles, the facade of a dwelling, and the color of a sunset can have elaborate meaning and value; the kind of beings who endlessly recreate and reshape materials in ways that carry interpretations of the world which guide individual action and community life. The process of experiencing-interpreting-creating is not a synthesis of logically prior or more fundamental processes; it is fundamental and non-derivative.

Second, human culturality involves each individual in a communal and historical process and makes the individual the inheritor of a fund of historical meanings and media. Culture connects human beings not only with things, but with each other and with dead generations whose products are reinterpreted and reinvested with meaning by the living.

The cultural theory of human being suggested by these thinkers has definite implications for the philosophy of mind, experience, and knowledge.

The 'problem of knowledge' that has been the primary concern of much of philosophy since the seventeenth century has been strongly influenced by subjectivist categories. The problem, classically formulated, is to understand how it can be shown that the contents of subjectivity, the subject's ideas and perceptions, are true of the non-subjective world, given the utter distinction between individual consciousness and non-subjective (presumably material) reality. Early-modern thinkers tried to solve this problem by: first, distinguishing between the subject's thoughts and sensations, the latter being caused by contact with external realities (experience); second, positing the existence of a transcendental capacity of subjectivity which made knowledge of the object possible; and, third, postulating criteria that, when met, would assure that particular thoughts and sensations validly represented the object.

This view, often called the representational theory, exhibited two features that deserve emphasis. According to it, the relation between knowledge and experience on the one hand, and their objects on the other, is purely external. At best, knowing and experiencing reflect, represent, or picture (in concrete or abstract terms) non-subjective things and/or their relations. Furthermore, this approach promoted an internal dualism of the mind, a distinction between the order of receptive experience that contacts or is affected by external things (an empirical order) and the order of spontaneous thought insulated from direct contact with things and thus capable of organization and analysis of ideas (a formal, logical or analytic order). The empirical order of sensations provided the raw material and the analytic order provided the organizational form for the house of knowledge.

In the eighteenth century, Hume raised the problem of the relation between these two orders, arguing that they are entirely distinct and cannot be synthesized by any 'transcendental' capacities (reason). Kant then attempted to surmount this and other difficulties by claiming that objects conform to our knowledge, rather than the other way around, and that there is a spontaneous, conceptual order which pre-determines the empirical order, named the synthetic *a priori*. However, in addition to the many problems Kant had in trying to demonstrate this point, he was forced to restrict his analysis to the *appearances* of things, excluding things-in-themselves from discussion. The appearances of experienced objects conform to knowledge, not the things as they exist independent of our experience.

Many twentieth-century philosophers have attacked the representational theory and the distinction between the empirical and analytic orders. Wittgenstein himself made such criticisms in his later work (for example, the discussion of "seeing as" in his *Logical Investigations*), and this became a dominant theme of Anglo-American philosophy after the Second World War, as seen in Quine's attack on the analytic–synthetic distinction, Sellar's critique of the 'myth' of the given, Kuhn's elucidation of the role of paradigms in scientific change and the attack by N. R. Hanson and others on the possibility of a theory-free observation language.[25] Philosophers became less able to accept the belief in an order of receptivity or observation that was free of predetermination by perspective, historical traditions, interpretive paradigms, and theoretical commitments. They recognized that the strict distinction of interpretation and perception that had been inherited from early-modern thought and applied in more extreme terms by logical positivism could not be maintained.

This recognition had also been a part of the continental philosophical tradition. Nietzsche expressed it in the late nineteenth century, asserting that, "No, facts is precisely what there is not, [there are] only interpretations . . . ." and "There are not facts . . . what is relatively most enduring is our opinion," and "Ultimately, man finds in things nothing but what he himself imported into them . . . ."[26]

This critique has returned philosophers to the original dilemma. How can we claim that we know or experience things as they are in themselves, as they exist independently of us, if all our attempts at knowing and experiencing are guided and shaped by the historical, cultural, and situational conditions that constitute us as knowers and experiencers? Do we know and experience the world in some primitive sense and subsequently interpret it, or do we only interpret it, never able to say that we encounter things as they are in themselves? Many philosophers have given up trying to answer this question. This is not an illegitimate response; there are other questions of import to be addressed. Yet, often the question is not really renounced, but is accepted as the insurmountable dilemma inherent in the philosophic project of improving our understanding of what is, and *this* project—the project of philosophy—is then renounced. That this question is today providing an excuse for some to deny the validity of philosophy as a whole is more than ample motivation for attempting a new approach to the problem.

A review of the various conundrums into which the numerous attempts at resolving this problem have led suggests that, if there is to be a solution, it is necessary to find a way to assert two seemingly incompatible propositions, in ignoring either one of which philosophy would make itself irrelevant to our understanding of the world. First, human beings *do* have experience and knowledge of things as those things exist independently of individual experiencers and knowers. To believe otherwise is to lead philosophy down the blind alley of claiming that we experience only experience, know only knowledge, and interpret only interpretations. This would deny validity to everyday experience and knowledge. If philosophy accepts epistemic criteria according to which there is no human knowledge at all, one must wonder about the possible justification for such criteria. But secondly, it is also undeniable that all knowledge and experience of things is influenced, conditioned, and guided by perspective, habits of thought, and patterns of interpretation that are historically, sociologically, and biologically conditioned.

How could these seemingly contrary propositions be simultaneously maintained?

Just as Kant borrowed the name of Copernicus as a way of suggesting a new philosophic approach to the problem of knowledge, a reference to Einstein's way of thinking about physical questions suggests an approach to this seeming contradiction. In his 1905 paper introducing special relativity, Einstein proceeded in an unusual way.[27] In trying to eliminate some "asymmetries" in Maxwell's electromagnetic theory, and to surmount the problem of the lack of experimental evidence for the existence of the "light medium" or ether, Einstein proposed two seemingly incompatible "conjectures" or "postulates": that the laws of physics are valid for all frames of reference *and yet* that the velocity of light is everywhere constant regardless of the motion of its source. He proceeded, on the basis of the conjunction of these two apparently incompatible ideas, to demonstrate how the original problems would be resolved if a host of other, seemingly uncontroversial physical ideas (length, time, mass) were radically reinterpreted in order to make his postulates compatible. In other words, Einstein proposed a seemingly impossible hypothetical solution and subsequently shifted the rest of physics to make it consistent with his hypothesis.

Suppose that in trying to solve the problem of knowledge, the two seeming contraries—encounter with things as they are and the conditioned nature of that encounter—are postulated or hypothesized to be *both* true. This is a hypothesis based on the conviction that the notion of philosophy as inquiry, the continuation of philosophy as something other than literary criticism, is in serious jeopardy if something like these propositions is not true. The question is, if these propositions were to be both true, what other ideas would have to be changed to make this possible?

The most promising point of attack is the concept of things, non-subjective objects. It is possible to maintain both propositions if things-in-themselves, the beings of which the world is constituted, are conceived to be *pluralities* that are constituted by their internal relations to other entities, including ourselves, and *yet* conceived as having existential integrity. If the manifold human experiences and interpretations of a thing are part of its being, a being which is plural or complex and nevertheless integral, then it is possible to say that we do know the things-in-themselves *and* that our knowing is limited and guided by the manifold conditions on the knower.

Things are plural, complex, never exhausted by knowledge and experience. Their plurality is due to their internal relations to other entities, relations which are constitutive for the things. Because such relations are indefinitely many and changeable, there is always more to know about the thing, more perspectives from which to see it, more connections to other things establishing more contexts within which it functions. Each limited, historically conditioned perspective, each theory-laden observation, each "seeing as" *does* reveal the thing-in-itself, the reality of an independently existing object, the true nature of a thing. It simply cannot reveal *all* of the thing, and thus cannot reveal how its own perspective stands within and compares to the totality of the thing's contextual adventures, a totality which can never be encountered.

The implications of this view for metaphysics will be explored in the next section. At present, its implications for epistemology and the philosophy of mind are at issue. What kind of relation between mind and things is made conceivable by this pluralistic-relational conception of the objects of human encountering?

Epistemology can surmount the representational theory while maintaining the possibility of knowledge and experience of pluralistic things-in-themselves only if the activities of knowing and experiencing are conceded to have an internal relation to their objects. The rejection of subjectivism, a view that requires an external relation between mind and things, would clear the way for this approach. The assertion of the internal relatedness of the modes of human encountering and the things of the world means that human knowing-interpreting-experiencing activity is internally related to the being, the nature of encountered entities in their independent existence.

This idea is not tantamount to idealism or to phenomenology, each of which asserts the internal relation of mind and *intentional* objects, that is, objects whose natural, material existence has been denied or bracketed. The hypothesis now under consideration asserts that human knowing and experiencing are internally related to, are a constitutive part of, encountered things in their very *natural, physical existence,* that these human activities are a part of what encountered things *are.* This claim is the antithesis of the modern subjectivist conception of the relation of mind and things. It is not a new idea; in a sense, it is a return to pre-modern lines of thought.

In *On the Soul* Aristotle based his theory of human knowing on the notion that the inner form of knowable objects is actualized in the mind through the activity of knowing. The nature of the independently existing entity comes into community with the knower in the act of knowledge. The form of the mind and the form of the object become "one and the same activity" or actuality. It is for this reason that Aristotle could write that the mind is capable, in a sense, of "becoming all things."[28]

For Aristotle, the mind has an internal relation to the things themselves. Aristotle conceived of this relationship through the idea of form, or more precisely, the "what it is to be" the thing (*to ti en einai*).[29] The form of the object becomes actual or active in the mind of the knower. The knower and the known remain distinct "in their being" but become identical in their form.[30] The human mind is involved with, performs a function for, the things it knows. In the act of knowledge, mind and thing achieve a kind of community.

The pluralistic-relational conception of things described above replaces the Aristotelian notion of form with an indefinitely large plurality of aspects, features, and functions of each thing, all of which are dependent on the thing's relations to other entities and persons. This conception retains the Aristotelian conviction that human knowing-interpreting-experiencing activity exists in communion with things and that this communion is by no means incompatible with the existential integrity (for Aristotle, the substantiality) of the human knower and the things encountered.

The cultural view of human being further alters the Aristotelian picture by asserting that the knowing-interpreting-experiencing activity of each human individual is funded by a pluralistic cultural heritage and subsists within a communal-communicative-cultural context. On this pluralistic-cultural view, every act of human experiencing and knowing is a kind of communicative encounter between a human being and a thing such that the act of knowing or experiencing, which always operates within a pluralistic and changing cultural context, brings selected historical-cultural meanings into a creative interactive grasping of an existing integral entity, as that entity stands or functions within a particular context of changing relations. The human being doing the encountering and the thing encountered are each pluralities (by virtue of internal relations to other things and persons) with existential integrity. The human being's plurality is cultural; among the totality of traits and relations the human being brings to the encounter with the object, cultural traits and relations predominate.

To summarize, something like the pluralistic-cultural approach is required if philosophy is to reject subjectivism and philosophical narcissism without also rejecting the project of presenting a philosophic account of human knowledge, experience, and interpretation. The manifold modes of human encountering can be regarded as conditional and yet revelatory of the things-themselves if: 1) things human and non-human are conceived as pluralities functioning in diverse relational contexts *and* as nevertheless possessing existential integrity; and, 2) the modes of human encountering are conceived as primarily cultural and occurring within a cultural context.

Culture and Nature

It is instructive to recall the etymology of the word 'culture'. The English 'culture', like the German *Kultur* and the French *culture,* derives from the Latin *cultura. Cultura* referred to the care, cultivation, and tilling of the soil. This original meaning is preserved in the English 'cultivation', 'agriculture', and the use of 'culture' in biology. Unlike 'civilization', which is rooted in the Latin *civitas* or city, culture's etymology connotes the human involvement in and cooperation with natural processes and their redirection for human use.

Agriculture is a philosophically interesting phenomenon. Plant growth is a natural process that proceeds independently of human beings, whether we want it or not, an ever-recurring process that existed long before human beings and most likely will continue long after our collective demise. In agriculture, humans step into this process in certain select places and times and try to influence and control it for our own ends within a limited frame. We select what will grow and when and, to some degree, how. But we never fully control the process; rather, we ride piggy-back on a planetary process of growth which we try to organize into a humanly usable form.

Culture's etymological connotations are not reflected in its common philosophical interpretation. Culture is commonly understood as a subjective, mental, non-natural phenomenon, thereby amalgamating it to a dualistic scheme according to which the creative, spiritual, and uniquely human aspects of human existence are considered antithetical to the natural, material, bio-physical aspects of human life.

This antithesis is due not only to prevailing notions of culture, but also to the subjectivist interpretation of nature. The legacy of the subjectivist tradition dictated the the non-subjective world is devoid of all traits that are considered uniquely human or subjective (for example, meaning and value). At the dawn of modern science, Galileo and Descartes theorized that physical existences are characterized only by the mathematically treatable 'primary' qualities: volume, mass, velocity, quantity, and spatio-temporal location. All qualities, such as color, are properties of the subject, not the physical object; they are the effect of the object on the senses of the subject, but do not represent the true nature of the object. Modern science and modern philosophy of nature have consistently attempted to interpret nature in quantifiable, material and, until recently, mechanistic terms.[31] The possible exception to this is biology and its related fields, in which there have always been some pockets of conceptual resistance to the project of translating all life-processes into mathematico-mechanical terms.[32]

The conviction that the mathematical description of matter exhausts all there is to know about nature is the dominant modern attitude toward nature, and this dominance foredooms any attempt at bridging the gap between the spiritual-cultural and the natural dimensions of human being. This dominant conviction dictates that natural existence is best understood through concepts that are particularly inappropriate to the interpretation of the specifically human aspects of human existence. It thereby reinforces the theoretical schism between human and natural existence, and makes this schism seem intractable. The very community of scholars and the presumed unity of knowledge have been fractured, split into "two cultures" of research, humanists and scientists, who cannot communicate with each other.[33]

The recent history of physics suggests that it would be naive to believe that science has now achieved the final and true paradigm for the understanding of nature. No one knows what model of the constitution of nature will be accepted by scientists three centuries hence. Consequently, the dualism of mind and nature that has been dominant in the science of the last three centuries—according to which the mental realm is either outside of and irrelevant to the understanding of the natural realm, or is reducible to mathematical-material processes as in psychophysics or strict behavioral psychology—may be someday overturned by natural science itself.

The mutual ignorance of the human and the natural sciences is reason enough to make one doubt the adequacy of either as they stand today. The mandate of each obligates them to understand their subject matter in relation to the other if they are to be complete, since no one can deny that the subject matters are intimately related. Human beings are part of nature. Consequently no natural theorist who aspires to completeness can legitimately renounce the relevance of understanding human phenomena to his or her own project, just as no humanist can legitimately renounce the relevance of understanding natural processes.

Yet, natural scientists are typically as unconcerned with their inadequate ability to explain the production of a sonnet through atomic or neural processes as are humanists to fathom the bio-chemical bases of love or the physical bases of the technologies whose social impact they criticize. In practice, humanists and scientists simply ignore each other's work. This is not without reason, for the methods of the human and natural sciences have become so divergent and the volume of research on each side so immense that the task of relating the two seems super-human. Among twentieth-century philosophers, only a handful have been able to embrace both.

Despite these difficulties, the notion that culture and nature are unrelated cannot be reasonably defended.

Culture is clearly a part of nature. It is the product of a naturally existing creature, is composed of physical media, and subsists within a natural universe. It is the habit of conceiving of culture as subjective, free, and ideal, and of nature as material, deterministic, and value-neutral, that makes the two seem unrelatable. Given this dichotomy, most attempts to treat culture and human phenomena as part of nature have been materialistic: if nature is material and deterministic, then a naturalist interpretation must reduce human creation and interpretation to deterministic material processes. Humanists, generally loathe to accept this reduction and unwilling to leap into an idealist interpretation of nature, usually acquiesce in the inevitability of a dualistic approach to reality and accept the impossibility of the human and natural sciences dwelling under the same theoretical roof.

Philosophy has not always surrendered to the necessity of choosing between dualism and reductivism. Aristotle classified the study of the human soul as a bio-physical project. For Aristotle, the soul (*psychē*) is the animating principle, the characteristic life-activity of a being. The human soul incorporates the intellectual, passionate, sensitive, and vegetative aspects of human being. The study of the soul of that kind of animal which is rational he groups under biology, the study of living natural entities, and physics, the study of natural entities in general.

Aristotle was able to take such a view and yet remain a humanist because his concept of nature was neither materialistic nor deterministic. In his view all material, natural entities contain within themselves a principle of movement and change, their material being determined by an innate teleology. Aristotle could interpret the human soul as natural because his philosophy of nature was not incompatible with essential features of the human process.

That Aristotle's doctrine of substantial forms and teleological conception of nature may be untenable today does not mean that his non-materialistic, non-deterministic approach to naturalism was wrong-headed. A number of recent philosophers have taken up this approach, proposing metaphysical and cosmological schemes that emphasize the complexity, plurality, contextuality, and indeterminacy of natural entities and processes as a more promising basis for fitting human beings back into the natural picture. The pluralism of William James, Whitehead's philosophy of organism, Dewey's humanistic naturalism, J. H. Randall's functional realism, and Justus Buchler's ordinal naturalism (or "radical naturalism," as Sidney Gelber has called it) are examples of this approach.[34] In each case, the proposed ultimate categories for the understanding of all beings (human, natural, cultural) impute indefinite complexity and plurality, and hence indeterminancy, to things, such that they cannot be reduced to the status of material simples whose nature is unrelated to context, function, and subsistence in an indeterminate number of orders. It would not be misleading to see in this tradition a vestige of the Romanticist interpretation of nature, insofar as the latter emphasized the efflorescence, the indeterminate and ever-expanding fullness and creativity of nature.[35]

One of the common features of these recent theories is the recognition of the reciprocity of the existential integrity of things and the internal relatedness of things. The notion that reality is composed of "actual occasions" which contain within themselves constitutive "perceptions of all other occasions" (Whitehead), or "natural complexes" subsisting in an indefinite number of "orders" (Buchler), or "situations" out of which the objects of experience and the act of experiencing are subsequently abstracted (Dewey), or cumulative "histories" (Randall)—each of these notions presumes the reciprocity, the mutual indispensability of the integrity of entities and their relatedness to other entities.

The pluralistic approach of these thinkers, if combined with the principle of the reciprocity of integrity and relation, can provide a basis for conceiving the relation of culture and nature. Human cultural activity, including human experiencing-interpreting-knowing, can be conceived as internally related to its objects in their natural, physical existence. The cultural interpretation of these objects is a *part of* what they are. It is not *all* of what they are, since each entity is indefinitely plural. Culture does not 'determine' the nature of things in an idealistic fashion, since the nature of the things is pluralistically indeterminant. Nevertheless, some of the orders in which a particular thing may function may be cultural orders, and so the cultural activities that establish such orders are a part of the nature of the thing, part of what it is.

Likewise, the things taken up into human cultural activity are internally related to the nature of those human beings engaging in the cultural activity. The artifacts, words, and material things which are culturally experienced, interpreted, and created are part of the human beings who experience, interpret, and create them, part of what they are. They are not all of each human being who relates to them, since each human being is indefinitely complex. Nevertheless, they are part of the constitution of cultural human beings, such that individual human beings would not be the same beings they are without them.

Culture is not a spiritual activity. It is always both mental and physical, always the interpreting or creating of a physical entity with meaning and value. It is the activity of a natural creature in a natural world, a creature whose nature it is to be cultural. The integrity of the natural, human individual presupposes involvement with natural, cultural artifacts and the community which creates and interprets them. The natural things which become artifacts or are culturally interpreted are also involved with, are affected by, and constituted by, manifold relations with the cultural community.

In summary, a number of the problems of contemporary philosophy are caused either by a continued reliance on subjectivist categories or by a belief that philosophy is inseparably wedded to those categories and so should be abandoned or subsumed by other disciplines (logic, intellectual history, literary criticism, theology).

Philosophy is not inevitably subjectivist. Philosophers can choose not to base their inquiries on the categories of subject and object. Rejecting subjectivism will not, however, usher in the philosophical millennium. Philosophy will never reach a final, unimprovable state, it will never attain certainty. This is not a failing, for philosophy does not need to attain these unattainables to be valuable and important. Philosophy is one of the cultural activities of humanity, along with cooking, weaving, oratory, and sculpture. It is not the least of these, nor is it the best; it is merely unique and indispensable. Philosophy is a hypothetical attempt to enhance our understanding and appreciation of the world in general terms. In this sense, it is hard to imagine philosophy coming to an end before the human race does. Alas, as Levinas says, today no one can underestimate the possibility of that.

Epilogue: Humanism, Democracy and Culture

The notion of anti-culture has been poignantly expressed by the Czechoslovakian writer-critic in exile, Milan Kundera.[1] He writes that western Europeans have almost completely failed to notice the Soviet destruction of the culture of central Europe. The reason for this failure is that the West had already lost the belief that culture *mattered*. Even before the Russian tanks bore down on Czechoslovakian culture in 1968, Western Europeans had ceased to feel that their own culture, or culture in general, had any intrinsic value. Western Europe has become "post-cultural." Kundera laments:

> I arrived in France [after the Russian invasion] and tried to explain to French friends the massacre of culture that had taken place after the invasion: "Try to imagine! All of the literary and cultural reviews were liquidated! Every one without exception! That never happened before in Czech history, not even under Nazi occupation . . . ." Then my friends would look at me indulgently with an embarrassment that I understood only later . . . . If all the reviews in France or England disappeared, no one would notice it, not even their editors. In Paris, even in a completely cultivated milieu . . . people discuss television programs, not reviews. *For culture has already bowed out.* Its disappearance, which we experienced in Prague as a catastrophe, a shock, a tragedy, is perceived in Paris as something banal and insignificant, scarcely visible, a non-event.[2] (my emphasis)

Kundera points out that the reason we can even speak of Western Europe as an entity is that until recently it has shared a common cultural heritage. In the Middle Ages that unity was provided by the religious and cultural force of the Roman church, which eventually tied together the entire region from Poland to England to Portugal. This unification was maintained throughout the modern period, although by a different force. He writes that:

the Medieval God has been changed into a *Deus absconditus*, religion
bowed out giving way to culture, which became the expression of the
supreme values by which European humanity understood itself,
defined itself, identified itself as European.[3]

Modern Western culture was "founded on the authority of the
thinking, doubting individual, and on an artistic creation that expressed
his uniqueness."[4] But now, in our time, "Just as God long ago gave way
to culture, culture in turn is giving way."[5]

Kundera is not certain what, if anything, will succeed culture as a
unifying force in the modern West. But he does suggest one of the forces
that is subjugating culture, that is forcing it out of its modern phase.
This force is politicization, the tendency to regard all cultural phenomena as politically motivated and as having predominantly a political significance. Furthermore, the dominant political view to which culture is
subordinated is a simplistic "Manicheanism of the left and the right that
is as stupid as it is insurmountable."[6] Using my own terms, culture is
being subjugated to a political discourse which itself has already been
subjugated to economic categories. That is, culture is being subjected to
a political discourse whose terms and distinctions are solely determined
by the contrast between two allegedly antithetical economic systems,
capitalism and communism.

This is why, Kundera feels, "there is something conservative, nearly
anachronistic [in the post-war revolts of Poland, Hungary and Czecho-
slovakia]: they are desperately trying to restore the past of culture, the
past of the modern era," the past in which Western cultural artifacts and
activities were felt by creator and audience alike to represent something
autonomously important for the Western community, something beyond
politics, economics, and private self-interest.[7] Kundera is entirely right in
claiming that these movements are regarded ambivalently in much of
'cultured' Europe and America as courageous actions committed in the
name of ideals whose names are written on all our public monuments,
but belief in which seems somewhat old-fashioned and naive.

In this connection Kundera relates the story of a friend, a Czech
philosopher, from whom the police had just confiscated a thousand-page
manuscript, the fruit of ten years' work. As the two men walked through
communist Prague:

> We talked about the possibility of sending an open letter abroad in
> order to turn this confiscation into an international scandal. It
> was . . . clear to us that he [should address the letter] . . . to some
> figure above politics, someone who stood for an unquestionable moral
> value, someone universally acknowledged in Europe. In other words,
> a great cultural figure. But who . . . ? Suddenly we understood that

this figure did not exist . . . there were great painters, playwrights . . . but they no longer held a privileged place in society as moral authorities that Europe would acknowledge as spiritual representatives. Culture no longer existed as a realm in which supreme values were enacted. We walked toward the square in the old city near which I was then living, and we felt an immense loneliness, a void, the void in the European space from which culture was slowly withdrawing.[8]

Kundera's remarks point to something vital. The progress of some aspects of modern culture (those connected with subjectivism) has led to an undermining of the context of modernity, an undermining of the sense and significance of culture itself. Simultaneous with the colossal achievements of modernity in science, medicine, technology, democratic enfranchisement, and economic well-being, Western societies exhibit a de-valuation of culture, a sense that cultural acts and artifacts can serve only private desires or economic functions.

The de-legitimation of culture reflects and promotes a de-legitimation of one of the cornerstones of modernity, namely, humanism. Human beings define themselves in and through culture. A loss of respect for the value of cultural acts and artifacts is an implicit loss of respect for human beings. Humanism, the belief in the inherent worthiness of respect and the rightful freedom of human individuals, is gradually being eroded by the same process that is de-legitimating culture. For, if what human individuals believe, say, do, and create is not intrinsically valuable, if it is all simply a product of the desire for private gain, then why ought we respect and value human individuals? The vitality of culture in the late-modern world, the vitality of humanism and the treatment of human individuals in late-modern societies are interconnected.

Jackboots on the Stairs

Modern humanism is the belief that the ultimate arbiter of truth, the ultimate source of value, and the ultimate repository of political authority is the human individual, and that the highest achievement of political history is the system of laws, administration, and social mores which reflects and promotes these convictions. It is a belief which has had a long run, and it has produced fruits which one can only hope few would attempt to deny, despite the fact that its tenets are constantly being violated by its adherents as well as its detractors.

Few modern ideas, except perhaps for the belief in the ether, phlogiston, and phrenology, have been attacked as consistently, by both theory and reality, as has humanism. From the theoretical side, humanism has been criticized as idealistic, logocentric, phallocentric, Eurocentric, bourgeois, rationalistic, satanic, reactionary, abstract, decadent, and the remnant of substance metaphysics and subjectivist epistemology. From the side of social reality, the twentieth century has made any pretensions to the sacral nature of human being seem ridiculous shams. The iron machine of History is what we believe in today, on both sides of the Elbe, in the street and in the seminar room, and not in the metaphysical illusions of dead writers. Human life has never been cheaper than it is at the present time. Today, no nation renounces the intentional killing of civilians in war as immoral, as seen in the universal acceptance of aerial bombing of urban centers, and some nations consider it virtually a sacrament. No one is innocent, no one has a right to be spared, therefore no one is morally culpable for atrocity. In the present time of uneasy peace, the rising tide of terrorism and civil war makes Tadeusz Borowski's chilling words from Auschwitz relevant to the whole world of today: "Observe in what an original world we are living: how many men can you find in Europe who have never killed, or whom somebody does not wish to kill?"[9] And for all advocates of extreme and immediate social change, liberal-humanist individualism is an obstacle to be circumvented or knocked aside in the pursuit of the reformulation of society in accordance with collective (class-conscious or racial-nationalist) ideals.

In philosophic and intellectual circles anti-egologists and anti-metaphysicians, following Heidegger, Foucault, and the structuralists, have attacked the conception of the integrity of the individual as an unjustifiable, anachronistic metaphysical claim.[10] The New Left, feminists, and various brands of Marxists have branded humanism an ideology of domination, as the ideology of the supremacy of adult Euro-American males with their self-proclaimed rationality and technical mastery. From the opposite end of the spectrum, the radical right claims that humanism undercuts any possibility of morality, community, and the recognition of super-individual values.

Much of the theoretical attack on modern humanism in this century has been wrongheaded. It has attacked a sham humanism and prematurely thrown out the baby with the bathwater. For humanism, like so much of modernity, has been traditionally interpreted in terms of the dominant philosophical tendency of modernity, subjectivism. The attack on humanism is an attack on *subjectivist* humanism. Insofar as humanism has been interpreted in terms of and conflated with subjectivism, it is rightly criticized. Yet this conflation is not inevitable, and thus an argument against its subjectivist version does not suffice to discredit the viewpoint or doctrine in general. The reason that humanism does not intrinsically involve subjectivism is simple: *the human individual is not primarily a subject.* Subjectivity is a feature, characteristic, or activity of human individuals, but this does not signify that human individuals are primarily subjects. Again, subjectivity is no more or less essential to human being than calcium, water, or love. The conception of human being as subjectivity is, on the contrary, *anti*-humanistic, since it is *prima facie* reductionistic and dialectically destructive to the concept of the existential integrity of the human individual.

If subjectivism is eliminated from the understanding of humanism, then humanism can be recognized as the belief which locates the ultimate value and the ultimate source of judgment in individual humans; not in their subjectivities or their minds or their reason or their souls, but in their total mental-physical integrity as members of a unique natural species. There is nothing in this conception which implies that it is humanity's birthright to destroy the natural environment, or to master and dominate the world, or that powerful individuals may justifiably control the less powerful and neglect community needs. Humanism does not imply that values and truths are relativistically projected by individual humans onto an otherwise, value-neutral world. Humanism is not anti-communitarian, for human individuals need not be understood as *a*communal. In short, a non-subjectivist humanism does not prejudice the case regarding these matters, but simply states that the judgment of human individuals is the only court in which they can legitimately be decided. Moreover, humanism makes this claim *not* by denying the value of super-individual realities, but by asserting the ultimate value of the individual and his or her decision-making process. That is, humanism is not primarily a skeptical, negative reaction to religious, communal, or environmental claims; it is a positive conviction regarding the inherent value of each instance of the human process.

Humanism cannot be proven to be true. It is a choice, a philosophical conviction whose legitimacy can only be established by its plausibility and its fruits. The fruits of modern humanism have been substantial. It would be difficult to conceive of the achievements of modern science, of Western standards of living, the energy and diversity of modern intellectual and artistic culture, and it would be impossible to conceive of Western democracy and civil liberties, without the pervasiveness of humanism in modern Western culture.

It is not illegitimate to question, critique, and even reject humanism, depending on the reasons given for this rejection. It is, however, myopic for theorists to reject humanism without considering the practical import of such a rejection; and a number of humanism's attackers have been guilty of this myopia. The question of the viability of humanism is not a merely academic issue; it reaches into the very life and death struggles of the twentieth century. Today, humanism stands as one of the few intellectual obstacles to regressive political and technical forces that threaten to dominate and to destroy human individuals in increasing numbers. Many of humanism's critics seem unaware that in denying the validity of humanism they are eliminating the main existing cultural barrier to movements from which they themselves would recoil: forms of fascism, collectivism, political violence, and the techno-bureaucratic domination of individuals. This does not mean that humanism ought not to be attacked, but that it ought not to be attacked glibly.

Those who have actually heard the sound of jackboots on the stairs may not find the question of humanism esoteric or anachronistic. They take philosophy somewhat more seriously than many critics. Experience has shown them that words and symbols have concrete meanings, that texts refer to realities outside of themselves, that a speech at a rally, a mark in a ledger, a star sewn into an overcoat can signify the end of one's private life, can mean barking dogs, starvation, and murder. They know that ideas can have brutal meaning, that romantic ideals of national unity and purity at which intellectuals may laugh have a direct translation in terms of iron and blood. They are aware that the impact of a rifle butt on an apartment door is the most eloquent argument for the validity of humanism and for its definitive position within the intellectual basis of modernity.

Anti–Culture and American Democracy

The adoption of a cultural philosophy of human being and of humanism throws new light on the manifold problems of humanistic and democratic societies.

Democracy is, as Dewey points out in his important volume *Freedom and Culture,* a cultural project.[11] The existence of democratic legal-political institutions is not a sufficient guarantor of the continued existence of democratic society. If these institutions are not embedded in a democratic culture, then their survival is precarious.

What is a democratic culture? It is, first of all, a culture in which the belief in the ultimate value of the human individual, the belief that individuals are the ultimate sources of truth, value, and political authority, is a dominant and pervasive cultural theme. It is a culture in which plurality, diversity, and creation of new cultural themes and traditions are not only tolerated but encouraged. It is a culture which places the highest premium on the creativity of individuals and groups. These tendencies would seem centrifugal and anarchic, except that democratic culture is above all a culture of *communication.* Democracy stakes its existence on the conviction that open, free, and never-ending discussion can bring together its disparate cultural elements, *not* in agreement, but simply in the act of communication between equally free citizens. It is the ideal of universal participation in the forum, in the arena of public discourse, which brings together the diverse strains of democratic culture, regardless of how vociferous are the disagreements in that forum.

Democracy is a gamble that the fact, the act of on-going communication and open deliberation as a form of self-rule is a sufficiently integrative social force, regardless of the content of the communication, regardless of the degree of disagreement and discord in the discussion.

Democracy is a commitment to talking, to communication as an end in itself. The on-going discourse of the community about itself and its future is, in a democratic society, the locus of all political authority. Democracy is not a final perfect state of human relations to be achieved and maintained; it is a "*method,*" as Dewey saw, a process of interaction which attempts to solve communal problems.[12] This method of discussion is hypothetical, experimental, and never-ending; it makes no claims on a "final solution." Because every individual citizen must have access to the forum, the debate cannot be arbitrarily controlled or limited, and nobody has the last word.

This cultural viewpoint flies in the face of the prevailing view of politics as a struggle in which individuals and groups engage merely in order to satisfy their own private ends. The liberal tradition beginning with Locke, just as much as the Marxist tradition, has misunderstood the relation of the public and private realms in a free society.[13] The public arena is not merely an instrumentality in service of private aims, a contract into which individuals enter solely in order better to preserve what is their own, nor even to promote the common good. A free, democratic society is committed to the public discourse, the forum of discussion in a self-determining society, as an *end-in-itself.* To fail to conceive of politics in this way, as primarily discourse, and of democracy as the discourse open to all individuals, is to accept a debased notion of both politics and democracy.

Many philosophers, following the lead of Nietzsche, Marx, and Michel Foucault, maintain that the ideal of a free and open discussion is untenable because all discourse is determined by power. It is naive to suppose that discussion can be free and equal since power differentials always exist between discussants, and the powerful can influence even the medium, the language, of the discussion, not to mention its agenda. Indeed, they argue, power created the language and the forum of discussion in the first place. There can be no discursive arena free of power, no power-vacuum, in which a free and open discussion could take place.

This critique judges the democratic idea against a false standard. Power and freedom are not incompatible. The forum of democracy does not need to be, and does not aspire to being, a power-vacuum devoid of influence and manipulation. As Nietzsche would say, power is indistinguishable from energy, from creativity, from life itself. Public discourse is an expression of power. The democratic forum merely requires that the most powerful discussants be unable to fully control access to the forum, and thereby fully control the debate. As long as no group can do this, an *attempt* to do so can at any moment *itself become the topic of* public debate. That is, democracy requires that the forum be inclusive, that it not be limited by the powerful, and the best measure of a democracy is whether the extent of its democracy (its openness or inclusiveness) is itself a topic of debate within the forum.

Democracy is not, as Plato and Nietzsche believed, a system by which the majority of mediocre individuals band together to control the few exceptional individuals, to prevent them from expressing and creating power. It is a system by which all individuals, both mediocre and exceptional, band together to prevent any members from inhibiting and preventing the expression and acquisition of power by others. Democracy aims to encourage the widest possible and most unfettered acquisition and expression of power, not its elimination.

The democratic commitment to the intrinsic value of every individual and that individual's cultural contribution will always be the object of attack for those longing for utopia. A utopia is a place of perfection, harmony, and the absence of conflict. But all utopias produce dystopias. For, as Milan Kundera tells us, the creation of a "magic circle" of harmony, a perfect "ring" within which there is no conflict, inevitably requires the creation of a little gulag off to the side, for those who fail to live up to the standards of the utopia.[14] Stalinism and Nazism exemplified the horrors of totalitarianism only for those *outside* the circle, and for those in the circle who had begun to doubt. But for those true believers on the inside, for those who kept burning within their hearts the flame of faith in the new world to be created, there was instead of horror a "collective delirium," a mystical brotherhood dedicated to progress and perfection, even to love.[15] The jackboots marched toward the ideal of a better world, entranced by what Kundera calls the "poesey of totalitarianism."

Democracy is not only non-utopian, it is in principle anti-utopian. Democracy and the humanism that serves as its intellectual base is a radical acceptance of ineradicable imperfection and everlasting conflict. Democratic individualism is the negation of any and all utopian visions, for it bars the state, majority, or collective from politically excising the anomalous individual. Democracies can never be clean; they are always soiled by the stain of the recalcitrant. A democracy can never know internal peace, for free individuals inevitably complain and agitate and band together to seek their collective satisfaction, forcing other free individuals to combine to oppose them if their own interests are threatened.

America is not fully a democracy. It is a partial and potential democracy, a democracy-in-progress. This is not solely because democracy is an ideal which America has not yet fully reached. It is because democracy is, first of all, a method or process and not a state. But further, democracy is a process which is inherently self-threatening. Participants in democracy are free to *try* to control the forum of democracy, to limit the access of others to it, and to determine the topics of debate, for their own ends. Nearly all participants hope to exclude some group's voice from the forum, thereby increasing their own power. Democracy is thus constantly threatened from within, not by anti-democratic forces, but by the very freedom that it is democracy's purpose to encourage.

What holds the self-threatening, seemingly anarchic system of democracy together? The institutional-legal system is only part of the answer. It is the prevalence of a democratic *culture,* the pervasiveness of the belief in the intrinsic value of participation in the forum of democracy that provides the centripetal force. The sense of the inherent value of self-government and of the inherent meaningfulness of each individual's cultural contribution to the on-going conversation of that government is the glue that binds democracy together. This sense or belief can be expressed in an indefinite number of ways in the cultural activities and artifacts of members of the society. When this sense is not prevalent, when people begin to lose the conviction that participation in the forum is an end in itself, democracy begins to fragment and public life becomes desiccated.

The effect of the late-modern anti-culture on democracy is a tendency toward self-disenfranchisement, toward a withdrawal from participation in the forum. The decreasing percentage of eligible American voters who actually vote is one indication of this tendency. The pervasive cynicism about public political discussion is another. This withdrawal from political discourse is one phase of a progressive de-legitimation of the value of participation in public culture in general. The sense, which is today becoming pervasive especially in urban American, that the public realm is impersonal, uncontrollable, and dangerous, and that one is free only in privacy, is a negation of freedom and of the whole achievement of the modern democratic tradition.

If one is free only in privacy, then one is not free. Freedom in public and freedom in private are inseparable. There can be no meaningful creativity in private if there is no freedom to selectively encounter, absorb, and reinterpret the materials of the public realm. For it is only in culture, which is public, that individuality develops. When we conceive of democratic public culture and political life as merely an arena for the struggle of individuals to achieve private ends, with no other intrinsic value, we not only desiccate the idea of public life but also deprive individuals of the source of meaningful living which is the peculiar achievement of democracy. Private life is itself composed of the individual's selection and creative modification of publicly available images, ideas, and meanings, and democracy opens the public realm to the active participation of all individuals to an unprecedented degree. If human life is cultural, then there is no private life in the absence of public, communal life. Without the public, the private is an empty shell. This simultaneous devitalization of public and private life is part of the general decontextualization of modernity's interpretive categories, the loss of the sense that cultural processes provide a context for the interrelation of the individual and the society at large. It was this cultural context which supported the notion of democracy as a forum in which otherwise disparate individuals shared a common experience of the value of self-government.

The failure to recognize the intrinsic importance of the cultural dimension of human social life is evident in the public discussion of a number of contemporary social problems.

Contemporary higher education suffers from, among other things, a disagreement over whether its primary aim should be vocational or the traditional goal of a liberal education. This debate is not new, but it has become more polarized in recent years as vocational education has come more and more to mean *technical* education, and as the public outcry for education in "basic skills" has been added to the demands on the higher educational system. The idea of a liberal education has been criticized as elitist and as failing to meet the needs of the majority of contemporary students, for whom college is primarily a key to economic advancement. The humanities faculty has often responded by attacking vocational aims as destroying the cogency of the curriculum, as leading to lowered standards, and as negating the educational system's ability to transmit a common cultural and intellectual inheritance to new generations of citizens.

This debate is based on a false dichotomy. Vocationalism and the humanities are not incompatible, even in spirit. They are both part of the development of the student as a complete person. The humanities play an essential role in vocational learning because they develop communication skills, give the student an irreplaceable cultural background that will inform and bring significance to their experience and, not to be overlooked, make the student a more intelligent, interesting, and intellectually sophisticated individual. Those who suggest that the humanities are a waste of time for low-income students seeking a career are placing an arbitrary limit on the future lives of such students. They assume that all such students will ever need are technical skills, that low-income students will never compete with the wealthier graduates of prestigious schools for managerial and executive positions that require far more than mere technical competence.

Those who presume a bleak dichotomy between humanistic and vocational education imply that the fruits of a humanities background—enhanced communication skills, general knowledge, intellectual sophistication—are vocationally irrelevant. This unrealistic attitude is all too common. It is implicit in the arguments of those humanities professors who can think of no other justification for humanities education than that it is time-honored and valuable in itself, and who regard their students' failure to accept this justification as a sign of stupidity or barbarism or both. The humanities are intrinsically valuable, but they are also instrumentally valuable in that they generate a more intelligent and complete person, and more intelligent and complete persons tend to achieve more intelligent and complete careers.

Higher education is subject to the same *cult of technique* that afflicts much of American life, a cult which regards technology and technical expertise as so supreme as to make non-technical skills and processes irrelevant, obsolete, and unimportant. This cult magically transforms means into ends; it regards the technological means of achieving humanly desired ends as ends-in-themselves that supplant the original ends in importance. This cult is not restricted to the worship of high technology. It has convinced many students that their vocational success will depend on their technical expertise alone, leading them to ignore the fact that the vast majority of students will obtain jobs in which more time will be spent interacting with people, communicating, making value decisions, creating novel approaches, and dealing with broad social and economic realities than performing non-communicative, non-interpretive technical tasks. This will be even more true if they wish to obtain managerial and executive positions.

Anti-culturalism is at work here. It is at work in the belief that the humanities, the cultural study *par excellence,* are irrelevant to life. It is at work in the narrowing of the concept of vocation and vocational education. The concept of vocation implies the notion of a "calling," implies value-choices and a redirecting of one's life, and often signifies service to the community. In contemporary education, the idea of vocation is shrinking towards the notion of a value-neutral, asocial, impersonal, technical skill. This shrunken notion is essentially what the concept of 'work' would be *if* work were removed from its embeddedness in a cultural, communicative context.

These developments do a grave disservice to students, contributing to the impoverishment of human experience by denying the recognition of the connectedness of different areas of life. This fails to prepare students for the future, a future that will expect them to be capable to complexity of thought, breadth of knowledge and subtlety of communication.

The importance of attending to the cultural dimension can be seen in a very different area. It is often remarked that native-born black Americans are a uniquely underachieving portion of American society. All other ethnic immigrant groups have managed to find their place in the American sun, including the recent wave of black West Indian immigrants, who seem to be prospering while a large segment of urban American-born blacks, more than a century after emancipation, have become ever more impoverished and enmired in severe social problems. It is argued by some that one hundred and twenty years is a sufficient time to have expected the effects of slavery to have been transcended, and that there is no good explanation, or excuse, for black underachievement in the light of other groups having surmounted great obstacles in a much shorter time.

This argument fails to notice one powerful fact. Black Americans are unlike the immigrant groups in one sense: they are the only Americans who, upon entry into this country, were deprived of virtually their entire *cultural heritage*. African slaves brought to America were systematically denuded of many forms of their pre-slavery cultural life, including the most fundamental ability to communicate with others in their own tongue. In general, only African musical traditions (and oratory as it was music-related) were retained, but even these without the knowledge of their origin. Virtually all other American ethnic groups have been able to maintain the linguistic and cultural traditions of their homeland, thereby retaining a sense of continuous cultural history on which to draw and define their individuality and self-respect. And a shared cultural heritage encouraged *economic* growth by providing a basis for group unity and interaction which made possible the economic intragroup development by which Jews hired and purchased from Jews, Italians from Italians and Poles from Poles. In each case the preservation of cultural and linguistic community, far from preventing economic advancement and so-called "assimilation," made these gains possible by promoting the economic self-development of the group up to the point of minimal self-sufficiency and beyond.

In contrast, the average black American thinks of his or her own historic homeland more or less in the same terms as the average white American, as an undeveloped land of pre-literate ignorance and superstition which produced few cultural forms from which we could learn anything today or take pride in as genuine cultural achievements. It would be difficult to find an Italian, a Jew, a Pole, a Korean, or a Hispanic who feels the same about his own homeland. As a culture, we are, both black and white, just as ignorant of African history and culture today as were the newly freed black slaves over one hundred and twenty years ago.

We fail to appreciate how destructive the truncation of black cultural heritage has been. There are today creative and diverse cultural strains in black society, just as there was cultural activity among blacks even during slavery. These cultural movements have been rich and powerful, and should not be underestimated. Much of the inherited culture the Afro-American community has today is relatively new, having been created since arrival in the new world. As such, contemporary black culture is a great human achievement when compared to the long traditions on which other groups have to draw. But it remains truncated by being split off from its earlier history, and by the continuing effects of that evisceration. A human being can exist without culture, can go on living from day to day. But it is extremely difficult for an individual to achieve, to create, to step beyond the role bequeathed him or her by society, without having participated in a cultural tradition from which resources and creative strength can be drawn.

It is characteristic of the anti-cultural strain of our culture that this fact is given little attention. The study of African history and of Afro-American cultural achievements are regarded by many as window-dressing, as less than crucial to the development of black American society and black-white relations. Such study is often regarded as having merely psychological value, as a sentimental celebration of the black community's "roots," as harmless but irrelevant to political and economic progress.

Culture is the context for individual and group activity and is essential to the cooperation required for a community's economic development. Culture is not an economic instrumentality, but neither is it unrelated to economic activity. Economic activity, especially in the late-modern world, is fundamentally and pervasively communicative. Business creates and depends upon the communication of shareable meanings and values; that is, business is cultural. The anti-culturalism of late modernity obscures this fact by interpreting economic activity *sui generis* as divorced from any cultural or communal context, as nothing other than the acquisitive adventures of individual subjects in the material world. Today, a number of black leaders and groups are recognizing the link between cultural reclamation and economic self-determination.

The anti-culturalism of late modernity ought not be overestimated. Culture is not dead. In millions of homes and towns around the late-modern world, human beings continue to create, to interpret, and to define themselves and their species through an uncountable number of individual cultural acts and artifacts. Communities and whole nations continue to derive sustenance from grand cultural artifacts and themes purveyed through oral traditions or mass media.

The ever-increasing ethnic-cultural diversity of American society, our openness to absorbing the new ways of immigrant groups, is testimony to the vitality of American culture. This openness is not absolute, but neither is it superficial. Compared to the rest of the world, ours is an open society. "Assimilation" is a misnomer; immigrants do not typically assimilate themselves into the dominant American scene, the American scene accommodates itself to newcomers. The culture changes and evolves under the impact of immigrants, because America does not force immigrants to give up their cultural heritage. What America requires is that all newcomers make money; beyond this, one is free to maintain one's native culture and to inject it into mainstream American culture. This freedom is not specious, it is real. America does not merely tolerate this diversity, it revels in it. The new wave of Hispanic, Caribbean, and Asian immigration in the 1980s has created ripples across the country, bringing with it the new problems and new promise that are the hallmark of every expanse in diversity. This newest enrichment of American diversity is fully in keeping with the best in the American cultural tradition; it is as American as apple pie, bagels and bratwurst, tacos and pizza, ribs and fried rice.

Along with the new ethnic diversity, the last decades have witnessed the enfranchisement of black Americans and the opening of most sectors of American life to women. Despite the continued prejudice against both groups, despite the continuing problems of the black underclass and gender barriers, and despite the fact that the highest rungs on the ladder of power remain white, male, and Protestant, progress in these areas has been, when seen in perspective, fast and far-reaching. Thirty years ago, few Americans would have voted for a black or female mayoral candidate, few whites would have paid money to root for a predominantly black sports team, few men would have been willing to hire a female lawyer or work for a female manager, and few whites would have accepted the principle that racial discrimination in housing is unjust. Now all these are commonplace.

Late-modern American culture exhibits its greatest beauty and morality in its ever greater openness to diversity. In any major American city, on any given day, we can witness the following characteristically late-modern event. A newly equipped city bus stops at a curb and, in the midst of rush hour traffic, the passengers quietly wait as a paraplegic in a wheelchair is slowly lifted into the bus by a mechanical platform that they have paid for with their tax dollars. The passengers may grumble, but none of them complains to the driver or attacks the paraplegic. In this simple moment, the achievement of late modernity is confirmed: the passengers almost universally accept the principle that, despite the inconvenience and the cost, society ought to open itself to the participation of all members, including the handicapped. They may not be happy about the wait, but one senses that most would respond, if asked, that it is right. It is this sense of the rightness of this accommodation to and inclusion of the handicapped, and not the mere technological capacity embodied in the bus, that reveals the true achievement of late modernity.

The anti-culture is only a segment of late-modern culture, but it is a prominent and fast-growing segment. It lies like the top layer in a cake on top of on-going cultural creation and interpretation, truncating and muting the meaning and value of the latter. The anti-culture makes it harder and harder for people engaged in cultural activity to justify, to describe the sense and significance of their activity in communicable, public terms.

An example of the effect of anti-cultural trends on public discussion was told to me by a New York City law student. His law school class had been asked to discuss a hypothetical proposal to replace natural trees in city parks with artificial trees. Students were to present arguments regarding the proposal. A number of students proceeded to cite the fiscal advantages of artificial trees in terms of park maintenance, reduced chance of fire, etc. The student telling this story recounted his growing frustration that, as the discussion evolved, it gradually became apparent that none of the students felt able to suggest that natural trees were simply better than artificial trees, that natural trees had an intrinsic value not possessed by artificial trees, even if the latter were virtually indistinguishable from the former. Even though, according to this student, most of the participants believed in the superiority of the natural, living trees (and would loath to put artificial plants in their apartments), none of them could think of a way to justify this belief, to quantify it, and so no one made this objection. The students, feeling unable to answer the question as to why natural trees are superior, were content to regard their value judgment as a private, unjustifiable preference, and acquiesced in a determination of public space by the value-neutral, objectified language of dollars and cents.

This is an example of anti-cultural de-legitimation. The students would no doubt have engaged in spirited discussions of the value of natural versus artificial plants in their homes. But in the public world of the classroom, discussing the public work of city parks, they felt their own valuative and cultural interpretations to lack a publicly articulable legitimacy. Intelligent and otherwise articulate young people felt unable to venture a communal, cultural determination for the organization of community life.

Not an Epitaph

The failure to attend to the cultural dimension is also a failure to attend to the human process of living creation. This is a failure we can no longer afford, for the technological and organizational innovations of modernity continue to create new potentialities for the influence, control, and destruction of human life, potentialities that far outstrip the imaginations of earlier generations. In non-democratic societies the consequences of these innovations have often been catastrophic, while in democratic countries existing institutions have absorbed and helped to channel these new powers and their social impact. But, as Dewey reminds us, the continued existence and effectiveness of these institutions depends upon the vitality and expansion of humanistic culture.

The humanist ideal may very well offend the formalistic and allegedly critical spirit that has increasingly become *de rigeur* in the so-called "humanities." What Kundera calls the post-cultural nature of our time is tantamount to the rise of a post-humanist culture, a trend that the human studies have not only failed to oppose, but to which they have actively contributed. In this context, the aim of the present study has been to alter contemporary intellectual culture, to legitimate and promote the place that a particular strain of interpretation of human life and the world has within our diverse culture, to shift the currents and swells of cultural tides in a certain way. It is important that humanism be revitalized, that the intellectual portion of literary culture shift toward it, rather than continue to shift away from it. This means that we must rehabilitate the concept of culture itself and that such a rehabilitation speaks directly to the special historical needs of our culture at this time.

Philosophy has a unique role to play in this process. That many philosophers refuse to take up the yoke of this role, refuse to see their discipline as involved in the life of society or culture in general is indicative of the state of philosophy today, but it does not alter the fact that there is a vacuum in contemporary culture where philosophy used to be. Rarely in history has philosophy impacted directly on the mass of people, but it has always affected them indirectly, steadily, and meaningfully, through various cultural intermediaries, scientists, artists, and political leaders. Philosophy has formed a unique part of the dense cultural fabric of every period in Western history. Today, culture had developed in such a fashion that it particularly lacks precisely what philosophy does best. The function which philosophy has filled in the past and could fill again is today a glaring, gaping absence in our cultural fabric.

Our culture is fragmented. It is not merely diverse, which is a good thing; it is fractured into components increasingly incapable of communicating with each other. Natural science, art, sport, media, economics, politics, the human sciences, technology, and religion have each developed their own specialized languages, which grow more and more divergent each year. Each of these languages, with its own implicit categorial scheme and guiding concerns, is split off from everyday discourse and practices. And each field is itself expanding into fragmented subfields in an orgy of specialization. The problem is not that these cultural activities are divergent, but that we have lost the ability, motivation, and even the hope of communicating across the divisions, of comparing and integrating, of *relating* the fields of human activity. How many people today, even from highly educated backgrounds, have a basic knowledge of or feeling for several diverse cultural fields, for example, international relations, poetry, handcrafts, and science? How many philosophers have a sufficient knowledge of contemporary physics and chemistry—of the best knowledge our society has about the physical world—to theorize about such matters intelligently? In each case, the answer is a mere handful.

Philosophy is uniquely suited to bring alive in contemporary culture the process of relating diverse cultural activities, a function that it has always performed, even without intending to do so. Philosophy is the only discipline which can aspire to the level of generality required to relate the diverse fields of cultural endeavor. This does not mean constructing a single meta-theory that will finally and permanently reconcile all of the fragmented pieces of our culture. First of all, what is needed is to relate the diverse cultural fields, to bring them into communication, not to unify them. But further, every systematic attempt to relate them, every constructive philosophy will eventually be found wanting and be superseded by another, because every historical community, faced with its own unique intellectual problems, will have need of a new kind of synthesis. The fact that a constructive integrative philosophy is eventually found wanting does not negate its value, no more than the fact that no work of art or craft is final, that each work is followed by other, new creations, effaces its value. In the very particularity and inevitable limitation of each philosophical construction, its historically determined and local character, there is revealed the eternal and universal function of philosophy, of the never-ending process of the creative, interpretive human response to the vicissitudes of the day.

This historical particularity and corrigibility does not make the task of interrelation illegitimate, nor does it negate the tremendous need our culture now has for it. Philosophers must restore, in their own minds, the legitimacy of this kind of synthetic, cultural philosophy, a philosophy which is not afraid of big questions and big answers, which is not afraid of speaking to non-philosophers, which is neither too agnostic and insecure nor too proudly abstract to take its rightful place among weaving, gymnastics, poetry, and physics as one more unique segment of human culture.

The philosophers of earlier epochs, whatever their shortcomings, were at least familiar with the best scientific knowledge of their time, and were not afraid to consider such knowledge as one of the factors to be incorporated within their systematic reflections. The contemporary drive toward specialization, while unbecoming to many fields, suits philosophy least of all. Declaring questions and topics out of court as illegitimate and unphilosophical in order to turn to narrow pursuits is a retreat from philosophy. This is not to say that philosophers cannot specialize. But we must wonder about the state of philosophy when general, systematic philosophy is actually frowned upon by much of the philosophical community, when philosophers have become specialists to the point that they no longer share a language with which to communicate among themselves, when most philosophers seem to have divided into separate monastic orders which do not consider the projects of the other orders to be legitimate philosophy at all.

A cultural conception of philosophy not only rejuvenates the philosophical project, but focuses philosophy's attention on that which needs it most, on the social life of human beings in this natural world. In the light of philosophy's role in that life, cultural philosophy is not only a search for knowledge but a commitment to the values and goals that are implicit in such a philosophy. In the world of the twentieth century, a century in which life is cheap and in which human individuals and their cultures are so much tinder awaiting the match, an acceptance of the cultural notion of philosophy draws us into an active, practical struggle.

Ernst Cassirer closed his 1935 Göteborg lecture with a poignant statement, words that became all the more meaningful four years after they were spoken, when the first guns were fired in a world war whose end Cassirer would never live to see. He spoke of an idea which throughout much of Western history has been virtually synonomous with philosophy and with the essence of the human, namely, the concept of reason. Cassirer's words on this subject can be taken as a statement on the project of philosophy and its place within human life. Contrary to Hegel's claim, Cassirer argued:

> reason is never a mere present . . . it is . . . a constant and ever *actualizing,* not a *given* but a *task* . . . . We can never grasp the true nature of reason in bare existence, in the finished and the extant. Instead we must seek it in the continual self-renewing work of spirit. This work is not one of a . . . metaphysical spirit which peacefully completes its immanent work . . . . It is the question of a problem which is placed before us and for which we must struggle, with the pledge of all our powers, with the exertion of rigorous investigation uncorrupted by prejudice, and with the whole weight of our will and our personality.[16]

Human beings are the kind of beings who are always presented with a choice between meaning and non-meaning, between regarding the world and their existence as significant and valuable and feeling them to be meaningless and valueless. This choice is not usually a conscious decision. It is more often a slipping into one or another alternative way of living, alternative realms into which a human being or a whole community can fall.

Culture is the primary way that human beings discover or express meaning and value. It is in the nature of being cultural beings that humans are prone periodically to question and even reject the meaningfulness of culture, to deny the mediate significance of human acts, to reduce their view of human existence to immediate gratification and survival. Then the intricate web of human communication and organization, of creations and passions, seems a tissue of fantasies and deceptions, appears to be, as Macbeth lamented, "a tale told by an idiot, full of sound and fury, signifying nothing."

This is a natural, inevitable, and permanent possibility for human beings, because meaning is a human creation. It is not inherent in the nature of things. Once it is discovered, it is discovered *as* inherent in things. We make the meaning and we discover it; discovery and creation cannot be separated. There can be no justification, no reason, no necessity for regarding life and world as meaningful, except that for human beings non-meaning is often tantamount to non-being. Choosing life means choosing meaning. And choosing meaning usually means choosing culture.

Modernity, the dominant cultural meanings created by the post-Renaissance Western world, cannot be proved to be superior to other cultures. Like every dominant culture it has its own beauty, its own achievements. The acceptance of the validity of modern humanism is a value choice, a conviction that human social life and the world are best and most beautifully exhibited when understood and reconstructed according to humanism. It is a conviction that the basic impulse of modern culture, its humanism, is superior to the basic organizing impulses of other cultures. The only reason for taking such a cultural stance is a sense of the value of its fruits.

Modernity will stand or fall with this idea. Someday it may become apparent that societies accepting the modern principles of individual rights, of open inquiry, of freedom to create, cannot successfully adapt to new world conditions or compete with societies that do not accept such principles. Then modernity will be superseded, will disappear or will become an unimportant actor on the world stage. This may not happen. But if it does, it will not negate modernity's value and achievements, no more than twenty-five centuries have dimmed the achievements of classical Hellenic culture.

If the noble achievements and the singular beauty of the modern world are to be re-invigorated and preserved in the face of its own destructive and deadening tendencies, modernity must evolve a new context of legitimacy for its basic ideas. This new context will not be found in a return to the transcendental, a leap into collectivism, or a gutting of the concept of human integrity. These alternatives simply negate the basic impulses of early and late modernity; they would push us into a new dominant culture, but it would not be the culture of modernity. Such negation is unnecessary, for there is ample room within the framework of modernity's basic impulses for wide-ranging re-interpretation. The problems of late modernity will be met with the tools that modernity itself has provided, not by recoiling from the frightening complexities modernity presents.

When, to use Spinoza's apt name for eternity, "God or Nature" writes the biography of human existence, modernity will reveal a mixed legacy as the era of humanity's greatest self-respect and creativity, and as the moment in history when apocalypse became, for the first time, a matter of human choice. The rope of modernity which we have tied into a noose to hang ourselves can also be untied and used to cross over the dilemmas that modernity has placed before us. We ought to preserve and take confidence in the humanistic roots of modernity's achievements, and to plumb their open-ended and unfinished promise, as we rush into humanity's unknown future.

Notes

INTRODUCTION

1. Karl Marx and Friedrich Engels, *The Communist Manifesto,* trans. Samuel Moore (New York: Washington Square, 1964), esp. pp. 61–63.

2. Marshall Berman, *All That Is Solid Melts Into Air* (New York: Simon and Schuster, 1982). Berman's title is actually a line from the *Communist Manifesto.*

3. Max Weber, *The Protestant Ethic and the Spirit of Capitalism,* trans. Talcott Parsons (New York: Scribner, 1958), p. 182.

4. Sigmund Freud, *Civilization and Its Discontents,* trans. James Strachey (New York: Norton, 1961).

5. See esp. Friedrich Nietzsche, *The Genealogy of Morals,* trans. F. Golffing (Garden City, New York: Doubleday, 1956).

6. Oswald Spengler, *Decline of the West,* trans. C. F. Atkinson (New York: Knopf, 1926–1928).

7. Theodor Adorno and Max Horkheimer, *Dialectic of Enlightenment,* trans. John Cumming (New York: Seabury, 1972).

8. Walter Lippman, *The Public Philosophy* (New York: New American Library, 1955), p. 13.

9. For the most comprehensive philosophical treatments of modernity, see: Hans Blumenberg, *The Legitimacy of the Modern Age,* trans. Robert Wallace (Cambridge: M.I.T., 1983); Gerald Galgan, *The Logic of Modernity* (New York: New York University, 1982); Jurgen Habermas, *The Theory of Communicative Action, Vol. 1, The Rationalization of Society,* trans. Thomas McCarthy (Boston: Beacon, 1984); and collections of essays on modernity in *New German Critique,* no. 22 (Winter 1981), no. 26 (Spring/Summer 1982), and no. 33 (Fall 1984); and *Independent Journal of Philosophy,* vol. IV, 1983.

For some of the psychoanalytic-political interpretations, see: the Marcuse-Fromm exchange in *Dissent,* vol. 2, no. 3 and no. 4 (1955), and vol. 3, no. 1 (1956); Herbert Marcuse, *Eros and Civilization* (Boston: Beacon, 1955) and *One Dimensional Man* (Boston: Beacon, 1964); and Norman O. Brown, *Life Against Death* (Middletown: Wesleyan, 1959) and *Love's Body* (New York: Random House, 1966).

French Structuralism and post-Structuralism have had a strong impact on one segment of the modernity debate recently. One might read any of the works of Michel Foucault, for example, *The Order of Things* (New York: Random House, 1970), or Giles Deleuze and Félix Guattari, *Anti-Oedipus*, trans. Hurley et al (New York: Viking, 1977). For a critical response, it is interesting to see that Habermas has branded this school of putative leftists, the "Young Conservatives;" see Jurgen Habermas, "Modernity versus Postmodernity," *New German Critique*, no. 22, Winter 1981, pp. 3–14.

A good introduction to the neo-conservative interpretation of modernity is Peter Steinfels, *The Neo-Conservatives* (New York: Simon and Schuster, 1979).

Those feminist writers who have made use of psychoanalytic theory in their critique of existing gender roles have contributed to the contemporary form of the modernity debate. See for example Juliet Mitchell, *Psychoanalysis and Feminism* (New York: Harmondsworth, 1974); Dorothy Dinnerstein, *The Mermaid and the Minotaur* (New York: Harper, 1976); and Nancy Chodorow, *The Reproduction of Mothering* (Berkeley: University of California, 1978).

Most provocative among the social-psychological commentaries on modernity are those employing the concept of narcissism in the context of a historical analysis. These works are, in effect, extensions of the dialectical theory, and will have a special place in my later chapters. They are: Christopher Lasch, *The Culture of Narcissism* (New York: Warner, 1979) and *The Minimal Self* (New York: Norton, 1984); Richard Sennett, *The Fall of Public Man* (New York: Vintage, 1978); and, Russell Jacoby, *Social Amnesia* (Boston: Beacon, 1975). It should be noted that Adorno himself suggested the connection of narcissism with late modern culture; see Theodor Adorno, "Sociology and Psychology," New Left Review, no. 46–47, 1967–68.

This employment of the concept of narcissism in social criticism has been very controversial, especially among feminists. For this sub-debate over the theory of social narcissism, see: Jessica Benjamin, "Authority and the Family Revisited: or, A World Without Fathers?" *New German Critique*, no. 13, Winter 1978; "A Symposium: Christopher Lasch and the Culture of Narcissism," with essays by Micheal Fischer, Larry Nachman, Janice Doane, and Devon Leigh Hodges, and a reply by Lasch, in *Salmagundi*, Fall 1979; Sarah Kofman, "The Narcissistic Woman: Freud and Girard," *Diacritics*, Sept. 1980; Stephanie Engel, "Femininity as Tragedy: Re-Examining the 'New Narcissism'," *Socialist Review*, no. 55, Sept.–Oct. 1980; Sandra Lee Bartky, "Narcissism, Femininity and Alienation," *Social Theory and Practice*, vol. 8, no. 2, Summer 1982; Bruce Mazlish, "American Narcissism," *The Psychohistory Review,* vol. 10, no. 3/4, Spring/Summer 1982; and Michele Barrett and Mary McIntosh, "Narcissism and the Family: a Critique of Lasch," *New Left Review*, no. 135, Sept.–Oct. 1982. See also Lasch's "The Freudian Left and Cultural Revolution," *New Left Review*, no. 129, Sept.–Oct. 1981, and the author's "The Sex of the Ego: Narcissism, Gender and the Critique of Enlightenment," *The Psychohistory Review*, vol. 13, no. 1, Fall 1984, pp. 30–39.

10. John Dewey, *Freedom and Culture* (New York: Paragon, 1979), p. 126 and p. 130.

11. See Czeslaw Milosz, *Native Realm*, trans. Catharine Leach (Garden City: Doubleday, 1968), and *The Captive Mind*, trans. Jane Zielonko (New York: Vintage, 1981).

12. Theodor Adorno and Max Horkheimer, *Dialectic of Enlightenment,* trans. John Cummings (New York: Seabury), p. xiii.

13. John Herman Randall, *The Career of Philosophy* (New York: Columbia, 1962), Vol. I, p. 7.

14. Ibid., Vol. I, pp. 10–11.

15. See John Dewey, *Experience and Nature* (Chicago: Open Court, 1925), pp. 27–28.

16. Admittedly, a philosophy may also affect the thinking of a community by being found to have a negative value. But, for the rejection of a philosophy to affect a community's thinking beyond the mere negative evaluation of that very philosophy, it could only do so by causing the community to also reject what it perceived as similar philosophies, which would otherwise have been found to have positive value. For example, rejecting Malebranche has a positive effect—as opposed to the *absence* of an effect—only if Malebranche is presumed to represent Descartes, and the community thereby rejects a Cartesianism that might otherwise be found to be enlightening.

17. Today the broadest possible social impact of a philosophy is very often effected, not by its creator, but through a chain of variously influential intellectuals: for example, the philosopher is read by a social historian, who is read by an economist, who one day works as an advisor to a United States Senator, etc.

18. The source of the power of conservatism can be seen here. Interpretation helps to reproduce the social realities that are consistent with it.

CHAPTER 1.

1. Fred R. Dallmayr, *Twilight of Subjectivity* (Amherst: University of Massachusetts Press, 1981), p. 1; Alfred North Whitehead, *Science and the Modern World* (1925; rpt. New York: Free Press, 1967), p. 140; Martin Heidegger, "Letter On Humanism," trans. Frank A. Capuzzi and J. Glenn Gray, in *Basic Writings,* ed. David F. Krell (New York: Harper, 1977), p. 229; and, John Dewey, *Experience and Nature* (1919; rpt. New York: Dover, 1958), pp. 13–15.

2. I mean 'thinking subject' as synonomous with 'personal consciousness' and 'faculty of representations'. I will in certain contexts use 'mind' as synonomous with those terms although mind in general is not equivalent. It will be seen that whereas thinking subject and its equivalents denote something private, for some versions of subjectivism mind incorporates the private sphere but also has the capability of transcending privacy, e.g., it has 'reason'. For Descartes and Kant mind is private in some of its functions and communal or transcendent in others.

3. See W. V. O. Quine, "Two Dogmas of Empiricism," in *From a Logical Point of View* (1953; rpt. New York: Harper, 1963).

4. The use of the term 'order' here derives from Justus Buchler. See his *Metaphysics of Natural Complexes* (New York: Columbia, 1966).

CHAPTER 2.

1. All references to Descartes' work, unless otherwise noted, will be to *Mediations on First Philosophy,* in *The Philosophical Works of Descartes,* Haldane and Ross translation (1911; rpt. Cambridge: Cambridge, 1979), vol. 1, hereafter abbreviated as HR.

2. *Oeuvres de Descartes,* ed. C. Adam and P. Tannery (Paris: Cerf, 1897–1913), 12 vols.; vol. III, pp. 297–298.

3. See Margaret Wilson, *Descartes* (London: Routledge, 1978).

4. HR, p. 149.

5. Ibid., p. 150.

6. The nature of mind for Descartes and its equivalence to consciousness will be discussed in the next section.

7. John H. Randall, *The Career of Philosophy* (New York: Columbia, 1962), vol. I, p. 392.

8. HR, p. 153.

9. Ibid., p. 153.

10. Ibid., p. 222.

11. Ibid., p. 223

12. Anthony Kenny, *Descartes: A Study of His Philosophy* (New York: Random House, 1968), pp. 68–69.

13. Randall, p. 393.

14. Kenny, p. 96.

15. HR, p. 353.

16. See Emerson Buchanan, *Aristotle's Theory of Being* (Diss., Columbia University, 1959).

17. Aristotle, *On the Soul,* in Richard MacKeon, ed., *Introduction to Aristotle,* trans. J. A. Smith (New York: Random House, 1947), Book III, chap. 2, 425b26, p. 209.

18. Ibid., Book III, chap. 2, 426a12, p. 210.

19. Ibid., Book III, chap. 4, 429a15, p. 217.

20. Ibid., Book III, chap. 5, 430a15, p. 220.

21. This dualism, which I will claim to be part of subjectivism, can, for example, be detected in the British empiricist tradition, which generally rejects the Cartesian metaphysics. It is also evident in the German idealist tradition. Wherever it appears—and this is the significance of tracing its appearance—parallel philosophical problems will come with it.

22. Randall, p. 393.

23. See, for example, Frederick Copelston, *A History of Philosophy,* Vol. IV (Garden City, New York: Image, 1963), p. 129.

24. See Aristotle, *On the Soul,* 425b20–426a20 (pp. 209–210) and 431a7 (p. 222).

25. It is interesting to see in Descartes the confrontation of the new modern dualism that eliminates substantial forms with older medieval notions. His theory of the pineal gland and "animal spirits" seems to me a remnant of the kind of medieval thinking apparent in, among other medieval ideas, the notion of the 'great chain of being'. That notion reflected the prevalence in the medieval mind of a sense of hierarchy and continuity rather than dualism; between the ultimate spirit and the lowliest matter there must be innumerable intermediate

forms of existence. The perceptible world itself contained variations, degrees of 'being' or 'perfection' (which two concepts were fused); thus there could be holy ground, holy artifacts, holy men. Descartes sundered that 'great chain' in two (or three, including God) categories. Non-mental things can no longer be holy in their essential nature. But Descartes then has difficulty with the relation between the two substances. He then tries to conceive (medieval-style) of intermediate existences: of a gland that is 'like' the mind in being indivisible, and of 'subtle' forms of materiality, namely, animal spirits. The problem is that he has done his work of bifurcation too well: once consciousness is made the essence of mind, and nature is purely extensional, mind and body must remain conceptually unbridgeable. There can be no "third thing," to use Kant's language, that can stand mid-way between them and share characteristics with each.

26. HR, pp. 142–43.

27. Ibid., p. 158.

28. Ibid., pp. 160–61.

29. By the "objective" reality of an idea Descartes means the idea as an object for mind. By formal reality he means the essence, the true nature or form of the existing thing which is represented in the objective reality of its idea. Descartes is here asserting that, while an idea in the mind may have been immediately caused by another idea, and another before that, ultimately there must have been some formal reality, something existing in itself and not merely a representation, that initiated the chain of more intermediate causal ideas.

30. HR, p. 171.

31. Ibid., p. 172.

32. Ibid., p. 184.

33. Descartes has already, by this point in the argument, given reasons why his own mind cannot be the cause. Nevertheless, his reason for why some other mind also could not be the cause seems to exclude the former possibility as well. That is, Descartes' preliminary exclusion of himself as the cause seems to be superfluous given the rest of his argument.

34. HR, p. 191.

35. Ibid., p. 191.

36. I mean to include here moral and aesthetic truths, which is to say, values in general.

37. See Immanuel Kant, *Critique of Pure Reason,* trans. Norman K. Smith (New York: St. Martin's, 1965), pp. 500–507: A592–A602, B620–B630.

38. It is interesting to note that God serves a similar function, although to be sure He serves others as well, in the systems of two other seventeenth-century thinkers who will not be treated in this thesis: Leibniz and Spinoza. For Spinoza, God makes possible the relation of mind and nature since God *is* mind and nature. In Leibniz's system God plays precisely the same mediating role that He does for Descartes. Leibniz declares that ". . . God alone constitutes the relation or communication between substances." Monads can only affect each other through the mediation of God. See Leibniz's *Discourse on Metaphysics,* trans. George Montgomery (1902; rpt. LaSalle, Ill,: Open Court, 1973), Sec. 32, p. 55.

39. As I have tried to show, Descartes' "proof" of his own existence is circular as well.

CHAPTER 3.

1. *Critique,* Axvii, p. 12. All references to Kant's text, unless otherwise noted, will refer to Immanual Kant, *Critique of Pure Reason,* Norman Kemp Smith translation, 1965 edition (St. Martin's, New York). The capital letters 'A' and 'B' will indicate the first and second German editions, respectively, as translated by Smith in his single volume, and the universal (German) page number will precede the Kemp Smith page, e.g. B10, p. 9. Where the passage is identical in both editions, the 'B' page will be given.

2. Ibid., Bxxx, p. 29.

3. Ibid., Bxxv, pp. 26–27.

4. Ibid., Bxvi, p. 22.

5. In the B preface Kant describes his project as an "experiment" in which the foregoing supposition is to be tested.

6. *Critique,* Bxx, p. 24.

7. Richard Rorty, *Philosophy and the Mirror of Nature* (Princeton: Princeton, 1979).

8. *Critique,* Bxvii, p. 22.

9. Ibid., Bxviii, p. 23.

10. Ibid., B1–2, p. 42.

11. For an example of this view, see Robert Neville, "Specialties and Worlds," *Hastings Center Studies,* Jan. 1974, vol. 2, no. 1. Neville neither endorses the objective version of the *Critique* as philosophically appropriate, nor does he believe it is the only appropriate reading of Kant, but he does seem to feel that it is the most fruitful construction of what Kant is doing in the Transcendental Analytic.

12. *Critique,* Axvii, p. 12.

13. Ibid., Axvii, p. 12.

14. By given reality I do not mean a finished reality known through a process of impression on a passive mind. Nevertheless, this model, which Kant is credited as being one of the major forces in banishing from philosophy, is not, in my view, as problematic as some of the models that have replaced it. It at least asserts that knowledge involves an interaction between a knower and a known, and admits the integrity and force of the object of knowledge, which some more recent subjectivist models make difficult or impossible to conceive.

15. For the distinction between *a priori* and empirical knowledge, see sections I and II of Kant's introduction to the *Critique.*

16. See Kant's Introduction, section IV.

17. See David Hume, *An Inquiry Concerning Human Understanding,* ed. Charles Hendel (1955; rpt. New York: Liberal Arts, 1957).

18. *Critique,* B620–31, pp. 500–7.

19. Ibid., B50–51, p. 92–93.

20. Ibid., B34, p. 65.

21. Ibid., B34, p. 66.

22. Ibid., B5, p. 45 and B35, p. 66.

23. Ibid., B33, p. 65. This is reminiscent of the empiricist dictum; see Hume's *Inquiry.*

24. To paraphrase Kant: Epistemology without psychology is empty; cognitive psychology without epistemology is blind.

25. See W. V. O. Quine, "Two Dogmas of Empiricism" in *From a Logical Point of View* (1953; rpt. New York: Harper, 1963).

26. The "Refutation of Idealism," Kant's proof of the real existence of non-mental objects-as-appearances, has an entirely different significance in the *Critique* than Descartes' proof of the existence of material substance in the *Meditations*.

27. *Critique*, Bxxvii, p. 27.

28. Ibid., A252, p. 270.

29. Ibid., B34, p. 65.

30. Ibid., Bxl note a, p. 34.

31. Ibid., B275–76, p. 245.

32. Ibid., Bxl–xli, p. 35–36.

33. Ibid., B276–77, p. 245–46.

34. One may say that the subjection of outer reality to *both* forms of intuition (space and time) gives inner sense and, consequently, the subject priority even within receptive consciousness. This may be; however, not only is this a weaker priority than that which will be apparent later when I turn to non-receptive consciousness, but the argument for a Kantian priority of inner over outer sense, and for the centrality of time in the *Critique,* will receive its greatest support from precisely those sections of the *Critique* where Kant is attempting to reconcile the worldliness of receptive consciousness with the foundational role he wishes to grant to apperception and the categories. I do not mean to deny the importance of time as a metaphysical, transcendental, or phenomenological factor. But Kant's turn to time and to imagination in the Deductions and in the Schematism is a direct result of the problem of reconciling understanding and intuition. Whatever the inherent priority of time and inner sense dictated by the transcendental project and by the Transcendental Aestetic, the motivation behind the elaboration and extension of that priority in later sections is based on the more fundamental problem of the relation of thought to receptivity.

35. *Critique*, Bxli, p. 36.

36. Ibid., B277–78, p. 246, note 2.

37. Ibid., A28, p. 73.

38. Ibid., B103, p. 112.

39. Ibid., B180–81, p. 183.

40. Ibid., A125, p. 147 and B165, p. 173.

41. Indeed, one can envision a romantic notion of nature here, e.g., that of Schelling. Kant's quote clearly implies, if we take it seriously, that the source of all transcendental synthesis, the schematism, is itself grounded in nature, a dark nature which antedates and is not susceptible to rational inquiry.

42. This is, of course, a simplification. We can, for Kant, know the moral law. We cannot, however, prove its actuality or necessity, nor its non-existence. Thus we can "think" it, and think ourselves as free to obey it.

43. Now, one could also say that this possibility would not threaten the moral project, because determinate thought or knowledge in general would not be possible for Kant in the absence of sensuous receptivity. To be sure, the

effacement of the latter's integrity would be intolerable in a variety of ways for Kant, and he would not allow the possibility of knowledge without intuitions. To think the possible consequences of the elimination of sensible intuition for Kant's system is indeed speculative, but it is instructive in that its theoretical consequences are suggestive of the paradoxical features of philosophical narcissism.

44. See Martin Heidegger, *Being and Time,* trans. John Macquarrie and Edward Robinson (New York: Harper, 1962), pp. 45–46, 246–48, 366–68.

45. Ibid., p. 45.

46. Ibid., p. 368.

47. Ibid., p. 250.

48. Excepting those passages, like the one previously noted, where Kant refers to a more potent, independent, 'naturalistic' nature.

49. *Critique,* Bxvi, p. 22.

50. It is interesting to examine parts of the *Critique* in respect to the comparative roles of the notions of "community," "causality," and "inherence" or "subsumption." They are Kant's three categories of relation and their juxtaposition can be seen to run like a thread through the architectonic of both the Analytic and the Dialectic. As the three "Analogies of Experience"—"coexistence," "succession," and "permanence," respectively—they form the cornerstone of the "Principles of Pure Reason." In the Dialectic, they appear as the absolute unity of the *system* of objects of thought in general, the absolute unity of the *series* of conditions of appearance and the absolute unity of the thinking *subject,* respectively; or, God, the world or freedom, and the soul or immortality. Thus, the Transcendental Ideas are derived from the three categories of relation.

Speaking somewhat metaphorically, one can describe various parts of the *Critique* in terms of the three kinds of relation. I have tried to show, for example, that the Refutation presents the thinking subject and "outer objects" in a relation of community, that is, of reciprocity or of interaction; whereas the task of the Deductions is explicitly to *subsume* reciprocity and thus, I suggest, community under the categories of the thinking subject.

51. For an example of a non-subjectivist account of synthesis, partially inspired by Kant, see Robert Neville, *Reconstruction of Thinking* (Albany: State University of New York, 1981).

CHAPTER 4.

1. God served the same function for Leibniz and Spinoza as well.

2. Max Horkheimer and Theodor W. Adorno, *Dialectic of Enlightenment,* trans. John Cumming (New York: Seabury, 1972).

3. Ibid., p. 82.

4. Sigmund Freud, "On Narcissism: An Introduction" (1914), trans. Cecil Baines, in *General Psychological Theory,* ed. Philip Rieff (New York: Collier, 1963), pp. 56–82.

5. Ibid., p. 63.

6. Heinz Kohut, *The Analysis of the Self* (New York: International Universities Press, 1971), p. xiii. Note: International Universities Press will hereafter be abbreviated IUP.

7. Freud, p. 57.
8. Freud, p. 58.
9. See James Strachey's "Appendix B" to Sigmund Freud's *The Ego and the Id,* trans. James Strachey (New York: Norton, 1960), pp. 53–56.
10. Freud, "On Narcissism", p. 80.
11. Ibid., p. 76.
12. Sigmund Freud, "Mourning and Melancholia" (1917), trans. Joan Riviere, in *General Psychological Theory,* pp. 164–184.
13. Heinz Hartmann, "Comments on the Psychoanalytic Theory of the Ego" (1950), in *Essays On Ego Psychology* (New York: IUP, 1964), p. 127.
14. Heinz Hartmann, "Contribution to the Metapsychology of Schizophrenia" (1953), in *Essays,* p. 192.
15. Otto Kernberg, *Borderline Conditions and Pathological Narcissism* (New York: Aronson, 1975).
16. See Jay R. Greenberg and Stephen A. Mitchell, *Object Relations in Psychoanalytic Theory* (Cambridge: Harvard, 1983).
17. Kernberg, attempting to retain the language of the drive theory, extends that language as far as possible to incorporate object-relations as primary, going so far as to argue that the latter precede the drives. His analysis of borderline conditions emphasizes the mechanism of defensive splitting and the need to attain integration of partial object-images. Kohut adopts a "mixed-model" approach, claiming that his new "psychology of the self"—derived from an object-relations analysis—complements and must be used in concert with classical drive theory; each is to be employed at different levels of explanation. For Kohut the key to development and therapy is the experience of the self, which results from satisfactory object-relations. Within his view, drives are the product of the "breakdown of [object-] relational configurations," the primary cause of which is a failure of the infant's caretakers to allow a normal and healthy narcissism to develop and become integrated into the child's experience of self. The task of the analyst is consequently primarily one of empathy, of allowing for the development and integration of grandiose, idealized "selfobjects" or self-images, a therapeutic aim which Kernberg would not accept. See esp. Ibid., pp. 327–72.
18. See Melanie Klein's "A Contribution to the Psychogenesis of Manic-Depressive States" (1935), in *Love, Guilt and Reparation* (New York: Dell, 1975), pp. 262–89; *Envy and Gratitude* (New York: Basic, 1957); and "Notes On Some Schizoid Mechanisms" (1946) in Klein, et al., *Developments In Psychoanalysis* (1952; rpt. New York: DaCapo, 1983), pp. 292–320.
19. David Winnicott, "Ego Integration in Child Development" (1962), in *The Maturational Processes and the Facilitating Environment* (New York: IUP, 1965), p. 57. Winnicott actually makes this remark about *all* infants at a certain stage in their development. But since it is, according to him and to other theorists, precisely at this stage that borderline conditions have their root, the remark is especially apt in the case of such patients.
20. Kohut, p. 33.
21. Kernberg, p. 233.
22. See Chapter 10.
23. David Winnicott, *The Maturational Processes and the Facilitating Environment* (New York: IUP, 1965).

24. Ludwig Wittgenstein, *Tractatus Logico-Philosophicus,* trans. D. F. Peas and B. F. McGuinness (1961; rpt. London: Routledge, 1977), par. 5.64, p. 58.

25. G. W. F. Hegel, *Phenomenology of Spirit,* trans. A. V. Miller (Oxford: 1977), pars. 202–6.

26. Jean Hippolyte, *Genesis and Structure of Hegel's Phenomenology of Spirit,* trans. Samuel Cherniak and John Heckman (Evanston: Northwestern, 1974), p. 190.

27. Hegel, pp. 124–25.

28. There are other examples: See Hans Jonas' discussion of dualism in his *The Phenomenon of Life* (Westport, Conn.: Greenwood, 1979), and Adorno and Horkheimer's *Dialectic of Enlightenment,* trans. John Cumming (New York: Seabury, 1972).

29. Hippolyte, pp. 186–7.

30. Kohut, p. 9. I have omitted the intermediate phases of development-regression from Kohut's original diagram which are irrelevant here.

31. G. W. F. Hegel, *Logic,* trans. W. Wallace (Oxford: Clarendon, 1975), sec. 87, p. 127: "But this mere Being, as it is mere abstraction, is therefore the absolutely negative: which in a similarly immediate aspect is just *Nothing.*"

CHAPTER 5.

1. Sigmund Freud, *The Interpretation of Dreams,* trans. James Strachey (New York: Avon, 1965). The similarity of the careers of Husserl and Freud is striking; not to mention the conceptual affinities between their systems. Both were born in Moravia, 3 years apart (Freud in 1856, Husserl in 1859), and died one year apart (Husserl in 1938, Freud in 1939). Both invented what they considered to be new sciences of the 'subject', and as "non-Aryans" both were persecuted by the Nazis.

2. See Edmund Husserl, *The Phenomenology of Internal Time-Consciousness,* trans. James Churchill (Bloomington: Indiana, 1964); and, Albert Einstein, "The Electrodynamics of Moving Bodies," in his *The Principle of Relativity,* trans. W. Perrett and G. B. Jeffrey (New York: Dover, 1952), pp. 35–65. Concerning the priority of time in the special theory of relativity, see Hans Reichenbach, *The Philosophy of Space and Time,* trans. M. Rei Chenbach and J. Freund. (New York: Dover, 1958), chapter 2.

3. Edmund Husserl, *Logical Investigations,* trans. J. N. Findlay (New York: Humanities Press, 1970).

4. The translation of the title is my own, due to the inadequacy, in my view, of the Gibson translation. See Edmund Husserl, *Ideas* (Vol. 1), trans. W. R. Boyce Gibson (New York: Collier, 1962).

5. Edmund Husserl, *Cartesian Meditations,* trans. Dorian Cairns, (The Hague: Nijhoff, 1977). The lectures "Einleitung in die transzendentale Phanomenologie" were given on February 23 and 25, 1929.

6. Edmund Husserl, *The Crisis of European Sciences and Transcendental Phenomenology,* trans. David Carr (Evanston: Northwestern, 1970).

7. Eugen Fink, "The Phenomenological Philosophy of Edmund Husserl and Contemporary Criticism," trans. R. O. Elveton in his *The Phenomenology of Husserl*, (Chicago: Quadrangle, 1970). The essay originally appeared in *Kant-Studien*, no. 38, 1933, pp. 317–83.

8. Ibid., p. 73–74.

9. The paper also helps to answer a question which has long puzzled me: why is Husserl so hostile towards—or so eager to ignore—Kant? Although the transcendental phenomenology introduced in *Ideas*, volume I, inevitably invites comparison to Kant, Husserl almost never refers to the latter. There is almost no mention of Kant in *Ideas*, I, and in *Cartesian Meditations;* and where there is mention, it is critical. Indeed, in *Ideas*, I, Husserl refers more often and more sympathetically to Hume than to Kant. It is not until the *Crisis* that Husserl discusses Kant's philosophy at length. The answer is, I believe, that there is indeed a strong affinity between the Kantian and Husserlian systems and yet, there is also a conceptual difference which for Husserl and Fink is a profound one. I tend to believe that Husserl did not completely understand the precise nature of this difference to his own satisfaction until late in his career. This late understanding was no doubt facilitated by the evolution of his conception of phenomenology. It is often the case, that a thinker who is close to one's own position, yet in disagreement with it, is treated more harshly than those with whom one has nothing in common. Add to this the dominant neo-Kantianism of Weimar Universities and the frequent comparisons made between Kantianism and phenomenology by commentators, comparisons that were no doubt irritating to Husserl. One gets the sense that such comparisons motivated Husserl to ask Fink to write the latter's 1933 essay.

10. Fink, p. 134.

11. Ibid., p. 124.

12. Ibid., pp. 130–31.

13. Husserl, *Cartesian Meditations*, p. 84.

14. Ibid., p. 85.

15. Ibid., p. 86.

16. See Husserl's *Crisis*, section 43, p. 155; also the translator's introduction, p. 3.

17. See also Husserl's "Vienna Lecture," on which the *Crisis* is based. It is appended to Carr's translation of the *Crisis*, pp. 269–99.

18. See Husserl, *Cartesian Meditations*, section 58, esp. pp. 134–36.

19. Husserl, *Crisis*, p. 127.

20. This view, especially as developed in *Crisis*, Part II, section 8–9 (concerning "Galileo's Mathematization of Nature") and in the essay "The Origin of Geometry" appended to Carr's translation of the *Crisis*, pp. 353–78, represents Husserl's most important contribution to the philosophy of science. Only today, almost fifty years later, is its significance beginning to be recognized: See, e.g. the work of Patrick Heelan, David Ramp.

21. Husserl, *Crisis*, p. 146.

22. Ibid., p. 148.

23. Ibid., pp. 151–52.

24. Ibid., p. 177.

25. Ibid., p. 144 (Husserl's emphasis).
26. Ibid., p. 157.
27. Ibid., p. 156.
28. Ibid., p. 178.
29. Ibid., p. 171.
30. See *Crisis*, section 50, p. 171.
31. Husserl, *Cartesian Meditations*, p. 1.
32. Ibid., p. 1.
33. Ibid., p. 4.
34. Ibid., p. 10.
35. Ibid., p. 12.
36. Ibid., p. 13.
37. Ibid., p. 14.
38. Ibid., pp. 15–16.
39. Ibid., p. 16.
40. Ibid., p. 18.
41. Ibid., pp. 20–21.
42. Ibid., p. 20.
43. Ibid., p. 21.
44. It is interesting to note that this is also part of Heidegger's criticism of Descartes. See Martin Heidegger, *Being and Time*, trans. John Macquerrie and Edward Robinson (New York: Harper, 1962), pp. 46–47.
45. Husserl, *Cartesian Meditations*, pp. 24–25.
46. Ibid., p. 30.
47. Ibid., p. 52, Husserl's note.
48. See Alfred Schutz, "The Problem of Transcendental Intersubjectivity in Husserl" (1957), in *Collected Papers*, ed. Maurice Natanson; trans. Frederick Kersten, with Aron Gurwitsch and Thomas Luckmann, (New York: Humanities, 1966), vol. 3, pp. 83–84. I must confess that there is an anomaly here that I cannot explain. In the 1957 lecture cited here, Schutz criticized that tendency of transcendental phenomenology to lead to ontology, while he continues to endorse a descriptive phenomenology of the life-world. In summarizing his position, Schutz refers to Fink—who was present and commented on Schutz's lecture—as supporting his own position in a paper published in 1951. Yet it is undeniable that Fink himself had given definitive expression of that very 'ontological' interpretation and foundation of Husserlian phenomonology in his 1933 essay in *Kant-Studien*, an essay to which Schutz also refers in his 1957 lecture. Fink's response to the Schutz lecture (see above, pp. 84–86) is one of polite agreement, so that one might presume his position to have changed from 1933 to 1957; yet there is a hint to the contrary at the end of his response, where he suggests that at the end of his life, Husserl was moving in a "Fichtean" direction. I am not familiar with the latter Fink essay of which Schutz expresses glowing approval [in *Problems actuels de la phenomenologie*, ed. H. L. Van Breda (Bruxelles, 1951)], and so have no resolution to propose for this confusing situation.
49. See Franz Brentano *Psychology from an Empirical Standpoint*, trans. A. C. Rancurello et al. (New York: Humanities, 1973).
50. Husserl, *Cartesian Meditations*, p. 40.
51. Husserl, *Crisis*, p. 166, Husserl's note.
52. Husserl, *Cartesian Meditations*, p. 41.

53. Ibid., pp. 30–31. Please note that in this quotation I have *avoided* using portions of Husserl's text which, according to translator Cairns, were marked by Husserl for deletion.

54. Ibid., p. 84.

55. Ibid., pp. 91–92.

56. Ibid., p. 93.

57. Ibid., p. 93.

58. Ibid., p. 94.

59. Ibid., pp. 104–5.

60. Ibid., p. 106.

61. Ibid., p. 114.

62. Ibid., p. 128.

63. Ibid., p. 130.

64. Alfred Schutz, "The Problem of Transcendental Intersubjectivity in Husserl," cf. note 48; and Michael Theunissen, *The Other: Studies in the Social Ontology of Husserl, Heidegger, Sartre and Buber,* trans. C. Macann (Cambridge: M.I.T., 1984).

65. Husserl, *Cartesian Meditations,* p. 149.

66. See Fink's response to Schutz's lecture on intersubjectivity in Alfred Schutz, *Collected Papers,* cf. note 48, p. 85.

67. Husserl, *Cartesian Meditations,* p. 115; see also *Crisis* section 53b, p. 185.

68. Husserl, *Cartesian Meditations,* pp. 126–27.

69. Ibid., p. 122.

70. This is the point made in Chapter 1. of the present study with reference to Hume. It may be noted that Husserl makes not a few favorable references to Hume; see, *Ideas,* volume I, and *Crisis,* section 23 and 24. One could argue that Husserl felt more philosophically akin to Hume than to Kant (cf. note 9 to this chapter).

71. Husserl, *Cartesian Meditations,* p. 114.

72. Ibid., p. 119.

73. Ibid., p. 96.

74. Ibid., pp. 98–99.

75. Ibid., p. 99.

76. Both the parallels and the contrasts between Husserl and Descartes become clear at this point. Within the transcendental realm, Husserl has located the natural world *within* the monad and bracketed the *Fremden*-world with the new *epochē.* Thus we have a repetition of the basic situation of the *cogito sum* of Descartes, with the natural existence of a world independent of the *cogito* still in doubt, except that in Husserl's case this situation occurs *within* the transcendental realm, so that the 'natural existence' of the world is not even a question.

Both Descartes and Husserl wish to avoid solipsism. Both wish to demonstrate the existence (or "constitution") of an 'Objective world'. Both discover that this can only be accomplished through an *intermediary:* in Descartes' case the intermediary is God, in Husserl's case it is the other ego or, more completely, the "community of monads." Of course, these are quite different "intermediaries." God is not a member of the finite world and has no natural body; the other ego is within the world and is perceivable through his/her body.

77. Husserl, *Cartesian Mediations,* p. 66.
78. Ibid., p. 68.
79. Husserl, *Cartesian Mediations,* p. 66.
80. Ibid., p. 66.
81. Ibid., p. 67.
82. Ibid., p. 67.
83. Ibid., p. 67 (Husserl's emphasis).
84. Jean-Paul Sartre, *The Transcendence of the Ego: an Existentialist Theory of Consciousness,* trans. Forrest Williams and Robert Kirkpatrick (New York: Farrar, Straus and Giroux, 1957).
85. Ibid., pp. 93–106.
86. Ibid., p. 93.
87. Ibid., p. 96.
88. Ibid., p. 98.
89. Ibid., p. 102.
90. Ibid., p. 96.
91. Ibid., p. 103.
92. Ibid., p. 103.
93. Ibid., p. 101.
94. Ibid., p. 101.
95. See Jacques Lacan, "The mirror state as formative of the function of the I as revealed in psychiatric experience," in *Ecrits,* trans. Alan Sheridan (New York: Norton, 1977). This lecture was originally delivered in 1936, the same year as Sartre's book appeared in *Researches Philosophiques.*
96. Sartre, p. 104. Here I have transliterated *epochē* from Sartre's Greek.
97. Ibid., pp. 98–99.
98. Ibid., p. 96.
99. Ibid., p. 93.
100. Husserl, *Crisis,* p. 187.
101. Ibid., p. 178.
102. Ibid., p. 179.
103. Ibid., pp. 179–180.
104. Ibid., p. 185.
105. Ibid., p. 180.
106. Ibid., p. 181.
107. Fink, p. 142.
108. Ibid., p. 143.
109. Ibid., pp. 104–5.
110. Ibid., p. 105. One is reminded here of a problem Kant bravely confronts toward the end of the *Fundamental Principles of the Metaphysics of Morals,* namely, why is it that human beings take an "interest" in the moral law? Kant's own absolute distinction between interest and duty has made it utterly perplexing as to why anyone should *want* to be moral. See Immanual Kant *Foundation of the Metaphysics of Morals,* trans. T. K. Abbott (Indianapolis: Bobbs-Merrill, 1949), pp. 77–78.
111. Ibid., p. 105. It is interesting to note that Sartre, referring approvingly to Fink's recognition of the unmotivated character of the *epochē,* interprets this character as consistent with his own view of the *epochē,* as an unavoidable

"anxiety" which requires no motivation, rather than as an intellectual decision or option which might indeed seem to require motivation. See Sartre's *Transcendence of the Ego,* pp. 102–3.

112. Ludwig Wittgenstein, *Tractatus Logico-Philosophicus,* trans. Peas and McGuinness (London: Routledge, 1961), stmt. 5.64, p. 58.

113. Husserl, *Cartesian Meditations,* p. 65.

114. Sartre, pp. 98–99.

CHAPTER 6.

1. Martin Heidegger, *Basic Writings,* ed. David Krell (New York: Harper, 1977), p. 26.

2. See Michael Zimmerman, *Eclipse of the Self* (Athens: Ohio, 1981).

3. Martin Heidegger, *Basic Problems of Phenomenology,* trans. Albert Hofstadter, (Bloomington: Indiana, 1982), p. 155.

4. Ibid., p. 175.

5. Ibid., p. 157.

6. Heidegger's problem with 'subjectivity' is similar to Dewey's problem with the term 'experience'. See p. 253 of the present study.

7. Heidegger, *Basic Problems,* p. 167.

8. Heidegger, *Basic Writings,* editor's footnote, p. 64.

9. Martin Heidegger, *Being and Time,* trans. John Macquarrie and Edward Robinson (New York: Harper, 1962), p. 29.

10. Ibid., p. 26.

11. Ibid., pp. 25–26.

12. Ibid., p. 25.

13. Ibid., p. 27.

14. Ibid., p. 32.

15. Ibid., p. 33.

16. Ibid., p. 33.

17. Ibid., p. 35.

18. Heidegger, *Basic Problems,* p. 176.

19. Heidegger, *Being and Time,* p. 56.

20. Ibid., p. 57.

21. Ibid., p. 57. Here, as in a number of places in *Being and Time,* Heidegger seems close to a kind of idealistic empiricism not unlike that of Berkeley. It is intriguing to note that it is Berkeley to whom Levinas refers in connection with his critique of Husserlian and Heideggerian phenomenology and ontology (see below, and Emmanual Levinas, *Totality and Infinity,* trans. Alphonso Lingis [Pittsburgh: Duquesne, 1969], p. 44.). This connection makes sense in terms of my account of subjectivism and philosophical narcissism. In very simplified terms, classical "empiricist" subjectivism (e.g., Berkeley) gives precedence to objectivity over subjectivity—while the so-called rationalists (e.g., Descartes and Kant) approached the subjectivist problematic, generally, from the side of the subject. *Both* are subjectivist. Husserl's narcissism—his radically purified subjectivism—comes from the side of the subject, so to speak. Heidegger, working out the implications of Husserl's phenomenology, starts out from the implicit negative of Husserl's scheme; namely, the object. Husserl and Heidegger

begin from opposite poles—but both poles are enmeshed in subjectivist dichotomy and narcissistic antinomy. If one removed all tendencies toward mechanism, naturalism, scientism, and atomism from classical empiricism, then similarities with Heideggerian phenomenology would, I believe, become quite apparent.

22. Ibid., p. 58.
23. Ibid., p. 58.
24. Ibid., p. 59.
25. Ibid., p. 59.
26. Ibid., pp. 60–61.
27. Ibid., p. 62.
28. Ibid., p. 75.
29. Ibid., p. 75.
30. Ibid., see note x, p. 490.
31. The eight strata are as follows:

1) Each human is Dasein (Being-there). Dasein is a being, or entity, with a distinctive mode of Being. The initially obvious, pre-analytic distinctiveness of Dasein is that Dasein is "pre-ontological"; that is, both an understanding and a misunderstanding of Being and of Dasein itself belongs to Dasein in its Being.

2) Being-in-the-world. Dasein is the only entity whose mode of Being is Being-in-the-world; that is, who 'has' a world and is 'in' the world it has. Dasein "projects" its world and is "thrown" into that world.

3) *Das Man.* The 'who' or 'self' of Dasein as average everyday Being-in-the-world is the 'they' or the anonymous 'one'.

4) *Erschlossenheit* (disclosedness, accessibility, opening-up-ness). Being-there "is its There," and as its There, it is disclosed. Dasein is a 'clearing' (*Lichtung*).

5) Existentiality, Facticity, and Falling. These three terms characterize the existential structure of Dasein as "falling thrown projection."

6) *Sorge.* Care is the defining unity of Dasein's existential structure of existentiality, facticity, and falling. Care is the mode of Being of "Being-Ahead-of-itself-Already-Being-In (a world)-as-Being-Alongside (entities within the world)."

7) *vorlaufende Entschlossenheit* (anticipatory resoluteness) is the existentiell possibility of Dasein's authentic potentiality-for-Being-a-whole. Dasein only becomes what it is, all that it can be, in this mode of Being. It is the "truth" of Dasein's existence.

8) *Zeitlichkeit.* 'Temporality', as the "meaning of authentic Care" and as the "primordial unity of . . . Care," is the most primordial condition for the existential constitution of Dasein as Care. The ecstatical structure of Dasein's authentic primordial Temporality is "letting itself come towards itself as having already been in making-entities-present."

32. Ibid., pp. 374–5. It is interesting that Heidegger here joins with Husserl, and with Kant in the latter's *Fundamental Principles of the Metaphysics of Morals,* in attempting to create a theoretical system which, while dispensing with all ordinary linguistic, quasi-biological terms for human being, nevertheless

clearly applies precisely and only to human beings. Husserl and Fink remind us repeatedly that transcendental subjectivity cannot be regarded as "human," Kant explicitly uses the term "rational being" so that his moral theory will not be restricted to the human species, and Heidegger wishes to avoid all anthropological, psychological, and biological connotations attendent upon "human being" and similar terms. In each case, a theoretical category is created which, while it is meant as a philosophical alternative to the terms 'human', 'man', 'person', etc., nevertheless finds instantiation *only* in the particular entities of a particular species, namely, human beings.

33. What is referred to here is the first two of the three existentialia: understanding (existentiality), state-of-mind (facticity), and falling. These three elements' of Dasein's existence and their derivatives run through *Being and Time* in much the same way as the three categories of relation run through the whole of Kant's first *Critique*.

34. Heidegger, *Being and Time*, p. 171.
35. Ibid., p. 80.
36. Ibid., p. 92.
37. Ibid., p. 119
38. Ibid., p. 120.
39. Ibid., p. 140.
40. Ibid., p. 140.
41. Ibid., p. 141.
42. Ibid., p. 143.
43. Ibid., see p. 235.
44. Again, like the categories of relation in Kant's first *Critique*.
45. Ibid., p. 171.
46. Ibid., p. 171.
47. Ibid., p. 167.
48. Ibid., pp. 164–67.
49. Ibid., pp. 306–8.
50. Ibid., p. 311.
51. Ibid., pp. 353, 357.
52. Ibid., p. 355.
53. Ibid., p. 343.
54. Ibid., p. 344.
55. Ibid., p. 402.
56. Ibid., p. 377.
57. ibid., pp. 321–22.
58. Ibid., p. 369.
59. Ibid., p. 369.
60. Ibid., p. 369.
61. Ibid., p. 370.
62. Ibid., p. 371.
63. Ibid., p. 374.
64. Ibid., p. 378.
65. Ibid., p. 377.
66. Ibid., pp. 401–2.
67. Ibid., p. 120. Notice Heidegger's use of the Kantian phrase.

68. Heidegger, *Basic Problems,* p. 126.
69. Emmanuel Levinas, *Totality and Infinity,* cf. note 21, p. 45.
70. Ibid., p. 44.
71. Ibid., pp. 44–45.
72. Ibid., p. 45.
73. Ibid., p. 45.
74. Ibid., p. 45.
75. Ibid., p. 45.
76. Heidegger, *Being and Time,* p. 371.
77. Ibid., p. 371.
78. Ibid., p. 255.
79. Ibid., p. 175.
80. Ibid., p. 177.
81. Ibid., p. 178.
82. Ibid., p. 184.
83. Ibid., p. 29.
84. Ibid., pp. 165–68.
85. Ibid., p. 98.
86. Ibid., p. 101.
87. Ibid., p. 94.
88. Ibid., see pp. 100–1.
89. Ibid., p. 101.
90. Ibid., p. 101.
91. Ibid., p. 92.
92. Ibid., p. 105.
93. Ibid., p. 105.
94. Ibid., p. 106.
95. Ibid., p. 94.
96. Ibid., p. 116.
97. Ibid., see pp. 116–19.
98. Ibid., p. 118.
99. Ibid., p. 118.
100. Ibid., p. 119.
101. Ibid., p. 120.
102. This is to say, all entities not within the world are *not Dasein.* Dasein itself is 'in', not 'within', the world. Dasein 'has' or projects the world it is 'in'; other entities are merely 'within' the world, they are intraworldly.
103. Ibid., p. 255.
104. Heidegger, *Basic Problems,* pp. 169–70.
105. Ibid., p. 169.
106. Ibid., p. 176.
107. Heidegger, *Being and Time,* p. 416.
108. Ibid., pp. 416–17.
109. Ibid., p. 254.
110. Ibid., p. 417.
111. Ibid., p. 255.
112. The passage in question occurs in section 15 of Heidegger's *Basic*

Problems, pp. 166–70.
   113. Heidegger, *Basic Problems,* p. 166.
   114. Ibid., p. 168.
   115. Ibid., p. 168.
   116. Ibid., p. 170.

CHAPTER 7.

   1. Max Horkheimer, *Eclipse of Reason* (1947; rpt. New York: Seabury, 1974). For a summary and general discussion of Adorno and Horkheimer's
theory see: Paul Connerton, *The Tragedy of Enlightenment* (Cambridge: 1980),
chapter 4; and Martin Jay, *The Dialectical Imagination* (Boston: Little, Brown,
1973), chapter 8. Connerton's summary of the theory expressed in *Dialectic of
Enlightenment* is especially good; see Connerton, pp. 66–71.
   2. Sigmund Freud, *Civilization and Its Discontents* (New York: Norton, 1961).
   3. Adorno, *Dialectic,* p. 68.
   4. Ibid., p. 26.
   5. Ibid., p. 82.
   6. Ibid., p. 26.
   7. Christopher Lasch, *The Culture of Narcissism* (New York: Norton,
1979).
   8. Ibid., pp. 369–70.
   9. Ibid., p. 64.
   10. Ibid., p. 133.
   11. Ibid., p. 160.
   12. Horkheimer, *Eclipse,* p. 176.
   13. Ibid., p. 174 and p. 183.
   14. Adorno, *Dialectic,* p. xiii.
   15. As Martin Jay concludes, "Theory, Horkheimer and the others seem
to be saying, was the only form of *praxis* still open to honest men," *The Dialectical Imagination,* pp. 275–80. See also, Jurgen Habermas, "The Entwinement of
Myth and Enlightenment: Re-Reading *Dialectic of Enlightenment*," *New German Critique,* no. 26, Spring/Summer, 1982, pp. 13–30.
   16. Adorno, *Dialectic,* p. xiii.

CHAPTER 8.

   1. David Winnicott, "The Location of Cultural Experience" (1967), in
Playing and Reality (London: Tavistock, 1971).
   2. Christopher Lasch, *The Minimal Self* (New York: Norton, 1984),
pp. 193–6.
   3. It is interesting to note that Bernard Henri-Levy, in his *Barbarism
with a Human Face,* trans. George Holoch (New York: Harper, 1979), sees
socialism, not as the antithesis of capitalism, but as a *species of* capitalism.
   4. For example, Japan has modernized economically. The Japanese
have not, however, experienced a cultural modernization along the lines of the

Western world. While we would have to expect that their economic development has affected their cultural development, and perhaps affected it in ways similar to the effects of economic modernization in the West, the overall cultural changes are not parallel. Thus, the same economic developments in different societies need not correspond to or produce the same cultural developments. Economy and culture may both be "modernizing," developing in a *related* direction, but this does not mean that the two lines of development are parallel.

5. Richard Sennett, *The Fall of Public Man* (New York: Vintage, 1974).

6. Lasch, *Culture of Narcissism* (New York: Warner, 1979), pp. 49–55, pp. 154–64, and p. 175.

7. Emmanuel Levinas, *Otherwise Than Being or Beyond Essence,* trans. Alphonso Lingis (The Hague: Nijhoff, 1981), p. 58.

CHAPTER 9.

1. See, for example, Wilfred Sellars, "Empiricism and the Philosophy of Mind" in *Science, Perception and Reality* (New York: Humanities, 1963); W. V. O. Quine, "The Two Dogmas of Empiricism," *From a Logical Point of View* (1953; rpt. New York: Harper, 1963); and, Richard Rorty, *Philosophy and the Mirror of Nature* (Princeton: Princeton, 1979).

2. Edmund Husserl, *Cartesian Meditations,* trans. Dorian Cairns (The Hague: Nijhoff, 1977), sec. 56–8, esp. p. 132.

3. Martin Heidegger, *Being and Time,* trans. John Macquarrie and Edward Robinson (New York: Harper, 1962), sec. 26–27, 14–18 and 73–76, respectively.

4. A. J. Ayer, *Language, Truth and Logic* (New York: Dover, 1946).

5. Ludwig Wittgenstein, *Tractatus Logico-Philosophicus,* trans. Peas and McGuinness (London: Routledge, 1961), stmt. 6.41–6.42, p. 41.

6. Edmund Husserl, *Ideas* (vol. 1), trans. Gibson (New York: Collier, 1962), p. 153.

7. Martin Heidegger, *Basic Writings,* ed. David Krell (New York: Harper, 1977), p. 228.

8. Wittgenstein, stmt. 6.53, pp. 73–74.

9. Ibid., p. 74.

10. Heidegger, *Basic Writings,* pp. 369–92.

11. The primacy of economics over social life and the consequent failure to develop an adequate theory of public political discourse within both liberal capitalist theory and Marxism is a theme of Kieran Donaghue, *State, Market and Politics,* Diss. State University of New York at Stony Brook, 1982.

12. See Marshall Berman, *All That Is Solid Melts Into Air* (New York: Simon and Schuster, 1982).

13. Richard Rorty, *Philosophy and the Mirror of Nature* (Princeton: Princeton, 1979).

14. Emmanuel Levinas, *Otherwise Than Being Or Beyond Essence,* trans. Lingis, (The Hague: Nijhoff, 1981), pp. 58–59.

15. Michel Foucault, *The Order of Things* (New York: Random House, 1970).

16. Giles Deuleuze and Felix Guattari, *Anti-Oedipus,* trans. by Hurley, et al. (New York: Viking, 1972).

17. Fred Dallmayr, *The Twilight of Subjectivity* (Amherst: Massachusetts, 1981).

18. Levinas, pp. 58–59.

19. Jurgen Habermas, "Modernity versus Postmodernity," *New German Critique,* no. 22, Winter 1981, pp. 3–14.

20. In this vein, much has been made of Heidegger's temporary alliance with the Nazis and of the question of whether or not his philosophy is implicitly connected with fascism. I believe the truth is as follows. Heidegger's philosophy, while not implicitly fascistic, was an attack on the rationalist basis of German liberalism, and this liberalism was one of the tenuous intellectual barriers to fascism extant in Germany in the 1920s and 1930s. Heidegger's error lay in his clearing away the supports for republican culture without offering anything that might replace them or without anticipating what the German alternative to republicanism would be. In opposing the rationalist-individualist ideals of the Enlightenment, Heidegger helped to open the door to something without first examining what it was that lay waiting on the doorstep. This is not an unusual failing for philosophers, who are often eager critically to tear up the parachute their culture is wearing without first looking to see if there is an alternative lying around.

21. Theodor Adorno and Max Horkheimer, *Dialectic of Enlightenment,* trans. Cummings (New York: Seabury, 1972), p. 82.

22. Ernst Cassirer, "The Concept of Philosophy as a Philosophical Problem," (1935), trans. Donald Verene, in *Symbol, Myth and Culture,* ed. Verene (New Haven: Yale, 1979), p. 60.

CHAPTER 10.

1. See Robert Neville, *Reconstruction of Thinking,* (Albany: State University of New York, 1981).

2. Justus Buchler, *Metaphysics of Natural Complexes,* (New York: Columbia, 1966).

3. Ibid., p. 32.

4. See Emmanual Levinas, *Totality and Infinity,* trans. Alphonso Lingis (Pittsburgh: Duquesne, 1969).

5. For a discussion of the various meanings of *ousia* in Aristotle, see J. H. Randall, *Aristotle* (New York: Columbia, 1960) and Emerson Buchanan, *Aristotle's Theory of Being,* Diss. (Columbia University, 1966).

6. See Aristotle, *Metaphysics,* trans. Richard Hope (Ann Arbor: Michigan, 1960), Book 9.

7. See Arthur O. Lovejoy, *The Great Chain of Being,* (Cambridge, Mass: Harvard, 1936).

8. David Hume, *Treatise of Human Nature,* (1888; rpt. Oxford: Clarendon, 1975).

9. David Hume, *Inquiry Concerning Human Understanding,* ed. Charles Hendel (New York: Liberal Arts, 1957) section 12.

10. We cannot escape the fact that an inevitable presumption of any philosophical inquiry, and a fact which limits the critique of any philosophy, is a

presumed aim of philosophical inquiry; when we engage in philosophic inquiry, we must have at least an implicit sense of the goal of what we are doing. Hume is thoroughly consistent in this regard; the only way to criticize his train of thought *at this point* is to assert that philosophy is or ought to be aimed at understanding the world. If we do assert this, then Hume's philosophy, however internally coherent, simply does not do what philosophies are supposed to do, and is therefore inadequate or invalid. Much in philosophical argument turns on this fundamental question, which is a question of *goals* and hence *value commitments:* is philosophy supposed to make sense of the world or not?

11. See the author's "The Sex of the Ego: Narcissism, Gender and the Critique of Enlightenment," *The Psychohistory Review,* vol. 13, no. 1, Fall 1984.

12. David Winnicott, "The Capacity to Be Alone," in his *The Maturational Process and the Facilitating Environment,* (New York: International, 1965).

13. In narcissism the ideal of reality and the content of reality both subsist, albeit as antithetical, and hence substanceless, phases of what is. Yet narcissism is an experience of that schism. Extending the psychopathological analogy further, one could ask, since beyond the borderline condition of narcissism is psychosis, a state in which the schism no longer exists because reality and appearance have entirely merged, whether there are contemporary philosophical parallels to psychosis, as there are to narcissism. I believe one could argue this. It is interesting in this regard that some contemporary philosophies explicitly enshrine psychosis as a philosophically-psychologically privileged state. I am thinking here in particular of Giles Deleuze and Felix Guattari's *Anti-Oedipus,* trans. Robert Hurley, Mark Seem and Helen Lane (New York: Viking, 1977).

14. Ruth Benedict, *Patterns of Culture,* (Boston: Houghton, 1959).

15. Winnicott, "The Location of Cultural Experience," pp. 95–103.

16. See David Winnicott, "Transitional Objects and Transitional Phenomena," in *Playing and Reality,* pp. 1–25.

17. It is interesting that Winnicott uses the term "experienc*ing*" in the same way as does John Dewey in *Experience and Nature,* to indicate that primary event from which subject and object are differentiated. See *Playing and Reality,* p. 2.

18. See Winnicott, "The Place Where We Live," *Playing and Reality,* pp. 104–10, which is a restatement of the "Location of Cultural Experience" essay.

19. Winnicott, "Location," p. 100, author's emphasis.

20. Ernst Cassirer, *An Essay On Man,* (New Haven: Yale, 1944), pp. 67–68.

21. Cassirer, *The Philosophy of Symbolic Forms,* trans. Hendel (New Haven: Yale, 1953–57).

22. John Dewey, *The Later Works: 1925–1953,* vol. I, ed. Boydston (Carbondale: Southern Illinois, 1981), pp. 329–64.

23. Ibid., p. 361.

24. Ibid., pp. 362–63.

25. Ludwig Wittgenstein, *Philosophical Investigations,* trans. Anscombe (New York: Macmillan, 1953); W. V. O. Quine, *From a Logical Point of View,*

(New York: Harper, 1953); Thomas Kuhn, *The Structure of Scientific Revolutions*, (Chicago, 1962); N. R. Hanson *Patterns of Discovery*, (London: Cambridge, 1972); and, Wilfred Sellars, *Science, Perception and Reality*, (New York: Humanities, 1963).

26. Friedrich Nietzsche, *The Will To Power*, trans. Kaufmann and Hollingdale (New York: Vintage, 1968), pp. 267 and 327.

27. Albert Einstein, *The Principle of Relativity*, trans. Perrett and Jeffrey (New York: Dover, 1952).

28. Aristotle, *On the Soul*, ed. Richard McKeon (New York: Random House, 1947), Bk. III, ch. 7, sec. 8, p. 225.

29. Emerson Buchanan, *Aristotle's Theory of Being*, Ph.D. Thesis, (Columbia University, 1959).

30. Aristotle, *On the Soul* p. 225.

31. See, for example, E. J. Dijksterhuis, *The Mechanization of the World-Picture*, trans. Dikshoorn (Oxford, 1961).

32. See, for example, Ernst Cassirer, *The Problem of Knowledge*, trans. Woglom and Hendel (New Haven: Yale, 1950), Part II.

33. C. P. Snow, *The Two Cultures*, (Cambridge, England: Cambridge, 1959).

34. William James, *A Pluralistic Universe*, (Gloucester: Smith, 1967); Alfred North Whitehead, *Process and Reality*, (New York: Macmillan, 1978); John Dewey, *Experience and Nature*, (New York: Dover, 1958); John Herman Randall, *Nature and Historical Experience*, (New York: Columbia, 1958); Justus Buchler, *Metaphysics of Natural Complexes*, (New York: Columbia, 1966); Sidney Gelber, "Toward a Radical Naturalism," *Journal of Philosophy*, LVI, 1959.

35. Conversation with Elizabeth Baeten, September, 1986.

EPILOGUE

1. Milan Kundera, "The Tragedy of Central Europe," *New York Review of Books*, vol. 31, no. 7, April 25, 1984, pp. 33–38. It is striking to note how many of the great thinkers dealt with in this present study were born or lived their whole lives in central and eastern Europe. Kant, Freud, Husserl, and Cassirer were all born in territory now segregated from the West by Soviet control (Königsberg, now Kaliningrad, is presently within the Soviet Union itself). What cultural luminaries, what potential Kants and Freuds, have been born since 1945, or will be born, whose contributions have been and are being lost to the West? The extent of the cultural price-tag attached to the political-military division of Europe will never be known; we will never know the depth of this loss.

2. Ibid., p. 37.

3. Kundera, p. 36.

4. Ibid., p. 37.

5. Ibid., p. 36.

6. Ibid., p. 36.

7. Ibid., p. 38.

8. Ibid., p. 36.

9. Tadeusz Borowski, *This Way to the Gas, Ladies and Gentlemen,* trans. Barbara Vedder (New York: Penguin, 1976), p. 122.

10. See Michel Foucault, *The Order of Things* (New York: Random House, 1970); Jacques Derrida, "The Ends of Man," *Philosophy and Phenomenological Research,* v. 30, 1969, pp. 31–57; and, Martin Heidegger, "Letter On Humanism," (1947), in *Basic Writings,* ed. David Krell (New York: Harper, 1977), pp. 189–242.

11. John Dewey, *Freedom and Culture* (New York: Paragon, 1979).

12. See Dewey, p. 128.

13. Kieran Donaghue, *State, Markets and Politics,* Ph.D. thesis, (State University of New York at Stony Brook, 1982).

14. Milan Kundera, *The Book of Laughter and Forgetting,* trans. Michael Heim (New York: Penguin, 1981).

15. Ibid., pp. 229–37.

16. Ernst Cassirer, "The Concept of Philosophy as a Philosophical Problem," (1935), trans. Donald Verene, in *Symbol, Myth and Culture,* ed. Donald Verene, (New Haven: Yale, 1979), p. 62.

Bibliography

Adorno, Theodor. "Sociology and Psychology." *New Left Review,* no. 46–47, 1967–68.

_____ and Max Horkheimer. *Dialectic of Enlightenment.* trans. John Cumming. New York: Seabury, 1972.

Aristotle. *On the Soul,* trans. J. A. Smith, in *Introduction to Aristotle.* ed. Richard MacKeon. New York: Random House, 1947.

_____ *Metaphysics.* trans. Richard Hope. Ann Arbor: Michigan, 1960.

Ayer, A. J. *Language, Truth and Logic.* New York: Dover, 1946.

Bartky, Sandra Lee. "Narcissism, Femininity and Alienation." *Social Theory and Practice.* vol. 8, no. 2, Summer 1982.

Barrett, Michele and Mary McIntosh. "Narcissism and the Family: a Critique of Lasch." *New Left Review.* no. 135, Sept.-Oct. 1982.

Benedict, Ruth. *Patterns of Culture.* Boston: Houghton, 1959.

Benjamin, Jessica. "Authority and the Family Revisited: or, A World Without Fathers?" *New German Critique.* no. 13, Winter 1978.

Berman, Marshall. *All That Is Solid Melts Into Air.* New York: Simon and Schuster, 1982.

Blumenberg, Hans. *The Legitmacy of the Modern Age.* trans. Robert Wallace. Cambridge: M.I.T., 1983.

Brentano, Franz. *Psychology from an Empirical Standpoint.* trans. A. C. Rancurello et al. New York: Humanities, 1973.

Brown, Norman O. *Life Against Death.* Middletown: Wesleyan, 1959.

_____ *Love's Body.* New York: Random House, 1966.

Buchanan, Emerson. *Aristotle's Theory of Being.* Diss. Columbia University, 1959.

Cahoone, Lawrence. "The Sex of the Ego: Narcissism, Gender and the Critique of Enlightenment." *The Psychology Review.* vol. 13, no. 1, Fall 1984, pp. 30–39.

309

Cassirer, Ernst. "The Concept of Philosophy as a Philosophical Problem." trans. Donald Verene. In *Symbol, Myth and Culture*. ed. Donald Verene. New Haven: Yale, 1979.

_____ *An Essay On Man*. New Haven: Yale, 1944.

_____ *The Philosophy of Symbolic Forms*. trans. Charles Hendel. New Haven: Yale, 1953–57.

_____ *The Problem of Knowledge*. trans. Woglom and Hendel. New Haven: Yale, 1950.

Chodorow, Nancy. *The Reproduction of Mothering*. Berkeley: California, 1978.

Connerton, Paul. *The Tragedy of Enlightenment*. Cambridge, U.K.: Cambridge, 1980.

Copelston, Frederick. *A History of Philosophy*. vol. IV. Garden City: Image, 1963.

Dallmayr, Fred. *Twilight of Subjectivity*. Amherst: Massachusetts, 1981.

Deleuze, Giles and Felix Guattari. *Anti-Oedipus*. trans. Robert Hurley et al. New York: N.Y.U., 1977.

Derrida, Jacques. *Speech and Phenomena*. trans. David Allison. Evanston: Northwestern, 1973.

Descartes. *Meditations on First Philosophy*. trans. Haldane and Ross. 1911; rpt. Cambridge, U.K.: Cambridge, 1979.

_____ *Oeuvres de Descartes*. ed. C. Adam and P. Tannery. Paris: Cerf, 1897–1913, 12 vols.

Dewey, John. *Experience and Nature*. Chicago: Open Court, 1925.

_____ *Freedom and Culture*. New York: Paragon, 1979.

_____ *The Later Works* (1925–53). ed. JoAnn Boydston. Carbondale: Southern Illinois, 1981. vol. I.

Dijksterhuis, E. J. *The Mechanization of the World Picture*. trans. Dikshoorn. New York: Oxford, 1961.

Dinnerstein, Dorothy. *The Mermaid and the Minotaur*. New York: Harper, 1976.

Donaghue, Kieran. *State, Market and Politics*. Diss. State University of New York at Stony Brook, 1982.

Engel, Stephanie. "Femininity as Tragedy: Re-Examining the 'New Narcissism'." *Socialist Review*. no. 55, Sept.–Oct. 1980.

Einstein, Albert. "The Electrodynamics of Moving Bodies." In *The Principle of Relativity*. trans. W. Perrett and G. B. Jeffrey. New York: Dover, 1952.

Fink, Eugene. "The Phenomenological Philosophy of Edmund Husserl and Contemporary Criticism." In *The Phenomenology Of Husserl*. trans. R. O. Elveton. Chicago: Quadrangle, 1970.

Freud, Sigmund. *Civilization and Its Discontents*. trans. James Strachey. New York: Norton, 1961.

_____ *Group Psychology and the Analysis of the Ego*. trans. James Strachey. New York: Norton, 1959.

_____ *The Interpretation of Dreams*. trans. James Strachey. New York: Avon, 1965.

_____ "Mourning and Melancholia." trans. Joan Riviere. In *General Psychological Theory*. ed. Philip Rieff. New York: Collier, 1963.

_____ "On Narcissism." trans. Cecil Baines. In *General Psychological Theory*. ed. Philip Rieff. New York: Collier, 1963.

Galgan, Gerald. *The Logic of Modernity*. New York: N.Y.U., 1982.

Gay, Peter. *Weimar Culture*. New York: Harper, 1970.

Gelber, Sidney. "Toward a Radical Naturalism." *Journal of Philosophy*. LVI, 1959.

Greenberg, Jay and Stephan Mitchell. *Object-Relations in Psychoanalytic Theory*. Cambridge: Harvard, 1983.

Habermas, Jurgen. *The Theory of Communicative Action*. vol. 1: *Reason and the Rationalization of Society*. trans. Thomas McCarthy. Boston: Beacon, 1984.

_____ "The Entwinement of Myth and Enlightenment: Re-Reading *Dialectic of Enlightenment*." *New German Critique*. no. 26, Spring/Summer 1982.

Hanson, N. R. *Patterns of Discovery*. London: Cambridge, 1972.

Hartman, Heinz. *Essays in Ego Psychology*. New York: I.U.P., 1964.

Hegel, G. W. F. *Logic*. trans. W. Wallace. Oxford: Clarendon, 1975.

_____ *Phenomenology of Spirit*. trans. A. V. Miller. Oxford: Oxford, 1977.

Heidegger, Martin. *Being and Time*. trans. John Macquarrie and Edward Robinson. New York: Harper, 1962.

_____ *Basic Problems of Phenomenology*. trans. Albert Hofstadter. Bloomington: Indiana, 1982.

_____ *Basic Writings*. ed. David Krell. New York: Harper, 1977.

Henri-Levy, Bernard. *Barbarism with a Human Face*. trans. G. Holoch. New York: Harper, 1979.

Hippolyte, Jean. *Genesis and Structure of Hegel's Phenomenology of Spirit.* trans. S. Cherniak and J. Heckman. Evanston: Northwestern, 1974.

Horkheimer, Max. *Eclipse of Reason.* 1947; rpt. New York: Seabury, 1974.

_____ "Traditional and Critical Theory." in *Critical Theory.* New York: Herder and Herder, 1972.

Hume, David. *Inquiry Concerning Human Understanding.* ed. Charles Hendel. 1955; rpt. New York: Liberal Arts, 1957.

_____ *Treatise of Human Nature.* 1888; rpt. Oxford: Clarenden, 1975.

Husserl, Edmund. *Cartesian Meditations.* trans. Dorian Cairns. The Hague: Nijhoff, 1977.

_____ *The Crisis of European Sciences and Transcendental Phenomenology.* trans. David Carr. Evanston: Northwestern, 1970.

_____ *Ideas.* trans. W. R. Boyce Gibson. New York: Collier, 1962.

_____ *Logical Investigations.* trans. J. N. Findlay. New York: Humanities, 1970.

_____ *The Phenomenology of Internal Time-Consciousness.* trans. James Churchill. Bloomington: Indiana, 1964.

Independent Journal of Philosophy. vol. IV. "Modernity." 1983.

Jacoby, Russell. *Social Amnesia.* Boston: Beacon, 1975.

Jay, Martin. *The Dialectical Imagination.* Boston: Little, Brown, 1973.

Jonas, Hans. *The Phenomenon of Life.* Westport: Greenwood, 1979.

Kant, Immanuel. *Critique of Pure Reason.* trans. Norman K. Smith. New York: St. Martin's, 1965.

_____ *Fundamental Principles of the Metaphysics of Morals.* trans. T. K. Abbott. Indianapolis: Bobbs-Merrill, 1949.

Kenney, Anthony. *Descartes: A Study of his Philosophy.* New York: Random House, 1968.

Kernberg, Otto. *Borderline Conditions and Pathological Narcissism.* New York: Aronson, 1975.

Klein, Melanie. "A Contribution to the Psychogenesis of Manic-Depressive States." In *Love, Guilt and Reparation.* New York: Dell, 1975.

_____ *Envy and Gratitude.* New York: Basic, 1957.

_____ "Notes on Some Schizoid Mechanisms." In *Developments in Psychoanalysis.* 1952; rpt. New York: DaCapo, 1983.

Kofman, Sarah. "The Narcissistic Woman: Freud and Girard." *Diacritics.* Sept. 1980.

Kohut, Heinz. *Analysis of the Self.* New York: I.U.P., 1971.

Kuhn, Thomas S. *Structure of Scientific Revolutions.* Chicago: Chicago, 1962.

Kundera, Milan. "The Tragedy of Central Europe." *New York Review of Books.* vol. 31, no. 7, April 25, 1984.

_____ *The Book of Laughter and Forgetting.* trans. Michael Heim. New York: Penguin, 1981.

Lacan, Jacques. "The Mirror State." In *Ecrits.* trans. Alan Sheridan. New York: Norton, 1977.

Lasch, Christopher. *The Culture of Narcissism.* New York: Warner, 1979.

_____ "The Freudian Left and Cultural Revolution." *New Left Review.* no. 129, Sept.–Oct. 1981.

_____ *The Minimal Self.* New York: Norton, 1984.

Levinas, Emmanuel. *Totality and Infinity.* trans. Alphonso Lingis. Pittsburgh: Duquesne, 1969.

_____ *Otherwise Than Being Or Beyong Essence.* trans. Alphonso Lingis. The Hague: Nijhoff, 1981.

Lovejoy, Arthur O. *The Great Chain of Being.* Cambridge: Harvard, 1936.

Lyotard, Jean-Francois. *The Postmodern Condition.* trans. Bennington and Massumi. Minneapolis: Minnesota, 1984.

Marcuse, Herbert. *Eros and Civilization.* Boston: Beacon, 1955.

_____ *One-Dimensional Man.* Boston: Beacon, 1964.

Marx, Karl and Friederich Engels. *The Communist Manifesto.* trans. S. Moore. New York: Washington Square, 1964.

Milosz, Czeslaw. *The Captive Mind.* trans. J. Zielonko. New York: Vintage, 1981.

_____ *Native Realm.* trans. Catharine Leach. Garden City: Doubleday, 1968.

Mitchell, Juliet. *Psychoanalysis and Feminism.* New York: Harmondsworth, 1974.

Neville, Robert. "Specialities and Worlds." *Hastings Center Studies.* vol. 2, no. 1, Jan. 1974.

_____ *Reconstruction of Thinking.* Albany: State University of New York, 1981.

Nietzsche, Friederich. *The Genealogy of Morals.* trans. F. Golffing. Garden City: Doubleday, 1956.

_____ *The Will to Power.* trans. W. Kaufman and R. Hollingdale. New York: Vintage, 1968.

New German Critique. no. 22 (Winter 1981), no. 26 (Spring/Summer 1982) and no. 33 (Fall 1984).

Quine, W. V. O. "Two Dogmas of Empiricism." In *From a Logical Point of View.* 1953; rpt. New York: Harper, 1963.

Randall, John Herman. *Aristotle.* New York: Columbia, 1960.

_____ *The Career of Philosophy.* New York: Columbia, 1962.

_____ *Nature and Historical Experience.* New York: Columbia, 1958.

Reichanbach, Hans. *The Philosophy of Space and Time.* trans. M. Reichanbach and J. Freund. New York: Dover, 1958.

Rorty, Richard. *Philosophy and the Mirror of Nature.* Princeton: Princeton, 1979.

Sartre, Jean-Paul. *The Transcendence of the Ego.* trans. F. Williams and R. Kirkpatrick. New York: Farrar, Straus and Giroux, 1957.

Schutz, Alfred. "The Problem of Transcendental Intersubjectivity in Husserl." In *Collected Papers.* ed. Maurice Natanson, F. Kersten et al. The Hague: Nijhoff, 1966.

Sellars, Wilfred. "Empiricism and the Philosophy of Mind." In *Science, Perception and Reality.* New York: Humanities, 1963.

Sennett, Richard. *The Fall of Public Man.* 1977; rpt. New York: Vintage, 1978.

Snow, C P. *The Two Cultures and A Second Look.* Cambridge: 1969.

Spengler, Oswald. *Decline of the West.* trans. C. F. Atkinson. New York: Knopf, 1926–28.

Steinfels, Peter. *The Neo-Conservatives.* New York: Simon and Schuster, 1979.

Salmagundi. "A Symposium: Christopher Lasch and the Culture of Narcissism." Fall 1979.

Theunissen, Michael. *The Other: Studies in the Social Ontology of Husserl, Heidegger, Sartre and Buber.* trans. Christopher Macann. Cambridge: M.I.T., 1984.

Weber, Max. *The Protestant Ethic and the Spirit of Capitalism.* trans. T. Parsons. New York: Scribner, 1958.

Whitehead, Alfred North. *Science and the Modern World.* 1925; rpt. New York: Free Press, 1967.

Wilson, Margaret. *Descartes.* London: Routledge, 1978.

Winnicott, David. *The Maturational Process and the Facilitating Environment.* New York: International Universities, 1965.

_____ *Playing and Reality.* London: Tavistock, 1971.

Wittgenstein, Ludwig. *Tractatus Logico-Philosophicus.* trans. D. F. Peas and B. F. McGuinness. London: Routledge, 1961.

_____ *Philosophical Investigations.* trans. Anscombe. New York: Macmillan, 1958.

Zimmerman, Michael. *Eclipse of the Self.* Athens: Ohio, 1981.

Index

Actuality, 38–39, 40

Adorno, Theodor (with Max Horkheimer): caught in subjectivist paradox, 192; criticisms of, 189–92; and cultural perspective, 198–200; *Dialectic of Enlightenment*, 4, 75–76; dialectical theory of modernity, 4, 17–18, 182–85; dilemma of, 18; on instinctual renunciation, 183, 189–91; and modernity debate, 4; paradoxes of subjectivism, 75–76; project of enlightenment, 182; reversal of enlightenment, 183–84; subjectivist presuppositions of, 190–91

Aesthetic concept of culture, 296

Afro-American culture, 275–77

Agriculture, 259

Alterity, 157

America: anti-culture of, 274–79; and black culture, 275–77; cult of technique in, 275; cultural diversity of, 277–78; culture of, 270–79; culture versus society, 197–98; and democracy, 270–74

Analytic-synthetic distinction, 54–58

Anthropological concept of culture, 246

Anti-culture: and American democracy, 270–79; definition of 209; de-legitimates culture, xv; and end of philosophy, 226–27; and Europe, 265–67; examples of, 210–11, 274–77, 279; in higher education, 274–75; in late modernity, 208–11; and philosophy, 209; in philosophy, 222–28; in political thought, 227

Anti-culture, philosophical, 224–27

Anti-egology, 268

Aristotle: versus Descartes, 38–39; non-reductive naturalism, 261; and pluralist-relational perspective, 258; relation of knower and known, 258; unmoved mover, 238; soul as 'act' of body, 40; substance, 237–38

Artifacts, cultural, 219

Asymptotic equatability, 86

Avant-garde, 227

Being: Dasein's mode of, 141–42; Dasein's understanding of, 140–41, 147; in Heidegger, 139–40; and intelligibility, 158–59; and meaning, 196; and nothing, 98; and phenomena, 156

Being and Time, 135–74

Benedict, Ruth, 246

Berkeley, George, 28, 299n.24

316